# Beyond Conservation

# Beyond Conservation
## A wildland strategy

## Peter Taylor

Earthscan Publications Limited
London • Sterling, VA

First published by Earthscan in the UK and USA in 2005

Copyright © Peter Taylor, 2005

The research for this book was commissioned by the British Association of Nature Conservationists, a 'think tank' of practitioners and publishers of the journal *ECOS*, where many of these ideas have developed. Contact ecos@easynet.co.uk and www.banc.org.uk

All rights reserved

ISBN: 1-84407-198-7 paperback
1-84407-197-9 hardback

Typeset by TW Typesetting, Plymouth, Devon
Printed and bound in the UK by Cromwell Press, Trowbridge, Wiltshire
Cover design by Susanne Harris
Front cover image: C. Dani and I. Jeske/Still Pictures
Back cover images: The Wilderness Foundation/www.wilderness-trust.org

For a full list of publications please contact:

Earthscan
8–12 Camden High Street
London, NW1 0JH, UK
Tel: +44 (0)20 7387 8558
Fax: +44 (0)20 7387 8998
Email: earthinfo@earthscan.co.uk
Web: **www.earthscan.co.uk**

22883 Quicksilver Drive, Sterling, VA 20166-2012, USA

Earthscan is an imprint of James & James (Science Publishers) Ltd and publishes in association with the International Institute for Environment and Development

A catalogue record for this book is available from the British Library

Library of Congress Cataloging-in-Publication Data

Taylor, Peter.
   Beyond conservation: a wildland strategy/Peter Taylor
      p. cm.
   Includes bibliographical references
   ISBN 1-84407-198-7 – ISBN 1-84407-197-9
      1. Wilderness areas – Great Britain. 2. Nature conservation – Great Britain. I. Title.

   QH77.G7T395 2005
   333.95′16′0941–dc22

                                                                                         2005011044

Printed on elemental chlorine-free paper

# Contents

# List of Figures

## Colour Plates (between pages 142 and 143)

# Foreword

This book has been long in the production and I owe a great debt to the British Association of Nature Conservationists (BANC), who commissioned it, for their perseverance since its inception in 1999. The original aim was to follow the initiatives of BANC and the National Trust that started with the conference Wilderness Britain at the Open University in 1995. BANC intended this work to continue on the path of Bill Adams' seminal *Future Nature*, which was sponsored by BANC and published in 1996. That book set the context for new thinking on wild nature, whilst celebrating and critiquing, where appropriate, the past history of nature conservation. One element emerging in the new conservation strategy was the prospective creation of larger and wilder areas where the processes of nature would be able to operate relatively free from managerial interference. However, schemes on the ground were few at the time, though several visions for wild areas were being pursued.

What was needed was to collate and network the various pilot projects that came under the rubric of re-wilding. At that time, the pioneering Trees for Life project in Glen Affric had stimulated similar visions of wild forest regeneration in Snowdonia, with which I was involved, and Adam Griffin had begun work on a vision for a wilder Dartmoor. There was also a fever of activity leading up to the Millennium, with Scotland embracing a Millennium Forest for Scotland. A plethora of projects spread across the country, some of which had a wildland ethos.

The following years saw a heightened activity in the purchase of land – especially strategic farmland – by a variety of organizations with an interest in wildlife. The Borders Forest Trust bought Carrifran and announced a pure wildland ideal for its regeneration; the Woodland Trust bought Glen Finglas and set about finding a balance between regenerating a forest (over 3000 ha) and maintaining grazing of domestic and wild herbivores; and the Royal Forestry Society of Scotland bought Cashel Farm as a strategic site for new woodland in the new Loch Lomond and Trossachs National Park; the National Trust for Scotland purchased the West Affric estate next to the Trees for Life project and Mar Lodge in the Cairngorms, with the intention of minimizing interference in natural processes in the former, and reducing the level of invasive impacts in the latter. In the last few years, the National Trust has bought land on Snowdon and announced projects in Ennerdale and the Cambridge Fens that have significant elements of wildland with minimal intervention.

Hitherto, wildland values had been secondary to those of amenity and biodiversity. At the Nature in Transition conference, organized by BANC and the National Trust at Lancaster University in 1999, a discernable shift in values towards natural processes became apparent. There has been much questioning of conservation programmes that maintain the status quo with management policies that work against natural processes and focus upon species that may be threatened by those processes, such as those of heath and reedbed. We are, however, at the very beginning of a major shift in emphasis, and much conservation effort is still focused upon the maintenance or creation of habitat that depends upon human intervention. In this book I have outlined the major practical initiatives and addressed some of the dynamic of policy and science that would underlie a major expansion of wildland in Britain.

In these years, there was a great deal of networking and discussion of practical initiatives. The pioneering Trees for Life project west of the Great Glen in Scotland had already mapped out a 2000 km$^2$ candidate area for large-scale ecological restoration, and had begun a ten-year programme of planting, fencing, collecting local seed, educational outreach, and cooperative projects with landowners and the Forestry Commission. This project sparked ideas for Dartmoor. In my homeland of Snowdonia, I helped to set up the Coed Eryri project aiming to develop the concept as it might apply to a largely cultural landscape of commercial forestry and hill farming. What was needed was a book that presented these projects in some detail – the differing visions and the different lessons learned, set in the context of recent conservation science and shifts in agricultural policy. At the outset I had hoped to make some prolonged site visits and a thorough review of these key projects, as well as researching other potential areas for re-wilding. There was also much relevant experience in the US and Europe, particularly with regard to large mammal re-introductions.

However, I have not had the opportunities I would have wished for detailed assessments on the ground, or for investigating European and American experience beyond collating anecdotes in journals, magazines and a few scientific papers, and the invaluable use of websites. And furthermore, the scientific and policy worlds of biodiversity and ecology, which have grown so influential in the last decade in the US 'wilderness' movement, have begun to take second place in my own mind to a set of values derived more from the rich cultural relationship to the land that is characteristic of Britain. Some of what I want to say is particular to these islands. We are a land of myth and deep poetry. We have given birth to much of the world's thinking on nature and wilderness, from Charles Darwin to John Muir, who was, after all, a Scotsman. These islands also gave birth to the great engine of industrialization and market economics that has wrought such enormous global change and currently threatens to eradicate all wilderness in its drive for renewable sources of energy. We in Britain, as much as any culture, are the source of modern rationalist and scientific society – where Nature is perceived as mechanistic and a resource to be exploited in the support of essentially human endeavours. Our scientific rationality has thus far not made headway against an industrial mentality that threatens not only our own countryside but the stability of planetary ecosystems of which we are all part. Whatever changes in values we may now manage to achieve here in Britain, we have the potential to influence what happens elsewhere, and this is the ultimate purpose of this book.

However, the ultimate process of re-wilding will be in our own hearts. What we create, or co-create, 'outside' will be a reflection of our own wildness. In the chapter on Coed Eryri I have given an account of my personal experience of transformation through my contact with wild land, and I have included, in amongst the more orthodox territory of conservation concerns, a chapter on the 'healing' dimension of the forest. These are no more than signposts to what I believe to be the ultimate work of 'nature conservation', where our contact with nature not only inspires and educates, but heals the wounds of a psyche damaged by industrial living and industrial mentality.

Of the many who have helped with the drafts of this book, there is a division between those who have been delighted by the shifts in style and tone from 'third' person to personal, and those who have been disconcerted. From the experience of the latter, I offer apologies in advance for the unorthodox mixing of poetic and scientific, subjective and objective. My reasoning has been that rather than write two books, I would try to build a bridge between two aspects of the psyche. Most of this book would sit happily within the realm of practical conservation biology, and it is from here that I have tried to extend the bridge, believing that it is conservationists who need to broaden their reach and their influence. Biologists and ecologists have good standing in the modern world. They, above all, have the open minds to embrace the connectedness of environment and psyche, inner and outer worlds, and concepts of healing that extend beyond the purely physical. And it is they who, surely, know how desperately important it is to bring the world into some kind of balance.

Peter Taylor
February 2005

# Acknowledgements

I particularly wish to acknowledge the persistence and faith of Rick Minter at BANC. Funding of the research and writing time was made possible by a private bequest from the estate of Frederick Eastwood to BANC. A review committee from BANC, consisting at various times of Rick Minter, Kate Rawles, James Robertson and Alison Parfitt has helped considerably in focusing the material. In addition, Jackson Davis, Professor of Biology at Santa Cruz, University of California; the environmental consultant Roger Kayes; Stanley Owen at Coed Cymru; Adam Griffin of Moor Trees and Alan Watson Featherstone at Findhorn's Trees for Life have all helped with readings, clarifications and encouragements. Derek Ratcliffe reviewed the first drafts and suggested a need for more detail on vegetation changes (not all of which could be included and this can be accessed at the wildlands component of the Ethos-UK website). However, this work represents my own views and not necessarily those of BANC, and I greatly appreciate this freedom.

I am indebted to the inspiring scholarship in the recent works of Derek Yalden, Tim Flannery, John Rodwell and Alan Turner, and the depths of natural wisdom revealed in Martin Prechtel's 'Secrets of the Talking Jaguar'. My friends in North Wales – the dramatist Iwan Brioc, the sculptor Meic Watts, and the educationalist Eric Maddern helped with the restoration of a truer ecological self in the wilds of that land.

Various initiatives were spawned by the original BANC conference – the Council for National Park's 'Design for the Wild' culminated in a conference at Newcastle University in 1999 and the work of Emma Loat has been central to carrying the message to National Park officers. In that year I worked closely with Rob Jarman and David Russell at the National Trust's head office, on *Call for the Wild*, which sought to present the ecological and spiritual value of wild land and to stem the tide of intrusive development. Recently a small group of practitioners, academics and consultants has formed The Wildland Network – details are available on the Ethos-UK website – and through discussions and information exchange, this book has been able to keep up to date with what is now a rapidly developing and evolving project throughout Britain.

And special appreciation in the final throes of production to the meticulous team at Earthscan.

# Glossary

| | |
|---|---|
| AONB | Area of Outstanding Natural Beauty |
| BANC | British Association of Nature Conservationists |
| BAP | Biodiversity Action Plan |
| BSE | Bovine spongiform encephalopathy |
| CAP | Common Agricultural Policy |
| CCW | Countryside Council for Wales |
| CEGB | Central Electricity Generating Board |
| CJD | Creutzfeldt–Jakob Disease |
| CSS | Countryside Stewardship Scheme |
| DEFRA | Department of Environment, Food and Rural Affairs |
| DNP | Dartmoor National Park |
| DTI | Department of Trade and Industry |
| EA | Environmental Agency |
| ERDP | England Rural Development Plan |
| ECOS | Journal of British Association of Nature Conservationists |
| ESA | Environmentally Sensitive Area |
| EU | European Union |
| FACE | Forests Absorbing Carbon Emissions |
| FC | Forestry Commission |
| FE | Forest Enterprise |
| FHN | Forest Habitat Network |
| FMD | Foot and Mouth Disease |
| GATT | General Agreement on Tariffs and Trade |
| GDP | Gross domestic product |
| GIS | Geographical information systems |
| GMO | Genetically Modified Organism |
| HLF | Heritage Lottery Fund |
| IPCC | Intergovernmental Panel on Climate Change |
| IUCN | International Union for the Conservation of Nature and Natural Resources |
| JMT | John Muir Trust |

| | |
|---|---|
| JNCC | Joint Nature Conservation Committee |
| KORA | Swiss Carnivore Project |
| LCIE | Large Carnivore Initiative for Europe |
| LEAP | Local Environment Action Plan |
| LIFEEU | Financial Instrument for the Environment (European Union) |
| LNV | Ministry for Landbouw, Natuurbeheer en Visserij (Netherlands) |
| LUPG | Land Use Policy Group |
| MAFF | Ministry of Agriculture, Fisheries and Food |
| NHLF | Natural Heritage Lottery Fund |
| NFU | National Farmers' Union |
| NGO | Non-governmental Organization |
| NNR | National Nature Reserve |
| NTS | National Trust for Scotland |
| NVC | National Vegetation Classification |
| PCB | polychlorinated biphenyls |
| PERG | Political Ecology Research Group |
| RRC | River Restoration Centre |
| RSPB | Royal Society for the Protection of Birds |
| SNH | Scottish Natural Heritage |
| SAC | Special Area of Conservation |
| SPA | Special Protection Area |
| SSSI | Site of Special Scientific Interest |
| TfL | Trees for Life |
| UKBAP | UK Biodiversity Action Plan |
| vCJD | Variant Creutzfeldt–Jakob Disease |
| WTO | World Trade Organization |
| WWF | World Wide Fund for Nature |

# Introduction

There is a quiet revolution underway in nature conservation. After decades of operating off the back foot, protecting and conserving a 'nature' perceived as under threat, conservationists are becoming proactive and creative. It is not that the threats have become less – indeed, losses have been continuous, particularly of once-common species in the broader countryside. The shift has arisen in part because of these losses and the realization that the current network of small isolated reserves will not cope with a greater acceleration of intensive agriculture around them, especially in the face of impending climate change, and in part because conservation organizations have grown sufficiently powerful in their own finances and political impact to be able to act creatively. There has been a significant movement towards land acquisition to enlarge reserves, and the promotion of strategies for linking reserves with wildland corridors.

In this endeavour, new habitat is being created, for example in native broadleaf woodland and reedbeds, or damaged habitat restored, such as natural river systems, heathland and wet pasture. Thus far this trend has been little documented and there is no overall national strategy. Furthermore, though there has been much debate, conservation thinking is still caught in the middle of a paradigm shift in values, with scientific thinking, hitherto focused largely upon species and diversity, now encompassing the importance of natural processes of landscape change. A willingness to allow natural processes a free rein appears to be evolving, with a desire to re-wild landscapes, including some of our tamer 'nature' reserves that are subject to the management ethos. In this there is a discernable emergence of spiritual values in a debate still dominated by concepts of environmental utility and economic services.

The paradigms of defensive 'conservation' and the marketing of nature's benefits to the economy have served well over the past half-century, when so much pressure has been exerted upon the remnants of near-natural land. At the very least, there is still a great diversity of species in Britain, if not a great abundance. However, this millennium presents new threats as well as new opportunities, and I believe these demand new thinking.

## Nature in reservations

Whatever the new-found strength of the conservation organizations, 'nature' as such is still marginalized. It exists as much in 'reservations' of the mind as in physical reservations in the countryside. It is still a minority interest, a hobby even, rather than an appreciation of the underlying reality of our existence – indeed, that which has given birth to all existence! In some sense, I believe, the whole nature conservation endeavour has been a category mistake, born of a false separation between what it is to be human and what it is to be natural. Having thus separated ourselves, we have lost touch with nature's processes both outside of ourselves and, more crucially, within ourselves. We think we know what nature is, and hence how we might conserve it – but afflicted by our separation, we see through the distortions of denial, and only now are we realizing how much has been delusion.

Virtually all of our nature reserves are unnaturally denuded of large herbivores, natural grazing regimes and big predators. They are too small to accommodate natural processes of fire, storm damage and climate shifts. Many are grazed by domestic stock and therefore managed according to human agendas of preference and interference with natural processes of succession. Furthermore, much of the food chain is underpinned by 'alien' introductions, such as muntjac, rabbit, hare, brown rat, pheasant and red-legged partridge. These reserves are themselves surrounded by ever-intensifying agriculture. Where 50 years ago there might have been a gradient of naturalness, with the reserves providing a nucleus, the boundaries have become steadily sharper, even in the relatively wild uplands where intensive grazing regimes have drastically altered vegetation patterns.

As a consequence, the land in-between nature reserves has become sterile, with huge swathes of species-poor acid grassland dominating the uplands; monocultural rye-grass replacing the ancient flower-rich hay meadows, even within national parks; and arable eastern England witnessing massive declines in once-common farmland species of birds, butterflies, moths, small mammals and amphibians. Ponds, hedges, river margins and woodland have been reduced, 'weeds' eradicated, and a great divide created between an eastern arable and a western pastoral Britain.

In response, conservationists have evolved a dual strategy of attempting to modify mainstream agriculture and make it less intensive on one hand, and creating new habitat such as reedbed, coastal marsh and heathland on the other. In my view, there is little chance that agriculture will be open to sufficient reform to do more than stem the tide of current losses, whilst the current strategy of habitat creation suffers from a lack of overall strategy, agreed goals or understanding of what is at stake. The key conservation organizations are open to cooperation but still pursue their own visions and values, many of which are rooted in the past paradigm of protectionism and maintenance of the status quo. Much of what conservation strives to protect or to restore is already the product of human management rather than natural processes. In this case, 'target' species and habitats are the main focus of action, with some species, such as domestic herbivores and even beavers, being brought in as 'management tools'.[1]

A great deal more could be achieved by a coordinated strategy, but more importantly, as Britain and Europe face unprecedented changes in the new millennium, I believe a great deal will be lost without one. Huge new pressures are beginning to mount. Perhaps the greatest and least appreciated is the shift from fossil fuels to renewable energy sources, most of which are located in wild places (if we consider sources such as wind, hydro, tidal barrages and wave power) or derived from new crops such as coppice willow and oil-bearing seeds. The scale of development required to meet a projected 50 per cent replacement of fossil fuels by 2050 is seldom discussed. In addition to renewable energy issues, global trends in agriculture are set to intensify production on good land even further, whilst potentially causing the abandonment of marginal production, especially of hill livestock.

Climate change is not preventable, despite much propaganda to the contrary among environmental groups backing renewable energy, often at the expense of landscape beauty and wildness. Periodic climate change is a feature of northern temperate ecosystems and there are major regional shifts even within the glacial and inter-glacial cycles. These climate processes have been a major force in shaping the floral and faunal communities over the last 2 million years of evolution.

The relatively minor changes seen so far (0.5°C on a global average of 15°C) *may not be due to carbon dioxide emissions*. The scientific committees of the Intergovernmental Panel on Climate Change (IPCC) give a 10 per cent chance for there being no real change (the current 0.5°C change would thus be an artefact of measurement protocols) and a 1 in 3 chance that, if real, the change is *natural*.[2] If it *is* carbon dioxide causing this observed rise, then the inertia effects of the global ecosystem mean more change is *inevitable*. Thus, whatever happens with emission controls, we have to develop policy relating to the vulnerability of isolated reserves, as well as to water demand, forestry policy, flood control on rivers and protection (or managed retreat) of coastlines.

## Crisis and opportunity

We are at a most crucial time for nature in Britain. There is a discernable public desire to eschew the road of ever-intensifying agriculture, as evinced by the opposition to GM crops. At the same time, marginal agriculture, particularly in the uplands, faces huge economic problems at a time when carbon sequestration and new forests on such marginal land can go some way towards compensating for Britain's emissions of carbon dioxide. Additional problems of flood control and water supply, worsened by climate change, also offer opportunities for landscape-scale change to natural systems of forest and wetland. Much of the new thinking in conservation recognizes the opportunities for natural processes, wildland and 'nature conservation' to contribute solutions to these problems.[3]

Conservation is thus emerging from its protective phase into a widespread but piecemeal operation of habitat creation and the wilding of forests, heaths, upland grassland and coastal marshes. However, this creative phase presents even further opportunities for restoring larger-scale natural processes and even for the re-introduction of lost species of large mammal such as the elk, wild cattle, primitive forest ponies, wild boar, beaver, lynx, wolf and even bear. For this to happen, there will need to be much greater levels of cooperation and strategic thinking among organizations and the whole-hearted support of both government and consumer.[4]

This book is an attempt to document the slow but steady restoration of the natural processes of wild nature, and it is also an appeal for us to restore something of the wild within our own hearts, for our spiritual well-being as well as for the sake of the planetary ecosystem upon which we depend. The task before us goes further than ecological restoration in Britain, for if our work cannot influence the current development paths of other nations, then we may enter a dark age more subject to natural law, but a lot less conducive to the human spirit. It is a paradox, that in our striving to sustain ourselves by co-opting the natural fruitfulness of the earth, we bring on its darker side of drought, flood, disease and famine. Hopefully, there is a middle way born of a greater humility and respect for these natural processes, rather than denial and control which has been our habit.

I would go further and argue that we need to break out of the category ghetto that sees nature as separate from ourselves, and hence something that needs to be conserved, protected or even enhanced. I say this because our current philosophy has condemned us, the conservationists, to the same 'reserves' as the conceptualized nature we seek to protect. We are not relevant to the mainstream of food production, water, timber, building materials, energy supplies and, above all, 'the economy'. We are still an afterthought, a concession hard fought when won from the departments of agriculture, trade and industry. It is as if nature is not necessary in modernity, other than in the services and jobs it provides.

In this book I can only leave signposts (in Chapter 9, The Healing Forest) to where that future thinking might lead in the themes of humanity and naturalness, denial and its consequences – as I wish to remain firmly rooted in the practicalities and limitations of nature conservation as it exists now, however much of a category mistake that may have been! The revolution that is unfolding has begun on the ground, in practical endeavour, but within the context of a larger dream.

Perhaps the way forward lies not so much in the abandonment of old concepts, but in the embracing of a new paradigm that builds upon the experience and understanding of natural processes gained from conservation biology. The challenge for conservationists will be to eschew management of these processes and allow nature to lead the way in some areas at least. These issues arise in each of the projects described and with different levels of intervention. However, this paradigm goes beyond that of the conservation biologist as landscape manager. There is something to be gained from allowing and respecting natural processes that is beyond utility, whether in pollution control, flood management or meeting biodiversity targets.

In the wilding of our land, we are also reaching into the realm of the heart and the province of the poet. All conservationists must ultimately act out of a love for nature, whether they operate scientifically or poetically, but the latter has somehow become lost in the ascendance of scientific reasoning. Within the three initiatives that I will describe in some detail – Coed Eryri (in Chapter 2), Caledon (in Chapter 3) and Dartmoor (in Chapter 4) – there exists a core belief in the spiritual value of wild nature and the necessity for recreating a connection that has been lost. These projects are at the wildest end of a spectrum: a potential for core areas that represent core values in the honouring of natural processes on a large scale.

In addition to these core-area projects and proposals, there are several smaller-scale core-area initiatives, such as Carrifran in the Southern Uplands, Ennerdale in the Lake District and at Wicken Sedge in the Cambridge Fens, as well as river and woodland 'corridor' schemes and landscape-scale strategies for wilder land, all of which are gathering pace. Some of these schemes – such as the Cambridge Fens – though initiated, will require long programmes of land purchase and conversion. Others – such as Ennerdale and Carrifran – are already under sympathetic ownership and are evolving long-term strategies. In the case of Carrifran, this is towards wildland with no exploitation, and in the case of Ennerdale, it is towards a spectrum of wildness where certain human use of the land could be regarded as 'natural', in as much as humans when not dominating natural processes can be described as natural. Some of our largest conservation land-holdings, such as the Mar Lodge estate (nearly 30,000 ha) in the Cairngorms, which was purchased as a sporting estate by the National Trust for Scotland, are currently debating management policies in the light of re-wilding issues such as the removal of bulldozed tracks, deer culling, removal of alien conifers, sustainable forest use and the degree of management for traditional sports.

These schemes, described in Chapter 5, presage a major shift in conservation thinking that will also require new science and more than a little risk-taking with pilot projects and experimental schemes. To this end, I have outlined the current science base for the restoration of natural vegetation types (see Chapter 6) – much of which has greatly benefited from the recent completion of extensive reviews – and attempted to explore the most relevant elements in relation to the dynamics of the changes we wish to see; I have also attempted to bring together the disparate data on experience with large herbivores (see Chapter 7) and carnivores (see Chapter 8), largely drawn from projects in the rest of Europe. Finally, I have outlined a strategy for large-area initiatives that is based upon the present undercurrents of change within agriculture (see Chapter 10, The Land In-between), forestry (see Chapter 11, Targeted Habitat Creation), and globalized markets (see Chapters 10 and 12, Stepping Stones to a Wilder Policy).

I believe that what we do in our own small landscape has the power to affect the greater debate on the future of the planetary ecosystem. We in Britain have a relatively stable population and a strong economy. Elsewhere, particularly in some of the most crucial ecological zones for the health of the planetary ecosystem, other nations are facing burgeoning population growth and dwindling financial resources. The forests of the Amazon, the Congo and South East Asia, and perhaps even the boreal fastness of Canada and Russia, are subject to increasing denudation, partly to accommodate people and partly to raise finance. The consequences to the planetary ecosystem of losing 50 per cent of that forest cover could be as extreme as the coming of an ice age. But having reduced our own forest cover to less than 10 per cent, and eradicated competing large herbivores or troublesome predators, with what authority can we speak and try to influence others?

Our own house is not in order. We have continued the destruction of the unenlightened past, when we exterminated several keystone species – the bear, lynx, elk and aurochs – as a consequence of deforestation, with the wolf, as it hung on and adapted to open country, being eradicated in the 17th or 18th century only by a determined effort.[5] The 19th century saw a veritable holocaust of a campaign against any predatory animal – hawks, falcons, kites, osprey, harriers, eagles and owls, as well as wildcats, martens, stoats, weasels and otters – all for the sake of an aristocracy that enjoyed the shooting of game, such that the balance of the countryside was radically altered. In the devastation of the last three centuries, deer disappeared outside of royal parks, the humble squirrel faced extinction in Scotland and had to be re-introduced, as did the roe deer to southern Britain.

In the past five years I have come to the view that if we are to influence policy on a global level, we have to do something very significant in our own backyard. If we were to restore some of our degraded forest ecosystems, bring back exterminated species and re-wild several large areas of land, we might have the power to change not only our own conscious relationship to nature, but also to influence others. In the final chapter I argue that a wildland strategy is also a strategy for the restoration of the human heart.

There are other nations at work on wilder-land programmes, particularly in North America and Holland,[6] but in Britain we have another contribution to make. We have a mythic heart. Our language is rooted in a literature of past relationship to the land – in Arthurian legend, in the romantic poets and in the Druid past of the Celts. I cannot but think that for us to have come so far down an irrational road of self-destruction, a road with so little heart, so little mystery, we must have laboured under some very great delusion of the psyche. It must lie in our separation not just from nature, but from the wild side of our own heart.

> My thought is
> that we are afraid
> afraid of the wild heart
> that we will not look into the fire directly.
>
> We live our job-protected lives
> behind the ramparts of a life insured
> and keep the wildwood at bay.
>
> Curious how our devil
> sports horns, goat's feet and dragon's tail
> red his favourite colour,
> whilst our hero is St George.
>
> My thought is
> he's science,
> scepticism his sword,
> hypothesis the lance that pins the dragon's head.
>
> Legend has it, when she of the three-fold way was lost to us,
> the Merlin held the magic,
> but then was lost to lechery,
> therein losing himself.
>
> No form now breaks the surface of the lake
> where Nimuë sleeps.
>
> Would that we could throw her not just sword,
> but lance and armour too,
> and walk this magic land,
> naked to the wild wild wood.
>
> *Author's introduction to the BANC Conference,* Wilderness Britain,
> *Open University, 1995*

# 1

# The Wild Side of Natural

Wild areas in which natural processes are left to reign supreme are commonly called 'wilderness', and in the US there exist designated 'wilderness areas' under the Wilderness Act, where no economic exploitation is allowed. The term is often used loosely in Britain, in which very few such areas are devoid of the present impact of agriculture and forestry, let alone past impacts. There has been much debate over definitions of wilderness and what is natural, and no conference on the subject of wilderness management has been complete without some academic discourse on its parameters and meaning.[1] However, 'wilderness' as a term, whilst useful to many, especially in America, is fraught with misunderstanding for the situation in Britain. This is perhaps because wilderness has both an ecological and spiritual dimension. For some, wildernesses are desolate places outside of the humanized realm, either to be avoided or brought under some kind of human dominion, and for others, they are places to practice humility, experience a certain vulnerability and acknowledge the creative and even destructive powers of the natural world.

I can see two dimensions of our being that are reflected in this polarity of meaning. As animals we are subject to nature's laws and natural processes, but as humans we have striven with apparent success to cheat those laws. Through technology, the human side of us has achieved control (perhaps only temporarily) of the natural cycles of abundance in food, the seasonal stresses of temperature and water supply, and, crucially, the exigencies of disease and childhood mortality. Nature seems to threaten these achievements, and much of the language of farming and resource use is couched in terms of a battle for dominance.

I will not here attempt to chart a course through these polarities, but will instead interject a hitherto oft-omitted ecological fact, lest we be tempted to build a practical philosophy of ecological restoration upon concepts of a pristine past. Historically, all the present wilderness areas outside Antarctica held populations of hunter–gatherers, hitherto assumed to have had minimal impact upon natural processes. Recent work has shown, however, that during the last glacial period (60,000–10,000 BP) huge changes were wrought throughout the Americas, Eurasia, Australasia and Oceania by the hunting to extinction of the mega-fauna (mastodons, mammoths, ground sloth, giant marsupials and large predators).[2] Once these animals were removed, further human hunting of medium-sized game and the use of fire continued to transform landscapes, particularly in the creation of open park-like forests and grasslands.[3]

Even the apparently pristine Antarctic ecosystem is today affected by chemical pollutants, which in the Arctic have already proven capable of altering the fertility of its major animal components, and in the recent past, whaling brought large-scale changes to the marine ecosystems upon which the landward ecology in polar regions is based. Commercial whaling removed over 90 per cent of the 'great' whales and with them virtually a whole trophic layer. There is so little data from that period that it would be difficult to say how much of any species' present abundance on that continent was not the result of the demise of those great competitors for the 'krill' and huge shoals of fish that underpin the ecosystem. Studies of the apparently pristine North Pacific coastal ecosystems of the Aleutians and Alaska have shown that the more recent whaling operation of 1949–1969, when half-a-million great whales, mostly sperm, were removed, caused major domino effects as orcas, the main predator of the whales, shifted predation to seals, sea lions and otters, causing rapid declines.[4]

In Britain and Europe, there are few areas to match North American wilderness. Most national parks support some present-day economic activity, such as farming and forestry, especially in Britain, and all receive large numbers of visitors and sustain significant tourist industries. A few have 'core areas' that would correspond to American 'wilderness areas', though there are none in Britain, and they also share a common prehistory of mega-faunal extinction.[5]

This 'hand of man' factor (noting the generally articulated gender bias) plays an important role in conservation management and the debates over minimal intervention. There has arisen a philosophy of 'natural' versus 'artificial' in which being human has been relegated to the latter. Thus, some have placed special value on the 'purely natural', whereas others value the artifices of human intervention in landscapes, such as open moorland, heaths, reed marshes and estuaries. James Fenton has argued that even these landscapes, though consequent upon deforestation and grazing, still present an array of perfectly natural processes, and that even domestic stock are adequate replacements for former herbivores that would have kept the land open.[6]

Until recently, the deep time perspective of palaeo-ecology has been missing from much of the debate. At what point do we decide that humans ceased to be 'natural'? We could choose the invention of stone tools, or the spear and bow, or fire, or place the point much later with the domestication of animals and the clearance of forest. We could categorize the mega-faunal extinctions as natural and similar to other major prehistoric shifts in the balance of species. But I am not sure that much is to be gained by the separation of artificial and natural. If we add our modern knowledge of the impact of human activity on inter-linked elements of the global ecosystem – such as the impact of carbon dioxide on the global climate; of the global distribution of toxins on immuno-competence, gender and reproduction of mammals, amphibians and birds; of the flux of basic chemicals such as sulphur dioxide, nitrogen and ozone upon vegetation on land and also upon marine life; as well as the more recent removal of mega-fauna from the oceans in the industrial whaling decades of 1949–1969 – then we must conclude, as did Bill McKibben in *The End of Nature*, that there are no purely 'natural' environments left.

Yet, if we abandon the concept of 'nature', so the argument goes, what then is the point of 'nature conservation'? Naturalness has been our yardstick and the main defensive weapon against competing demands on land use. Only since the mid-1990s have we really begun to take these factors on board and begun a necessary paradigm shift in values and perceptions. Firstly, it should now be clear that we cannot recreate the past, an oft-articulated aim of restoration ecology. For example, the Caledonian Forest of 6000 years ago was not just a matter of trees and National Vegetation Classification eco-type mosaics of habitat – it was a dynamic interactive process involving many species in a large herbivore guild with carnivores feeding upon them; as well as the hunting ground of extremely efficient human omnivores. The 'forest' was this entity and had evolved over millions of years of continuous interaction, but even this Mesolithic forest with its herds of wild cattle, forest pony, elk, wolf, bear, boar and lynx had already lost its mega-herbivores, the European temperate-forest elephants and rhinos as well as the very large carnivores, the sabre-toothed cats, that fed upon them.

It follows, therefore, that if we now seek to recreate or restore anything in nature, we do so as an act of co-creation, as an active agent in the future process of the forest. In a sense, we shall be restoring a relationship that has existed for tens of thousands of years, in which humans have altered habitats to suit both themselves and certain of their fellow creatures. Some would dress this up in the clothes of science – to set aside areas for the study of natural processes – or of politics, whereby we seek to influence the development agenda of a planet heading for ecological destruction, with humans included; others might argue that all species have a right to exist, and that we should set land aside for their needs. What I see under the surface of reasons is an act of love, or gratitude – in essence, a making sacred – something that shines out from all the initiatives that are reported in this book. It is a love that generally dares not speak its name, yet in acting out of love, at some risk to our own short-term interests, we can set the strongest example to others in a world that needs such leadership.

We are, after all, world citizens in a global process of development and loss of wildland, particularly forests, that now threatens the stability of our supporting ecosystems. It has so far not been enough to argue a case for wildland based upon this ecological or economic self-interest. After all, respected groups of UN scientists have been doing that for decades to minimal effect. We have to affect the development ethos itself, and to do that, I believe we have to reclaim the deeper spiritual sense that once connected us to the land, to nature and to a wilder heart.

The wild heart places death and comfort in a different perspective to that of the civil heart. Death is not something feared and avoided at all costs; rather, the heart is rooted in a spiritual sense of belonging that engenders an honouring. Only a wild heart is capable of living with the dangers of nature, of accepting the risks, and taking death or loss in its stride.[7] The wild heart thus honours the wolf, the bear and the panther. It does not seek to eradicate, because in acceptance there is no revenge.

In this, we need not look to Americans for guidance. They are essentially escaped Europeans, and they escaped from an overcrowded garden into what at first appeared to them a wilderness of plenty. North America, after a little more than 300 years of mass immigration, still has large areas of land with little or no economic exploitation, landscapes still essentially dominated by natural processes, even if somewhat depleted of their original mammalian inhabitants, humans included. We could add that even after the national parks were set up, an irrational predator 'control' policy all-but eradicated wolf, brown bear, lynx and puma from vast areas of wild country – there were limits to how wild wilderness could be.

When John Muir effectively gave birth to the modern 'national park' ethos, he was still a European awed by the beauty and majesty of wild nature, and disturbed at the prospect of its ultimate despoliation. Back home in Britain, the Victorians had just finished their massive onslaught on anything with claws or talons – from the diminutive polecat and weasel, to the buzzard, kite and eagle. England was finally a tame landscape, with nothing to challenge the supremacy of man as the main killer in the land. Whereas the founding fathers of New England sought refuge for their Puritan faith, old England set about turning the world into a market of commodities. The bucolic landscapes that inspired the Romantic poets were soon to be possessed by the demons of production – a process not yet ended. Wilderness became that which was non-productive and useless, the abode of biblical isolation and disturbance of the spirit. Where John Muir found spiritual solace, others were still infected by a spiritual dread of where the 'wasteland' begins.

There were other, darker elements at play in that early creation of wilderness sanctuary. The 'national park' movement has created wilderness by evicting or excluding people more often than it has preserved wilderness that was unused. The movement is essentially a product of civil society and of the expressed need for jaded industrialized souls to find solace in the purity of nature. We now have categories of wildness essentially defined by the degree of human absence. At its outset the concept was fallacious and imperial. Almost all wild areas, certainly in North America, supported nomadic hunters and gatherers, or in some cases were reserved by them as a sacred place for ceremony and vision.

The earliest European settlers appreciated this. A mixed-blood Native American storyteller I know has a repertoire not only of Chippewa myths, but also of Gaelic and Breton myths from the earliest nomadic trappers who intermarried with the indigenous peoples. However, European ideologies of dominion, custodianship, commodity, exploitation, markets and wealth rapidly followed upon the heels of the awe-inspired adventurer. As did that myopic superiority that saw no tribal culture worthy of the name human, and thus the slaughter and slavery began. Introduced diseases outstripped the guns and chains. By the time of the national parks movement many wild places were empty, and for the first time in 30,000 years.[8]

Our immediate forebears in the wilderness movement that birthed the national parks looked through eyes of ignorance at these empty or almost empty lands. They were not aware of the long histories of ecological change brought about by the thinly distributed hunters and gatherers. It was easy for them to mistake the depleted populations of Indians or Aborigines as peripheral in their impact, and perhaps as recent and marginal additions to the landscape. When Europeans arrived to define them, the teeming middle-fauna and park-like forests appeared as an apparition of Arcadia, or Paradise, a mythical past or a heavenly promise. Considering the overcrowded cities of Holland, Britain, France, Portugal and Spain, from which they had set sail, with their diseases, stench of excrement, and confined and enclosed lands, all owned, the people enslaved and caught in rigid hierarchies, small wonder the new lands seemed paradisiacal. But paradise *had* to be empty – as if Adam and Eve must find the mythic garden as they had left it. All over the world, indigenous peoples, settled and otherwise, have been moved out, traditional practices curtailed, and pristine people-free zones created for recreation or in the case of total exclusion zones, scientific study (noting that scientists can usually get access!).

## Nature as Mother

Just as modern day Native Americans hold no concept of wilderness, it is unlikely that our ancestral Celts felt anything other than the presence of the great nurturing power that so many tribal peoples call Mother, that which has given them birth and sustenance. It is a curious and perhaps unfortunate evolution of language that English has chosen the Latin *Natura* to represent the concept of 'nature' – that which we came to see as separate from ourselves; natural in opposition to artificial or man-made. For the Latin simply means 'to give birth'. The word *birth* comes from our Angle or Scandinavian roots. How different things might have been had we called the natural world about us, *Birther*! Wild 'nature' might then have felt less 'other' and our connection to its processes more fundamental and reverent.

We are a long way down the road that has led to the current despoliation and exploitation of our 'mother' earth. The poster with the wolf's eyes reads, 'in wilderness is the salvation of the world'. It is a plea for the survival of the greater ecosystem upon which we all depend and the plea is then defended by ecological truths. But in truth is this not a plea to the unfeeling and mindlessly destructive would-be controllers of the world? Most scientific ecologists think that the human species would survive without wilderness, but do not believe that an insensitive humanity would respond to their pleas to protect what they also love, unless humanity's own survival was at stake. The poster would be truer if it read 'in wilderness is the salvation of the heart', but the dominant ideology has yet to realize that there is a problem in the heart.

It should be obvious now that the pleas of ecological science to conserve biodiversity and wild places are failing to get through at the global level. They have become based upon a 'self-interest' argument: that if we lose some species from a complex structure of which our general understanding is limited, then the whole edifice that supports human life could crumble. Or we make claims for the future discovery of drugs that could save humanity from debilitating and potentially catastrophic diseases. I doubt these claims are treated with credence by the business-oriented minds that purport to run the global economy. If the new drugs can turn a profit, then tropical forests have a future; the same is true for elephant and ivory, and lions and eco-tourist potential.

We might have expected to get further with arguments relating to process, of the functionality of forests for carbon sequestration and climate control, and of the potential disasters for the global economy if the planetary ecosystem is destabilized. There is a mentality in the industrial-ized world that would see each and every component of our supporting ecosystems managed and engineered for our global benefit as expressed in a market of commodities and services. For those with this mentality, the Amazon constitutes a planetary climate control service.

Imagine we were to celebrate the fact that 'every component of our birth-mother is now managed and engineered'. Some eco-technicians have emerged with plans for global forest cover to be managed for optimum carbon efficiency – first, cut down inefficient old growth, store the carbon, and plant new and better forest genetically engineered for the task. In the face of climate change, agriculture could be made more robust and sustainable, but with modified genes, and housing and transport made less energy demanding with new technology. And there would be wind turbines, tidal barrages, hydro-schemes, and vast biomass fuel plantations. Deserts could be plastered with photovoltaic solar collectors to power the emerging hydrogen economy. And the wild? Little pockets of eco-tourism – service providers for the remnant sensitives.

If we are to avoid this soul-less future, I believe we have to move now and go beyond the utilitarian arguments of ecosystem dynamics. Few of the nature reserves of today, even the larger national parks of Africa and America, will provide robustness against climate change, let alone genetic drift for the isolated populations they hold. If we are to conserve the beautiful diversity of life, we will have to redress the balance in those areas outside the reserves – the vast areas of agriculture and industrial forestry, and even the cities themselves. And, most crucially, our energy, water and materials demands in the urban environment will determine the extent to which we can allow the wildlands to coexist. This balance is ultimately related to risk, loss, comfort and security rather than survival. These are issues of the heart. Perhaps that is the ultimate power of the wild: it forces a discourse. It will force us to marry the emotional with the scientific, the spiritual with the rational.

In Britain an ethos of 'wildland' is emerging in which human intervention is minimal and natural processes are respected. At times, as if caught between paradigms, these natural processes and even some re-introduced species (such as the beavers penned in a Kent nature reserve) are still viewed as 'management tools' in relation to some set of desired targets. Above all, any government-mediated change must meet socio-economic goals in the definition of sustainability. Any landscape-scale evolution of wilder land will set challenges with respect to economic losses and gains. But with the growing consciousness of respect for nature as teacher and healer, there is every prospect that such evolution will generate as much economic gain as loss, and perhaps more so where lands marginal to agriculture and forestry are concerned. On a world scale, the rich nations will have to develop more effective ways of funding protection and ecological restoration in nations that would otherwise face economic penalties in the non-exploitation of wildland. In this endeavour the world desperately needs a change of heart, and we in Britain have an opportunity to develop a working model.

# 2

# Coed Eryri

The emblem of the Snowdonia National Park is the arctic-alpine Snowdon lily *Lloydia serotina*, and this refugee from the arctic is found nowhere else in Britain. But the Welsh name for these hills is Eryri, the place of eagles. To the modern mind, an eagle, however spectacular, is just another species, but to the older culture of these hills, it held a special meaning: it represented visionary power. Eagles were eradicated in North Wales in the 16th century.

In February 1992, I wrote a pamphlet for a small group working on a vision for a Forest of Snowdon, Coed Eryri, inspired by Alan Featherstone's work in Scotland and by the success of Community Forests in England.[1] We aimed to draw together a number of disparate initiatives for re-wilding Snowdonia, but we had to work against an entrenched antipathy to natural processes. The National Park (see Colour Plate 1) held no core area of wildland and virtually no naturally regenerating forest due to the presence of sheep, and indeed, despite 30 per cent forest cover (mostly plantation), only 1 per cent remained of the ancestral indigenous oak.[2] After three years of discussions, I concluded that we were dealing not just with the economic interests of farmers and foresters, but with a deeper psychology relating to the need to dominate nature and to bring wild land into productive use:

> . . . the primary thing, the fear of listening, is a fear of Nature herself. In the Forest there are no voices but hers. This is not the Chapel to the Son, who will be our salvation, to a Father who will guide the righteous and judge the wicked, or to a Holy Ghost that forever sustains and promises a personal immortality. It is not a Cathedral of solid immovable stone set by architect and mason. Here there is darkness and constant motion. Here we may be reminded of our physical frailty, our death and decay. Here is the dark mother, not Mary the sustainer, but Ceridwen or Hecate, the destroyer. Here is where the male mind must surrender and meet its greatest fear. Here is the rebirth of consciousness.[3]

What began then was very much a personal rebirth, a personal journey of reconnection for each of our group, but particularly for me, blinkered by

years of scientific training and policy analysis. In our small group we began
to uncover ancient practices of listening, of storytelling, of drum and dance
and vision quest, and in so doing, sought our teachers among the Native
Americans, the yogis, and those few women who had kept alive the ancient
spiritual traditions associated with a deeper healing connection to nature:

> . . . from other cultures we have long sought to suppress and exterminate,
> we are now learning that this great mystery of nature cares for us, that her
> voices speak wisdom, that her servants, the animals and trees, have spirit
> voices that speak of love, with love. All along it was so, but we could not
> see through the mist of fear. The wolf and bear have medicine as deep as
> any herb. Raven and beaver will speak if we cup hand to inner ear. In
> dreams or quiet wakefulness they will come. They know our journey, they
> know love. Of course, how could it be otherwise? How could the divine
> not be everywhere, not be with them and with us unbounded by concept,
> by language, by time or space? This is not 'mysticism'. It is honouring the
> great mystery and is a deeper reality, a deeper ecology.[4]

And of course, that made it difficult for mainstream conservation, National
Park committees or farming communities to embrace our vision! My friend
Eric Maddern, however, developed 'Cae Mabon', near Llanberis, to
become a centre for education and the spiritual connection to the wildland
of Snowdon.[5] The vision of a wild forest is held firm in many hearts and
we must trust that what we have shared will influence those with
responsibilities for land management in Snowdonia. Coed Eryri's activities
have been primarily a 'visioning' process involving the core group,
educational outreach and discussions with various 'stakeholders' in the
National Park; this has been ongoing in relation to a core area in the
Rhinogydd (see Colour Plate 2).

However, in the slow metamorphosis from ecological vision towards
cultural change, I have also undergone a personal transformation in
understanding and values, and in this account of Coed Eryri I will depart
from the normal accepted form of conservation discourse and objectivity,
as I believe we, as conservationists, have to make such a transition on a
broader political level – we have to become central to human values in
areas in which we are now marginal. I do not believe that we can do it by
embracing economic 'services' or through some quasi-scientific conservation ethic. I have come to believe that through our work with wild nature,
we must restore something central to the human soul, something that has
the power to over-ride selfish and short-term motivation, as well as to
over-ride the great fear of nature still rooted in the psyche.

When I moved to Snowdonia in February 1989, I was struggling to live
with a severely split personal world. I had a scientific training in biological
sciences and had worked as a professional consultant in ecological policy
for over ten years, work that covered the fields of radioecology, chemical

pollution, climate change, renewable energy impacts and various industrial policy issues. I also had further degrees and academic training in social anthropology that had given me a perspective on man's relationship to spiritual and natural worlds. But I had become mired in these systems of thinking and was already engaged in the process of redeeming another, more intuitive part of my self. This other self trained in yogic 'sciences' with a Himalayan master, worked with Native American teachers, and ran groups developing techniques of spiritual purification and vision quest. My spirituality had begun as an essentially Eastern quest for the purity of heart and absence of mind, and much later I had confronted the reality of living in the West, the place of creativity and dreaming.[6]

I was to spend seven years slowly reconciling my two worlds and working with some remarkable people. The Coed Eryri group consisted of local artists, sculptors, storytellers, shamanic healers, community workers, foresters and woodworkers, about half of whom were native Welsh speakers.

On previous encounters with the bleak mountainous terrain – in the 1970s I took my students for hikes above Cwm Idwal – I had looked upon the land with the manipulative eye of a zealous ecologist: 'if only we could get the sheep off, rejuvenate the flower meadows, reforest the slopes. This place should by rights be forest. After all, it is a National Park where nature should be paramount.'

Instead, it is a national sheep reserve, overgrazed and ecologically impoverished. The answer was to recreate the forest with its ecological web intact. I set about making plans and finding allies. There were already many small independent initiatives, and if we combined, we could argue for major policy changes and the funds for ecological restoration. What Alan Featherstone was doing for the Caledonian pine, we could do for the Welsh oak!

Only about 1 per cent of Snowdonia National Park is remnant semi-natural woodland, yet there is 30 per cent 'forest' cover consisting of plantations, largely of alien Sitka spruce, Japanese larch or Scots pine. Outside these plantations, almost every nook and cranny is grazed by sheep or cattle, and very little of the remnant ancient broadleaf woodland is regenerating. Wild herbivores are few: there are some ancient feral goats in the rockier parts of the hills and fallow deer (not indigenous to Britain) in the Forestry Commission's Coed y Brenin in the south of the Park. The red deer and roe deer are extinct in the region. The grazing pressure from domestic stock prevents re-colonization of the bare hillsides by natural regeneration, and large areas have been invaded by alien rhododendron scrub.

The first response of conservationists in protecting existing woodland or planting new trees is to aggressively fence out domestic stock. I had an opportunity to compare open and fenced woodland along the ancient woodland ridge of Harlech near my home. Almost a third of the wood was fenced, another third or more heavily grazed, but the immediate area of about 20 ha around the house was lightly grazed by sheep and a small suckler herd of eight or so Welsh Black cattle. The third that had been fenced off from all stock had a thick shrub and herb layer of bramble and ivy, with few flowering plants and little regeneration; the heavily grazed section held little other than grasses and mosses, with no young trees; whereas the lightly grazed area was alive with flowering plants, regenerating young trees and a large variety of shrubs and ferns.

## Llety'r Fwyalchen – abode of the blackbird

That area of active regeneration surrounded my home, Llety'r Fwyalchen, the abode of the blackbird. Whilst I set about my plans and alliances, largely around the traditional model of conservation – how to get the stock off, erect fences, combine planting and natural regeneration, and take care over provenance – I would walk daily around the meadows and woods. I kept a diary not of the times of flowering or numbers of species, but of the moons and the inner dreams that came. I would walk out on a circuit from the house and visit first the old crab apple, casting her dense shade, the space below barely high enough to crouch, surrounded by the bracken and bright sunlight, to quietly feel the day's concerns drain away in the cleansing darkness:

> These woods are special in ways that cannot be measured. The scientist would find nothing unusual here, for here is a poetry of the commonplace. Yet a poetic masterpiece, a symphony of the most divine.
>
> We begin with Crab, the Old Lady, Hecate, alone in the witchy dark, to crawl beneath her black wings on the damp moss, she is the purifier and the entrance and here we ask the shadows to cleanse us of the dross we bring. On then to Grandfather Oak, its youth saw Glyndwr's rebellion, the securing of the Bardic land, if momentarily. Fissured bark. Huge girth, giant arms, broken and horned. Heart of Herne. Old Druid. Lend us strength for the journey.
>
> On to Holly. Boughs pink flushed grey tickling the sensual centre with erotic curve, a thigh to touch, delicate arm, rounded breast, or muscle bulging with power, flexed and waiting, man or woman? Here is mysterious coupling, knowledge beyond the veil.
>
> To the Alder grove. Ground sodden first flush of golden saxifrage. Her place. Red bleeds her wound. Kingcup in pools where the moon strikes through. Iris bed. Yellow her favourite. The owls nest here, bird of the coven. We come with no requests. This is not the place for asking, but of gratitudes, the return of love. Bathe deep in cold waters. Open to moon's silver, alders' shadows. Come when Luna is full and dances on the

surface of her pools. Slip softly under, let the water embrace. Here there is no asking. Kiss the moss between her thighs. She loves you, you are welcome, always. Then listen. She tells you how long she has waited, knowing your wild heart.

It is a bluebell spring. The foragers are late and the blue comes to full bloom. Beltaine brings a carpet of wonder, whites of anemone and woodsorrel, stitchwort and pignut, tiny stars of sanicle, woodruff and a foam of ramsons heavy with scent, and everywhere yellows of celandine, pimpernel, spearwort, buttercup and marigold, blue violets, pink herb robert and campion. So quick now. Each week brings someone to seed. Meadows of dandelion heads, daffodils long gone, snowdrops bent back to the earth, burying their green swelling womb.

Soon will come foxglove, meadowsweet, woodsage and valerian, tall to outpace the vigorous summer grass, the spreading ferns. And honeysuckle, queen of the woodland night high above her carpet, the enchanter's nightshade.

She is bright now with song. Mwyalchen opens the gap between the worlds. Winter loyal thrush, dunnock, robin and wren, joined now by throaty blackcaps, flute-warblers, flycatchers and jewelled redstart. You have come a long way for this. Pan's garden. Wild heart.

Every species was regenerating – ash, oak, willow, birch, alder, rowan, holly, hawthorn, crab apple, spindle, blackthorn and gean – and all holding their own against the prolific sycamore; yet the meadows were grazed and there were no barriers to entering the woodland. The small sloping fields among the woods were alive with musk mallow, marsh orchid, cranesbill and betony, and in the wet woods, in one small patch in May, I counted 13 species of woodland flowers along with many medicinal herbs such as valerian, wood sage and lady's mantle. You can walk for hours elsewhere in the National Park and not see a significant flower.

In the long-fenced section of the ancient woodland, you were also hard-pressed to find any flowers – the whole place was a tangle of brambles and ivy; however, it took several years for the significance of all this to sink in. Meanwhile the plan unfolded: draw maps of land use categories – the planning authority had maps of presumptions of consent for forestry (assumed to be commercial); develop strategies to get rid of the stock over large areas. The solution was clear: buy key bits of land (by approaching the John Muir Society, National Trust and Woodland Trust for help, and even by raising money locally), then fence and plant, or regenerate where sufficient seed sources existed. It might also be possible to get agreements from landowners (the National Trust owns significant acreage) to fence and regenerate small areas on the higher ground, especially beside streams. It would take a long time, but if all parties cooperated to a grand design, in 50 years we could see a new forest on the barren slopes.

Not much happened. The National Trust did great work on the upper reaches of streams by fencing and planting, but balked at purchasing redundant Forestry plantations with the aim of reconversion. The agencies of the National Park and Countryside Council for Wales thought our long-term plan 'unrealistic'. And of course, they were right. The difference between Caledon and Eryri, is that Eryri has hundreds of small-scale sheep farmers, myriads of stone walls and several centuries of human domination of the landscape. The traditional Welsh-speaking communities are also insular, rather cool towards incomers with ideas, deeply religious and totally dependent upon agricultural subsidies. Many of today's farming families were quarry workers in the Victorian heyday of slate mining, and for some, attitudes to the land had not evolved greatly.

In modern times a 'traditional' Welsh upland farm has no trees outside of the odd single-aged copse with no regeneration, billiard-table green swards of improved meadows of in-bye land and access to the moors where heather has largely been replaced with acid grassland. The farmers' kitchens are bare of dried herbs or bottled anything: no jams, honey, fruit or cobs – the culinary forest is smaller than the remnant ancient oaks. World-weary National Park ecologists and other assorted nature conservationists long settled for protecting what is left – the bats, and the twayblades hidden in the heather. Otter were getting scarcer, pine marten hadn't been seen for years and black grouse were on the verge of extinction. Though there was then no detailed species list and limited monitoring data for the National Park,[7] it was obvious that the old concepts were not holding ground and that the agricultural economy was both the historical villain and the main obstacle to change.

## The ancient forest, cattle and the Celtic heritage

If we were to transform Snowdonia, however, we had to have the farmers on board. This would mean a fundamental social and cultural shift. In realizing the need to integrate current farming communities in the vision, the 'forest' came to mean much more than my earlier scientific ecological training had provided for. Earlier concepts of primeval woodland replete with re-introduced herbivores – boar, roe deer, red deer and beaver –and maybe the odd lynx (Scotland was the only place big enough for bear and wolf), now gave way to the 'cultural' forest as a place where people dwelt and intimately used the forest whilst respecting its natural sanctuaries and wildlife. This was the forest of the original Celts. They were a cattle people and a forest people and respected the wolf and the bear as much as any tribal people in other parts of the globe respected the big cats and other dangerous species in the forest around them. Theirs was also a shamanic culture; the relationship between the human psyche and the creatures and plants of the forest was a two-way communication in the furtherance of healing and spiritual growth. The tribal healers entered into communion and alliance with the healing spirits of the trees, herbs, birds and other animals.

It is at this point that the 'superior' Western scientific mind starts to include tribal peoples in the same category as the twayblades and red grouse: objects for study. Social anthropologists make wonderful patterns with quaint comparative tribal data. Following the work of the anthropologist and popular writer Carlos Castenada, there have been a few dissenters, but generally, the world of the shaman is relegated to the realms of personal experience and cultural delusion.[8] Modernity knows where reality begins and ends. Yet, truly modern and open science knows that it co-creates the reality it purports to study objectively. Physicists tell us quite clearly that there are no boundaries to physical reality – that underlying everything is electromagnetic waveform and a gravity field – and the occasional psychologist has even put the scientific mind under scrutiny! The scientific worlds of measurement and metaphor, with their glorious technological spin-offs, have gained not just primacy as knowledge, but primacy of culture: the objective and consensual over the personal and the rational above the intuitive.

And although everything we ever conceive and make must first be dreamed, the dream is relegated. Our schools do not encourage dreamers nor teach intuition. No one is taught to expand their consciousness beyond the boundaries of their own personal mind. Odd really, considering that Galileo, Kepler, Copernicus, Mendeleyev, Newton, Einstein and Tesla were all dreamers, gaining their breakthroughs by deep intuition; most of them were ostracized for it at some time by the narrower-minded scientific or political fraternity.

In my mountain retreat, I began to relate to the underlying reality rather than to the surface form. The forest began to take on another light. Slowly we became conscious of what the forest had meant to the mythical ancestors of Snowdonia. It was a place of healing and spiritual retreat. In meditation, a communion was reached with animals and trees. They talked by reflection, but that reflection always held a greater wisdom. And in return came gratitude, respect and ceremony.

## A mythic heart

At the mythic heart of Britain lies Arthur the King. He sleeps, sometime to awake. He is the keeper of the dream, the essential soul matter of this land. Noble yet flawed, ever in service to the Grail Goddess, his sword of truth is now long lost beneath the waters of human consciousness. Something we know and treasure has retreated from this land.

'Aart' is bear in Celtic languages. Native American teachers call bear 'the keeper of the dream'. The mythic bear–king thus keeps the dream of Albion alive for a time when there will be a true relationship to the land, one of honouring, respect, reverence and celebration. The Grail is the deep feminine mystery, which the masculine must touch and be touched by in order for the land to be fertile (and the honourable man to be healed of his aggressive masculinity).

As I work on this book by the banks of the Artro (the bear) that runs from the heart of the Rhinog mountains, where Robert Graves went to primary school and later first dreamt of the White Goddess,[9] there is now a yellow digger grinding out new drains. All over the National Park, furiously religious men dig and scrape, hurtle about in four-wheel-drive jeeps or quad bikes, part of an 'industry' of producers, businesses and service providers. New conservation subsidies rebuild the walls that the Goddess has weathered and erect barbed wire as if at war. We are so very far from the balance of masculine and feminine.

But the blackbird still sings at Llety'r Fwyalchen. In the Druid oracle, the blackbird's song heralds the gateway between the worlds. Many people arrived there for that journey into the Otherworld of dream. For four days and four nights in the woods, with no food, some would refuse bedding and just sit, still, quiet, until the forest revealed itself in the quest for personal vision. The ancient Celts and Native Americans knew that in meditation, in active lucid dreaming, with nature all around, a unity of consciousness can be reached in which the presence of animals and plants influences the dream. The ancients would ascribe to each participant in the dream a spirit reality, an essence of their medicine and healing influence drawn from direct dream experience.

Ten years ago, the scientific mind scoffed more than it does now. The arrogant edifice has crumbled a little – the ozone hole, global warming, acid rain, dying seals and forests, gender-bending chemicals, BSE, HIV and the funeral pyres of foot-and-mouth disease. The techno-world is vulnerable to nature as well as to its own follies. But there has to be something more – perhaps a realization that science has elevated itself too far above the personal and subjective, wherein dwells the soul and through which man reaches to the soul in all about him.

Yogis, Native American medicine teachers and Shamans of all cultures have no problem with this. Not because of some theory, but because it is their practical experience – they can dwell in the unified field of consciousness. In that field, the voices of oak and ash, raven and eagle, are not separate from our voice and each has its own particular character – they do not simply reflect, they heal – they hold 'medicine'.[10] We return to this theme in Chapter 9, The Healing Forest.

And in that realm of healing, God is not a postulate, a belief or a hypothesis, but the direct experience of presence – a feeling, a seeing of connectedness and of beauty, and above all, of love. There are no cultures that have nurtured this expanded consciousness and have not felt and named this presence, be it Great Mystery, Great Mother, Wakan Tanka or Pancha Mama.

This, of course, takes us even further from the problem of the cultural tradition that is Welsh sheep farming – and which in its current form of smallholdings and enclosed land is only a few hundred years old. Here, God is definitely a man, and a very orderly one: a shepherd, a husbandman, a guardian or a steward. Nature conservationists settled on the latter and tended to disappear when talk came round to recreating wilderness – to have done otherwise would have been political, and perhaps even social, suicide. Nevertheless, in this unpromising environment, the small group called Coed Eryri was formed with the intention of holding the vision and promoting discussion. Our time would come when the Common Agricultural Policy (CAP) dissolved and the uneconomic farms went to the wall. Only in times of decline and distress are communities open to new ways. Meanwhile, we needed to develop the vision to address the political realities of our community.

## Integrative regeneration

In this respect, an opportunity arose in the form of a derelict but very fine building in the heart of Snowdonia. The former slate mining town of Blaenau Ffestiniog, an enclave of industrial dereliction (and a major tourist attraction with the former deep mines and caverns), had growing social problems of unemployment and disaffected youth. The building in question was an old market hall. It was stone built with a huge vaulted roof, housing what had been at various times a ballroom, a cinema and a war-time production unit for uniforms. The old market was on the ground floor and the upper storey, supported by pillars, held a magnificent sprung wooden floor. The roof and walls were still sound, but all the windows were gone and boarded up and significant repairs were needed. The council could not bear the costs and had decided to knock it down unless a buyer or custodian could be found.

We had already witnessed the parents of the Snowdonia Steiner School design and build a 'science unit' for the school – a large and wonderful building on wooden piles with a shingle roof in which all the timber had been cut from local larch forests and shipped in using the 'tourist' railway (formerly built for transporting the slate). We approached the County Council with ideas of restoring the building using local materials (slate and timber) and local skills in carpentry. The eventual use for the building would be as a community and educational centre, perhaps with its own theatre group. It would provide a most excellent performance space. The youth theatre project could focus upon issues of regeneration and the relationship to nature as well as issues of dereliction and social dysfunction (use of drugs among young people was fast becoming a problem in rural Wales).

We began researching the feasibility of an idea that had great potential for regenerating links between the urban areas of Snowdonia and the natural resources as well as the natural beauty of the Park. I visited a pioneering project in mid-Wales, where the National Trust was restoring a large country house and estate that had been bequeathed to it. There, the local director of the Trust had eschewed immediate large inputs of money to renovate the derelict buildings in favour of smaller, timed allotments to finance a community-based programme of restoration. Timber from the estate was to be harvested and milled to provide for a team of locally recruited craft carpenters who would replace the fittings. Such old skills were in short-supply and many retired people were enlisted to train modern apprentices. When I visited the site at Llanerchaeron it was a hive of activity, a ready example of integrative regeneration of skills, meaningful work, cooperative endeavour and connection to the land.

Sadly, what was an innovative opportunity for one National Trust director was a potential headache for another; the North Wales regional director, after much consideration and several site visits by some of the Trust's more forward-thinking officers, would not take on the Market Hall, though it was offered by the Council for a nominal £1 and there were obvious sources of funding for its renovation and management.

The interest in the Hall sparked alternative schemes by local interests centred on a 'heritage' experience – effectively a pay-at-the-door tourist attraction. At least our involvement was instrumental in generating this interest, and the building was eventually preserved and renovated by the Council and serves now as a community arts centre, but the opportunity for a truly 'integrative regeneration' was not taken. This brief attempt to reconcile urban life with the forest, the past with the future, and to reach a disaffected youth, taught us the important role that individual personalities and politics plays in any history.

In many respects, the former industrial history of Snowdonia affects current policies – there are large communities within or on the edge of the Park that look to a future of high-technology companies, energy resources or tourist developments such as narrow-gauge railways and artificial ski slopes, rather than any kind of relationship to nature itself. Indeed, since its inception, the National Park has been blighted by major installations such as the nuclear power station at Trawsfynydd, an above-ground hydro-pipeline on the very slopes of Snowdon itself, a massive pumped-storage scheme, power lines, 'improved' roads and a plethora of new applications for small-scale hydro schemes on the rivers, many of which were in use in the industrial past. If the future of the National Park is to include a re-wilding, a way ahead must be found whereby there is an integration of development with local resources and skills.

## Re-evaluation and vision

The time at Llety'r Fwyalchen thus evolved as a dance between the two worlds of personal initiation and a community ecology. Occasionally, the one world would inspire change in the other. Values began to change. My own political ecology became more human-centred. I came to learn that the essence of a shamanic relationship is the human journey of love and caring. All ideas of the expulsion of humans from nature, to leave it pristine, were thus long gone. But what then of domination, of over-use and the acute lack of honouring of nature's processes? We began to formulate a more integrated approach to a wildland ecology, and at the same time, to untangle an ideology of the 'natural' forest.

The forest must be grazed to be natural. A sapling that has grown tall and never in its youth been munched is as unnatural as any alien Forestry Commission plantling. Its form will never be natural. Use of Tulley tubes may gain a few years growth, but the seedling will be weak and untested by wind or nibbling teeth. The vital growth spurts of young trees, shrubs and herbs all evolved in a battle against the forces of innumerable nibblers – aurochs and tarpan, wood bison, moose, two or three species of deer, boar and beaver and as we were later to realize, mega-herbivores such as temperate forest elephants and rhinoceros.

The primeval forest had a plethora of grazers, browsers, diggers and dammers – beaver created wetland; boar opened ground for seedling development; roe deer, red deer, forest pony and forest cattle kept the balance between glade and thicket; and the wolf kept them all moving around such that no one place was overgrazed. Where then is our English Nature Reserve? The process has been emasculated, evolution interfered with and alien minds put in charge! Grazing and browsing, crushing and trampling, damming and flooding – they are integral to the beating heart of the forest.

So, why make the farmer redundant? If Llety'r Fwyalchen had such a rich flora and the patchwork maintained itself, it could act as a model for all the valley woods and farms. The open moorland would remain fundamentally open and kept under lesser grazing pressure by removing sheep, introducing wild cattle and red deer, and licensing culls for the local organic meat market. Beaver could be introduced to the wetter valley bottoms, and once again, cattle could be farmed on the meadows. Ultimately, a grazing system based upon cattle would be robust enough to bring back the lynx and the eagle. Initially this could be done in one large area; the Rhinog hills, with no major roads running through, nor settlements in its heart, looked ideal.

A vision began to form that sought to maintain a balance of land use within the National Park – the northern areas of Snowdon (the peak) and the Carneddau would remain under hopefully less-intense grazing regimes as recreational areas for walkers, ramblers and climbers and would support the remnant populations of moorland birds; the southern areas of Cadair Idris and Coed y Brenin would remain as open hill country and commercial forestry, but hopefully with a more-enlightened choice of indigenous species. But in the centre, at its heart, there was space for a re-wilding.

## Cultural shifts: from grass pasture to wood pasture

The vision as articulated may be fanciful on a cultural level, but is economically and ecologically feasible. Virtually all Welsh upland farmers are effectively paid by the state. Their inputs cost as much as they earn from their output, and any real income is courtesy of the European Union or the UK taxpayer. The average income for UK farms in the 1990s fell from £10,000 to £4000, and in Wales the figure is likely to be significantly lower. In addition to agricultural subsidies, therefore, most farmers are on income support. If the average farm size is 100ha and a decent new forest were to cover 20,000ha of wood–pasture mosaic, then the cost of maintaining farmers as managers of such an area would be £800,000 per annum – the amount that they are being paid now by the EU anyway! More realistically, double that income and a farm of twice the size would be required, with the farmers encouraged to supplement the income as managers with eco-tourism or craftwork. This sort of money is available and paid today either under the CAP or various Welsh stewardship schemes such as Tir Gofal to provide for marginal food production, land management, wood-land creation and rural economic and social aid.[11]

There is no a priori reason why the same farmers could not be retrained to manage a regenerating forest, the introduction of former species, eco-holidays and conservation work camps, as well as shepherding small herds of prime organic beef (the last three activities confined to the buffer zones around a core area). There are models of silvo-pastoral systems in Portugal and in the famed *dehesa* of Spain. Shepherding communities co-exist with bear, wolf and lynx in both these countries, as well as in France (lynx in the Vosges), Germany (lynx in the Bavarian forest), Austria and Slovenia (bears in the alps), Italy (wolves in the Abruzzo National Park) and the great carnivore stronghold of Romania. The key to success is adequate wild prey and effective guard dogs. We would not advocate the wolf and bear for Snowdonia, but there is certainly room for the lynx.

However, we cannot assume that the current level of social subsidy will persist under the free-trade dominated international market conditions that are only now beginning to make their presence felt. Food subsidy has somehow maintained political favour, as it apparently led to cheaper food – something that the international market now purports to provide. Social subsidy for an uneconomic industry is less attractive, and there are adequate precedents, even in Wales, of whole communities, such as the coal miners in the south, having to face redundancy and adapt. Whether a social subsidy could be sold as maintenance of landscape, recreation, ecosystem restoration and obligations under the EC Habitats Directive remains to be seen. Current Wales-based stewardship schemes exist (Tir Gofal, see Chapter 10 on strategy), but have only a limited vision: primarily of maintenance of the social and environmental fabric as it currently exists, but with a marginal improvement in meadows and woodland.

But of course, the real barrier is not ecological or economic – it is cultural. Re-wilding is seen as a step backwards. Farmers have seen themselves as producers, an 'industry', and operate as self-employed small businessmen. They are fiercely independent, yet massively dependent! Few know their flowers or birds, though every field has a name and a history. Much as their heart might belong to a bygone Celtic poetry, their minds are focused by chapel and the protestant work ethic. At Harlech the highlight of the young farmers' year was the banger-racing fest. Chemicals are macho, organics are for dreamers. One successful neighbour of mine worked all hours but spent two weeks in Florida before the lambing. The unsuccessful work all hours for little reward, and severe stress is common with broken marriages, disaffected children and a rising suicide rate. If wildland advocates are to orchestrate changes in land use over wide areas such as the Rhinogs, they must address the disintegration of the present cultural framework. The repair work began for us at Cae Mabon, but such centres are far removed from the inclinations of most indigenous working people in North Wales.

## Cae Mabon and rites of passage

When I first visited Muriau Gwynnion, Eric Maddern's home and centre for new approaches in education located above the lake at Llanberis, it was to participate in a gathering of 14 men intent upon recreating something once integral to human psychology, and like our ancestral ecology, long lost in the past. As men, there was still something within us that had never become adult, though we ranged in age from mid-thirties to mid-sixties. We had come to realize its absence when confronted with the task of guiding 14 year-olds through powerful initiations of vision quest and the scary ordeals of being alone with the mountain and forest. We all felt at ease with nature's wildness, but the initiations we were working with involved boys gathering together with men; their trials and quest were witnessed both by their peers and their mentors. Few of us had had the same opportunity when we were young. Or, in my case, that opportunity had been on a God-forsaken Scottish moor, with a Lee-Enfield rifle and a platoon of rain-soaked would-be commandos in the Army Cadet Force. I recall, on the long forced-march into headwind and sleet, glancing down-slope at some hawthorns amid which huddled dozens of exotic Waxwings, rare vagrants from the Russian boreal forest, and then cursing our intrepid leader; no time to stop.

In my misguided youth, I lost all poetry, all sensitivity to love and any hope of a truly open meeting with the opposite sex; the natural landscape became simply a backdrop to the endless games of ego. Initiation there had been, but into the blind world of men separated from their women and from the land. At Cae Mabon, with my friends Eric Maddern and Iwan Brioc, we came to appreciate that the real barriers to realizing our visions were laid down in our uninitiated youth.

Meeting Eric and his co-conspirator, Alex Wildwood, provided an opportunity to work with two great pioneers in the enormous task of providing an initiation for young men into the mysteries of their divinity and their relationship to the land, to each other and to women. In that first gathering in Eryri, we, as grown men, set ourselves the task of rediscovering 'initiation' – firstly, of who we truly were, and secondly, of how we relate. Each of us recounted our life history, its hopes, fears, trials and successes; crucially, we also spoke of what we felt was missing or unhealed and unattained. Then each of us in turn left for a two-hour sojourn in the woods, and whilst away, the group devised a ritual, a piece of theatre, a task or perhaps even an ordeal, that would address our need. None of us would know what to expect. All were participants in the initiatory process; everyone was a witness.

In some sense, we were developing a school of 'male mysteries'. We were already well aware of the pioneering work of our women friends and teachers in developing their own 'wild women' courses and initiations. The women were rediscovering their sisterhood and the deeper feminine power so long abandoned in the Western world. We had shared with them the sweat lodge, the shamanic journeys and the vision quest process, and for some, even the fire walks and earth burials. Yet, something always divided us and eluded us, some level of meeting. It was as if the mysterious elements of deep feminine power that were being liberated bred a separation. As men, we had all learned a great deal from female teachers. Some men had suffered an oppressive guilt of maleness in a world devastated by the mentality of domination. We were now involved in an inner process of rebalancing, a part of which was the discovery and liberation of the feminine within ourselves.

At its heart, we had to learn to mother ourselves, to liberate ourselves from deeper psychic needs that inevitably prevented a truly equal meeting with woman. As long as this remained unachieved, we were still boys. I came to believe that without this inner liberation, which embodies a level of acceptance, receptivity and trust in the essential abundance of life, men will always seek to dominate Nature, to control her and even to take out some unconscious revenge upon her. In some sense, it was as if their own mother had let them down; they were still her boys, for she had not taught them to find the mother within themselves, and that had bred a vicious resentment now projected out upon the earth itself, and all too frequently, at deep psychic levels, upon the women in their lives.

I know of no sociology to support these suppositions, other than the obvious correlation of such deep imbalances within 'Western' materialist culture and its continual rape of the earth's resources. I cannot prove by scientific means that rebalancing such disoriented psyches will lead to stability and satisfaction such that the goal of 'economic' growth and ever greater consumption is replaced with less damaging values. These things are perhaps beyond science – for how would it be possible to conduct appropriate surveys, isolate factors and ultimately prove causes and effects? Science has always been limited when applied to the human psyche, and for that matter, to the complexities of human health and the environment.

Eric Maddern's centre slowly became Cae Mabon, a cluster of low-impact dwellings in the forest clearing above Llyn Padarn and below Elidir Fawr in the western mountains of Eryri. An Iron Age roundhouse has been built for gatherings, music and storytelling, and over the years, Eric has added a straw-bale hogan and some nomadic tents. It is an ideal setting for gatherings now devoted to 'creative expression, healing and spiritual wellbeing, traditional arts and crafts, environmental awareness, rites of passage and personal transformation'.[12]

After 12 years of development, Cae Mabon produces a rich programme of events with activities taking place most weeks of the year. In 2001, the John Muir Society held its third camp there for young people between the ages of 16 and 24, exploring the deeper 'magic' of the wilderness. My friends Iona Fredenburgh and Elisabeth Brooke held workshops entitled Plant Spirit Medicine, which explored the healing power of plants. There are workshops in five rhythms – dance, masked drama and clowning, Zen, yoga and the perennial rites of passage for men. Cae Mabon has become a place where East and West meet and where the ancient Celtic heart of Wales is being recreated.

In Eryri the wildwood is still a remnant. For it to return amid all the competing needs of a farming community, 'economic' forestry and a tourist culture, the forest must first grow in the hearts of the people who make their living or find recreation in Snowdonia. This is the essential work of Cae Mabon, but as I put forward at the outset, I believe that elements of initiation are essential if we are to liberate ourselves from the fear and denial that drives our current relationship to nature, our culture's essential disrespect for the wild.

## New green shoots of change

There are some new signs that our vision has not been entirely dismissed. The Countryside Council for Wales recently put out to tender a contract for ways of implementing a doubling of Snowdonia's natural forest cover. The National Trust recently bought 3000 acres on Snowdon and is committed to re-establishing woodland up to the natural tree line. The Trust also has an active interest in applying minimal intervention practices in large areas that it owns elsewhere (for example, in Ennerdale, see Chapter 5) and of large-scale habitat restoration in the fens of Cambridgeshire. Coed Eryri lives on as a vision – now held by a motley assortment of educationalists, artists, writers, poets, sculptors and the occasional forest ecologist. It is an open and evolving concept that must embrace culture, community and ecology.

We are now more acutely aware that the temperate forest ecosystem evolved in the presence of the now extinct 'mega-fauna' and that the forests of Snowdon in that former natural totality cannot now be restored. In all of my earlier work I had failed to appreciate the extent to which the mega-herbivores processed the forest – keeping it open and free of accumulated vegetation. Parts of Europe must have resembled the wooded savannah of Africa and been teeming with game. If we now wanted to restore the primeval ecology, we would need to genetically manipulate some safari-park elephants and rhinos, recreate the tarpan and aurochs from their descendents, and import a few Asiatic lions!

What place now does the argument against alien species have when Snowdonia's hills are covered in rhododendron and Sitka spruce, the streams colonized by Japanese knotweed and Himalayan balsam, large numbers of the planted oaks came from Poland and there have even been sightings of escaped panthers? Our benchmarks have been blown away. What we now create can hardly be justified by the narrow confines of a rather mutable ecological science.

It had been part of the Coed Eryri dream to bring back lost species. A small group of us began to think about the reintroduction of beaver, and in 1992 in the company of Alan Featherstone and the more adventurous agents of Scottish Natural Heritage, we visited re-introduced colonies in Brittany. After eight years of contemplation, the Scottish authorities have agreed to a re-introduction programme and there is a small scheme in Kent (see the later sections on species in Chapter 7). Beaver is a builder at the base of the ecosystem. In the animal medicine of North America, it teaches the value of a strong foundation and industriousness. Ecologically, beaver transforms habitat and provides a foundation for a web of diversity.

If there is success in Scotland, then we can promote again something similar in Snowdonia. The bear and the wolf may one day return to Scotland, but for Wales, the dream is of eagle and lynx. Eagle is associated with poetic 'vision' and lynx is the 'keeper of secrets'. Only when there is a poetic vision to match the divinity of the Welsh language, and when the great mystery of nature is hallowed and not hounded by science, will we have the will to bring them back.

In Wales I learned that our soul and our future are intimately bound with the wild. As we rediscover ourselves, we shall safeguard and sanctify the wild places, and not out of some ecological sense of doom if we don't but because of our love and expanded awareness. In the ancestral Celtic forest, I learned that the animals, trees and herbs held healing powers, the whole environment was alive with spirit and there was no boundary between the human mind, the forest and the greater cosmos. I came to see that we had lost that consciousness, and in so doing, we were moving towards the endgame of a planet-wide destruction of our very life support systems.

Coed Eryri taught me that there is no environment to be studied, managed, conserved or restored – the environment is not a thing, not an object, other than as a human concept. It has been a category mistake, something we have separated from ourselves and set apart from other categorized things, such as 'the economy', industry or business. As such it will always come second, as something we must protect while getting on with what really matters now that 'the economy' has become God.

The major part of Coed Eryri's work now lies in the projects at Cae Mabon: to apprehend the truth that we are a part of nature, to rediscover the rituals of appreciation and the joys of reconnection. But the vision is held and will one day help to integrate all the disparate workings of foresters and nature conservationists who strive gradually to enhance the wildwood of Eryri.

However, immediately to the south of the Rhinogydd, in the North Cambrians, there are signs that 'wildwoods' and the concept of core areas (see Chapter 5 on the work of the Land Use Policy Group) are gaining local advocates, and this may yet revitalize proposals for the Rhinogydd, which has the advantage of a cluster of 'public' lands in the form of Forest Enterprise holdings and National Trust land in the southeast corner, and one or two large estates in the centre and north. These may yet provide focal points for management of wild areas with the introduction of deer, ponies and wild cattle, the conversion of plantations and the regeneration of upland vegetation.

# 3
# Caledon

Any search for the wildest land in Britain would begin in Scotland. There are several areas of land in excess of 1000 km² in the Western Highlands and the Flow Country with little obvious imprint of man. The Cairngorm Mountains contain some of the largest near-natural forest remnants and montane plateau areas, and this area, together with the Western Highland areas of Ben Eighe and Inverpolly, contain the largest nature reserves in Britain. However, even these apparently natural areas share with Snowdonia a history of systematic denudation.[1] The wildest country is now virtually treeless, and although deer are abundant, several key herbivores are missing, as are all the large carnivores.

Outside these nature reserves, the denuded state of the land is maintained by managerial policies aimed primarily at the economic returns to be made from grouse shooting, deer stalking or marginal sheep farming. The large nature reserves, such as the island of Rhum and Ben Eighe on the mainland, are only beginning to regenerate their natural tree cover. The absence of predators has meant that deer overgraze the remnant forest and there is little natural regeneration unless deer numbers are severely culled or areas fenced off.[2] The wildness of the Cairngorms, though still rich in biodiversity, is compromised by tourist developments and high numbers of visitors, with winter skiing requiring an infrastructure that now penetrates to the core of the mountains. Conservationists fought long and hard against a funicular railway that would take skiers and walkers up onto the high plateau with little effort – the latter factor perhaps the only real safeguard for wild areas.

Although we shall focus upon the Trees for Life project in the relatively untouched Glen Affric region, there is considerable progress being made within the Cairngorms by both the National Trust for Scotland (who are also active in Glen Affric) at Mar Lodge and the RSPB at Abernethy. These two organizations are fostering increased natural regeneration of the pine forests with policies of deer culling and fencing over several thousand hectares. The NTS management allows for traditional economic exploitation from grouse shooting and fishing, whilst the RSPB land represents a core of habitats subject to natural processes.

## The Trees for Life vision

Nevertheless, Scotland provides by far the greatest opportunity in Britain for recreating a functional wild ecosystem and it is here that the most advanced re-wilding initiative was founded in 1987 by Alan Watson Featherstone and the Trees for Life project at Findhorn. An area of approximately 2000 km² was identified west of the Great Glen and away from the traditional tourist hot spots in the Spey valley and Cairngorms. Here the Trees for Life group built upon Finlay MacRae's pioneering work with the Forestry Commission in Glen Affric and upon a long-held vision to regenerate a significant fraction of the former glory that was the great Caledonian Pine Forest.[3]

The ancient pine forests of Caledon have inspired many conservationists over the decades to dream of restoration, especially in the face of massive commercial afforestation of the Highlands with exotic species in plantations of dreary monotony and disrespect for landscape form and beauty. Few, however, thought of the forest in its natural dynamic, with the original fauna of large herbivores and carnivores restored, and those who could embrace that vision, such as Derek Yalden, were never very optimistic that such a project could prevail against the interests of large landowners. Yalden was led to suggest a rejuvenated functional ecosystem with all the mammals returned, but safely quarantined on the island of Rhum, a national nature reserve, but even this exciting proposal found no support among government agencies.[4]

At the outset, the Findhorn group embraced not only the politically problematic carnivores but also the spiritual dimension inherent in any such renewal project and were not afraid to make this a major tenet of their vision at a time when few people talked of re-introducing extirpated animals, and even fewer talked of the spiritual values of nature. Alan began with an unabashed holistic vision of the forest that included the eventual return of such keystone species as beaver, boar, wolf and bear, and then sought support from traditionalist foresters in the Forestry Commission and National Trust.

The Trees for Life project would have been easily dismissed as New Age dreaming were it not for the dedication and hard work of its volunteers in growing trees, raising money, talking good science and getting out in all weathers. The project is now a world-famous, award-winning endeavour, but this has come after many years of labour on the part of a team working with the full knowledge that the fruits of their 200-year vision would not be seen for generations to come.

## The Millennium Forest for Scotland

In addition to the pioneering work of Trees for Life, Scotland has also proven fertile ground for other relevant initiatives unique to Britain and perhaps also Europe. In the late 1980s a nationwide initiative to reforest Scotland was set up. Reforesting Scotland grew out of the *Tree Planters' Guide to the Galaxy*, a magazine devoted to the many small tree-planting groups, in particular, small nurseries and schemes such as that of the founders, Bernard and Emma Planterose, who then lived on the almost totally denuded West Coast of the Highland Region. As the millennium approached, the ever-growing organization of small-scale planting groups, combined with the more radical critics of land ownership, began to find a resonance that was reflected in a millennium grant from the lottery as part of a wider 'Millennium Forest for Scotland'.[5]

Reforesting Scotland held a broad vision of community woodlands, with a focus on regenerating sustainable, economic, but local uses of woodland and increasing biodiversity. There was room in the vision for wildland initiatives, and indeed, a smaller-scale project of about 800 ha, Carrifran, was developed in the Borders region of southern Scotland (see Chapter 5).

In addition to these new radical developments, the traditional conservation bodies have also been actively creating larger areas of land reserved for wildlife with policies of minimum intervention. The National Trust for Scotland received government support for buying the Mar Lodge Estate in the Cairngorms, thus adding a substantial area with the prospect of linking up with the large holding of the RSPB at Abernethy. Other significant developments have been the crofters' movement to buy estates commonly owned by absentee landlords, the most important being Knoydart on the west coast. The John Muir Trust has also purchased significant areas of land on the Isle of Skye.[6]

Some of these broader-based initiatives have mixed implications for the wilding of these large tracts of land. Different organizations have different visions. The John Muir Trust, for example, has yet to embrace active regeneration of ecosystems on a large scale; the National Trust for Scotland carefully balances wildlife and habitat requirements with its obligations to the local economy and traditional rural practices, and the RSPB, though commendable in its approach to all wildlife on its land, is fundamentally oriented towards bird conservation, access and educational facilities for its members. The voluntary sector now has a large membership and a commitment to access and interpretation that can compromise areas formerly little known, remote and inaccessible. Whilst a sense of wildness may be lost, species remain, and the visitors are an important element of a local economy that needs to see changes in land use that safeguard community life in the Highlands. In general, the last decade and the new millennium has seen a major shift in awareness, new thinking and practical initiatives in Scotland that are not seen in Wales and are only just beginning in England.

## Land and ownership: iniquity and opportunity

Perhaps the greatest opportunity in Scotland arises from what many regard as the country's greatest cultural and environmental problem – the iniquitous pattern of land ownership.[7] Virtually all wildland in Scotland is privately owned by large estates in the hands of often-absent landlords. These estates are managed essentially for economic uses such as grouse shooting, salmon fishing, deer stalking and, under former more generous tax regimes, plantation forestry. However, such large estates regularly come on the market and represent major opportunities for large-scale wildland initiatives at a time when conservation bodies have only recently found the resources to match the several million pounds required for such purchases. These opportunities do not exist in the smaller-scale, more fragmented ownership patterns in England and Wales, where land values are also much higher.

It is crucial, however, that conservation interests do not focus solely upon an exclusive biodiversity agenda. First, as I shall argue, that agenda requires some reassessment in the light of future climate change, the fragmentation of habitats and the dysfunctional nature of present ecosystems. Second, there is an important political and cultural issue relating to 'wildness' that needs to be addressed. Many of these now wild lands were formerly inhabited and were cleared by the imperial powers of England. There is a rich cultural and linguistic heritage in the ancient Celtic relationship to animals, plants and nature generally, much of it long dormant. In my view, it would be a mistake for the conservation community to approach wildland entirely from a conservation biology standpoint. It would be an opportunity missed for education and for a relevant input to the land 'in-between' that we shall argue is of equal importance to the core areas of wildland.

There are many people within the broad church of Reforesting Scotland working for a balance that keeps people on the land, and as in North Wales; I believe that this can be fruitfully combined with the creation of natural sanctuary areas in which there is essentially no human domination or economic exploitation. This is especially the case for community-owned, small-scale forest enterprises meeting local needs with the wood pasturing of livestock (see the Woodland Trust's Glen Finglas plans in Chapter 5), and which, along with eco-tourism and education, could be the main economic activity in the buffer zones and corridors around core areas.

## Scottish Natural Heritage: a policy on wildland

In 2002, Scottish Natural Heritage (SNH) issued a policy statement on wildland, *Wildness in Scotland's Countryside* (Policy Statement No. 02/03), in response to the government's National Planning Policy Guideline NPPG 14, which specifically identified wildland as an aspect of landscape character to be protected through land-use planning. The policy statement considered the value of wildness to society and its significance as a distinctive part of Scotland's natural heritage. It is a most succinct and clearly written argument for conserving wildness: linking people to the physical realities of the natural world, the importance of solitude and sanctuary, closeness to nature and wildlife, lack of disturbance and tranquillity, and wildness valued as a quality in its own right. It also distinguishes between 'wildness' as a feature that can apply to quite small-scale features, even those close to urban life such as wild areas in cities or on the urban fringe, and 'wildland', a term SNH prefers to 'wilderness' with its historical connotations of emptiness.

The document then goes on to consider how best to safeguard these areas – looking at the threats of hydro-electric development, afforestation, bulldozed roads, tourism (for example, helicopter tourism in the Cuillins), aquaculture and renewable energy installations, such as wind turbines – and enunciates a policy aim, that:

> There are parts of Scotland where the wild character of the landscape, its related recreational value and potential for nature are such that these areas should be safeguarded against inappropriate development or land-use change.

In its policy of safeguarding wildness and wildland, it will assume a strong presumption against any development that compromises the quality of wildness, especially in those areas that currently bear no obvious effects of human activities. It also talks of the potential for *enhancement* of nature. In its initial assessments, maps showing the distances of wildland from public roads and private tracks have been produced. These show clearly the recent impacts of privately bulldozed roads in the Highlands and acknowledge the efforts of the National Trust for Scotland in Mar Lodge, where such intrusions have been removed, as an example for other areas to follow.

## Scottish Wild Rivers

Scotland also hosts some of the major initiatives for restoring wild rivers – the WWF Wild Rivers programme and a major scheme of the River Restoration Centre (RRC), an EU-backed programme of effective re-wilding. Most such projects have been on 'reaches' (small stretches where meanders can be restored to canalized sections of river) or floodplains that are restored to their original function; on the Tweed, in contrast, a catchment-based approach is being pioneered. We shall look in more detail at the work of the RRC in Chapters 5 and 11, as it has the potential to form a major element of a more general wilding strategy in the provision of wildlife corridors and networks.

## Restoration ecology and appropriate economic development

The political environment in Scotland has thus shifted towards a greater embrace of the value of wildland, but the pressures from other directions are still severe. Renewable energy development, in the form of wind turbines, are planned for large swathes of the western coastline and hills – with a recent application for very large machines having been approved on the Isle of Skye, despite strong local opposition. The heavy urban bias of Scotland's population, coupled with desires for modernity and economic growth, mean that wildland values will struggle against the drive for sustainable livelihoods in rural areas. With careful siting, there need not be great conflict because most of the wind resource is accessible offshore and there is no pressing national need to develop onshore wind; onshore wind power, however, appears cheaper, easier and quicker, despite the long history of planning delays seen in England. Moreover, current wildland undoubtedly contributes to Scotland's economic wellbeing through tourism, and further enhancements can be expected to have economic value.

Fifteen years ago, the Trees for Life team were truly voices in a wilderness; now they are an integral and inspiring part of a major movement in restoration ecology in a country big enough to embrace a whole range of restoration initiatives, from community forests and sustainable use, through publicly accessible large-scale nature reserves to the 'core wilderness' concept, which is the basis of the Trees for Life project. In some ways, the existence of multi-purpose regeneration schemes in other parts of Scotland aids the creation of more remote and radical wildland projects. In areas where wildland is scarce and under pressure from a multitude of uses, such as the English and Welsh National Parks, compromises are made to appease the powerful lobbies of economic forestry, bird preservation, hill livestock farming, recreational use and military training. In Scotland there is a potential for diversity of uses. Such a large area as the Cairngorms, though managed as a wild 'core area' and surrounded by forestry and shooting estates, already accommodates a range of uses within its boundaries – Mar Lodge has retained some traditional economic activities and there are extensive tourist developments for skiing, walking and bird-watching. This area may act to siphon off visitor pressure and provide employment and thus make wilder-land initiatives elsewhere more acceptable. Furthermore, the gradual creation of a wider reforesting mentality that embraces community use may create more appropriate buffer zones for core areas that might one day re-introduce mammalian predators such as the bear, lynx or wolf.[8]

## Pioneering re-introduction of predators

Scotland has already hosted a pioneering re-introduction project for a controversial predator in the return of the white-tailed eagle to the Western Isles. In the late 19th century, this eagle was commoner in north and west Britain than the golden eagle, with over 100 eyries in Scotland and about 50 in Ireland. It was persecuted and finally eradicated in 1916.[9] Re-introduction attempts began in 1959 using birds from Norway, but the first successful breeding took place in 1986. About 11 pairs are now breeding regularly along the west coast of Scotland.

The white-tailed eagle, or sea eagle, had an undeserved reputation as a lamb-killer, and this programme managed to overcome historical prejudices. The eagles feed mainly upon hares, rabbits, seabirds and fish. A programme for Eryri should be considered as part of the wildlands ethos.

Scotland has also made a major contribution to Britain's fauna by the careful nurturing of returning ospreys in Speyside. This species was also persecuted and eradicated in Britain, and the Scottish success has led to breeding successes in England.[10] Scotland has also hosted a re-introduction programme for the red kite, parallel to successes in returning this predator to England.

## The wild heart of the Highlands: Trees for Life and the Glen Affric core area

The Trees for Life vision embraced the concept of 'whole ecosystem regeneration' from its inception and did not shy from the thorny question of re-introduced predators. The forest was more than the trees – it was a community, an ecosystem, the health of which depended upon the interaction of grazers and predators. Moreover, the 'forest' was conceived as a living entity, not just as a collection of 'species', but as a community of beings that had a dimension in spirit. However magnificent a regenerated landscape of Caledonian Pine might look, it would be populated by ghosts of a past greater magnificence if the bear, wolf, lynx, moose and beaver were still absent. Thus, Trees for Life committed to the regeneration of the wild not only as a biodiversity obligation, but as the retrieval of something lost in the *human* heart, the consequence of which is a particular loneliness of spirit that comes from the absence of animals for which that heart has always had reverence.

Fifteen years ago, there would have appeared little hope of early acceptance of such species re-introduction, but today, Scotland is engaged upon the re-introduction of the beaver – the first re-establishment of an eradicated mammal since the red squirrel was re-introduced to Scotland in the 19th century. There have been initiatives to canvas the return of the

**Figure 3.1** *Alan Watson Featherstone and the Trees for Life Vision: regenerating willow high in Glen Affric*
Photo: Alan Watson/Forest Light

wolf and to fund research on the feasibility of its acceptance and survival (see Chapter 8). Scotland is a country of deep conservatism *and* radical ideas that have a habit of leading the rest of the world. It is the birthplace of John Muir and the National Park movement, and thus it is fitting that it should inspire a regeneration of the spiritual as well as the practical reconnection to the natural world.

In this particularly Scottish tradition, the Trees for Life project has also won numerous conservation awards and influenced land management in adjacent areas as well as abroad. Alan now travels and lectures extensively on ecological restoration.

## Practical regeneration: the Glen Affric project

The success of the Trees for Life project owes a great deal to the availability of land on which to begin the project. The Forestry Commission owned large areas of Glen Affric and in the early 1980s had already decided to reserve this area as the core of its native woodland regeneration plans (see Colour Plate 3, which shows land ownership and planting projects in the Glen Affric core area). The Commission began to fell non-native conifers and to exclude deer from areas that could then regenerate. The scene was set for a cooperative endeavour. Trees for Life began with a native trees nursery that included not only Scots pine, but also key species for the

**Figure 3.2** *Trees for Life nursery at Plodda*
Photo: Alan Watson/Forest Light

colonization of open ground – birch, rowan, willow and aspen. The latter had become rare in the highlands as it suffered from excessive browsing and largely propagated itself by suckering. The volunteers set about finding remnant seed trees, collecting seed and establishing nurseries.

Glen Affric lies at the heart of a large area of the Highlands that is not crossed by roads and where there is little agricultural activity. A number of large sporting estates rely upon deer stalking as the main economic activity. It was thus an ideal place to centre the vision of a large ecosystem restoration project. About 1500 km² of relatively wild country is bounded by two major roads running from east to west, and in the west, though separated by a main road, lies the large National Nature Reserve of Ben Eighe, a reserve also subject to native woodland regeneration.

## The problem of red deer

The remnant native woodland of Glen Affric had limited regeneration due to the heavy grazing pressure of excessive deer numbers. The problem of deer has long been recognized but only recently have major efforts been made to address the excess. In a review of the problems, SNH produced what I regard as one of the best-designed scientific policy documents aimed at communicating ecological issues to a wide audience of stakeholders – a document worth procuring for that reason alone (*Red Deer and the Natural Heritage*, SNH, Policy Paper, June 1994).

Red deer numbers in Scotland have been rising steadily for several decades. Objective counts began in 1953, but records go back to 1900, when open country deer numbered about 150,000. This figure remained the estimate until 1963, after which there was a steady rise until 1989 when numbers peaked at 300,000, including estimates of deer in forestry plantations.

Red deer now occupy more than 40 per cent of the land area of Scotland, or about 3 million hectares. The main factors affecting their increase appear to be a decline in sheep numbers, under-culling of hinds, and a sequence of mild winters and dry summers. Animal density ranges from 5 to more than 30 per square kilometre, with winter densities in favoured areas being much higher. Scotland's red deer population represents an estimated 28 per cent of the total European population (most of which are confined to woodland).

It cannot be emphasized too much that the current landscape and ecology of large areas of Scotland is dysfunctional. The landscape may look wild and the deer may look wild – but this is deceptive, a fact readily appreciated by ecologists. Deer are now so numerous that forest structure has been severely degraded. Large vistas can be seen with one or two isolated old pines and some areas of extensive woodland have no young trees at all. It is not just a matter of failure of trees to regenerate; the whole under-storey of shrubs has been degraded. In particular, berry-bearing species have been over-grazed and are now either absent or unproductive, and upon these a whole host of other species rely for their well-being, such as capercaillie and black grouse. Above the tree-line, montane scrub and tall herb communities have been severely degraded. Lush riparian vegetation has also disappeared. These formerly diverse plant communities are essential for such mammals as bear, beaver and wild boar, as well as for a host of insect and birds.

## Deer control

The culling of red deer for sport or for range management purposes is regarded as a significant factor in their ecology, with 6–12 per cent of hinds and 10–17 per cent of stags killed each year. The total annual cull increased from 24,000 animals in 1973 to 70,000 in 1992, and the Red Deer Commission considered that the cull of hinds equalled recruitment for the first time in 1990; however, there remains an imbalance in the sex ratio. There is some debate about carrying capacity – it is generally considered that deer numbers would continue to increase in the absence of culling, but that density-dependent mechanisms operate to limit post-natal growth, the age of first conception and the number of hinds in milk. On the island of Rhum, fecundity fell from 80 per cent to 30 per cent as hind numbers increased from 900 to 1200.

The excessive density of deer is regarded as the main factor accounting for the lack of regeneration of Scotland's native woodlands, estimated at only 2 per cent of land cover. Damage to commercial forestry is substantial – costs are estimated at £5 million net of revenues from culling in plantations, with half of this figure made up of the cost of rangers and fencing and half being direct damage to trees. This represents 7 per cent of total revenue from forestry in Scotland (1990 figures).

Thus, any large-scale forest regeneration scheme has to address the deer problem. Remnant Caledonian pine in the valleys provides over-wintering shelter for open-country herds and densities can be very high. If these woods are to regenerate naturally, then either deer numbers must be reduced or fencing must be used to exclude them; both options are expensive.

In Glen Affric, Trees for Life gained permission from the Forestry Commission to fence off areas for regeneration, and the first exclosures were created in 1989. Deer were driven from the enclosed areas and the sites monitored for re-entry (often fairly easy for the deer when winter snows drift to the height of the fence). The effects were apparent within a very short time – birch, rowan and pine seedlings shot up within a few years.

The Trees for Life strategy was to fence off areas with good seed sources to allow natural regeneration and to enclose some areas far from seed sources where planting of reared seedlings could occur. By 1999, volunteers had planted over 250,000 seedlings. In the nearby privately owned Wester Guisachan Estate, similar numbers were planted by professional planters over a two-year period. Trees for Life had also influenced the National Trust for Scotland's (NTS) purchase of the West Affric Estate and had negotiated agreements for exclosures in the open country west of Loch Affric. Thus far, about 500 ha of new woodland regeneration and planting has been added to the Glen Affric remnants. A further 135 ha are planned for West Affric, where NTS also instigated rigorous culling to bring deer numbers down to a level at which natural regeneration takes place outside the fences. Once this is established, all fences will be removed. In areas where there are still black grouse and capercaillie, culling is preferred to fencing because these birds have a propensity for flying into them, a source of high mortality.

Ideally, a regenerating forest will progress most naturally under some kind of grazing regime. However, the relationship between deer numbers and forest regeneration is not known in any detail. The consensus among naturalists and from limited research is that with densities above 5 animals per square kilometre no regeneration will take place. Almost all open forest areas currently exceed this level, but where deer culls have been instigated in the Cairngorms (the RSPB and Mar Lodge reserves have begun a radical programme) there is already extensive regeneration. SNH's management of deer at the 4000 ha Creag Meagaidh National Nature Reserve since acquiring the important Site of Special Scientific Interest status in 1986 has mainly relied upon the culling of hinds to drastically reduce deer numbers and produce significant regeneration. It has also shown that hefting of hinds to a particular area meant that no significant numbers were drawn in to this vacuum from neighbouring estates. The Woodland Trust has instigated similar policies of natural regeneration in the presence of reduced deer numbers (based on five deer per square kilometre) in a plan to afforest over 3000 ha at Glen Finglas.

Any large-scale ecosystem regeneration, for example, over the core area envisaged, will have to reduce deer numbers to less than 5 per square kilometre. This will require cooperation from estates where deer stalking is the main function and an important local source of employment. Currently, estate managers are following policies that have allowed overall deer numbers to increase and allowed females to predominate. SNH have argued, in their review, that half current numbers would provide the same level of stalking and potentially bigger stags – stag size reduces as density increases.

For the Caledonian Forest to come back, deer numbers in the core area envisaged by Trees for Life would need to be less than 7500, whereas if the area now has an average population density, there will be 15,000 deer present. The resultant 'forest' deer would, however, be larger and provide better stags, and because stalking success is related to the number of beaters and overall effort rather than to absolute deer numbers (in areas where deer numbers have doubled, stalking success has remained constant), there should not necessarily be a conflict of interest in the buffer zones that other estates currently provide.

## Re-introduction of other herbivores

There are, however, some keystone herbivores that have been eradicated. Elk disappeared from Scotland before the Roman period and boar went the same way in medieval times. In the past, beaver were probably also present in the Spey valley and perhaps also in the more mountainous streams of Trees for Life's core area. Boar have a profoundly beneficial effect upon the natural regeneration of trees, providing scrapes and disturbed ground from their digging where seedlings can get a hold. Trees for Life have recently begun a study project in the glen in which wild boar have been introduced to enclosures to study these effects. Beaver also modify habitat in such a way that benefits other species – moose especially benefit from wet pastures and still pools with emergent vegetation.

Two more herbivores, the wild forest horse, or tarpan, and cattle are now extinct, and if the full grazing and browsing spectrum were to be recreated, then functional replacements might be found in the Exmoor pony and among the various breeds of semi-wild cattle (the issue of specific status is discussed in greater depth in Chapter 7). Such additional herbivory, whilst diversifying grazing and forest structure, would raise questions of population control in the absence of predation, particularly for elk, which can increase rapidly – this is also dealt with in more detail in Chapter 7.

## The question of carnivores

The excess of deer has been cited as a good reason to bring back the carnivores, although Trees for Life would be happy to see them back because they are of value in their own right. This issue of predators and control of numbers is not at all clear and it may well be that the presence of small numbers of wolves and even smaller numbers of bear would have little impact on the population size of the deer. Red deer numbers are more likely to be limited by the quality of the range and the severity of winters or dryness of summers. However, wolf predation certainly affects the habits of deer herds and may lead to a higher deer density threshold for woodland regeneration as they keep animals from overstaying in one particular sheltered location. It is certainly true, however, that the current numbers of red deer will support a population of wolves (see Chapter 8 on the wolf and other predators)!

Lynx will also take young red deer and adult roe deer, and there has been much less publicity about their potential re-introduction. Indeed, there are rumours that hunting activists, rather than conservationists, have already begun a restoration programme of their own. There are regular sightings of lynx in Scotland, as well as sightings of 'big cats' of the pantherine lineage. We shall discuss this at greater length. The re-introduction of lynx to such a wild and semi-forested area should raise few questions of conflicting interests. Where wild prey are abundant, lynx seldom predate domestic stock, and given the above-mentioned factors affecting deer stalking, the re-introduction of lynx would not be in conflict with that interest either. It is also clear that there is ample room for a small population of these carnivores, and there are data to show that lynx can significantly reduce the density of smaller deer, such as the roe.

The brown bear is more problematic. Although it will take young deer, it is an omnivore with a substantially vegetarian diet. It requires a rich indigenous flora – nuts, apples, berries, roots and tubers, as well as insect grubs, bees, wasps and honey. However, it would not take much effort to review the successful Swedish endeavours to rebuild bear numbers, particularly in the more open country of the northern arctic birch forests, and to gain useful insight relevant to Scottish upland habitats. There are relic populations of bear in the Pyrenees and northern Spain that are confined to smaller areas than the proposed core area. However, on the down-side, small populations are vulnerable to genetic isolation. I would like to see SNH at least commission a review – but there was little enthusiasm for the idea when last I raised the issue.

The return of predators, however, will be contingent not only on local landowner support (which could be problematic, although again, in theory the quality of deer stalking would not necessarily be impaired and may even improve) but also upon the attitudes of the wider land-owning fraternity.

Wolf, bear and lynx will naturally wander from the core area and colonize other areas. To the west lie significant areas of national nature reserves that might welcome the return of native predators. However, there are also significant sheep farming areas in the Western Highlands – over 2 million sheep are estimated to share the overall 3 million hectares of land occupied by red deer alone.

A future forest of 2000 km² in the core area might support 10,000 red deer (half the current average density), with a potential recruitment of 2000 animals – enough to support between 10 and 50 wolves. Theoretically, 100 wolves eating 3 kg per day would require 1000 adult deer at 100 kg each per year and thus the area might support up to 200 wolves. However, the wolves will utilize other food sources and take a mixture of adults and calves. In addition, there are other factors limiting wolf numbers such that the most likely resident population would be between 10 and 50. Wolf kills in open country will also benefit carrion eaters, which include golden eagles – a species that would be negatively impacted by reduction in sheep numbers and the extension of forests, though the Caledon area is not an area of particularly high density for this raptor.

Lynx will also take red deer, though its preferred prey is roe deer, hare and large game birds such as grouse. It is likely that lynx could coexist with wolves quite happily and that the area would support between 2 and 20 territories. Bear, as noted, is an omnivore, chiefly vegetarian, requiring a large home range, and is not dependent upon deer, though it will take young and the occasional adult animal. The core area would support perhaps one territory (see sections on bear and lynx in Chapter 8). In the case of these predators, their future genetic health and chances of persistence would be enhanced by, and perhaps dependent upon, populations in contiguous areas such as Knoydart, Ben Eighe and Inverpolly.

## Other species issues

Scotland possesses about half of Europe's golden eagle population, with ca. 400 pairs occupying much the same range as the red deer. It is a species that might suffer reduced territory or breeding success if tree cover were more extensive and deer numbers reduced. The availability of red deer carrion is a major factor in the occupation of territories, though the eagles depend on live food, mostly hare and grouse, for the success of the nestlings.

The 2000 km² of the core area would represent about 6 per cent of the golden eagle's breeding area. However, even if completely reafforested, significant areas of open montane heath and bog would remain above the tree line. Furthermore, reduced deer numbers may produce a higher yield of young animals in a less dense deer population.

In any major habitat change there will be 'winners' and 'losers'. A regrowth of heather moor over grassland and an invasion of drier bog areas by birch would favour those species that need cover for nesting, such as merlin and hen harrier, over those that require open short-cropped grassland, such as golden plover and dunlin. Red grouse appear to require shorter heather and numbers respond to burning but are reduced by over-burning and over-grazing, whereas black grouse numbers could be expected to increase with the return of birch upon whose shoots they feed; the capercaillie could expand as better habitat increased.

The wider extent of forest and larger numbers of mature trees could support the return of the red kite (recently re-introduced to Scotland) and the goshawk (colonized from falconry releases) and benefit the expanding osprey population. Pine marten and wildcat numbers would benefit from the greater forest cover. The indigenous Scottish crossbill would also benefit as it is limited to native pine forests.

On balance, the small potential reduction in numbers of golden eagle, golden plover, dunlin and red grouse (and again the core area is largely peripheral to their main areas of habitation in Scotland), could be offset by better prospects for the endangered capercaillie and the currently declining black grouse. If the forest were eventually to come into its near original state over a much wider area, then the (unnaturally) large numbers of eagle and red grouse would reduce but be complemented by forest predators such as goshawk, the two forest grouse species, the mixed country red kite, and of course, the potential return of forest-dwelling bear, lynx and beaver.

There is also some evidence to suggest that the native flora would be richer in such a balanced habitat range of trees and open country, especially as a result of lower grazing pressure from deer (SNH in its study referred to 11 susceptible plant communities and to the rare *Homogyne alpina* in particular). As the eventual vision includes the return of the full spectrum of large mammals, including additional browsers and grazers, the eventual gains and losses are probably beyond the predictive power of current ecological science, which is limited when applied even to well-researched assemblages (see Chapter 7). If beaver were re-introduced, there are acknowledged benefits for floral diversity in riparian habitats. Elk (moose), 'tarpan', forest cattle and wild boar would modify habitats considerably, contributing to the open structure of the forest and adding to the overall biomass and hence to the availability of carrion and prey for predators.

## Other initiatives in the core area

In other parts of the core area envisioned by Trees for Life, landowners have become active in regenerating the forest: the Strathconan and Brahan Estates have projected an increase in native woodland from 150 to 2800 ha, with the possibility of cooperation in aspen survey work and use of Trees for Life volunteers with the native woodland projects. Trees for Life have influenced regeneration and planting projects in the adjacent private estates of Wester Guisachan, Mullardoch, Hilton, Ceannacroc, and Balnacarn, whilst SNH have a management agreement for regeneration in Glen Strathfarrer (see Colour Plate 3).

In all of Trees for Life's work, the aim has been to recreate a natural forest structure for the purposes of wildland conservation, rather than for economic use. In this process, nature is mimicked – there is a focus upon natural patterns of regeneration and pioneer species rather than on maximizing numbers of trees planted. To some extent these aims are compromised by the deer problem – unnatural fences are necessary to establish seed trees until deer numbers are reduced. Furthermore, as we have noted, other grazers and browsers such as moose, beaver, wild forest cattle and horse are absent. However, establishment of tree cover and the recovery of the shrub layer from over-browsing are the essential first steps in this ecosystem recovery process.

There is also an ongoing process of research and mapping (now using geographic information systems – GIS – with academic support from Scottish Universities). Of particular interest are the mountain top communities of dwarf birch, juniper and willow; hazel and aspen in the valleys; and the presence in the lower broadleaf woods of oak and alder.

There is every chance that the core area conceptualized by Trees for Life could come about. It may well be that Glen Affric alone would represent the unutilized heartland of wild forest, and that surrounding estates would still practice deer stalking, but these surrounding areas could in theory coexist and even flourish with the return of the forest and a decline in deer numbers. It is unlikely that sheep farming will be a serious barrier to the future vision for the area, and forestry practices have evolved to value native woodlands and wildlife. The Forestry Commission in Scotland has pioneered community involvement in management and is committed to the regeneration of native woodland.

## Economic exploitation: Hydro-electric dams, roads and reservoirs

The Glens of Affric and Strathfarrer were opened up in the last century to hydro-electric development with the damming of the rivers and the construction of tunnels and roads. The resultant electricity production in the core area is small and is insignificant at the national level. Conceivably, following a more general acceptance of the wildlands ideal in the longer term, such items of hydro-electric infrastructure could be decommissioned so that the rivers could find their natural flow and the lochs their natural level. Such policies may sound fanciful in the current climate of greenhouse gas reduction, but they have been a feature of re-wilding in the US, where even quite large dams have been decommissioned. The access roads to these reservoirs could be left open to facilitate walkers and bicycles, but would ideally be closed to motor traffic. Where such access has become a major aspect of local recreation, access to vehicles could be limited by license (with keys for barriers), or electric-vehicular access provided.

The large adjacent sporting estates may come on the market and prove attractive to conservation organizations concerned to further large-scale nature reserves. Alternatively, even within traditional land ownership, the potential for wildlife watching might prove as attractive economically as deer stalking and would be more in keeping with the ethos of the core area (there would likely remain a need for culling of deer numbers). These aspects are addressed in more detail when we come to consider future strategies in Chapter 10.

## Inspiration

The Trees for Life vision has proven inspirational across Britain and doubtless to many people concerned for wild areas in other parts of the world. In my own experience of working in the very different environmental and political situation in Wales, the steady year-by-year successes of Alan's project in Scotland did a great deal to counteract the frustrations of so little happening on the ground in Wales. The Caledonian pine forest existed as much in our own hearts as did the wildwood of Eryri, and thus each increment bolstered our strength and vision.

Adam Griffin has felt similarly encouraged in the setting up of Moor Trees in Dartmoor, where there is a bewildering array of powerful stake-holder interests, each fighting their corner, so that the status quo tends to prevail. Further afield, at least one foreign initiative was also inspired by Alan's work, the safeguarding of the Yendegaia, 38,780 ha of degraded forest in southern Chile.

A crucial element in this inspirational work has been the outreach driven by the superb photography of trees and wild forest around the globe, and the effective marketing of professionally produced calendars, diaries and cards that have carried the message. Justice has been done to the original beauty of the forest, and it is this that strikes the greatest resonance. As Alan would be the first to acknowledge, whatever inspiration people find in his work, he owes to the inspiring presence of the Caledonian forest itself! It is in the spirit of the great tree itself – in its aromatic presence the automatic response is to breathe it in, as if welcoming life itself in all its glory, the true healing power and meaning of inspiration!

# 4

# Dartmoor

Dartmoor is in many ways a perfect example of an English 'wilderness', and the term is frequently used in promotional literature for visitors to the National Park. The area of the Park, at 950 km² holds virtually the entire 'natural area' of the Dartmoor massif, consisting of high moor to above 500 m, river valleys and woodland.[1] This 'wilderness' has several roads crossing the central parts (see Colour Plate 4), and the National Park as a whole attracts over 2 million visitors per year. It is an area of upland heath, grass moor and blanket bog, drained by steeply inclined river valleys containing some of the most extensive ancient oak woodland in England. This area is less 'wild' than the Rhinogydd in Wales (which are of comparable size), and much less remote than the Caledonian forest in Glen Affric. The moors are subject to heavy recreational pressure from visitors holidaying in the many hotels, centres and camping sites on the periphery. In addition to recreational use, extensive areas of common land support high numbers of cattle, sheep and ponies; there are also large areas subject to military training, reservoirs for water supply and some small areas of commercial forestry.

Even so, there are parts of Dartmoor that are quiet, little visited, of marginal use to agriculture and unsuitable for forestry. These areas hold large Sites of Special Scientific Interest (SSSI), designated either for blanket bog or upland heath communities. The diversity of the area, with ancient woodland, torrent rivers, wet and dry pastures, heath and bog, together with the distinctive granite outcrops, make it an exceptional candidate for a wildlands project. However, as with virtually all upland habitat in Britain, a hands-off approach to management, relying upon natural processes of regeneration, would significantly alter the balance of species and community structure: heathland would be colonized by birch and rowan, pastures by bracken and eventually both would become woodland. This succession would likely be opposed by interests protecting open sub-climax communities either for communal grazing or bird protection (or other species identified as important for biodiversity such as butterflies, flowering plants, lichens and mosses), as well as by ramblers and preservationists concerned with elements of an archaeological and cultural landscape. The area is rich in Bronze Age and Iron Age sites and has been farmed since Neolithic times. Any proposal for large-scale wilding will have to take on board these competing interests. In this sense, Dartmoor is very different from Glen Affric, and more extreme than the much quieter Rhinogs in Snowdonia.

At first site, it would appear a less promising prospect than wild areas of the North Pennines, Lake District and the Dales. It has, however, one of the most fundamental requirements of a major wildlands project, and that is a local community-based organization – Moor Trees, which has a strong vision and an active membership – and despite the competing interests in the area, there is a large sector in the southwest of the Park that could accommodate a significant wilding project involving the regeneration of the native Atlantic oak wood.

## Moor Trees: a local re-wilding initiative

As will be seen when we look at other candidate wild areas, there are quieter places in England – in particular in the Cheviot Hills and North Pennines. However, Dartmoor has spawned an active local group that has already begun the uphill task of reconciling the various and conflicting interests. Moor Trees began work in the early 1990s with Adam Griffin gaining inspiration from Trees for Life's work.[2] By 1999 they had instigated a major conference that was attended by all concerned parties, ranging from government agencies, the Park authorities, voluntary bodies and local commoners, all of whom showed a willingness to enter into constructive dialogue (*Toward the Wild*, November 1999). Thus, the millennium started with encouraging signs that re-wilding had become an acceptable part of the conservation agenda in England.

Moor Trees has started without a specific long-range plan, other than to have more trees on Dartmoor and the restoration of a more natural landscape. Its main aim at this early stage is to generate a consensual process whereby a feasible long-range plan could evolve. Since the 1999 conference, it has begun to draw together stakeholder interests. On a practical and educational front, local tree nurseries are being set up and school children are involved in collecting seed. The most immediate aim is to set up a demonstration project covering 100–500 ha and to commission a professional feasibility study to select the most appropriate area.

Given this bottom-up consensual approach, there is an opportunity to provide an input to developing discussions. We shall return to the issue of how change has been furthered among a plethora of competing interests in a later chapter. For present purposes, I will outline the problems that Moor

Photo: Moor Trees

**Figure 4.1** *Tree nursery on Dartmoor*

Trees will face and make some suggestions on possible sites and the process of consensus.

Firstly, in the simpler task of just increasing tree cover on the moors and in the river valleys, a great deal of potential exists without conflicting interest. The Dartmoor National Park Authority already has a goal of an additional 100 ha of new broadleaf woodland by 2005.[3] This modest target will also be supplemented by management agreements to reduce grazing pressure and this should ensure some additional natural regeneration. There are large areas of poor pasture invaded by bracken which could quite happily succeed to woodland, and will slowly do so under present management and trends. It is when a large-scale scheme is considered, involving the return of native herbivores and perhaps also predators, that difficult policy decisions will have to be made among competing interests.

## Military training grounds

One of the most important of competing interests on Dartmoor is military training. The largest and 'quietest' area in the northwest of the Park is used as a firing range for small arms (the use of heavy artillery recently ceased). Given the scarcity of such areas for military use, it can be assumed that the army will be present on Dartmoor for the foreseeable future. Although the Ministry of Defence has taken on board its responsibilities, particularly under recent Biodiversity Action Plans, it is unlikely to want large-scale intrusion of woodland. Its lands, however, consist largely of upland heath and grassland, with some blanket bog, with a considerable area designated as an SSSI. Whilst military training grounds hardly qualify as a core area that would uplift the spirit, the open moor and quiet on non-firing days is, for many people, an effective counterpoint to the over-used tourist zones. There is some possibility of enhancing the area and it could act as a contiguous zone for populations of animals in the other candidate zone.

## A potential core area

Dartmoor divides into two major upland zones – the northwest and southwest, with the smaller wooded region in the southeast also being important. The southwest bloc is bounded by a major road that splits Dartmoor north and south, and another that cuts NW/SE, with the main Exeter–Plymouth road effectively forming the southern boundary of the Park. This southwest bloc contains a large tract of SSSI designated for its blanket bog, as well as grass moor and heath. There are small tracts of ancient oak woodland in the valleys. This area has the advantage of no military training and the presence of a major conservation-oriented landowner in the National Trust. It would be my suggestion that this bloc be a candidate core area (see Colour Plate 4). The question then arises as to the nature of the changes envisaged and other conflicts that might arise.

## Non-intervention

If it were feasible to get agreement for the whole bloc marked by the orange line in Colour Plate 4 to be left to itself, one benefit would ensue: we would have an opportunity to watch nature 'doing its thing'. There would be natural processes of succession and decay (eventually), fire, drought, storm damage and processes of climate change. Over a period of a few decades, we would see extensive change, and over a century or two, some eventual balance (for however long the climate and other factors such as disease and invading species remained stable). Given that domestic stock would be removed, though wild ponies would remain, grazing pressure would be reduced such that natural regeneration would allow the woodland cover to extend up the valleys – closed-canopy oak in the bottom and birch, willow and rowan forming open woodland on the heaths and grass moor. There would be a rich shrub layer of heather and bilberry. The blanket bog would remain relatively free of trees, unless it dried out as a result of climate change.

There is a possibility that pony numbers would increase and suppress regeneration – it appears an open question, with the most likely outcome being a density-dependent suppression of fecundity. However, in the case of red deer, this self-limiting process does not kick-in at the low densities required to sustain regeneration of woodland. There is no current population of red deer on the moor, but they ought to be a feature of the wild area. The neighbouring Exmoor ponies are very much left to themselves, but any combination of herbivores such as wild cattle, deer and ponies would require some control of numbers to safeguard natural regeneration. There is a current discussion concerning woodland and grazing dynamics, which is outlined in Chapter 7.

If applied generally to Dartmoor, this policy would impact upon a number of other conservation goals:

- sites of ancient settlement, such as hut circles, burial mounds and field systems
- species-rich flower meadows, in particular Rhos pasture, with its characteristic floral assemblage and nationally rare insect fauna
- a number of open-country birds, such as dunlin, golden plover and ring ouzel, which are part of the Dartmoor National Park (DNP) Biodiversity Action Plan
- rambling interests concerned with 'open-views' and unfettered access
- commoners' grazing rights.

However, perusal of the DNP maps for the Biodiversity Action Plan (BAP) shows that considerable potential exists within the southwest bloc on land not crucial to any of Dartmoor's priority BAP species.[4] For example, the majority of dunlin, golden plover and ring ouzel are in the northern zone, and the major areas of Rhos pasture (important for the marsh fritillary butterfly and narrow bordered bee hawk moth, as well as rare flowering plants) are in the east and southeast; the bog specialists are largely in the northern areas, and denizens of the special valley mires, such as scarce dragonflies, would not suffer from expansion of woodland near such sites, which would remain protected. Many of these bird and insect species are also at the edge of their range in Britain and Europe, being more numerous in the Pennines and Scotland, and constitute a very small percentage of the British (and European) populations. There remain, however, significant archaeological sites.

Furthermore, BAP species that depend upon mature Atlantic oak woods would eventually benefit, and these include the blue ground beetle as well as mosses, lichens and liverworts and characteristic birds such as the pied flycatcher, redstart and wood warbler.


## Managed re-wilding

In this option, the goal of a more natural climax vegetation is achieved by managed regeneration, in which domestic stock are removed and replaced with special breeds, augmented by re-introduced herbivores, and the overall pattern of grazing is used to reproduce a more open woodland. In this case, zones of planting and protective fencing would also be used, which could speed colonization of treeless moor as well as safeguarding natural regeneration in the valleys. Most fencing could be removed after about 20 years when natural regeneration would occur, provided that herbivore numbers were controlled.

In this scenario, several original herbivores, or their equivalent special breeds, could be re-introduced; wild forest cattle (either Hecht from Germany, or if possible, a third Chillingham Park herd), near-natural ponies (the Exmoor pony is regarded as the closest to wild stock), and red deer would be the main browsers and grazers, with wild boar and beaver also being present. The degree to which special breeds would need to be protected from interbreeding with other ponies and cattle would require study. The area may be too small and not diverse enough for elk, which would tend to wander and would represent a major hazard on roads and an unwelcome intruder on farmland, although given attitudes in England generally, this also applies to boar and deer.

With the presence of special breeds and the need to control herbivore numbers, there is a role for present farmers to be involved in range management – particularly in the harvesting of venison, organic beef and wild boar. Appropriate grazing regimes could also be used to keep the most important archaeological sites open. Large areas of Dartmoor form part of the Duchy estate of Prince Charles, who is disposed towards organic production and conservation issues, but tenant farmers have a great deal of autonomy, and commoners' rights are notoriously difficult to harmonize with large area conservation schemes (a large-area native woodland regeneration proposal in the Brecon Beacons foundered on this issue).

The Dartmoor area could in theory support a small pack of wolves and this has been proposed by some commentators, but the wolves would range outside the core area and predate domestic stock and ponies, and their offspring would have no contiguous areas to emigrate to. In my view, the general area is too small, too intensively used by people and too isolated from other wild areas to be considered for wolf re-introduction. It is too small for bear for the same reason. However, the area is not too small to support a viable population of lynx, and there is sufficient woodland and numbers of deer in surrounding farmland for emigration to other suitable areas. Predation of sheep by lynx would doubtless take place, but at a level that could be tolerable and would be in line with European experience in France, especially if buffer zones and forest corridors were established. There is already evidence of naturalized puma on the moor (see Chapter 8).

Appropriately managed, the southwest bloc has the potential for greatly extended cover of the important Atlantic oak woods and the regeneration of heath with open woodland. There could be 'conservation' gains whilst safeguarding species of current concern: in particular the locally extinct black grouse would have sufficient habitat to return, as would goshawk, red kite and possibly also osprey.

With about one-third of Dartmoor designated as a wild-zone, there could emerge a balance of interests between farming, commoners' land, military, open country rambling, and specialist conservation interests. There would exist a further potential for the military land to be subject to a wild-grazing regime involving special breeds of cattle and pony; however, it would probably require the whole of the upland zone to be under this regime, and for a buffer of beef- or dairy-only pasture land in the rest of the National Park, before the return of lynx would be practicable.

# 5

# The Potential for Networks and Corridors

The wilding ethos has gathered such momentum in the first five years of the 21st century, that there are now many projects on the ground of varying degrees of wildness, encompassing a variety of visions, ranging from small-scale programmes on particular reaches of rivers and urban wildlife corridors to habitat network initiatives relating to woodland, reedbeds and coastal marshes. Many of the smaller schemes are indicative of a general wave of change in cities, the urban fringe, the community forests, wetland restoration, coastal retreat, the wilding of farming and even wild gardens. In this chapter, we shall look at those larger schemes of relevance for linking core areas with corridors of land that, although not necessarily free of human use, would be wild enough to allow movement of animals between these core areas and also to provide buffer zones with more appropriate economic activity. Each of the following schemes, though separately conceived and not yet part of an overall strategy, will provide important lessons in implementation, particularly for landscape-scale initiatives outside traditional nature reserves.

These networking initiatives are fostering partnerships between land-owners, government agencies, wildlife trusts, local councils and the industrial sector. The different schemes illustrate a variety of cooperative endeavours between voluntary bodies such as the large landowning National Trust, Woodland Trust and RSPB; the campaigning organizations such as WWF, which have supported purchases of land; the Water Companies and associated civil engineering companies supporting the re-wilding of rivers and catchments; the County Wildlife Trusts with targeted land purchase and some landscape-scale plans; specialist trusts such as the Vincent Wildlife Trust and the Otter Trust, which have been concerned with species re-introduction and breeding programmes; Local and Municipal Authorities, and government agencies such as the Environment Agency (very active with regard to catchment-based local plans); and the Forestry Commission, playing a pivotal role with its major holding of public lands and schemes to convert plantations of exotic species into multi-purpose wilder forests of native species. In addition, the Heritage Lottery Fund (HLF) has taken an interest in large area schemes and supported many of the above initiatives.

Out of this plethora of wilding schemes of varying scale, there are two major initiatives that have the potential to further the creation of corridors and buffer zones for a broad strategy: the inter-agency Working Group on New Wildwoods (Land Use Policy Group – LUPG, consisting of English Nature, the Countryside Agency, the Environment Agency, the Forestry Commission, Countryside Council for Wales, Scottish Natural Heritage and the Joint Nature Conservation Committee) and the work of the River Restoration Centre, supported by the agencies and Water Companies, as well as by private-sector engineering companies.

## The Land Use Policy Group and new wildwoods

The Land Use Policy Group investigated the potential for new wildwoods in England and Wales largely in response to a failure of government incentives to create significant new native woodland outside of Scotland. The LUPG reported on its research and seminar series *New Wildwoods* in July 2002.[1] The Scottish successes had indicated that there was a public demand for wilder, more natural woods. After considering definitions and principles, the group did a preliminary survey of key areas in Britain, looking at current initiatives and the potential for a new policy of wilder woodland – preferably on a large scale (1000 ha) and with the further possibility of incorporation into a Forest Habitat Network on an even larger scale. The definitions of wildwood have been left open – essentially the woods must be primarily native species, the main purpose being conservation and recreation rather than commercial use, subject to minimal managerial intervention and as large as can be achieved.

One of the current initiatives earmarked for study was 'Wild Ennerdale' in Cumbria, a joint venture between the landowners: the National Trust, Forestry Commission and United Utilities (a water company). Although this is not described by the partners as a re-wilding project as it intends continued economic exploitation for timber and livestock farming, there is some separation of wilder land and buffer zones that could prove instructive for larger-scale projects. Perhaps because of the nature of the grouping of agencies, the LUPG gave less attention to Carrifran, which we describe below, which is perhaps the closest to the wildwood ideal. The Woodland Trust project at Glen Finglas also received little attention, yet at 3000 ha, it is one of the largest woodland regeneration projects in Britain and one that could have much relevance for the study of both domestic and wild herbivore interactions.

## Ennerdale in the Lake District National Park: a cooperative project of the National Trust, water companies and Forestry Commission

This project has been highlighted in the LUPG report as providing a good model for Wildwoods both in terms of the general philosophy of what is being proposed and the structures being developed to implement it. A major aim of the Ennerdale project is to increase the sense of wildness in the area, to use this as an asset and to integrate wildland with existing land uses.[2] It is an integrated rural management project (or catchment management), rather than being specifically a native woodland or re-wilding project. Some areas of existing conifer forest are currently being felled as they are seen to detract from the sense of wildness and will be replaced by more open woodland, established through either natural regeneration or through 'kick starting' by planting in areas where the broadleaf seed source is lacking. Some areas of conifers will also be retained as public opinion had demonstrated that conifer trees can add value to the experience of the valley as a 'wild' place. In addition, the partners are keen to see cattle (likely to be Highland cattle) introduced into the valley to facilitate habitat change through what (at present) is a missing natural process of 'dynamic disturbance'.

Ennerdale is a remote, rugged valley in the Western Lake District drained by the River Liza and including Ennerdale Water, a public water supply for West Cumbria (see Colour Plate 4). The upper part of the valley is historically unpopulated. The higher slopes are used for grazing for fell sheep, while the lower slopes and valley bottom are dominated by commercial forestry and farmland. There is an area of semi-natural ancient oak woodlands on the north facing side of the lake and an attractive sprinkling of small woodlands and mature hedgerows.

The original native woodland cover was oak–birch and alder, important as hunting grounds and later for generations of charcoal burners and iron smiths. Through the 19th and 20th centuries the valley was an important water supply for the growing communities in West Cumbria and the level of the lake was raised. Sheep grazing also supported a number of farms. Commercial forestry began in 1927 and transformed the nature of the valley.

Ennerdale is distinctive for its sense of wildness due to the grandeur of the fells, the remoteness from public roads and habitation, the presence of a forest that is big enough to get lost in and the wild nature of the river Liza. However, there are also features which detract from these special characteristics, such as overgrazed fell vegetation, stark forest boundaries, dense plantations and clear-felled areas, fences, signs and occasional man-made features. The valley is also a place of work for people through

Photo: National Trust

**Figure 5.1** *Ennerdale in the Lake District National Park: a cooperative project of the National Trust, water companies, and Forestry Commission*

farming, forestry, water supply, tourism and recreation as well as conservation-focused land management, with the latter three becoming more dominant over the past 40 years.

The project developed from initial discussions between the National Trust and the Forestry Commission about how the two organizations could work together better in the valley, sharing resources and working towards a common vision. These discussions developed over a number of years and more recently included United Utilities (the water authority which owns and manages Ennerdale Lake) resulting in the formation of the Wild Ennerdale partnership in 2002. The vision of the partners is to 'allow the evolution of Ennerdale as a wild valley for the benefit of people, relying more on natural processes to shape its landscape and ecology'. A memorandum of understanding was agreed between the partners in September 2002 and forms the basis for the future management of Ennerdale.[3]

## Land ownership and management

The land ownership pattern is remarkably simple in the upper valley with the National Trust and Forestry Commission owning the fells (National Trust owns a small area of oak woodland) and Forest Enterprise owning the lower forest land. This gives a potential for managing the valley as a single unit, with landowners and others (including local farmers and community groups) sharing long-term objectives and planning management on a whole-landscape basis.

Management is aimed at finding ways of enhancing the area's unique qualities of wildness and remoteness while still creating opportunities for social and economic activity. The partnership sees the Wild Ennerdale process as a philosophy of management which is still developing, rather than identifying a fixed end point and trying to achieve that in as short a time as possible. It is also about recognizing that 'wilding' is a process of change that involves reducing the intensity of human intervention and allowing natural processes greater freedom to operate. Following on from this is the concept that Wild Ennerdale will continue to be a place in which people live, work and play but that they will do so in a way that is in keeping with the scale and nature of natural processes. It is further argued that anthropogenic processes can then be seen as becoming part of the range of natural processes that operate. There is a feeling amongst the partners that Wild Ennerdale has an important message to communicate in the re-wilding debate: that it is not always necessary to see natural and human processes as completely different things, and that it has been the scale and nature of human processes (particularly the involvement of the internal combustion engine) that marks human processes out as being different. Thus, if new principles can be established in the valley by which people operate, then human activity need not necessarily be seen as competing with natural processes, but as complementary to them.

Wild Ennerdale is a unique cooperative vision, and much experience could be gained from the management process in different zones of the valley in terms of vegetation changes, the role of herbivores, and species gains and losses. The intended result will be a wilder landscape, a more diverse and robust environment and a major enhancement of the sense of wildness and remoteness of Ennerdale. It can act as a model for development in other areas where similar land holdings exist, and is certainly relevant for Dartmoor and the Rhinogydd. Experience gained from the grazing of domestic stock, local marketing of products and eco-tourism will be of relevance to buffer zones for large core areas where there is no human influence.

## The Carrifran wildwood project

The LUPG make little mention of the important Carrifran project in the Southern Uplands of Scotland, yet this is precisely the kind of project LUPG have in mind, and a thorough perusal of its history, methods of finance, management structure and ecological restoration plan reveal a model for virtually all other developments on ecologically degraded pasture lands in

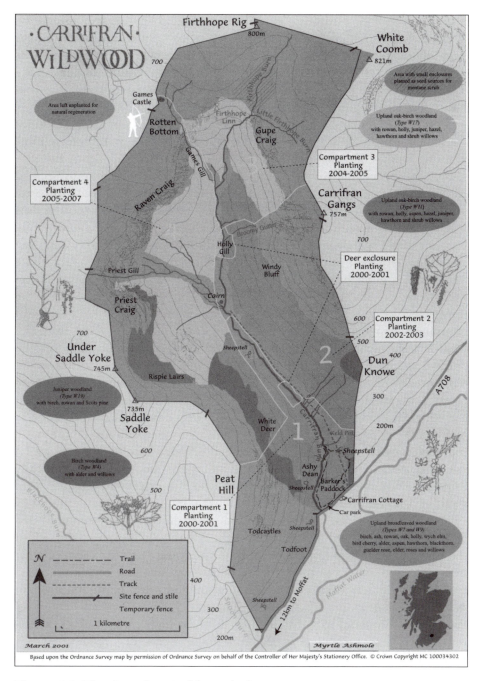

**Figure 5.2** *The Carrifran Wildwood planting programme*

the uplands. This is a fascinating project, taking account of distant
ecological history, advances in vegetation science over the past two decades,
making use of all recent opportunities for cooperative endeavour and

general ecological restoration ethos and strategy. It is a rare combination of the vision of a small professional group of committed eco-foresters, the sharing of that vision and creation of a large support group in communities local and regional (from which 80 per cent of the initial land purchase price of £400,000 was raised) and the gaining of support from agencies and NGOs for ongoing funding and management.[4]

This project arose when the charitable Borders Forest Trust set up a wildwood group and looked for an opportunity to purchase suitable planting land. This was in the mid-1990s and in the lead up to the new millennium when there was a veritable feeding frenzy of groups seeking Millennium Funding from the National Lottery for a wide variety of forest schemes in Scotland. Carrifran could not get onto that bandwagon in time and decided to raise the money through a founders' share scheme – 600 people bought a half-hectare share for £250 or more, and the Carrifran valley site of 650 ha was purchased in 1998.

The valley is in the upper watershed of the Tweed in the Ettrick Forest and ranges from the valley bottom to 800 m, containing the complete upper catchment area. It is virtually treeless, with acid grassland and relic montane heath over a variety of upland soils, including some base-rich flushes and calcareous outcrops. The valley and heights are a Site of Special Scientific Interest and a candidate Special Area for Conservation, in an area with as little as 0.4 per cent native woodland and large areas of forestry plantation and sheep pasture. The montane heath communities are of great conservation interest, containing dwarf willow, cloudberry and some rare northern plants at their southern limit. There is a population of feral goats hefted to the valley, blue hare on the tops and a few ring ouzel and black grouse, but otherwise the area is ecologically impoverished. The Tweed catchment is also the subject of a major wild rivers project (see below).

This is precisely the kind of situation found in the North Pennines, the eastern parts of Snowdonia, in part of the Rhinogydd and in very much of the Cambrians. In this respect, the Carrifran project is, in my view, of great relevance and deserves more detailed monitoring and review. This is particularly underscored by the detailed management plan; the level of professionalism is exemplary and addresses all the critical issues of large-scale woodland establishment in areas of high conservation value – but where that value has reflected a focus upon degraded secondary habitats maintained by domestic livestock management practices. In Carrifran there are few deer and although there are 180 goats, these, as well as the sheep, will be gradually removed.

The ensuing expected vegetation changes consequent upon planting about 300 ha of the 650 ha site (there being few seed trees) have been mapped in detail (see Figure 5.2); the scheme allows for a patchwork of habitats: the conservation of base-rich flushes (for rare plants), bog and archaeological remains, together with the natural regeneration of montane heath and, eventually, scrub woodland to 800 m, so that important open eco-types are not planted. Tree species for planting are scrupulously related to soil nutrient and soil moisture conditions, National Vegetation Classification (NVC) type and ecological factors, with a self-admitted purist zeal for seed provenance and palaeo-ecological evidence for appropriate species. Scottish Natural Heritage were supportive of the plan to alter the entire ecology of a large section of a Site of Special Scientific Interest (now a candidate Special Area of Conservation), provided botanically rich flushes and areas with rare montane plants were conserved.

This group of experienced foresters and ecologists has openly embraced wildland concepts – the valley is to be returned to as near original state as soil and climate allow and will not be furnished with interpretation and visitor facilities, though access will be open to all. Despite this puritan zeal, the Borders Forest Trust have won support from Scottish Natural Heritage (for funding of the project office), the Forest Authority (with grants for planting), WWF and the John Muir Trust, as well as Millennium Forest for Scotland grants. On top of the £400,000 purchase, planting will cost an estimated £300,000 and MFST will contribute £125,000 to management. The ongoing management cost for ten years is estimated at £1.1m, generating five full-time job equivalents over eight years for 300 ha of planting.

In addition to these important data on costs, management, structure, cooperation and committed vision, the project will generate valuable scientific monitoring data on conversion of acid grassland and regeneration of montane heath and scrub. The NVC woodland types in the mosaic of plantings are clearly set out, with expected transitions from grassland and heathland. Colonization of these woodlands by woodland flora, birds, insects and mammals will be of great interest. Eventually, the project might be persuaded to consider beaver, boar, wild cattle, forest pony, elk and perhaps lynx! At this stage, however, the priority is to establish a woodland in the face of nibbling voles, hares, roe and sika.

The project is ideally sited for linking with a future Forest Habitat Network in the Southern Uplands, as the commercial enterprises in the border region become more wildlife friendly. The land to the east is owned by the National Trust for Scotland (NTS), and although managed for sheep, it will one day, perhaps, be subject to a wilder management regime. Carrifran also illustrates the importance of identity. The fund-raising brochures are wonderful examples of the use of evocative photography, a concise message and convincing organization to inspire and galvanize local people not only in support of the project, but in the embrace of a wildland ethos.

## Glen Finglas: a Woodland Trust site in the Trossachs

The Woodland Trust acquired the Glen Finglas site in 1996 prior to the area becoming Scotland's first National Park. It is a 4039 ha former hill sheep estate. Support for the purchase came from the Heritage Lottery Fund, and management makes use of woodland grants from the Forestry Commission as well as agricultural subsidies.

The project is described by Angela Douglas in *Reforesting Scotland* as having five objectives: to restore native woodland across its full natural range; to promote the concept of sustainability as it relates to multi-purpose land use; to promote many and varied opportunities for access and public enjoyment; to promote participation by the local community and others, fostering a sense of stewardship; and to demonstrate and attract international interest in a range of woodland establishment techniques as well as forestry, agriculture and tourism integration.

At the time of purchase, only 235 ha of neglected ancient semi-natural woodland remained on the estate. The Trust aims to re-establish over 3000 ha of native woodland (70 per cent of the land cover) over 40 years, creating the largest native broadleaved forest in Scotland. Woodland will range from lowland wood pasture, wet woods, Caledonian pine and the full altitudinal range to sub-montane scrub of willows and juniper.

Livestock grazing will continue with both wild and domestic stock in order to maintain a mosaic of open ground. The use of livestock will also maintain employment and skills locally. Visitor management also offers opportunities for employment and involvement in the project. Access and 'public enjoyment' facilities are being developed and the glen is within one-and-a-half hour's drive of 85 per cent of Scotland's population.

There are three different glens on the property and each is planned to demonstrate different means of regeneration. Lendrick Hill, 580 ha ranging from 100 to 630 m of broken rock, will be the core area for a new native Caledonian pinewood. There are remnants of birch, rowan and hawthorn, with some holly and aspen with 44 ha of birch. A traditional approach to deer fencing is being taken until the new woodland is established. Glen Casaig rises from the Glen Finglas reservoir to the summit of Ben Ledi at 850 m. There is gorge woodland, but otherwise it consists of treeless grass and heather slopes. The area will continue to be grazed but at a lower level to allow natural regeneration and maintenance of open spaces (there is an important population of black grouse). In another valley, Glen Meann, rising to the summit of Ben Vane's 811 m, a mosaic of open ground and trees (mainly alder and birch, but with some old elm, aspen and guelder rose) will be maintained. Archaeological remains, a public right of way and old drovers' routes make this a major area for walkers. Sheep and cattle grazing will continue, but with various combinations of exclosures, scarifying and seeding to study different strategies of natural regeneration and planting under varying conditions, such as distance to seed source, exposure and herbivore pressure.

Glen Finglas itself is relatively well wooded and extends to 670 m, with mainly birch and alder, hazel and bird cherry. This area has been pasture woodland for many centuries and this has resulted in a diverse flora and fauna. All the trees are of significant age (with the largest hazel bole in Scotland at 5 m), thought to be the result of pollarding practices. In this area, sheep grazing and deer numbers will be controlled to allow natural regeneration and the maintenance of the wood pasture conditions. Sheep will be removed from the eastern part of the glen and the area stock fenced, with sheep introduced in May at a density of 1 per hectare; cattle will also be grazed for short periods. On the western side of the glen there is a hefted (attached to a particular area) population of hinds and this will be reduced to five deer per km$^2$ to allow vegetation to recover; all sheep will be removed. The floor of the glen will be grazed at normal levels to maintain open views and to secure the archaeological remains.

This project is thus on a scale and variety worthy of close study; it should provide much useful comparative data of relevance elsewhere. It may well be that in the future, the wilder areas could accommodate the re-introduction of other wild herbivores such as Exmoor pony and Heck cattle to diversify the grazing. The continued use of domestic stock, whilst detracting from the wildland potential, will at least provide experience relevant to buffer zones around core areas. The expected influx of visitors will also offer a model for management of buffer-zone tourism in the National Park areas of Snowdonia and Dartmoor.

## Cashel

The Royal Scottish Forestry Society purchased Cashel Farm on the shores of Loch Lomond in 1996 with a major grant of £800,000 from the Millennium Forest for Scotland (funds supported by the National Lottery in the lead up to the millennium). The total cost is estimated at £2 million and the project is supported by the Forestry Authority and Scottish Natural Heritage. At about 1500 ha, the project is smaller than the Woodland Trust project but shares similar aims of multi-purpose use, encouraging conservation, amenities and rural recreation whilst establishing new woodland but with a greater focus upon sustainable timber production.

There will be a substantial area of new Scots pine woodland, mixed broadleaf woods and new sub-montane habitat with dwarf species. This project will therefore provide a useful model for the purchase and conversion of farmland in buffer zones where the maintenance of local employment and timber supplies is important – such as adjacent to Coed y Brenin in Snowdonia and areas in the east of the Affric core area.

## The National Trust fenland project in Cambridgeshire

I have focused upon the wildwoods project in terms of potential large-scale core areas and corridors, all of which are in the uplands, but there is another more advanced initiative on low wetland in Cambridgeshire that involves a mix of wet pasture, fen and carr. The vision relates to a number of fragmented holdings by the National Trust in the fens east of Cambridge, centred on the National Nature Reserve of Wicken Fen.[5]

The fens are an artefact of human engineering on a regional scale, having been drained in the 16th and 17th century by Dutch engineers, and then heavily utilized as arable land. There are fragmented pockets of old fen, mostly alder carr, sedge and reed-swamp, where the reed and sedge were formerly cut for thatch or peat extracted for fuel, but which now curiously perch above the water table in a land that has gradually sunk all around them as peaty soil has dried, oxidized and shrunk. Much wildlife-rich habitat in the area relies upon complex systems of pumps to drain and reflood, much as the Somerset Levels and Ouse Washes, two other major artificially maintained wetlands.

The National Trust has been looking at a large area with a view to wilding their agricultural holdings and creating a large bloc of wet woodland, reed and riparian meadow habitat (see Colour Plate 5). A feasibility study was completed in 1999,[6] and two farms totalling 215ha have been bought at a cost of £1.7 million with substantial help from the Heritage Lottery Fund. It is a major challenge given the complex hydrology, but lessons learned in this project will be of relevance to other wetland areas. Ultimately, however artificial the water regime, there is an opportunity to bring in large herbivores. The ideas of the Oostvaardersplassen project are being taken up (see Chapter 7), and a small herd of Konik horses has already been established at Wicken, with Highland cattle to follow. The site manager, Adrian Colston, thinks it unlikely the project could include beaver and boar as these would cause economic damage to dykes and nearby crops, but elk would be a possibility.

The major limitation of the project is that the area is cut off from other fenland and forest and it would not be an easy task to link the enlarged reserve to other sites or to the Broads in the east or Thetford forest to the north. In this respect 'nature-mapping' exercises, drawn from Dutch experience, which outline potential expansions of wildlife sites, can be used to garner local support and strategic funding (Simon Bates, *Nature mapping in ECOS* 25 3/4 2004). Such links would be necessary to support truly wild herbivore populations. Nevertheless, an enlarged reserve diversified by grazing and disturbance regimes might allow re-colonization of some key species that have been lost in the last 100 years, such as the swallowtail butterfly and Montagu's harrier.

## The North Pennines and Sussex wildwoods

The northern Pennines contain some of the largest expanses of 'wild' country in England, most of it grassland and moorland managed as sporting estates for grouse, and with important conservation interests for species associated with these managed habitats. There is also a substantial area of commercial forestry, particularly further north along the Scottish borders in the Cheviots. A large area of the Kielderhead forest was not planted because growing conditions were deemed poor, and part of this 3500 ha area has had no domestic stock for 30 years, though feral goats have maintained a relatively treeless heath. This area is now a Site of Special Scientific Interest grazed by wild goats and could form the basis for wildland management with other wild herbivores if neighbouring farmed areas were incorporated. In neighbouring Geltsdale, the RSPB has a large reserve of moorland bordered by remnants of ancient woodland in the valleys. There are already moves to link woodlands and recreate traditional pasture woods, once a feature of Geltsdale Forest, with domestic stock – 200 ha having already been planted.

This area of the North Pennines is a patchwork of commercial forestry, remnant ancient woodland, grouse moors and fell sheep farms with extensive areas of bog and heath under conservation agreements. It would repay study of the potential for networks and enlargement, for wild herbivores and, given the extensive Kielder Forest, for the role of lynx as top predator.

The Sussex Weald has been studied for the potential of smaller-scale networks linking ancient woodland – and the Sussex Wildlife Trust has an EU-funded project of land purchase, habitat creation and corridors currently at the planting stage, but intends to incorporate hardy breeds of domestic and then wilder cattle once the trees are established.[7]

## Wild rivers

Next to the various initiatives to re-wild forestry and extend woodland cover, there has been a parallel movement among conservation bodies to re-wild rivers. Many schemes are small and local 'reach-based' projects and costs are high, but some schemes involve long-term planning across whole catchments and present opportunities for coordinated habitat creation along ideal wildlife corridors that could link core areas.

Rivers and forests are inextricably linked in the planetary water cycle. In Britain we have taken our rainfall and water supplies for granted, but in areas where rainfall is not so reliable, intact forests are vital for regulating the cycle. Our largely urban populations have long ago become used to denuded uplands as their primary source of water, and reservoirs, water supply, quality and demand have adjusted to the accelerated run-off from the resultant apparently stable grasslands. River systems have then been engineered to ensure this water flows to the sea as quickly as possible and with minimum disturbance to agricultural land or damage to property. As a result rivers have been dammed, canalized, impounded and denuded of their natural vegetation. A natural wild river is now a rarity in Britain, and indeed, in southern England some rivers cease to flow at all in dry summers as a result of heavy abstraction.

This situation would have mattered only to nostalgic ecologists were it not for significant environmental changes that became serious in the last two decades. Firstly, despite no statistical change in rainfall patterns, there have been several years of disastrous flooding causing great personal distress to homeowners as well as very high costs to the insurance industry. In addition, a number of other problems are evident and increasing:

- Pollutant runoff in the form of sulphates and nitrates has seriously affected water quality for drinking, fisheries and wildlife, both on land and in the near-shore environment; this has resulted from a combination of atmospheric deposition from industrial activities, particularly the burning of fossil fuel, fertilizer use in the uplands and intensive farming in the lowlands.
- Pesticides from sheep-dip and commercial forestry, as well as heavy metals, PCBs and toxic metals in atmospheric fallout contaminate the watersheds.
- Intensive livestock rearing in the uplands has increased problems from disease organisms such as *Cryptosporidium*.

The suspicion exists that increased flooding is caused by a combination of erosion, field drainage and stream canalization, with restricted floodplains and inappropriately sited development, and the relevant agencies are now looking to traditional catchment management to alleviate the problem and the costs.

Given this general shift in socio-economic significance, a hitherto esoteric interest on the part of river ecologists to re-wild rivers has begun to have wider appeal. The WWF-inspired Wild Rivers Programme – based largely in Scotland – has now found resonance in a UK-wide River Restoration Centre (RRC) at Silsoe College (Cranfield University), with the support of the EU-LIFE programme, the corporate engineering sector and government agencies.[8] The RRC started in 1998 as a networking operation to share the experience of a series of small pilot projects on the reaches of the Skerne in Durham, the Cole in Wiltshire and the Ogwen in Snowdonia. Four years later it was networking over 500 projects with 2000 professional contacts, following a massive upsurge in appreciation and awareness. It estimates that river restoration work now accounts for about £3 million per year in expenditure.

A great many of these schemes are small-scale reach-based restorations of the natural line and flow of rivers, correcting the heavy engineering bias of the past, and with water quality, fisheries, anglers, recreation and flood alleviation in mind – small-scale re-wilding to be sure, but there are also some larger schemes of more direct relevance to large-area ecosystem restoration.

Chief of these is the catchment-based approach on the River Tweed, where the whole river system has been walked, surveyed and prioritized in terms of both economic value for game fishing (mainly salmon) and nature conservation generally. The catchment encompasses 5000 km$^2$ with 3000 km of watercourses. The coordinated operation, led by the Tweed Foundation and funded by EU and local enterprise monies, has focused on opening up spawning and feeding areas, removing over 1000 artefacts, creating riffles and meanders, fencing streamsides and restoring riparian vegetation and woodland.[9] The project has £4 million to spend over three years and is addressing a game fishery worth £12.5 million annually with 500 local jobs. This initiative has led to a wider operation under the umbrella of Tweed Forum called The Tweed Rivers Heritage Project, which now oversees 50 schemes promoting the natural, built and cultural heritage of the Tweed and with a spend of £9 million, half of which comes from the Heritage Lottery Fund.

A great deal of the work on the Tweed relates to habitat enhancement of benefit not only to fish, but to woodland, birds and insects. Wet meadows and floodplain woodland have been surveyed and cooperation with the Borders Forest Trust has led to riparian corridors being planted with a strategic opportunity to relate this work to Forest Habitat Networks being promoted for the Southern Upland headwaters (see Colour Plate 5 and photographs of the river Twill, before and after rewilding, Figure 5.3).

A useful survey of other catchment schemes could be made: the Tamar in Devon is subject to a wide-ranging cooperation of stakeholders, particularly the farming community; the rivers Devon and Black Devon in Clackmannanshire have an integrated management scheme; the tributaries of the Mersey are subject to a 25-year programme of enhancements; and there are reach-based schemes where techniques of re-wilding meanders, floodplains and riparian forest are being advanced. The upper Wharfedale has attracted £200,000 of EU-LIFE funding, with the Wye, Medway, Seaton, Brent (an urban scheme near Wembley), Till (tributary of the Tweed) and Ogwen among the more notable schemes. The Wildlife Trusts have recently instigated a £600,000 programme funded by water companies, landfill tax and British Waterways on 580 wetland sites.

We have not the space to explore and analyse this rapidly expanding work, but its strategic importance is clear – riparian habitats, especially riparian woodland, have great potential to link wild areas and to provide corridors for wildlife, often well into urban areas. We return to this in the

Photo: Tweed Foundation

**Figure 5.3** *River Twill, tributary to the Tweed in the Scottish uplands: before and after rewilding by the Tweed Rivers project*

final chapters relating to the land in-between our nature reserves and to a strategy for wilding the countryside. I believe very strongly that this large number of seemingly small initiatives has as much power as a few large and charismatic schemes – they involve millions of people and provide, through catchment-based projects, a sense of local identity and focus and the opportunity to work with local businesses as well as schools. They also create a groundswell of conscious awareness of the ethos of restoration and wildness.

There is also a meaningful environmental gain – in the 1980s it became evident that the answer to widespread pollution of the marine coastal environment lay in a myriad of small house-keeping operations in the watersheds of rivers. It was not very glamorous work, but the UN's centre for Clean Production in Paris focused attention on river catchments, pollution clubs, industrial audits and simple, cheap managerial changes, to the effect that by the turn of the century, major river systems such as the Thames and Mersey were once more populated by salmon and the coastal environment began to recover.

The same factors of identity, focus, management, funding and involvement that have made catchment-based audits for pollution control successful are now benefiting habitat enhancement and wilder river restoration schemes. In catchment-based pollution control, after decades of being the laggard in Europe, Britain could justifiably claim to have taken the lead, and perhaps the same will apply to the re-wilding of rivers.

## Coastal retreat: Abbott's Hall Farm, Essex

Coastal salt marshes and mudflats present large areas of remote and wild country, often with important populations of breeding and wintering bird species. With the expected sea level rise due to global warming, wave erosion will reduce these areas substantially. At the same time, there are high costs involved in maintaining sea defences for farmland along these coastal strips, and a considered option is to combine 'managed retreat' of the sea defences with the creation once again of salt marsh. There is some considerable potential for re-wilding areas of Britain's lowland wet pasture and salt marsh, especially in the Wash, Suffolk, Essex and north Kent.

In this regard, a project of the Essex Wildlife Trust involving over 350 ha of arable and pasture land at Abbott's Hall Farm on the Blackwater estuary (representing Europe's largest coastal retreat experiment) will prove instructive. Here, sea defences along a 3.5 km stretch of sea wall have been breached with the aim of creating 84 ha of new salt marsh (see Figure 5.4). The rest of the farm will be managed for low-intensity livestock with some arable land (140 ha). The project has been supported by grants from the Heritage Lottery Fund, the Environment Agency and the Wildlife Trusts, with the farmland attracting grants from DEFRA for low-intensity use as an Environmentally Sensitive Area.

This area is typical of Britain's coastal marshes, which have lost 40 per cent of wilder land either to intensive farming or to erosion. In Essex, a

Photo: Chris Gomersall

**Figure 5.4** *Abbot's Hall Farm: a coastal retreat project*

reduction from 4800 to 2600 ha has occurred in the last 25 years alone. There is an obvious potential to recreate larger areas of coastal marsh, wet meadow and carr woodland that could provide sufficient habitat for wild herbivores such as aurochsen, ponies and boar, following the Dutch model. In this regard, rather than maintain domestic grazing and secondary wetland habitat of grassland behind the dykes, the coastal marshes could be bordered by more open grazed woodland without the sharp demarcation between coastal marsh and farmed grassland. Such linked projects occur along the Suffolk coast where the RSPB has been extending its holdings and has also recently brought in Konik horses to help maintain habitat diversity.

## Concluding on networks

These initiatives demonstrate the progress made in the last ten years in extending reserves in a more strategic way that involves corridors and networks between isolated sites. Strategic farmland is being purchased and allowed to go wild. Natural processes of grazing and disturbance are being enhanced by semi-wild horses and cattle, although usually as 'management tools' or as a more economic means of maintaining habitat targets. However, the idea of large areas with charismatic assemblages of wild herbivores is taking root (see Trevor Lawson's 'Back to the Future' in *BBC Wildlife*, October 2004), and it now requires just a little persistence and courage to take this vision forward. In Scotland, there are already areas sufficiently large and cohesive: Forest Enterprise and NTS land in Affric and the RSPB and NTS land in the Cairngorms; in Wales there are areas that could be linked and managed along the Ennerdale model, for example the Welsh Assembly (Forestry Commission) and National Trust land in the Rhinogs and around Snowdon. In England, Ennerdale is already under a form of wildland management that will eventually bring in semi-wild breeds such as Highland cattle and could include Exmoor ponies; Forest Enterprise and Northumberland National Park at Kielderhead could readily follow suit. No area yet has the full guild that would include boar (present in Kent), beaver (penned in Knapdale and Ham Fen, Kent) and truly wild and risky cattle such as Aurochsen, though wild Chillingham have been translocated to Savernake Forest (see Chapter 7). Few managers want to take on the headache of restoring red deer or re-introducing elk. And with regard to carnivores to complete the restoration of natural processes – there is finally a somewhat secretive discussion of lynx as a first appropriate step in Scotland. There is a growing realization, now pursued in a 'Wild Britain' proposal by Toby Aykroyd, that charismatic assemblages of large mammals in large-area schemes could offer major economic advantages in tourism and employment.[10]

# 6

# Restoring Ecological Processes: Regeneration of the Core Vegetation

The core areas and smaller initiatives that we have reviewed represent some of the wildest country in Scotland, England and Wales, yet the land in each has experienced centuries of progressive degradation of its vegetation. The Glen Affric core area proposed by Trees for Life is one of the least degraded as it has several thousand hectares of old Caledonian pine, but overall, Caledon has only a small proportion of original forest cover. Eryri, including most of the Rhinogydd, is far less natural, with large swathes of plantation forestry (all exotics) and hillsides denuded of trees, with ancient woodland confined to remnant patches on the lower slopes of the valleys. Dartmoor has been similarly deforested and grazed by domestic stock to produce a species-poor acid grassland on most of the high ground, with relic but in places extensive patches of ancient woodland on the hillsides and along the lower reaches of the rivers.

Restoration of these core areas must therefore begin with the regeneration of the vegetation. The indigenous plant communities of these areas and indeed of most of Britain would, in the current climatic period, produce almost entirely forest and montane scrub habitats with very little land remaining open. Forest or scrub would extend to about 750 m upslope, with extensive grassland and heath confined to areas of the coast or higher mountains. As forests became re-established after the last glaciation, pollen studies show that by 7000 BP there was very little open grassland or woodland glades (this issue is discussed at length by Yalden in his *History of British Mammals*). It could be expected that some riparian meadows and scrub would have existed as a result of the activity of beaver, moose and forest cattle, but the influence of the mega-herbivores of previous inter-glacial periods was absent.

Each of our core areas thus requires a programme of regeneration of the forest cover. However, simple tree planting, though necessary in the early stages, would not lead to a natural forest. A forest is more than trees: it is a dynamic relationship between vegetation and herbivory, with the latter influenced by predators.

## Woodland, grazing and pre-history

It has been recently argued by Franz Vera, of the Netherlands Strategic Policy Division in the Department of Agriculture, that assumptions of extensive closed-canopy lowland forest in Europe may be wrong and that large numbers of herbivores would have produced a more open park-like landscape.[1] A dynamic may have existed whereby gaps created by dying trees were grazed into glades, with the forest edge retreating as more trees died. Regeneration would have taken place only when sufficient thorny scrub had developed to protect tree seedlings from herbivores. Vera is articulating a more extreme form of something palaeo-ecologists have supposed for some time: that even in the absence of the mega-herbivores, cattle, bison, tarpan, elk and deer would have kept the forest more open than we are used to seeing.[2] Dutch nature conservationists are now engaged upon enlarging and linking their bigger reserves to accommodate mixed herds of deer, wild cattle and wild ponies.[3]

England's New Forest, which has substantial grazing by horses, cattle and deer, may represent such parkland. In the uplands, the use of fire by human hunters would be expected to have maintained more open montane heath. However, pollen analysis shows little evidence for significant areas of grass prior to the first agricultural clearances, and recent arguments that the current landscape of the British uplands with its large populations of domestic herbivores is not far removed from the 'natural' landscape structure have yet to be substantiated.[4]

## The indigenous British temperate forest

The indigenous British temperate forest would have varied in the assemblage of tree species and their respective abundance according to soil and climate factors.[5] In the north, along the Atlantic seaboard of Scotland, the high rainfall and cooler climate favoured a temperate mixed deciduous forest of sessile oak, birch, hazel and alder; whereas inland in the drier and colder central and eastern Highlands, the vegetation was characterized by pine and a flora closer to the boreal conditions of Scandinavia. In the more southern regions of Scotland, north and western Britain, the mixed deciduous woodland was dominated by sessile oak and birch on the wetter more acid soils, with alder on swamps and along rivers, and ash woodland where more base-rich and drier soils prevailed, such as on limestone; in the drier south and east of Britain, the deeper soils produced a high forest of mixed deciduous trees with an original high frequency of tall forest trees such as lime and elm in oak woods on the clays, with beech on the chalk. The southeast of Britain has elements of a central European vegetation, whereas the western Atlantic oak was part of a temperate forest type that extended down through western France to Portugal – where the oaks are steadily replaced by warmth-loving species.

As a result of great efforts by vegetation specialists in the decade 1980–1990, we are now in the fortunate position of having an accurate idea of the floral assemblages that would be found in British forests according to these varying factors of climate and soil.[6] However, given the diversity and abundance of the original Atlantic forest fauna, a purely botanical approach runs the risk of not seeing the forest for the trees.

This original temperate forest fauna and flora evolved over a two-million-year period of cyclic expansion and contraction in the northern hemisphere, with the last three inter-glacials representing the culmination of that process in terms of genera and their ecological relationships. The fauna had a somewhat Indo-European flavour with herds of large cattle, horses, deer, beaver, wild boar and forest bison, with forest elephant and rhino; among the predator guild were a European race of lion, leopard, spotted hyena, hunting dog, wolf and bear, as well as the sabre-toothed cat *Homotherium*. African elements included the hippo, with populations of dwarf species on all the Mediterranean islands. In the previous inter-glacial, jungle fowl were found as far north as Britain, and the climate was about two degrees warmer than the current Holocene. Such modern day 'aliens' as hemlock and Norway spruce, as well as rhododendron were also present.

Thus, in the 'deep time' perspective of previous inter-glacials, hippo were common on the major rivers of England as far north as the Yorkshire Ouse, and these animals create extensive riverside grassland that would have attracted herds of other grazers, such as cattle, horses and deer.[7] The European forest elephant *Palaeoloxodon antiquus* and rhino *Stephanorhinus hemitoechus* would have contributed to keeping these meadows open as well as to the maintenance of a more open park-like woodland. The warmer mean summer temperature may have been enough to alter the dynamics of fire sufficiently for this to contribute to a more open forest where lion and hyena were regular features.

In the post-glacial re-emergence of forest in this current inter-glacial (Holocene) it is not a simple matter to discern a 'natural' forest structure. In the first millennia after the ice retreated, the temperature was as warm as the previous inter-glacial (marked by the appearance of the European pond tortoise in Britain), and the large expanses of post-glacial typically Boreal birch and willow scrub gave way to continuous forest of birch and pine in the northwest of Scotland, to Boreal pinewoods in the eastern Highlands and to oak, alder, lime and elm in the south.

Until Flannery's ground-breaking work (1995, 2002), most naturalists would have assumed that a snapshot of British forests from 7000 BP, as gleaned from pollen studies, would have given us a picture of a pre-agricultural 'natural' forest structure. However, we had reckoned without the widespread human-induced extinction of the elephant and rhino in the contracted glacial refuges of Spain and Southeast Europe. Furthermore, the absence of forest bison and the scarcity of horses may also have been a consequence of such human interference.

The situation is further complicated by the simultaneous arrival of agriculturalists with domestic stock and a rapid change in the climate. The warm period immediately following the disappearance of the ice was followed by a climatic shift to cooler and wetter weather. This climatic change was largely coincidental with accelerating forest clearance by Mesolithic migrant peoples who brought domestic breeds of cattle and pigs.

It is now thought that a combination of climatic and human factors led to a shrinkage of the northern forests, particularly in the west, as peat bog developed and produced a more open landscape. In the south, forest structure altered both as the climate became cooler and wetter and as humans cleared areas and grazed their stock. Agriculturalists began the clearance of forest around 4500 BP in southern Britain, with some parts of upland Britain cleared by fire and the development of blanket bog between 5500 and 5000 BP.[8] Agriculture reached the western Highlands by 2500 BP, too late, it is thought, to have had a major influence on the shift to tree-less sphagnum bog that became extensive in the uplands around 4500 BP.

In this combination of human and climatic influences, lime and elm lost out as the dominant canopy tree in the southern areas, with oak becoming commoner and more continental species such as beech forming woods, particularly on chalk. The resultant patchwork of woodland over most of England, whilst reflecting its origins, became much modified by the removal of large trees, the grazing of stock, the opening of the canopy and the practices of coppicing and pollarding. By the time of the Romans, near-natural remnants remained only in the less accessible Welsh mountains and Scottish Highlands.

Thus, the natural or indigenous forest communities were always changing with climatic shifts, and were subject to various herbivore regimes, at first natural (but with the incoming herbivore guild possibly already depleted by Neolithic hunters operating in the glacial refuges), and later, very unnatural, with fragmentation, exploitation and the eventual reduction of deer numbers (virtually eliminated throughout England by the 18th century), as well as the early elimination of boar, beaver and wild cattle.[9]

In the past two millennia, intensive grazing and cropping regimes, as well as a long history of economic exploitation of woodland for timber, charcoal, hurdles and firewood, have left none of the indigenous forest structure – even the remote Highland glens have been subject to timber extraction and the introduction of exotics. Many types of habitat simply no longer exist even as remnants – such as high forest on good soil, typified by the original presence of lime trees, or extensive flood plain forest, dominated by alder. On a large scale, the more mobile mammal and bird fauna of the predominantly oak woodland may have used the wet forest habitats as an important source of seasonal food plants.

Added to the problem of such widespread absence of keystone species and long-term economic uses that have transformed the remnant woods is the presence of introduced trees such as sycamore that now feature as a major element of even old woodlands, as well as the widespread planting of trees outside their normal ranges. In Scotland it is less complex: though much of the original Caledonian Forest was felled, there are sufficiently large remnants that are likely to be close to the original plant communities, if somewhat modified by over-grazing by deer and the absence of beaver and boar.

Thus, British woodland has a long history of evolution since the time of the natural wildwood, and it is not an easy task to discern from the remnant structure what the wildwood was like. Modern classifications of woodland types and their relation to conservation practice have tended to accept the current pattern and structure, with a growing focus upon history and treatments in relation to maintenance of diversity. Only very recently has there been coordinated thinking on extension of large areas and rejuvenation of natural forest processes.

Three major studies of ancient woodland, those of Oliver Rackham (1980), George Peterken (1981), and D.N. McVean and Derek Ratcliffe (1962) for the Scottish Highlands, have taken an essentially historical approach and provided invaluable insights into the original wildwood and to the dynamics of forests as affected by human activity. The most recent and exhaustive classification of woodland (and other) flora by John Rodwell of Lancaster University (1991), although taking the modern context for granted and being less concerned either with history or destiny, provides clear insights into the relationship of basic woodland types to soil and climate such that the diversity of the wildwood patchwork can be appreciated.

These studies do not go much further than an account of plant species composition in relation to climatic and edaphic factors and to the effect of human treatments, including grazing of stock – there is simply not enough intact forest with the original fauna present for studies of natural forest dynamics in Britain. Where there are native herbivores, such as red and roe deer, the predators are absent and numbers are excessive; in addition, other browsers such as moose, forest cattle and forest ponies are absent. The nearest we can get to a picture of the ancient wildwood *structure* may well have been the Royal Parks or hunting reserves that kept grazing ponies, pigs and cattle among the wild deer, but, of course, large predators were still absent.

Rodwell's *British Plant Communities* (1991), building upon the previous works, describes 23 basic types of woodland and scrub community in Britain, classifying the associations according to the dominant trees and typical floral associates and showing how each type reflected soil and climatic factors. Some of these basic types have sub-types related to the changes wrought by heavy grazing – usually by domestic stock. In this classification, 16 of the communities are of relevance to the core areas under consideration: 6 basic types of mixed deciduous oak–birch communities; 7 wet woods of alder, birch and willow; and 1 of Scots pine, together with 2 high-altitude scrub communities. Woodland types reflecting continental elements located in southern and eastern Britain, such as beech, oak with hornbeam, and yew, would only be relevant for our purposes were it possible to develop large core areas in these regions, though some networks, such as the Sussex pasture woodlands, will involve these associations.

Rodwell's detailed review provides data on basic types and their variants according to the nature of the field and shrub layers, and as noted, a practical manual has been drawn from this work by the Forestry Commission, thus aiding planting programmes in their need to take account of soil and climate factors. Remnant habitats within our core areas can readily be identified and can serve as seed sources and centres around which natural regeneration can occur (some details collated from Rodwell are available on the Ethos-UK website: www.ethos-uk.com). In planting and regeneration programmes, it will also be important to glean data on the time periods over which growing forests are colonized by woodland flora and how this might be encouraged. Different tree species both require differing soil chemistry and themselves alter soil chemistry and hence the colonization process. Birch, for example, is capable of colonizing acid grassland and heath, and then as the birch woodland matures, the acid soil is ameliorated and shade is provided for other tree species to colonize.

Each climatic and edaphic zone has, over millennia, selected genotypes for its particular set of conditions – and a great deal of genetic variation is hidden under the simple title of an 'oak' or 'pine' species. There has been great emphasis of late upon 'provenance' of seedlings for restocking, with preferences for native stock. However, in past decades large numbers of seedlings have been planted without regard to provenance, for example, oak from Poland and Scots pine from Scandinavia. In addition, although native stock may be preferred for core areas, we shall have to consider the unnatural extent of future climate change, as well as the semi-natural regimes that may exist in corridor forests that will likely have multiple uses.

Furthermore, after centuries of deforestation and heavy grazing, soils have been altered, perhaps in some cases irreversibly, and the original species structure would be difficult to re-establish. In particular, the great rainfall, high ground and siliceous rocks of the western hills, now for the most part completely denuded, have led to shallow, leached and very acidic soils. This land, along with lakes and rivers, has been further acidified and artificially fertilized by a century or more of sulphur and nitrate precipitation.

Our three candidate core areas are all in the west, but Dartmoor has southern influences and the Rhinogydd, though typically western, has elements of the English woodlands further east; the Caledonian communities are decidedly northwestern, showing some Boreal as well as Atlantic influences. Dartmoor and the Rhinogs are firmly in the oak–birch provinces, whereas Glen Affric is in the wetter more westerly pine province with some Atlantic deciduous woodland in the more westerly areas of the adjacent coastal glens. The higher ground in our Caledon area has remnant scrub of willow but is generally too wet for juniperous scrub. The Rhinogs have remnant juniper on the higher ground, but it is not clear what form of sub-montane community would have preceded the heath and grassland that exists today. Dartmoor's grassland and heaths are probably too low to have supported a sub-montane community. In the Carrifran project, which has the potential to stimulate a larger core area or network, tree and shrub species include downy birch, rowan, sessile oak, holly, ash, wych elm, aspen, alder, Scots pine, bird cherry, hazel, hawthorn, blackthorn, juniper, guelder rose and many species of willows. The lower part of the valley should eventually become upland broadleaved and oak–birch woodlands with strong representation of hazel (NVC types W7, W9, W11 and W17), with small areas of birch woodland (W4) as shown in Figure 5.2. At higher levels there will be juniper woodland (W19) with birch, rowan and some pine; above this there will be scrub of juniper and specialist willows, with montane heath near the exposed summits.

In addition to the basic woodland types of oak–birch, pine and ash, wet woodlands feature with alder as the dominant tree in riparian woodland and fen, and are of a more Atlantic type than wet alder woods on the continent. There are a further four basic types lying outside our candidate areas: three of beech and one yew woodland, but these types are not relevant to our sites. Some consideration should be given to the unique nature of British yew woodland – particularly the extensive canopies of 1000 ha at Kingley Vale in Hampshire. A case could be made for extending this forest and providing buffer zone protection purely on the grounds of its majesty and rarity.

Wet woodland of alder, willow and birch will be important in all three core areas, which contain extensive river systems and lakeside vegetation. These are the most over-grazed and depleted of habitats, particularly in Snowdonia, yet historically they were very rich in their associated flora. There are several types of woodland with dominant willow, sedges and reed that occur as succession stages at the edge of shallow lakes and this would be a feature of Cwm Bychan in the Rhinogs.

Rodwell's classic work of typing for British woodland is illustrative of the limitations of a species-oriented ecology. The major focus is upon the assemblage as it is, rather than on the processes of forest ecology and evolution. Whilst the species assemblages do relate to soil and climate factors, these factors are in a constant but long term cycle of change whereby forests are continually created and destroyed. Furthermore, although Rodwell gives useful indications of the impact of herbivores, the presence or absence of grazing animals is not a significant feature of the analysis.

Oliver Rackham's *History of the Countryside* provides a more historical perspective that relates to the 'original' wildwood of pre-agricultural times and changes wrought by man's exploitation. This historical perspective highlights the disappearance of high-forest lime and elm in favour of oak – we tend to think of the heartland of old English forest as oak woodland, whereas the original English wildwood was characterized by the tall canopies of these other trees. Peterken, also taking an historical approach, provides more perspective on the dynamic structure. He notes, for example, that the original forest was dominated by shade tolerant species – of which lime, elm and beech are chief, whereas he classifies oak along with the other shade intolerant species such as birch, ash and pine. These early forests would, Peterken argues, have been characterized by a patchwork of single aged stands, each patch of varying age, as the opportunities for regeneration were limited and furthered by wind-throw or periodic die-offs from drought. As the closed canopies degraded due to human influences, the oak replaced the lime and elm.

It is important to note however, that this ancient lime–elm high-canopy woodland may not have been typical of the north temperate forests that formerly included elephant, rhino, hippo and beaver, the activities of which created glades, riparian meadows, and perhaps park-like forests supporting large populations of grazers and browsers that may then have favoured oak. The pervasive effect of grazers on forest dynamics is now the subject of much rethinking, led by the Dutch ecologists with their large-scale projects (see Chapter 7).

## Beneath the trees: the importance of woodland flora

It is also clear that any re-afforestation programme must aim to restore the whole range of characteristic woodland flora for each type. Rodwell's classification of assemblages (known by NVC or National Vegetation Classification numbers) is a starting point based upon the present day, and there may not be a better indication of what the wildwood would have contained. The Carrifran project now has detailed mapping of planting proposals according to NVC categories, taking account of the base flushes, soil and aspect.

We have not the space to outline the floral associations of all the woodland types of relevance to our core areas, and certainly not the vast range associated with Forest Habitat Networks that would include heath and grassland. However, some idea of the floral complexity associated with restored vegetation can be gained (drawing on Rodwell's work) by looking at the basic mix of montane scrublands, pine, oak and ash woodland that would constitute the most substantial elements.

## Montane willow and juniper scrub

Scrub does not have quite the status of forest or woodland, yet it is an important habitat in the montane zones that would form our core areas, and in its natural state, extremely scarce. In the absence of over-grazing, as we can infer from continental habitats, it would be the predominant cover between 400 and 900 metres in the uplands. Thus, large areas of the Caledonian forest would have been a patchwork of willow scrub of several species above the tree line grading into sub-arctic grassland and heath above 900m. This form of tree-cover is quickly degraded by heavy grazing pressure and now exists in remnants in the NW Highlands, the central and southern Highlands, the Moffat Hills and on Helvellyn in the Lake District. It would be expected that the Rhinogydd with its peaks between 700 and 800m would have had little natural grassland and that some form of willow scrub would dominate, and that Dartmoor, with its highest point at 500m would also have had willow scrub on the peaks with areas of grassland confined to the bogs. It would be important to map any remnants to identify the type and serve as seed sources.

The sub-shrub and herb layer in this low canopy can be especially rich where grazing is not severe and is characterised by large mats of the woodrush, especially on rocky slopes, bilberry, cowberry, bog whortle-berry, crowberry and ling ; and among the taller herbs, lady's mantle, water aven, wild angelica, northern bedstraw, mountain sorrel, alpine saw-wort, golden rod, devil's bit scabious, meadowsweet, valerian and frog orchid.

This montane scrub with its tall herb layer is especially worthy of study in relation to habitat for the chiefly vegetarian bear as it is rich in berries, juicy stems and rhizomes. Bears in other mountain areas spend time above the tree line seeking food and these habitats could be crucial for the maintenance of a viable population in the Highland zone. In ascertaining the potential for the Glen Affric area to support bears, studies of their food preferences in such areas as the Sarek National Park in Sweden would be of great assistance.

In the drier eastern Highlands, the dominant montane scrub is character-ised by the presence of juniper, with wood sorrel in the field layer. This type of low scrubby woodland is restricted to the Cairngorms and Monadhliath, with small remnants in the Pennines and Lake District. Rodwell notes that water-logging is strongly inimical to juniper and supposes that in the western Highlands above the tree line it is replaced by willow scrub. However, I have found remnant juniper high up in Snowdonia, and as he also notes, in its natural state these community might have been as widespread and tolerant of more varying conditions as it is in Scandinavia. He has found remnants existing widely as a scrubby fringe between pine woodland and montane heath or grassland, and calls for more research using enclosures to determine the relationship of grazing and burning to its persistence and potential re-colonisation of the montane zone. There is no doubt from observations of the absence of seedlings in grazed areas that this woodland is peculiarly susceptible to high grazing pressure.

In some areas heavy grazing has opened up the juniper stands and the field layer is reduced to grassland. Under less intensive pressure, the relatively unpalatable juniper offers some protection to the field layer, which is characterised by *Vaccinia* species, heather and an abundance of ferns and mosses. The rare *Linnaea borealis* and the wintergreens *Pyrola media*, *P. minor* and *Orthillia secunda* are associated with this habitat.

## Pine woodland

The native pine woods of Scotland have been variously surveyed and classified and represent a mixture of stands, few in a semi-natural state, almost all affected by the removal of mature trees, the opening up of the canopy, and varying degrees of grazing pressure either by over-abundant deer or domestic stock. Large areas of relic pine forest are very open and Rodwell follows McVean and Ratcliffe in their studies by setting a lower limit of 25 per cent cover to distinguish the woodland type from larger areas of ericoid heath with isolated pines. Semi-natural stands tend to have less than 70 per cent canopy, and the more closed canopies are noted in plantations. It is likely that under natural conditions closed canopy occurred only in the more sheltered locations with better soils. The woodland is notable by being made up of quite well segregated age-classes – as in other semi-natural high forest, and McVean and Ratcliffe noted three major arrangements at the time of their survey in 1962: even-aged stands, 80–150 years old; two generation mixtures of pioneers, 150–200 years old with straight-stemmed offspring 80–100 years old; and pine-heath stands of varying densities but composed of broad-crowned pioneers 150–200 years old, (few individual pine trees live as long as 300 years).

In most locations the canopy is only 13–15 metres high, and up to 20 m on better soils. Associated tree species in the western reaches are brown or downy birch, rowan, sessile oak at lower altitudes, holly and on wetter ground and stream-sides, alder various willows *Salix* and aspen. The shrub and field layers divide into several types according to soils and a general east–west Highland divide of rainfall, but are also strongly affected by treatments – such as plantation stocking density, and grazing. Rodwell notes three major elements in the associated flora: the grass *Deschampsia flexuosa*; ericoid shrubs; and bryophytes. The grass predominated in shady stands, with bilberry, cowberry, and ling in the more open canopies. In dense stands these shrubs can be eliminated and leave a field layer of bryophytes and *Deschampsia*. The more open semi-natural stands also contain more rarely crowberry and *Erica cinerea*, bog whortleberry and bear berry *Arctostaphylos uva-ursi* (the latter a must for returning bears!).

In denser stands the ericoid shrubs disappear and a rich byrophyte flora is characterised by the moss *Hylocomium* along with about twenty other species, and the ferns *Pteridium* and *Blechnum*. Interesting herbs, though generally infrequent, are lesser twayblade and the various wintergreens *Pyrola minor*, including the nationally rare *P. media* and *P. rotundifolia*, *Moneses uniflora*, *Orthilia secunda*, the northern montanes *Linnaea borealis* and creeping lady's tresses. The wintergreens, and northern montanes such as *Linnaea* have their stronghold in these pinewoods and some of their rarity may be due to the reduction in the extent of the forest.

An important factor in the natural dynamic of pinewoods is the occurrence of fire – some experts considering pine a fire-dependent species. Natural regeneration is largely confined to the more open forest and fire helps seedling establishment by removing the felted mat of *mor* and recycling nutrients.

Herbivores browse pine seedlings and the tops of young trees emerging in the shrub layer, and although it is clear that current deer numbers as well as the former grazing of cattle and ponies, and the later use of sheep, have all contributed to the general lack of regeneration throughout the Caledonian Forest, it is also the case that under natural conditions there would have been a strong herbivore presence of deer, moose, and forest cattle. Wild boar would also have been an important element in the disturbance of ground enabling the germination of seeds. In this case, the harrying actions of wolves may have been a deciding factor in keeping herbivores from congregating for too long in particular areas. Clearly, the forest regenerated naturally despite the presence of so many herbivores.

## Oak–Birch woodlands

There are three basic NVC types of oak–birch woodland that are of relevance and these combine a range of former descriptions of birch, hazel and oak woodland types from authors such as Tansley, McVean and Ratcliffe, Birse and Peterken. We will follow Rodwell's synthesis as it provides a good indication of the floristic variations and the nature of the oak woods in our three core areas in the west. All of our sites are in areas of high rainfall and relatively acidic leached soils. In Caledon, oak woods are chiefly a feature of the more temperate coastal zone in the western Highlands, and of valley woods in the eastern Highlands, but come in on the better soils to the north-west of the Glen Affric core area. In the Rhinogydd it would be the dominant forest over much of the core area and likewise on Dartmoor. In Scotland, the climate is cooler, although the coastal oakwoods benefit from the Atlantic milder winters; in the Rhinogydd the climate is also ameliorated by the proximity of the sea, and we have already seen that the ash woods hold elements in common with more southerly and eastern woods; in Dartmoor the southern influences are more strongly shown by the occurrence of the pedunculate oak *Quercus robur*, rather than the sessile oak *Q. petraea*.

The three types represent variations due essentially to climate and soils, although they grade in to each other, and in the case of the Welsh hills, several types are present. Silvicultural treatment and grazing regimes also contribute to a convergence of types. Indeed, most birch woods are regarded by Rodwell (following Ratcliffe) as 'oak–birch' with the oak removed. I found thus surprising, as I had previously thought, regarding their prevalence in northern Scandinavia, that Highland birch woods were an altitudinal feature of the Highlands. This will have some relevance to regeneration schemes in the core areas.

In the main type of woodland for the western areas of Britain either sessile oak or downy birch may predominate, and it is associated with leached acidic soils. The canopy is often low, at 20m or less. On Dartmoor, curiously, *Q. robur* forms some of the higher altitude wind-stunted stands, as at Wistman's Wood, and this species may also feature in the eastern Highlands and North Wales (where it may be the result of old planting regimes). All of these woodlands have been subject to centuries of exploitation of oak for charcoal and tanning, where large trees (and hence seed sources) have been removed and many multi-stemmed trees attest to former coppicing. *Q. robur* was the foresters' preferred species for planting even in the natural range of *Q. petraea*.

Other tree species include rowan and silver birch scattered through the canopy; holly where there is less grazing and browsing; and hazel as the main component, along with saplings of the other species in the usually patchy and low under-storey. This woodland has been colonised by *Rhododendron ponticum* in many places where this alien has been introduced – particularly in North Wales where it often forms a dense under-storey shading out all other species and boding ill for the future regeneration of the canopy trees.

The field layer has three components that make up the distinctive type – grasses, bracken and ericoid shrubs. The bracken is not so prevalent as in eastern and southern oak woods on better soils, being limited by the thin soil and prominence of boulders and rocks. Likewise, bramble and honeysuckle are present but not in abundance. The ericoids demarcate this woodland from the eastern and southern sub-types. These shrubs are very sensitive to grazing pressure and readily give way to such grasses as *Agrostris capillaris* and *Holcus mollis*. Herbs in the field layer include heath bedstraw, tormentil, cow wheat, wood sage, devil's bit scabious, goldenrod and the rushes, *Luzula pilosa*, *L. multiflora*, *L. sylvatica*. Bluebell is generally scarce and wood anemone restricted to base-rich flushes.

Ferns are a major feature, especially in ravines, with *Blechnum spicant* dominant in the field layer and *Polypodium vulgare* as an epiphyte. However, the mosses often form distinctive mats over boulders and rock faces and on the forest floor where there is excessive grazing. There is an abundance of moss species – Rodwell lists over thirty as well represented, and in one sub-community, considerably more, including national rarities which give these moss-woodlands their unique character.

These woods are typical of our Welsh core area, Dartmoor and also west of the Great Glen. In all cases they have been subject to removal of large oak, oak coppicing, and heavy grazing. It is typical to find very few saplings – usually among the protection offered by boulders. The bryophyte flora, though of conservation importance, has benefited from excessive grazing by the suppression of grasses and woodrush. Reduction in grazing pressure leads to saplings of birch and rowan with occasional oak seedlings, but they often fail to prosper where the moss carpet prevents access to the soil.

Oak with dominant bracken and bramble is typical of central and southern Britain on deeper clay soils, but it features in a few places in North Wales and on the fringes of Dartmoor. *Q. robur* is the commonest tree, although *Q. petraea* may also be present, and hybrids are a feature in the zones where both occur. The next commonest tree is the silver birch, especially characteristic of those communities that have colonised open ground and the most frequent invader of gaps in the canopy. Ash and field maple are generally scarce, with sycamore often colonising gaps and reaching into the high forest canopy in the wetter areas. Wych elm is frequent in the north and west, and hornbeam and lime in the drier south-east, as well as the introduced sweet chestnut. In places, the past history of plantings, removals and coppicing has left hornbeam, lime or chestnut dominated woods. Other sparse associates include holly and rowan, which may contribute to the canopy, and where adjacent to the natural zone of beech this tree may also contribute. Yew is sometimes present as a patchy lower tier; alder in less well-drained areas; gean which Rodwell notes can sometimes reach magnificent size; and the crab apple.

In the Harlech woods there are some large specimens of gean, as well as a few old lime trees, with some yellow archangel in the field layer, and the adjacent scrub containing spindle and crab apple – all indicative of the milder climate and more continental influence.

The shrub and field layers are species poor – shrubs being often absent in the more park-like grazed woods. Saplings are generally confined to gaps in the canopy and usually dominated by birch or sycamore. In the high-forest, though the canopy is not dense, oak seedlings are very scarce. However, these are the 'bluebell' woods *par excellance*, and this is the vernal dominant, except for wood anemone on the wetter ground. This type of woodland is quintessentially British, occurring in the rest of Europe only in north-west France and Belgium. In late spring and summer the field layer is characterised by bracken, bramble and honeysuckle.

The field layers tend to vary according to the degree of canopy shade, soil moisture and grazing – being at times grassy, dominated by high bracken, a mass of bramble and honeysuckle, or carpeted by ivy. Ferns of *Dryopteris* are frequent but the bryophyte flora is much reduced and the herbs also, with greater stitchwort red campion, hairy wood rush, golden rod, ground ivy, yellow archangel, foxglove. The latter can be abundant, especially where the canopy is reduced.

This forest is the nearest to the natural high-forest of the English lowlands (without the elm and lime of the original wildwood). As such it occurs on the fringes of Dartmoor on the better soils, and features of it are also present in the western Rhinogydd, such as bramble, bracken, and honeysuckle, as well as yellow archangel, abundant red campion, ground ivy, stitchwort and foxglove.

## Ash woodland

Although oak–birch woodland is the dominant type south of the pine province, it gives way to a characteristic ash woodland wherever the soil has sufficient base enrichment – as on limestone or in base-rich flushes among generally base poor soils. Rodwell notes that the woody component of these communities is among the richest in British woodland. I have found such ash woodland near Harlech on the western edge of the Rhinogydd and Rodwell's maps show occurrence in eastern Dartmoor of the ash–field maple–dog's mercury variant that is more characteristic of the south-east divide. These woods do not appear in the western Highlands, except along the coastal zone on and near Skye, but consideration in planting regimes should obviously be given to areas where there is base-enrichment in any of the core areas where these woods may have disappeared.

The range of woody species includes downy birch and alder, wych elm, hazel, sycamore, sessile oak, silver birch, hawthorn, and elder, holly, bird cherry, the sallow *Salix cinerea*, and aspen. The field layer is particularly rich and Rodwell lists over thirty species of flowering plant in a shrub layer that is generally 38 per cent of cover to 5m and a herb layer of 40 cm at 76 per cent cover. The type occurs up to 350m, almost always on slopes.

The characteristic plants of the field layer are dog's mercury, wood sorrel, common violet, bluebell, enchanter's nightshade, wood avens, herb robert, wood false brome, primrose, wood anemone, barren strawberry, germander speedwell and wood speedwell, globe flower, the thistle *Cirsium helenoides*, sanicle, yellow pimpernel and sweet woodruff. Rodwell cites the yellow archangel as characteristic but confined to southern examples, yet I have found it in small patches in the Harlech woods.

Several rarities are associated with this woodland type – the baneberry, the soft hawk's-beard, yellow star of Bethlehem and whorled Solomon's seal.

These ash woods so characteristic of some of the Welsh mountain slopes where flushes of base rich water appear in an otherwise relatively base-poor environment dominated by oak woods, when not grazed-out by sheep, have given me some of the most wonderful, magical moments – from the early spring abundance of anemone, celandine, primrose, marsh marigold, violets, and wood sorrel, followed by the bluebells, speedwells, yellow pimpernel and herb robert, to the eventual carpet of enchanter's nightshade, this woodland floor is a natural garden of delights and quite different from the more rugged oak woods on the greater part of the hills. Around Llety'r Fwyalchen, this floral abundance was maintained despite a lack of fencing and ready access for a small suckler herd of cattle and a larger flock of sheep. Grazing pressure was intermittent, but enough to keep back bramble and ivy, and not so heavy as to convert the field layer to grasses. In adjacent, more heavily grazed woods of this type, the grassy carpet held virtually no flowering plants until the summer when foxgloves predominated.

I have tended to associate the berry-bearing bushes black currant, red currant and gooseberry with these wet woodlands, as well as large patches of raspberry, but they do not feature strongly in the data gathered by Rodwell. The red and black currant feature in the alder-wood species lists, but not the gooseberry, and the raspberry in the alder-nettle community which are essentially lowland woods. Perhaps these species are very sensitive to grazing and have become less frequent in the uplands – I have found blackcurrant, raspberry and gooseberry in isolated locations where there is no access to sheep in the lower Rhinogydd streamsides, and as they are an important element of floral diversity, as well as containing food plants for birds and a favourite feeding ground for bear, I have often wondered at how much more widespread they would have been in the original wildwood.

## Restoration and creating anew

We should, however, be aware that not only can we not expect to recreate what has passed, but that there may be little merit in trying to do so. We are starting with an impoverished soil and a fauna denuded of keystone species. Furthermore, the climate is undergoing an accelerated change. In my view we need to consider the *functional* element of our future forest as well as any species we may re-establish. In this regard, the forest canopy can be seen as protective of the flora beneath, which in turn supports the diversity of invertebrate and vertebrate species. When we consider areas outside of the wildwood core, then the forest will take on functions relating to human uses such as the provision of timber, wood pasture, hunting and recreation.

The functional forest is thus a vessel for the rich diversity of life its structure supports – including humans. In this respect, the field layer becomes as important as the trees. Some forests will have the primary function of providing buffer zones and corridors for large vertebrates and for roaming carnivores. In terms of this function, the floral diversity of the field layer or the near-natural nature of the canopy is of less importance – and a forest primarily managed for timber, rather than for naturalness, would fulfil that role.

A forest with a strong recreational function – such as a Community Forest, would be served by the establishment of a rich field layer of flowering plants such as bluebell or anemone. Where near-natural conditions are aimed for in the core areas, it may take many decades for the diverse field layer to develop in regenerated areas and hundreds of years in the case of the planting of open grassland.

In any restoration project it will be important to ascertain the prevalence of remnant seed sources for these field layers, as there may need to be planting programmes for the missing herbs and shrubs. It is known that some species can survive for several decades under conditions unfavourable for flowering – wood spurge, for example, has reappeared after 125 years of suppression by closed canopy. Some woodland flowers colonize at very slow rates – oxlip for example, though not a feature of our western woods, progresses at 1m per year. Translocation or seeding may only be successful when mature woodland soil conditions evolve. There are precious few studies of the recovery of this woodland diversity after centuries of grazing, particularly in comparing exclosure with reduction in grazing pressure.

## Dynamics of regeneration

We have argued that herbivore pressure is a constant feature of natural woodland. All species present in the woodlands today evolved within the context of that dynamic. If that grazing and browsing pressure is suddenly reduced, the vigour that has evolved to counter that pressure is suddenly unleashed – in the herb layer, the most vigorous can quickly eliminate those plants requiring a closer-cropped sward, and diversity usually falls. Likewise, the shrub layer is adapted to browsing and a certain browsing pressure keeps the bushes low and rounded and, as any gardener keen to procure the maximum floral show knows, the nipping of the end shoots promotes a denser-flowering and thus berry-bearing shrub. Saplings are also adapted to this pressure, with some species being resilient to the loss of a leading shoot and others being more affected and producing smaller, more-branched trees.

This natural dynamic presents something of a dilemma in the early stages of re-establishing a functional forest. Forest regeneration will be hampered by grazing and browsing animals, especially in the absence of predators, but if regenerating woodland is fenced off, the resultant growth will not be natural in form and the field layer will be less diverse. Fences are also inimical to the ethos of wildland, although they can readily be removed later. Ideally, where high grazing pressure exists, it needs to be reduced by the removal of stock and the culling of deer, but some fencing will be required in most situations. Areas with no natural herbivores show the reverse side of this coin: trees may do well, but the understorey will be dominated by vigorous species. In the case of new plantings, there will often be little choice but to protect the evolving woodland until such time as it is robust enough for large herbivores to be introduced; the project at Carrifran has taken this approach.

However, as will be appreciated from the sections on woodland classification, regenerating a near-natural forest will be a long process. In the western uplands we have less of a problem than if we wished to restore the high forest of elm and lime of the English lowlands – and in any case, elm has been decimated by Dutch elm disease. In our core areas the relic oak and pine woods can readily act as centres for natural regeneration, and this process can be seen in adjacent meadows and heaths where seedlings are establishing themselves. This process is slow for spreading oaks and pine, more rapid for birch and rowan but would take a very long time to naturally colonize large areas of acid grassland on heavily degraded soils. In these cases, planting programmes could establish patches of woodland through the use of whips and standards – using birch and rowan with small numbers of oak, ash and alder according to soil conditions. Scarifying and sowing of birch seed would accelerate colonization of open ground far from seed sources.

One technique pioneered by the National Trust in Snowdonia is to fence off streamsides and plant with alder and oak using Tulley tubes. Thus, moorland areas can be colonized through the network of streams and gullies. In these enclosures, the ericoid shrub layer regenerates rapidly, as does the streamside vegetation of meadowsweet, purple loosestrife, valerian and other herbs. In Caledon, Trees for Life have set up large fenced exclosures and seen rapid regeneration of pine, birch and rowan. Where fencing has been used in Snowdonia to exclude sheep, for example in the Cader Idris range, there is a clearly marked reversion to ericoid heath with isolated rowan and birch. Such areas would, over decades, develop into mature forest.

Large areas of bracken exist in Snowdonia and Dartmoor in places where grazing pressure has reduced, and this species indicates relatively good soil for woodland. It has proven very expensive to reclaim these areas for grazing, and woodland would be a better option. I have seen quite remote bracken-infested hillsides successfully planted with oak, birch, rowan, holly and alder in the Cambrians, with only spiral guards for protection inside the stock-proof fence.

In one of our candidate core areas, the Rhinogydd, there are large plantations of exotics, mainly Sitka spruce and Japanese larch. These blocks often come onto the market and are close to felling age; some belong to Forest Enterprise. Observation shows that if simply left after felling, birch and rowan colonize rapidly and seedling exotics (as well as the unwelcome rhododendron) could be readily pulled out. The forest rides have already been colonized by many of the woodland herbs, grasses, ferns and mosses, although the characteristic flora of ancient woodland would be very slow to appear. Some of these margins become self-sown with oak at some distance from the nearest seed trees – perhaps as a result of the habit that jays have of burying acorns.

Fencing and protective tubes are expensive, and over much of Scotland, reduction of deer numbers by the culling of hinds is required. Browsing will still be present, but in large areas adjacent to woods in the Cairngorm Mountains, much reduced browsing has not prevented regeneration. However, where culling is impractical or where intensive grazing of domestic stock on open hill land is the problem, fencing off domestic stock from remnant but overgrazed woods, or newly planted areas, is the only option. Fences can be removed once trees are established, but the natural dynamic and structure of a self-regenerating forest will necessarily take centuries to evolve. In the Rhinogydd and on Dartmoor there are considerable areas of common grazing land and the only option for systematic reduction of stock is either conservation agreements with the holders of grazing rights or the purchase of strategic farms and their rights, such that the overall grazing pressure is reduced.

The dynamic between a regenerating forest and domestic or wild herbivores has received limited study and should certainly be a focus of ecological research over the coming decades. English Nature, spurred on by Dutch experiments, has begun some research and has introduced Chillingham cattle (see Chapter 7) into the forest reserve at Savernake, near Marlborough.[10] Again, however, herbivore numbers and grazing patterns are strongly affected by the presence of predators, especially wolves, and relevant research on complete forest ecosystems for Western Europe is virtually non-existent. There may be relevant studies in the eastern forests of Bialowieza or the Rhodope Mountains of southern Bulgaria where some of these elements still exist. Similar arguments apply to the rooting activity of boar and the natural scarifying of the ground such that seedlings can take hold, as well as to the wetland-creating propensity of beavers. In this regard the introduction of boar to enclosures in Glen Affric and beaver in pens in the Kent Wildlife Trust reserves, both as management tools, may yield useful data.

This general absence of relevant research on forest dynamics, the absence of key species, the presence of alien introductions, and the necessary compromises over domestic stock and human use in buffer zones and corridors, all mean that our mooted large-area programmes are going to be essentially experimental. The Ennerdale project makes a point about not being 'prescriptive' and leaving the future 'open'. This may go against the grain of modern conservation practice with its preference for predictive computer models and simulations, but it is unlikely that either sufficiently robust data will exist from past studies or that the past is necessarily prescriptive of a future under a progressively changing climate.

In those areas of Wales and England under consideration for large-area initiatives, the long history of over-grazing may have so seriously denuded the native vegetation that recovery will require more than tree planting and fencing. Studies need to be carried out on the distribution of seed sources for a wide range of plants in the understorey, in the shrub and field layer of the forest and in much-denuded riparian habitats, and suitable nurseries need to be established. In my own limited work in Coed Eryri I came across small pockets of relic woodland in the Rhinogydd that held a few plants only of native blackcurrant, raspberry and gooseberry, and noted how easily local genetic variability could be lost. There was one small area of base-rich ancient woodland in the Rhinog, near Harlech, that held old lime trees and gean (with many seedlings lost to grazing and no regeneration), with some spindle on the nearby *frydd*, again with no sign of young trees – these three species would be hard to find in the rest of Snowdonia.

One is led to wonder at how extensive these now scarce species would be in a natural ecosystem. Berry- and nut-bearing species and the often scarce crab apple would be important food plants in any area considered for the re-introduction of bears. There are a host of tuberous species upon which bears also feed and the British equivalent of a rich habitat for this species would require some detailed research.

Generally, however, given the long time scale over which these large-area initiatives would be developed, these matters should not present major problems. In the upland areas, birch forest and alpine scrub should be relatively easy to establish within a few decades, whereas a mature oak wood will take over two hundred years. We may never have access to large areas of deep soil to recreate the lime woods of lowland England or the riparian forests of the flood plains, but in the three candidate areas that we are looking at in more detail, we have an opportunity to recreate something closely resembling the past structure and diversity.

The Glen Affric project area would have pine woodland (with important species such as aspen) in the sheltered glens and dwarf willow on the higher ground, with grassland on the areas of bog; the Rhinogydd would be predominantly oak–birch woodland, though some high ground would remain open under sufficient grazing pressure as grassland, moor and heath; Dartmoor would also primarily be oak, but has extensive secondary grassland and heath that has accrued high conservation status and would thus need to remain open.

Detailed inventories of the ancient woodland in Snowdonia and Dartmoor exist, and Trees for Life has begun an inventory of the flora for the Glen Affric project. This data will be required to appreciate the variations present within the various woodland types and to orchestrate planting and seeding regimes within core areas, buffer zones and wildlife-friendly corridors.

A key part of the strategy for regenerating these areas will be to strike the right balance between grazing and browsing regimes; planting compared to natural colonization; and the fencing of domestic stock or wild ungulates. We might expect the Glen Affric area to respond quickly to reduced grazing pressure, but very large areas in the northern section of higher ground lack seed trees. In the Rhinogydd, in the absence of stock, regeneration led by birch and rowan would be rapid in most areas close to the woods, and there would likely be conservation pressure to keep grazing on the higher ground. This could be effected by naturalized goats supplemented by Exmoor ponies, wild cattle breeds and the re-introduction of red and roe deer. In Dartmoor there are large areas in the southwest of wet acid grassland, but eventually these would be colonized by birch and willow where domestic stock intensity was reduced.

Although there are no red deer in the Rhinogydd, there is a healthy population of rather majestic feral goat in the northern part; on Dartmoor red deer are infrequent wanderers from Exmoor, but semi-wild ponies are widespread. At some stage, red deer herds should be established in these core areas, but not until forest regeneration or planting has had two or three decades to extend the cover. Ultimately, the forest structure will only approach its natural processes and diversity when both the larger spectrum of grazers and browsers and their predators are returned and in some kind of balance with the vegetation. In practical terms, however, it is likely that all large herbivores will require active control if the vegetation status is to be maintained. Although predators may not ultimately control herbivore numbers, which are forage dependent, they can influence spatial density such that regeneration is assured; however, one of the main safeguards for herbivores in the temperate forest would have been the ability to migrate to lower ground in times of harsh weather, and the provision of adequate corridors connecting our core areas to richer pastures will be an important element in their sustainability. In the next two chapters we shall look at the potential for returning the full herbivore guild and some of its predators, in order to restore the *processes* of a natural forest dynamic.

# 7
# Restoring Ecological Processes: The Herbivore Guild

There was a time when 'forest' did not mean so much a place of trees as a place for deer and other game. Indeed, the medieval meaning still applies to large expanses of almost treeless 'deer forest' in Scotland. With the disappearance of deer and other large herbivores over much of Britain, the modern vernacular use of the word has come to mean little other than the trees. The sense of a functional forest, both as an ecological entity or a cultural one, has been lost along with the large mammals.

In the previous chapter we discussed the role of large herbivores as an integral part of evolving temperate and boreal forests. That herbivore guild included elephant, rhino and hippo, and it is unlikely that we could find the space for their functional equivalents. Although it should be said that 2000 km² of a dedicated natural area (the size of some of our national parks and the Affric core area proposal, compares well with some reserves for extant relatives of these species, such as the Asian elephant and the Indian and Sumatran rhino. It is therefore worth stating at the outset that any ecological functionality to which we aspire will be missing these powerful structural elements of the forest.

Of the range of large herbivores that we would normally expect to find – two species of deer, forest horse, forest cattle, woodland bison, wild boar and beaver – most British forests and certainly most smaller woodland have few if any representatives of the original guild. Even European forests within the larger natural areas in the cores of national parks do not have the full guild: the forest horse or tarpan (*Equus ferus*) is extinct as are forest cattle or aurochsen (*Bos primigenius*); the wood bison or wisent (*Bison bonasus*), like its cousin the American buffalo, was until recently restricted to small herds in zoological gardens; beaver were eradicated throughout western Europe. Only the wild boar has remained common, and even that species has had a history of persecution and disappearance, followed by a recent return to its former range.

We can therefore appreciate that the natural forest had a very different structure from anything likely to be seen in Europe today. Cattle, horses, deer, elk and bison all have different feeding niches as they graze and browse the forest. Perhaps the closest in Britain would be the New Forest, which has been used for centuries to graze ponies and cattle. This is surprisingly little commented upon in treatises relating to restoration of ancient woodland. Often, one of the main stated purposes of restoration is to recreate indigenous or near-natural forest, but 'forest' is seen almost entirely in terms of tree cover, rather than in terms of an inclusive dynamic relationship between plants and animals.

Some conservationists have been arguing for the use of wild herbivores as a natural method of management to maintain biodiversity in the control of scrub. Whitbread and Jenman set out proposals for an extensive patchwork of Sussex woods drawing on the Oostvaardersplassen experience in Holland (discussed in more detail below).[1]

We cannot now expect to restore the functional equivalents of the extinct mega-herbivores to Britain, for example, by breeding cold-adapted Indian rhino and elephant, and there are no temperate zone populations of hippo – though we could usefully look at the potential of setting up areas large enough to contemplate a project in Europe. Even in areas such as Bialowieza in Poland, celebrated as the last great European forest wilderness, the largest herbivores are missing. (The beaver was absent until re-introduced in 1955.) Not only are forest elephant and rhino extinct, but so are the aurochs, tarpan and, very nearly, the wood bison. Only in the last century have the reconstituted aurochs-like Heck cattle, forest horses (Konik ponies) and wood bison been re-introduced in Bialowieza, and although wolf, lynx and apparently bear are present, the bear had to be re-introduced and is still absent from most modern references.

Bialowieza is also surprisingly small – about 500 km$^2$ of forest, roughly half the size of Dartmoor National Park, with the primary reserve being only 50 km$^2$ or 5000 ha. Considering that an important factor relating to abundance of herbivores is their ability to migrate, this reserve is extremely small. In pre-agricultural times, large herbivores could have undertaken long-distance migration to avoid severe winters or drought.

Nevertheless, as Derek Yalden (1999) has pointed out, Bialowieza gives us some guide as to the abundance of herbivores in relation to forest size. He quoted data from Polish sources showing that 580 km$^2$ contained 14,274 large herbivores: 250 bison, 3710 red deer, 2730 roe deer, 170 elk, 7375 boar; 19 lynx and 20 wolves.

There are references in popular articles to the recent re-introduction of both tarpan-like Konik horses and aurochsen (Heck cattle) as well as bear, but I have no data on their numbers.[2] Thus, for this forest there are about 25 large herbivores per square kilometre. This may not be an accurate guide to abundance for our core areas when fully restored as they would differ in forest type, soil fertility and climate. Bialowieza has a truly ancient and diverse mixed forest structure on what may be more productive soil with warmer summers, but these advantages may be offset by the harsh winters. It may, therefore, be cautiously assumed that our Snowdonian (ca 150 km$^2$) and Dartmoor (ca 300 km$^2$) core areas might hold 3750 and 7500 large herbivores respectively, and Caledon (ca 2000 km$^2$), where a large proportion is above the tree line, might hold 10,000–20,000.

Herbivore behaviour and abundance may also be affected by the absence of large cats. The post-glacial lion *Panthera leo* ranged as far north as Holland, but was presumably an open-country predator that disappeared as steppe gave way to forest. However, it is not clear what happened to the post-glacial leopard *Panthera pardus* in Europe – fossils are known from Italy, but in former inter-glacials it occurred as far north as Hungary.[3] Although wolves will take sick, injured or very old adult elk, cattle and pony, a fit adult is seldom attacked, whereas the lion could tackle all sizes of herbivore as well as young pachyderms. Lynx are known to suppress roe deer numbers in forest and also to affect behaviour of pasture-grazers that avoid the forest edge.[4] There are also post-glacial fossil records of hyena and hunting dog in central areas of Europe.

Given the potential for eco-tourist development, we should at least contemplate and research the possibility of a large-area initiative in Poland and Belarus that would recreate the ancient European 'Serengeti' of forest, grassland and forested savannah, with an all-important wildlife corridor linking these areas to the refuges of southeast Europe that would be needed during any periods of future glaciation. Such thinking has recently emerged on a smaller scale in Holland and Belgium with regard to large herbivore populations.[5]

For Britain, we can start with our baseline of a herbivore guild that evolved over the last three or four glaciations to occupy the temperate, largely broad-leaved forests. This group has its origins in the dynamic relationship between cold tundra, boreal forest, temperate forest and forested steppe, which we see today as static geographically located ecological zones, but which exist in a constant longer term flux. As the ice retreated, cold tundra at first became warm, virtually treeless grassland with arctic willows and dwarf birch – this was rapidly colonized by the cold steppe fauna of central Asia: horse, steppe bison *Bison priscus*, saiga antelope and red deer (and in the more distant past, steppe mammoth and the steppe rhino *Dicerorhinus*). These species then gave way to forest types as the open country was colonized by boreal pine, spruce and birch, with temperate oaks and beech coming later. In mountain regions, the latitudinal zoning is repeated with altitude. Thus, as the inter-glacial advances, the cold-adapted grassland species retreat to the Asian steppe or to tundra and alpine habitats.

Within this dynamic, the various herbivore genera have either evolved ecotypes (sub-species) or separate species adapted to each habitat. Kurten considered many of the supposedly separate species identified in the fossil record as sub-specific, differing only in size (horse for example). The elephant and rhino had different species each adapted either to grazing or browsing. Red deer had smaller forms in open country and larger forms for forests (with dwarf types evolving on islands). The bison were at first thought to have separate steppe forms (*Bison priscus*) and forest forms (*Bison bonasus*) but are now considered conspecific (we deal with some of the implications of specific status later). Cattle appear to have had only forest forms, although modern domestic stock, drawn from that gene pool, are well adapted to open country.

In the course of ten such ice ages, this faunal assemblage had proven its adaptability, with the warmth-adapted forest types having their refuges in southern Europe during cold periods, and the cold-adapted open-country forms having refuges during the warm inter-glacials in the eastern steppe, the northern tundra or alpine zones. The two types often replace each other at a given location in the fossil record of Britain.

It is worth reiterating that this rhythm of steppe and forest will, as far as we can predict, repeat itself within a future time frame perhaps equivalent to the period of agriculture that we have known over the past eight thousand years.[6] It is not common to find any conservation thinking or planning on this timescale! And this may seem at first rather fanciful and scientifically questionable given the uncertainties, but in many other areas of environmental concern, such timescales are not uncommon, for example, waste management strategies in relation to chemically toxic and radioactive materials have to incorporate predictive modelling over tens of thousands of years despite the uncertainties regarding human populations.

During these natural oscillations the abundance of these species would have altered drastically. The glacial refuges for European species, for example, are very small: only the southern parts of Spain and Portugal and the southern tips of the Balkan peninsula held closed-canopy forests. This means that forest species would have had their numbers considerably reduced, whereas open country species would have proliferated. In the immediate post-glacial period, for example, steppe horses, bison and saiga antelope formed vast herds that extended from southern Britain across Europe and Asia. As the forests returned, these species retreated to the steppes and forest species proliferated. What will a future oscillation look like?

In the past 8000 years, farming has transformed Europe's habitat and vastly increased the human population. When the ice returns, humans, as well as forests, will migrate south! What chance is there that we will leave sufficient forest for the fauna and flora to find their traditional refuges? Certainly, without planning, there will be a zero probability. In terms of scientific conservation, therefore, a forest corridor linking the northern and central European forests to the southwest is vital, as is the conservation of remnant forests in the southern Balkans – areas such as the Rhodope in northern Greece and Bulgaria. The Carpathian arc also has great significance. It is crucial, therefore, that infrastructural planning in an extended European Union takes this into account. The central Asian steppe fauna will also become the European fauna at some future time. Indeed, it may well be that some forest eco-types regularly disappeared at glacial maxima and were replaced by evolving eco-types from the steppe – this is certainly possible for tarpan and wood bison.

## Rebuilding the herbivore guild

In our more modest ambitions for Britain we cannot expect to rebuild the complete herbivore guild (see Figure 7.1). However, we are capable, given the political will, of creating a very large area for conservation in Scotland and significant cores in Snowdonia and Dartmoor that could go some way towards re-establishing a functional forest ecosystem. We might note, at the outset, however, that the future-oriented argument works against our conservation ethic, as we do not know how the past British fauna adapted to an oncoming ice age. Migration would have been impossible until the English Channel had been reduced by the lowering of sea levels, and it may well be that the British fauna was extinguished only to be replaced my incomers in the next cycle. If, however, the deteriorating climate coincided with falling sea levels, there may have been time for migration – certainly the onset of an ice age has generally been much slower than its post-glacial transition.

We have to take on board, therefore, that anything we do for species conservation in Britain may ultimately be of no account in an evolutionary perspective. Unless, that is, what we do here can influence values and practices in eastern and southern Europe and perhaps also, equally crucially, in the Middle East and near Asia. Certainly, what we can do in Britain is to set up models and advance thinking on the functionality of forest ecosystems.

In this respect, we need to look more closely at how a guild of herbivores makes use of the range of niches present in the habitat: from the branches and leaves of trees and leaves of shrubs (browsers) to grass meadows and glades (grazers), luxuriant riparian herbage (beaver) and roots and bulbs (pig). The presence of the herbivore guild modifies the *structure* of the habitat:

- elephant can uproot whole trees, open the canopy and create a more parkland type of forest. In drier areas the sheer amount of herbage cycled through them may have had an important restraining effect on the ferocity of forest fires – and although temperate forests generally do not burn, a more open shrubby understorey would have been more susceptible

Drawing: Peter Taylor

**Figure 7.1** *The British temperate forest herbivore guild and its ghost species*

- hippos create extensive close-cropped riverside grasslands (and would have ranged throughout the major river systems of the lowland forests)
- large browsers and grazers can trample vegetation and keep the understorey more open (rhino, aurochsen and bison)
- deer can inhibit growth of tree seedlings on the forest floor and, by pruning the shrub layer, increase the berry crops
- wild pig can open up ground to aid germination, as well as thinning out the acorn and beech mast crop substantially
- beaver create riverside water meadows of lush vegetation and virtually coppice the surrounding willow.

Without this guild of herbivores, the forest is denser and darker. If only the largest are absent, such as elephant and rhino, the canopy can be expected to be more closed and the shrub layer less developed. If the large aurochsen and bison are absent, this effect will be greater still, although the denser forest might favour larger numbers of deer and pig. Thus, we can have very little predictive knowledge of the carrying capacities of the kind of habitats we would recreate in large-area initiatives.

Our modern British forests are either large plantations of conifers, usually in blocks of a single age structure and species, or much smaller tracts of 'semi-natural' or 'ancient' broadleaf woodland in a patchwork with pasture and arable land. In the conifers outside of the Caledonian

Forest and northern England, there are usually only a few deer. Apart from the fallow deer in Coed-y-Brenin, Welsh conifer forests are devoid of deer. In the broadleaf woodland, deer numbers can be a problem for regeneration in areas of lowland England where populations of roe and the naturalized muntjac *Muntiacus reevesi* have increased.

Absent from British woodland, apart from a few parkland estates, and most of continental Europe, are the wild cattle, bison, elk (moose) and tarpan. We have no wild boar other than a small population of escapees in Kent and, as yet, no free-living beaver. We thus have the most unnatural forests (and nature reserves) in Europe.

The first step, therefore, towards creating a 'balanced ecosystem' would be to restore the natural herbivore guild in those areas that could support it. There is an argument for restricting that to species we knew made it to Britain after the last ice age, which would exclude bison, but we could also usefully re-evaluate our old paradigm of naturalness in the light of a more functional wildland ethos.

If we are to set up a whole and fully functional ecosystem, then we could argue it should contain all components of the guild that evolved with it. This would mean seeking substitutes for the now extinct forest elephant and forest rhino! In the case of forest horse and aurochs, breeding programmes have come close to recreating the primitive characteristics and we shall review these below. The large pachyderms are obviously more problematic, but we should consider the issue carefully rather than rejecting it out-of-hand.

Clearly, though, a fully functional forest ecosystem with these elements present would require not only a large core area, but an effective system of corridors so that these animals could migrate and maintain their abundance. It is unlikely that even were we able to breed suitable replacements for the forest elephant and rhino, not even Scotland could provide a large enough area for a sustainable population. However, such a concept would not be so outrageous as part of a central European core area and corridor scheme along the Polish–Belarus border with corridors running down to the Carpathians.

For the 'smaller' herbivores – elk, wild cattle and tarpan, a core area such as Glen Affric would need to have corridors out to western areas of Knoydart, Ben Eighe and Inverpolly. An eastern corridor to the Monadhliath and Cairngorm massif is more problematic, but these areas could also support the return of these herbivores. The National Trust for Scotland's Mar Lodge estate covers 30,000 ha of forest and open moorland, with good connectivity to the RSPB reserves in Abernethy, but the National Trust for Scotland's management is committed to 'traditional' Highland employment in grouse shooting, deer stalking and fishing, thus limiting the potential for a return to entirely natural processes and re-introductions.

The core areas of Wales and England would be able to accommodate only the smaller species, but these could include forest cattle, horse, wild boar and perhaps beaver, as well as re-instated deer. There are many small-scale nature reserves that include special breeds as part of their conservation strategy, although used largely to limit scrub and keep important species-rich grasslands open.

## The herbivore species

### Forest elephant and rhino

We shall deal with these species briefly rather than dismissing them without some reflection. First, as we have noted earlier, the temperate Atlantic forests of all previous inter-glacials held the forest elephant species *Palaeoloxodon antiquus* as well as an early forest rhino *Dicerorhinus kirchbergensis* (Merck's rhino) and the later *Stephanorhinus* (*Dicerorhinus*) *hemitoechus*, as well as a temperate population of hippos with no marked skeletal differences to the modern day African species.[7] The three mega-herbivores were constant companions in the fossil record of Britain's lowland forests. It is important to realize that these temperate broadleaf forests were little different from those of today – with Britain enjoying marginally warmer temperature regimes somewhat akin to the Atlantic region of France – and that the larger mammals would have had seasonal migrations. Elsewhere in Europe the woodland elephant gave way to a steppe species *Mammuthus trogontherii*. Both elephant species were present during the early part of the last glacial period in Spain, where both types of habitat must have existed, but died out, presumably exterminated by man. The European hippo, once present on the Ouse, Thames, Rhine and Rhone, and having survived previous glacial cycles, disappeared at the same time.

Unlike browsing ungulates, elephants are able to eat the woody parts of plants, such as branches, saplings and bark, as well as being able to bulldoze small trees to get at their branches. They also eat fruit, grasses and leaves. Their dung-heaps left in clearings would thus provide a ready germination site for seeds of the fruits they had eaten and for other colonizers to take hold. The diet of browsing Indian rhinos is about 20 per cent woody material and also includes fruit, leaves and grasses, whereas the Sumatran species is an exclusive browser of woody material, leaves and fruit.

The British and European rhino were of the browsing type – rhino are either grazers with heads held low like the so-called white rhino *Ceratotherium simum*, or browsers with heads held high, such as the black rhino *Diceros bicornis*, the Indian *Rhinoceros unicornis*, the Javan *R. sondiacus* and South East Asian species *Dicerorhinus sumatrensis*. The Sumatran form (and the warmest zone) appears to be the closest relative of the extinct European species.

The normal range of these rhino genera today obviously coincides with warmer climes, and historically, the Asian elephants extended only as far as northern Iraq. Although this area of the Middle East can have harsh winters, it must be assumed that the animals could readily have migrated to avoid them. Some Asian elephant inhabit montane forests that have cold winters. And we know that the family generally can adapt to cold with woolly coats, given evolutionary time. Temperate forests were certainly warmer in Britain in the past inter-glacials, but not such that the habitats in which these pachyderms lived were significantly different floristically – winter temperatures were cool and there would have been some periods below freezing. Thus, any northwestern populations would have evolved a hardiness to deal with the seasonal climate, much as cattle and horse breeds have done.

The question arises, therefore, as to how feasible it would be to breed a hardy population of rhino and elephant from the current species? By at least asking the question, we may be led to some research strategies. African rhino species are regularly kept out of doors in 'safari parks' in England and there must be a wealth of experience with regard to their temperature tolerances. Elephant have not generally been so free-roaming, but there may be useful data on montane forest populations in the Himalaya. Both these species are under threat in their native ranges and the rhino are kept in Zoological Gardens, ostensibly for conservation purposes.

If we take a long-term perspective, an argument can be made for setting up European breeding populations of browsing rhino in large enclosures, much as forest cattle, bison and tarpan were conserved in medieval times in Europe, and until such time as large areas exist for their return as functional elements in the ecosystem.

## The European wisent or wood bison

The European bison is a classic example of the historical importance of 'zoological parks' and enclosures in protecting a species from extinction and then through careful breeding, restoring populations in suitable wild habitat. The last wild-living wood bison disappeared from Polish forests in the 1920s and from the Caucasus Mountains in the same decade. As late as 1857 there were said to be about 2000 animals in Bialowieza, and this population dwindled to 700 in 1914, only to be wiped out during the ravages of the First World War. Sixty animals remained in zoos, some having been cross-bred with American bison *Bison bison*. The Caucasian form was a distinct sub-species adapted to the mountains, *B.b. caucasicus* and was smaller than the lowland form.

As early as the 1920s, breeding programmes were oriented towards repopulating the ancient Bialowieza forest, with enclosures set up close to

**Figure 7.2** *European wood bison or wisent*

the reserve. The first animals were released in 1952 and numbered 20 by 1959. The former Soviet Union embarked on similar operations in the Caucasus and by 1959 there were 30 wild-living animals. In 1971 captive and wild populations had reached 1500 with about half in the wild in ten different localities in Poland and Russia.

The European bison with its plains and woodland forms must have once rivalled in numbers those of the American west when European settlers first began their systematic slaughter – indeed, it would appear that the American plains bison was a post-glacial Eurasian invader crossing via the Bering land bridge.[8] The European plains bison became extinct in the most recent post-glacial period as it was a favourite quarry of humans, but the woodland form held on in the forests of Scandinavia until AD 1000 and in eastern and central Europe until the 15th century, gradually being restricted by the 16th century to a few royal hunting reserves and eventually to Bialowieza.

*The bison in Britain*
The bison's history in Britain is somewhat mysterious. It was certainly a feature of the inter-glacial forests, and the steppe bison occurred during the warmer phases of the glacial period at around 40,000 BP. The woodland form appears not to have returned with the advancing woodland – a consequence of its late arrival in relation to the land bridge or of predation in Western Europe. Given that the elk, which shared a similar range and habitat, was able to return, as were the woodland-dwelling

aurochs, there is no clear reason why the bison should not have returned. It may be a matter of the poor fossilization potential of the woodland species – it was thought that woolly mammoth had also not returned in the last glacial period, but in 1987 the record had to be revised when new fossils were found in Shropshire dating to 12,800 BP.[9] The bison is such a charismatic animal that a case can be made for its presence in a restoration programme for Britain. It is also an important animal ecologically, both as a forest grazer and a browser.

## Bison ecology

Typically, herds number 30–40 and are dominated by a bull, with the young bulls either forming small herds or wandering off alone. Each herd tends to remain within a home range of 25–35 km$^2$ depending upon food supplies. In earlier times the wood bison underwent migrations from lowlands to higher and drier ground in winter, but the Bialowieza herd is now confined to the inner core area of wilderness. The animals are both grazers and browsers (capable of browsing conifers, which cattle and horses are not), preferring mature mixed forests with a rich understorey of shrubs.

In Europe the woodland animals browse leaves and new shoots of trees such as willow, elm and oak. They also eat grasses, herbs and lichens during the summer, supplemented by acorns and beech mast in autumn and heather, bark and evergreen foliage in winter. In Yellowstone glades it crops the grass and improves productivity of the meadows, fertilizing them with its phosphorous-rich faeces and urine. It is also prey for Yellowstone's wolves, and carcasses from wolf kills are also an important food source for scavenging bears.

There are, however, some crucial problems with the species. As a bovine, it can harbour diseases that would threaten livestock interests. In Yellowstone, problems have arisen because of the propensity of the population, which harbours brucellosis, to disperse into rangelands. The disease causes fever in humans (seldom fatal) and abortions in cattle and is subject to strict regulatory control: infected herds must be destroyed. In the severe winter of 1996–1997, 1100 dispersing bison were slaughtered by federal officials. This led to corrals being constructed at the edge of the park to hold dispersing bison for slaughter. Any programme for a larger European population would likely encounter similar problems.

## Forest cattle: the aurochsen

Cattle are fundamentally forest animals, despite the images of pasture and open-range grazing we get from domesticated stock; the range of form manifested in domestic cattle are the result of two lines of domestication from one now extinct forest species – the aurochs, *Bos primigenius*, whose range extended from the Atlantic to Pacific coasts of Eurasia, North Africa and India. The aurochs was a constant feature of British forests during the previous inter-glacials, returning in the immediate post-glacial period as soon as a patchwork of woodland existed to support it. Its fossil bones begin to appear as soon as the first birch and alder woods feature in the pollen record, at about 9400 BP. It shared this early woodland habitat with elk, roe and red deer, boar, beaver, wolf and bear, and continued to do so throughout the Mesolithic period, when it was quarry, along with deer and boar, for the sparse population of human hunters and gatherers.

With the arrival of Neolithic farmers and the rapid destruction of forests, it became steadily scarcer, until, by the time of the Romans, its large bones were a rare feature of town middens – the last being recorded in North Wales in the 4th century AD. In the rest of Europe it experienced a similar decline as the forests receded, and by the 10th and 11th centuries had disappeared from Western Europe. In the following centuries it gradually became confined to a royal hunting reserve in the Jaktorow forest of Poland, where by 1599 the herd had dwindled to 24 animals. In 1603 only four remained and the last survivor, a cow, died in 1620.[10]

Because it survived into the historical period we have a good idea of its appearance and behaviour – it is depicted in numerous bas-relief work at Roman sites in central Europe and there is even a 16th century painting of a bull. The males were blackish brown with a yellowish stripe along the spine and were large, almost 2 m at the shoulder and weighing up to 1000 kg; cows were reddish brown and about 25 per cent smaller. Herds are thought to have numbered about 30 individuals – the last Jaktorov herd had 22 adult cows, 5 calves and 11 bulls, 8 of which were fully grown. Its lifespan is thought to have been 20–25 years. Calves were born in May or June and were suckled for six months, following the mother until the next calf was born.

The horns of the aurochs were formidable weapons and the animals had a reputation for ferocity when hunted by man or when threatened by predators, as they were fleet of foot and intelligent. They were fundamentally grazers, and from studies of feral cattle of today, we can assume that they could feed on a wider range of coarse grasses and herbage than can domestic animals. Many sub-fossil remains in Scandinavia are associated with water, and it is likely that the herds were dependent upon riparian pastures and the lush herbage associated with these habitats. In this regard, they would have benefited considerably from the presence of beaver.

## The wild white cattle of Britain

Britain is blessed with a unique breed of feral cattle, the origin of which has been the subject of long debate and still presents something of a mystery. G. Kenneth Whitehead's monograph *The Ancient White Cattle of Britain and their descendents* reviewed the history and status of the herds in 1953.

**Figure 7.3** *Lascaux's 'white' cattle*

Several herds of wild white cattle have existed on private estates in northern Britain and central Scotland since records began at the time of the enclosures of land in the 13th century – the herd at Chillingham Park has a documented history of 700 years. Prior to the enclosures, wild white cattle were commented upon at different times as a feature of these northern forests: by the Earl of Warwick in 924; by Canute in 1042, particularly in the southern counties of England such as at Enfield Chase; and by Hector Boece in 1527 as a feature of the wild Caledonian Forest in particular. Yet, as far as is known, the early cattle of the Celtic tribes were reddish brown or black, and the first records of white cattle relate to the Roman period when they were certainly imported and were of a type known as Piedmont and were important for ritual sacrifices.

The likeliest origin is that after the Romans left Britain in the 4th century, these herds became feral and populated the remaining wild forests of Northumberland and Caledonia. The possibility that these ancient white cattle were a distinct sub-species of the wild aurochsen and evolved in Britain, or were present in Europe but had their last refuge here, has been championed by some. There are several factors that count against this: the animals are much smaller than aurochs; they share certain skull characteristics with domestic breeds, such as the occipital angle, and they retain the domestic trait of round-the-year breeding.[11] The first two are not necessarily convincing as these genetic traits may also have been present in the original aurochsen gene pool from which all domestic breeds have their origin. The changes in breeding pattern, however, are more convincing, as it is hard to see how such changes would have conferred any advantage in the harsh northern climate. Further, Derek Yalden (1999) presents data showing how cattle bones from Neolithic middens in Britain show a distribution of bone sizes that do not overlap with that for aurochs, suggesting that Neolithic settlers brought domestic stock with them that did not interbreed with wild aurochs, which were by then probably confined to wilder Scotland and Wales.[12]

On the wild side of this speculation, the naturalist Rod Lawrence recently drew my attention to cave paintings at Lascaux (ca 15,000 BP, see Figure 7.3) that could be interpreted as depicting white 'aurochsen' with black noses and, curiously, spots on their neck similar to those appearing on the park herds (the artist used the white rock as body colour and black outlines). The majority of aurochs paintings including some in the same cave, involved infilling the body colours, either black for bulls or red for cows. The possibility remains, of course, that these drawings involved a form of artistic license. Despite their potential origin from domestic stock, the Chillingham herd have re-acquired the aurochsen wild traits of herding dominance, with bulls fighting for control of the females, sometimes to the death; a great wariness of humans; ferocious protection of young by cows; and an ability to survive on much rougher forage than domestic stock (they will not accept pelleted food at all). These stocks of wild cattle thus present a unique potential for restoring wild cattle to future forests – they are well accustomed to British conditions and have proved themselves robust despite centuries of inbreeding.

However, as with the aurochsen, they are dangerously protective of their young and are thus unsuitable for areas with frequent public access. In this regard, Highland cattle, equally robust, but tame by comparison, have been used in preference at a number of conservation sites.

## Heck cattle: reconstituted aurochsen

There are, however, other potential sources of wild stock from breeding schemes on the continent. As early as the 1920s, the brothers Heinz and Lutz Heck, German zoologists, began a breeding programme: one brother in Munich zoo crossing Scottish Highland cattle (small and red with long hair) with Hungarian steppe cattle (the largest breed and white with short hair) and a few others that contained different elements of the aurochs; the other in Berlin crossed Spanish fighting bulls with other Mediterranean breeds. The Hecks were surprised at how quickly their programme produced a dark very aurochs-like form, the same for both of the programmes. By 1932 a male and female of the type were mated, and to the brothers' even greater surprise, bred true to type instead of throwing up the mix of types that had gone into the pot. The males developed the blackish brown colouration and even the yellow stripe, and the females were reddish, both with the typical aurochs shape of horns. Herds were quickly built up of the reconstituted aurochs – identical in all respects but for size, as the brothers could not reconstitute the enormous height of the bulls (see Figure 7.4).[13]

Thus were born the Heck cattle that have been used by several conservation programmes to replicate wild grazing regimes, including the major initiative of Oostvaardersplassen in Holland. Here the 5600 ha reserve hosts 300 head of Heck cattle, as well as 200 Konik horses (representative of the original tarpan, see below) and 150 red deer. These herds are unmanaged and exist within a patchwork of reedbeds, willow

Photo: Hans Kampf

**Figure 7.4** *Heck bull: reconstituted aurochs*

carr and alder woodland that began growing on reclaimed polder land in 1968. The bulls fight and sometimes seriously wound and kill each other and carcasses are left on the reserve (or were until this fell foul of the local veterinary laws).[14] The different grazing and browsing patterns have created an open woodland structure, with deer tending to keep to scrub and the cattle and ponies keeping to the meadows.

These parkland herds and cross-breeding programmes have provided us with some useful insights: that an isolated and inbred population can survive for several centuries and that relatively small areas can sustain them. The Chillingham herd occupies about 300ha (formerly twice that area), which it used to share with red deer, but which it now only shares with fallow deer. Today there are 50 or so individuals, including 13 mature bulls, but at certain points the population has fallen to critical levels – in 1947 it was down to 13 following extreme blizzards, and at one point in the 18th century, when there were only three bulls left, one of which was infertile, the other two killed each other in a fight and the herd's continuation depended upon male offspring from the pregnant cows. Upon sexual maturity, the bulls establish territories of 40–50 ha shared with non-dominant bulls and then attract females. The dominant bull controls access to the females, but will eventually be challenged for dominance, though fights are usually ritual affairs only rarely resulting in death.

The Dutch habitats are a mosaic of reedbeds, lagoons and woodland where 300 head occupy 5000 ha at a crude density of one animal per 16 ha (see Figure 7.5), compared to one animal per 6 ha at Chillingham (where there is no competition from red deer and horses). If we add deer and

Photo: Hans Kampf

**Figure 7.5** *Aurochsen at Oostvaardersplassen*

horses, then the Dutch reserve has a similar one animal per 7 hectares, and at 14 animals per square kilometre, this compares with the Bialowieza data of 25 large herbivores per square kilometre.

In Caledon, although we may be looking at 200,000 ha (2000 km²), a great deal of this habitat is above 600 m and has a very low presumed carrying capacity. Likewise, the Rhinogydd, although much lower and further south, consists of large expanses of treeless grassland, with perhaps one quarter of the 20,000 ha eventually providing a suitable woodland habitat. Dartmoor's potential woodland zones are of the same order as those of the Rhinog, although its moorland might be more conducive to cattle. It can readily be seen, however, that Heck or Chillingham cattle would have ample space.

Some British nature reserves already use rare breeds – essentially primitive cattle able to survive with minimal attention, in order to diversify habitats. However, in large-area initiatives, an important element of wilding is to leave the herds subject to natural selection, including the periodic scarcity of feed, winter temperatures, disease and wounding. This may raise issues of animal welfare – more likely in the case of tame breeds, and perhaps less so with those bred specially for the purpose such as Heck or those with a long pedigree of survival in wild conditions, such as the wild white park cattle.

## Wild forest horses or tarpan

The wild forest horse *Equus ferus* is another enigmatic animal, with less data than for cattle, which is curious considering the popularity of horses.

I have come across anecdotal reference to extant herds of tarpan in similar zoological situations to the wisent in Poland or Romania, but all academic references assume that the forest horse or tarpan became extinct in the wild at much the same time as the wood bison.[15] There have apparently been cross-breeding programmes between primitive ponies *Equus caballus* and Przewalski's horse which have achieved near-tarpan form but without the upright mane that is known from historical records as characteristic of the tarpan.

Judith Kolbas, writing in *Wildlife* in September 1997 about her encounters with wild horses in Mongolia, describes four types of post-glacial horse: the Scandinavian 'forest' type, the central European tarpan, Przewalski's steppe type, and a 'tundra' type – the tundra type is shown by her as grey and spotted. There are 'spotted' pale horses drawn in Lascaux paintings, which, as with the pale and spotted cattle, may just be artistic licence – but a licence not extended to any other animals such as bison, elk or deer.

The pre-history of the horse in Britain is also somewhat mysterious. The wild horse depicted in Continental cave drawings is of the Przewalski type with a tan coat, pale muzzle, striped forelegs and dark upright mane, and hence is the 'steppe' form. This form is well represented in late glacial fossils in Britain – the time when, as the ice melted, large areas of warm tundra grassland developed and when other steppe species, such as the saiga antelope, were found as far west as Somerset. Later, as scrubby willow, birch, alder and hazel woodland developed, horse fossils are at first common but become progressively more scarce and eventually are associated only with higher ground in the Mesolithic of about 9300 BP, after which the animals either disappeared or were too scarce to be represented in the fossil record. Typical woodland species such as the aurochs, elk and boar continued to be represented in the archaeological record and hence coexisted with man for thousands of years.

If the woodland form of the horse is known to have persisted in the forests of central and eastern Europe into the 19th century, why then did the upland tarpan of Britain disappear? There is a possibility that it did not disappear entirely. Some writers have considered the wild Exmoor pony as a direct descendent of this upland type. The tarpan's absence may simply be an artefact of the imperfect archaeological record between 9000 BP and 4000 BP when bones and teeth of the identical early domesticated forms first appeared, associated with the numerous middens of the agricultural settlers.

Derek Yalden, although preferring to believe that the Exmoor pony is derived from feral stock (i.e., from escaped domestic imports) largely because of its floppy mane (which all domestic breeds have) concedes that within that gap of several thousand years when there were no domestic breeds, there are a smattering of teeth that are difficult to date. Rod

**Figure 7.6** *Lascaux's 'Exmoor' pony*

Lawrence has shown me photos of cave paintings of floppy-maned horses in Lascaux, and though they are indistinct, they clearly lack an upright mane (see Figure 7.6). The Exmoor Pony Society argues that whorl patterns on the coat, as well as the floppy mane and hooded eyes, are adaptations enabling rain to be dispersed more easily – and it is clear that horses adapted to the British uplands are going to require adaptations from any ancestral steppe animal. Joep van der Vlassaker of the Large Herbivore Foundation, based in the Netherlands, believes the Exmoor pony to be the most primitive horse available for wildland projects. This foundation is active in the breeding and re-introduction of feral horses, mostly Polish Koniks, aurochsen, wood bison and a range of endangered ungulates across Eurasia.[16]

To some extent the question is academic – the Exmoor pony ought to be treasured for its uniqueness whatever the provenance. But conservation science leans towards the academic and it is not treasured. If that population were regarded as 'pure' tarpan, it would be classified as an endangered species and strictly protected.

Przewalski's horse has itself suffered persecution and presumed extinction in the wild, and has been rescued by zoological collections. This horse has two more chromosomes than *E. cabbalus*, though offspring are still fertile. In the last decade, a re-introduction programme has been ongoing in Mongolia from pure bred stock from the world's zoos, all of which are derived from just 13 parents. Initially a wild herd was established by taking animals from Britain's Marwell zoo to a site in the Cevennes Mountains of France in 1989. The first releases in Mongolia occurred in 1997, and there are now two herds, one in relatively lush grasslands, with 140 head, and another in semi-desert, with 25 head.

## Ecology of upland forest ponies

The Exmoor pony is, in any case, regarded by many commentators as one of the most tarpan-like of the feral horses, with characteristic pale muzzles and a large head and jaw structure; they also breed true to type (see Figure 7.7). It is able to survive on extremely poor fodder and its presence would appear to go back beyond historical records. The small herds roam an area

Photo: Toby Hickman

**Figure 7.7** *Exmoor ponies*

of about 300 ha on poorer grassland, down to 150 ha on better land. Herds comprise a stallion and 8–18 mares plus foals, although matriarchal groups also exist. The ponies graze grass swards and gorse in the summer and aquatic vegetation, mosses and leaves in winter. There are a total of 1200 individuals of the breed, but only about 180 of these are free living; they are rounded up in October for inspection, branding and registration. The free-roaming herd is unmanaged and subject to the natural processes of selection, leaving them very hardy. In the year 2000 about 30 ponies were released on the Downs above Lewes as part of a programme to improve the sward of chalk grassland, and several other conservation sites are grazed by small numbers of animals.

Feral ponies exist on many uplands of Britain, all with slightly different characters and histories of 'improvement'. The Carneddau in Snowdonia is a stronghold of the primitive Welsh breed of pale grey ponies, and Dartmoor has a much less primitive improved stock. The New Forest holds feral herds in park woodlands and provides study material for the grazing impact of horses on woodland vegetation. As might be expected, as primarily grazers of coarse grasses and sedge, horses transform the ground layer of woodland to a closer cropped sward and this is richer in herbs. The primitive Exmoor breed would thus be ideal as an animal to restore the functional equivalent of the tarpan to the core areas proposed, and by being dispersed to other areas, it would be in a better state to continue its evolutionary trends. However, aesthetics, at least, would dictate that care

Photo: Hans Kampf

**Figure 7.8** *Konik horses at Oostvaardersplassen*

be taken to protect the breed from breeding with feral ponies closer to the domestic types.

There appears to be a conservation preference emerging for the Konik, as used in Holland (see Figure 7.8), where there is now a surplus in the herds. This animal is closer to the pale-coated steppe form and has a semi-upright mane. It thrives in wetlands and is therefore appropriate for lowland heath and marshes. The NT reserve at Wicken and RSPB reserve at Minsmere have recently introduced small herds. However, it should be noted that Exmoor ponies also have extremely tough mouths adapted for gorse and holly, and in addition to coat structure and hooded eyes for protection against rain and wind, are better adapted to wet upland ecosystems.

## The elk

Elk, *Alces alces* (Moose in America, where the red deer is called elk) were a regular feature of Britain's Atlantic temperate forests, surviving the advances even of Neolithic agriculture until some time before the Roman occupation. The latest C[14] date for elk bones is 3925 BP in Scotland, but there are few fossil sites from this period, and it may have survived longer in northern parts of Scotland where there was much suitable habitat. It can be assumed that human predation was the cause of its demise.

In the rest of Europe they had been exterminated from lowlands and Germany by the middle ages, but survived in eastern Prussia until the 1930s with a population of about 1000 individuals.[17] These did not survive the Second World War, when it also became extinct in Poland. However it was re-introduced in Poland in 1957, and occasional animals now wander into Germany. In Scandinavia it was all-but exterminated by hunting when royal prerogatives were removed in the 18th century – it disappeared from southern Sweden and Norway and only a few were left in the northern forests. At the end of 19th century it began to recover due to protective legislation and staged a remarkable resurgence, aided also by modern forestry practices and the extermination of large predators, such that in modern Sweden 126,000 were shot in 1986 compared to 4000 in 1910.

## Elk ecology

Elk are primarily nocturnal browsers and grazers. Adult bulls at five years old in Europe may weigh up to 500 kg (in Canada they reach 800 kg) and stand 2 m at the shoulder. Each adult requires between 10 and 20 kg of food each day, browsing on shrubs of bilberry and heather; on bushes and trees such as rowan, aspen, sallow and willows in summer; and on pine and juniper in winter. They also forage for aquatic plants and are particularly fond of the roots of water lilies.

Population sizes are strongly related to suitable habitat, and tolerable densities in Scandinavia are also limited by the amount of damage they can do to forestry plantations from browsing on spring shoots. In Finland 4–7 animals per 1000 ha was considered acceptable in terms of forestry and also for traffic safety (these big animals are a motoring hazard in Sweden, where 5000–6000 are killed on the roads each year; they are also capable of serious damage to cereal crops). In many parts of Sweden densities exceed this: winter densities in northern Sweden were estimated at 11.4/1000 ha below the treeline and at 5.0/1000 ha above the treeline (animals will feed above the treeline up to 2500 m in summer). Natural densities in southern Sweden are about 8/1000 ha, but can be as high as 30/1000 ha in the royal parks. Elk will wander up to 50 km and can swim well.

Although a clear case can be made for the return of this charismatic animal to Britain, the currently overgrazed British uplands are perhaps not the best place to start! In the Caledonian core area it would be better to plan for the reintroduction of elk after one or two decades of lower red deer numbers and the restoration of the vegetation, particularly riparian habitat and the montane scrub zones. The return of the beaver would considerably enrich the habitat for elk, and the return of wolves should also predate their re-introduction in order to avoid a rapid growth in numbers. It is also apparent that introduced animals will quickly spread to other areas and that even with the presence of wolves in the core area, culling will probably be required. The core area might eventually support as many as 2000 animals. The animal is highly prized by hunters and could bring added revenues to the Highland stalking industry.

One animal we cannot consider for re-introduction is the now extinct Irish elk *Megaloceros giganteus* – not a moose-like elk, but a giant deer of similar proportions to the moose but with wider, deer-type antlers. This magnificent animal died out well before hunters could account for its demise. It existed in Ireland before the arrival of man and disappeared in the immediate post-glacial period, surviving there until about 10,000 BP. It was probably an open country animal and a genuine evolutionary casualty.

### Reindeer

The reindeer *Rangifer tarandus* was a regular feature of glacial Britain and survived into the immediate post-glacial, with the most reliable fossil record dating from 8300 BP. References in Norse sagas about red deer and reindeer hunts in Caithness in the 12th century have been taken as evidence for their continued existence there, but there is no fossil evidence.

Despite the loss of reindeer being most probably natural (although it was a main prey item for Palaeolithic hunters and must have been much reduced in numbers as a result), it has been the subject of a re-introduction programme in the Highland sub-arctic tundra zone of the Cairngorm massif, where the herd remains above the treeline. The animals were brought from semi-domestic stock in Sweden in 1952, but have been supplemented by wild animals from Norway and Russia.

### *Reindeer ecology*
In the rest of Europe the wild reindeer is quite rare – there is a montane sub-species *R.r. tarandus* that occupies a small area of southern Norway and the Russian Kola Peninsula. The forest reindeer *R.r. fennicus* survives in Karelia and Finland. Semi-domestic forms occur in northern Norway, Sweden and Finland, where they are herded by the Sami people of Lapland. This form of nomadic husbandry accounts for strong anti-predator policies throughout northern Scandinavia – affecting wolves, lynx, wolverine and bear. The Sami also persecuted the wild mountain reindeer to extinction in Sweden and Finland, because it competed with their stock. Conservation programmes brought the southern Norwegian and Kola wild populations to recovery levels of 60,000 by the 1970s, after numbers had dwindled in the 1930s to less than 3000. Larger herds of both forest and open country forms are found in Siberia, Greenland, Canada and Alaska (where they are called caribou).[18]

Reindeer are essentially grazers of mosses, lichens and grasses, but the forest form also browses leaves and shoots as well as riparian vegetation. In Norway the wild herds are hunted to control numbers, and yield 10,000 animals per year. They are also the natural prey of wolves, lynx and wolverine (especially the young animals).

Again, it would not be a wise move to add this herbivore to the core area of Caledon until its natural predators were in place, but the species could eventually add to the diversity of animals above the treeline.

## Wild boar

Wild boar are a characteristic feature of forests throughout central and southern Europe, France and Spain. They were also common in Britain throughout the Mesolithic and Neolithic periods, surviving until the Norman conquest in woodland throughout lowland Britain and Scotland. Their eventual demise in Britain is obscure due to the paucity of reliable records, but as they were considered an agricultural pest they survived in wild herds probably only until the 13th century when they were last recorded in the Forest of Dean, and then until the 17th century confined in a few royal parks and hunting preserves. This fate was paralleled in Europe by their disappearance from much of France, Germany, Austria, Hungary and the Balkans as well as Scandinavia during the Middle Ages.[19]

On the continent, however, they have been re-introduced to Southern Sweden (accidentally from farmed animals) and the Netherlands; Karelian populations have re-colonized Finland. Populations in France and Germany have increased considerably and large populations also exist in central and southern Italy and northern Spain. The species occurs across Eurasia and into South East Asia; it is also found in North Africa, and has been introduced to North and South America and Australia. It is regarded as a major game animal in Europe and from a population of 500,000, 400,000 are taken annually, a cull made possible by typically large litters of up to 12 young.

### Boar ecology

Their natural preference is for old deciduous woodland because they prosper on a diet rich in acorns, beech mast, seeds, fungi, grasses, roots and rhizomes, as well as insect grubs and carrion. In mixed habitat of woodland and arable land they can cause considerable damage to crops. The breeding range is limited by severe winters, at which time they are subject to high mortality.

A breeding male will control a territory of 1000 ha, with females and young roaming over 100–300 ha; one male may control several groups. Most animals stay within 5 km of the breeding territory, but excluded males may wander up to 10 km from the home range. A large male may be 1 m high at the shoulder and weigh as much as 350 kg, with females usually weighing less than 100 kg.

With high fecundity, good habitat and mild winters, their numbers can increase to pest proportions very quickly, and central European populations sustain intense sport hunting as a means of controlling numbers. Their natural predators are wolves and bear, with the young also being vulnerable to lynx, and although boar have a reputation for ferocity and can certainly inflict severe wounds with their tusks, they are shy and not dangerous unless provoked.

In recent times wild boar have been 'farmed' in enclosures to provide meat, and as with so many other penned or farmed 'exotics' some have escaped and become naturalized. There is now a thriving population of between 100–200 boar in ideal habitats along the Kent and Sussex border. Derek Gow reviewed this situation in *ECOS* in 2002, noting in particular that government departments were monitoring the situation with regard to crop damage and also to the potential for boar to harbour contagious diseases of stock such as foot-and-mouth disease and swine fever. He notes that in France, where they were long considered a pest species, a change of attitude occurred in the 1970s when they were reclassified for game hunting, with licence fees funding compensation for agricultural damage. Martin Goulding, an ecologist at Sussex University, in 2003 produced a useful monograph on the boar population in Britain, which he had studied in the field for the previous six years.[20] In Britain, the National Trust and RSPCA have supported the presence of boar, whereas farmers' organizations such as the NFU, and curiously, the shooting fraternity have called for their eradication.

Gow notes that the major public issue in these areas has been one of safety, and that both Kent and Sussex County Councils regard the animals as not dangerous unless provoked, and have simply put up notices in their woodlands to deter foolish behaviour. The animals are, in any case, typical in being nocturnal, shy and seldom seen. Gow goes on to make a case for keeping the boar (despite doubts about their genetic purity) under our obligations to return exterminated species, but also notes that Britain's globally important bluebell communities might be adversely affected. Boar certainly uproot bluebells and feed on the bulbs, but there have been no studies to assess the potential impact on this species. On the continent there are contradictory indications of inhibition of anemone communities – some studies showing a negative impact and others a positive impact from regeneration of fragmented rhizomes. Gow also makes the point that natural woodland evolved with boar and should thus be adequately robust or even improved by their presence. Some species may suffer from competition, such as badger, which has a similar diet, and some may benefit from the disturbed soil and wallowing that creates colonization opportunities.

Consideration should certainly be given to the return of this animal to wilder land in our three core areas, but with some caution: it would be wise to re-establish the natural predators and competitors first, such as wild cattle (which will also feed on mast and acorns), the wolf, bear and lynx in Scotland, and lynx in the Welsh and Dartmoor habitats.

## Feral goats and sheep

Neither goats *Capra aegagrus* nor sheep *Ovis ammon* are indigenous to Britain, and although the mouflon *Ovis musimon*, or wild sheep, is widespread in European forests, its natural distribution was limited to Mediterranean islands. Nevertheless, Britain has some very ancient natural-ized populations of charismatic 'breeds' that merit conservation status. Snowdonia is home to some very fine and distinctive feral goats, which can be quite shy of humans, and the Western Isles of Scotland harbour ancient and hardy breeds of feral sheep that are close to the original domesticated 'mouflon-like' stock.

These ancient breeds of sheep are often used as conservation tools for managing grassland swards, whereas feral goats, although tolerated, are generally regarded as a nuisance because of the need for constant surveillance of their numbers and effects upon vegetation. In the Rhinogydd, the goats make a unique contribution to the fauna, and although capable of extensive damage to new tree planting due to their great agility in mounting walls and fences, my own feeling is that they are so remarkable for their beauty and long history that they should be carefully conserved. They would contribute to conservation objectives in those hills particularly, where the montane heaths are regarded as of high value and should remain scrub free.

Likewise, Soay sheep are unique animals that could also contribute to the diversity of herbivores in large areas such as the upper parts of Caledon, the Rhinogydd and Dartmoor. However, more herbivory is hardly appro-priate until the vegetation status is improved and natural predators are present.

## The beaver

The beaver is about to become the first formerly indigenous mammal to be officially re-introduced to Britain. Scottish Natural Heritage and Forest Enterprise have instigated a project in the forest of Knapdale (Mull of Kintyre) that will act as a pilot scheme.[21] If 'successful', other sites will follow. The first animals were scheduled to be released in the spring of 2003. This scheme follows ten years of fact finding and consultation since the idea was mooted by, among others, Alan Featherstone of Trees-for-Life at Findhorn, as part of the longer-term vision for the Caledonian forest.

Beaver were once extensive residents on the major rivers and wetlands of Britain, and well into the Scottish highlands. They were trapped to extinction by the 13th century, for their musk as well as their fur. Derek Yalden (1999) gives a detailed account of their history including place names related to beaver and the archaeological evidence for their general distribution. They were already scarce by Saxon times. The question is – to what extent could they re-establish themselves in former habitats such as the Broads, the Somerset Levels and marshes around the Humber? Most English wetlands are now a complex of levees, dykes and pumping stations with small nature reserves where water regimes are artificially regulated. In the fens, some reserves such as Wicken stand above the surrounding terrain, and in the Somerset Levels, newly engineered reed beds are as much as a meter below the water level in the main dykes. In these highly engineered systems, beaver would be rather chaotic management tools.

In the core areas under consideration, however, they would be more contained and could act as a test bed for other areas, just as the Knapdale scheme is intended to do. Upland zones are, at first, not obviously ideal habitat, but observations in the Parc d'Armorique in Brittany were instructive. The programme there began in the 1970s following successful introductions elsewhere in France, and the Parc was still engaged in a programme of extension, focusing on purchasing suitable habitat, when we visited in 1992. Beaver had colonized a variety of sites ranging over small streams in meadowland, reed-fringed lakes (one with a nuclear power station, much like Trawsfynydd in the Rhinogydd), and most remarkably, some steep boulder-strewn mountain streams reminiscent of Dartmoor. Small dams were evident on the smaller streams, but there were no large beaver ponds and lodges – European beaver do not generally build large dams, but seem content with small pools, wet meadows and even mountainous terrain, where they engineer at most a series of still reaches and generally wetter meadows.

## Beaver ecology

Above all, beaver require luxuriant streamside vegetation for their summer feeding (for example, meadowsweet, willow herb and thistle) and ample supplies of usually small trees for winter feed when they strip the bark from twigs. They are not limited to flat-reaches of rivers or lakes – in the Parc d'Armorique, Alan Featherstone and I saw some lodges on steep wooded streamsides that were reminiscent of Dartmoor.

## Re-introductions

Beaver populations have been re-established throughout Scandinavia, southern Germany, Austria and Switzerland. However, attempts to interest the Countryside Council for Wales in a Snowdonia project (and to steal a march on the Scots) demonstrated what lay ahead. Nobody wanted to stick their necks out – the line being 'the Scots are leading on that one', and officialdom was glad to keep out of any controversy. SNH persevered, however, and set up the obligatory consultation process, which finally found an approving public and a willing participant in Forest Enterprise. Even so, there have been reports in the press of neighbouring landowners in Knapdale campaigning to have the programme stopped on the grounds of potential impact on sport fishing. This despite an extensive educational programme that should have allayed such fears – salmon and trout can benefit from the enhanced riparian habitats.

The Scottish project now has some Norwegian animals in quarantine and in 2005 still awaiting approval from the Scottish Parliament for their release. However, I was surprised to discover that Kent Wildlife Trust are about to let beaver loose in one of their reserves; no consultation process, no computer models, no messing! Except on closer inspection it is not a 're-introduction' programme – the beaver are 'management tools' in a wider scheme to re-wild near-natural areas and use herbivores (Heck and Highland cattle, wild ponies and roe deer). The beaver will be penned and carefully monitored to assess their effectiveness. The Trust now has several animals through the quarantine period.

In Native American lore, the beaver symbolizes the building of strong foundations (the foundations of its dams are extremely resistant to winter floods), industrious activity and the maxim of always having more than one exit from any situation. Native Americans would study the habits of animals and become imbued with their spirit, so it is interesting that for those who have worked hard to get the beaver re-introduced here, there are so many caveats and exit points for this re-introduction programme! It is, however, the foundation upon which other re-introduction schemes for the missing mammalian fauna will be laid.[22]

## Red, roe, fallow and other deer

It is worth noting that our indigenous deer species, keystone species in any habitat, have been exterminated throughout much of their former range, and crucially, are absent from many nature reserves and areas of high conservation status. In the Rhinogydd, for example, where large areas are designated a UNESCO Biosphere Reserve, there are no native deer and only stragglers from the fallow deer population in the Forestry Commission's Coed y Brenin to the southeast. Thus, the so-called natural habitat of such great importance is not grazed by any natural herbivores, though the upland pastures and heaths support a considerable number of alien sheep. Red deer are absent from Snowdonia, having been exterminated in the 19th century outside of private parks on the periphery (Vaynol Estate near Caernarfon may still hold some, as well as a stock of relatively tame white park cattle), and the roe deer have been absent there since their overall extinction south of the Scottish border in the 18th century.

Red deer are scarce on Dartmoor, there being a few wandering individuals from Exmoor to the north, which has held one of the very few wild remnant herds in England, outside of deer parks (the other herd is in the southern Lake District). This species has, as we remarked, expanded its population in Scotland after severe reductions following the introduction of sheep to the highlands in the late 18th century. There has been a concomitant severe impact upon natural forest regeneration. Despite high costs of management, approaching £3million per annum for fencing plantations, almost £2 million is added to the economy through stalking, and as with policy on the continent, deer are now regarded as an economic resource for shooters rather than as an agricultural or forest pest to be exterminated.

However, sport shooting is not effective at controlling numbers, and professional culling or some other form of licensed shooting is required. The advent of stalking effectively saved the Highland red deer from extinction, as some estate owners turned away from sheep when the market collapsed in 1870. The problem is that the population, at over 300,000, is too dense to allow adequate regeneration of forests and natural plant associations, and only in recent years has the Deer Commission instigated sufficient culling operations to stabilize the population. Conservation interests around the Cairngorms (the RSPB and the National Trust) have begun culling programmes in moves to regenerate the natural forest cover and these are proving successful, whereas culling in Affric has been less effective due to in-migration.

In England, the red deer suffered as soon as royalty's interests switched from deer (with severe penalties for poaching animals of the royal chase) to trees (especially oak for timber) and deer were systematically eradicated from the royal forests and were poached elsewhere. They were effectively extinct in the wild some time in the 18th century – there is evidence that even the Exmoor herd stem from continental imports, or at least are not free from having been so augmented.

The red deer was replaced to some extent in England by fallow deer escaping from deer parks. This is now the main species in the New Forest, where it too had a precarious existence, the population having fallen from 7000 in 1670 to 200 around 1900. Numbers are now up to 1000 under controlled culling.

Roe deer suffered much the same fate – becoming extinct in England by the beginning of the 18th century and scarce in Scotland. They were re-introduced to Dorset from Scotland in 1800 and to Norfolk from Germany in 1884. At the present time they have spread west to Devon and north to the Midlands and Welsh border at a rate of 1 km/year. Scottish animals have re-colonized the central lowlands and northern Britain. They are thus absent from Snowdonia.

## Deer ecology

Considering the extent to which deer are keystone animals of the forest, having profound effects upon the understorey as well as providing the mainstay of large predators, their historic scarcity is an important determinant of many conservation values and priorities – a great many British 'nature' reserves are far removed from any natural dynamic of vegetation–herbivore–carnivore interactions. When, therefore, deer do return, they are regarded as causing considerable 'damage' to conservation interests as well as to commercial forestry. They are particularly destructive in areas of coppicing, a once-commercial practice now kept alive by the conservation community to benefit the vernal herb layer.

This latter problem is exacerbated by the introduction of two alien species, the Indian muntjac *Muntiacus reevesi* and the Chinese water deer *Hydropotes inermis*, the former having exploded in numbers and spread rapidly through lowland England, largely through human agency. Muntjac are now present in Snowdonia (1969) and Dartmoor (1979).[23] Yalden reports that this species tends to suppress numbers of roe deer and is an even greater source of trouble to woodland conservationists, having an impact on bluebells, primroses and orchids, as well as on bird and butterfly diversity. The muntjac is a shy and elusive animal that is difficult to cull humanely. Chinese water deer (a rare species found on riparian grassland in China) has established small populations in the Broads and fens of East Anglia (from where it is unlikely to spread).

Another exotic, the sika *Cervus nippon*, which was introduced to Scotland in 1914 and to Dorset in 1896 (escaping by swimming to the mainland from Brownsea Island), with a further herd established in the Forest of Bowland in 1906 (and spreading towards the Lake District), presents problems of a different kind.

The sika raises important questions relating to 'aliens' and 'natives'. The species was at first confined to the areas where it was introduced, but began to spread in the 1970s with the maturing of large areas of conifers. It appears peculiarly adapted to this (alien) habitat in ways that red deer and fallow deer are not, and it has become a forestry pest because few plantations have been designed with deer control in mind. It is very difficult to locate and cull the animals humanely.

However, it also presents a problem for conservation: the 'species' is inter-fertile with red deer and the hybrids prosper. Hybrid herds now exist throughout Scotland, and even apparently native red deer have been found with sika genes. This is now not a reversible process, and it is likely that in the future the entire British population of *Cervus* will consist of these hybrids. Derek Yalden speaks for many conservationists:

> Many of the hybrids are unrecognisable as such. . . . This seems a very sad way to lose our largest native land mammal.

and refers to the 'hybrid swarm' spreading to 'threaten the genuine native red deer'.

Of course, the red deer do not view the sika in this way! Quite the contrary, given the hybridization rate. And, equally, we are not losing our largest native land mammal, but simply watching it being transformed to a species better adapted to the varied British environment. Our red deer are, in any case, already altered by being much smaller than their continental cousins, which dwell in more intact forest ecosystems with more efficient culling and less over-grazing, and in some cases, the presence of effective predators. This is a classic example of scientific conservation values drawn from an old paradigm of an almost nationalistic taxonomy, rather than from functional ecology.

The whole situation with deer species will require a careful appraisal. Many conservationists are also concerned for animal welfare and rights, and object to shooting, some in all circumstances, including even profes-sional culling, and others only to sport shooting. Yet, without control, deer numbers will prevent regeneration of native woodlands and impact upon the ground flora, birds and insects. Furthermore, high winter densities of deer will lead to high mortality and suffering during harsh winters and also to high rates of disease and parasitic stress.

Policies with respect to alien species, culling, sport shooting, licence fees, compensation for damage, animal welfare in hard winters and traffic hazards will be particularly relevant to buffer zones around core areas and to wildlife-friendly corridors. These aspects will also apply to elk, boar, wild cattle and horses.

Conservationists now have to reckon with the 'tiggywinkle effect' – following a public outcry by animal rights and welfare groups, led by the special trust of that name set up for hospitalized hedgehogs. That species, having been disastrously introduced to ground-nesting bird areas of the Hebrides, was marked for eradication by SNH. The welfare group organized rescue operations to carry animals caught by the trapping programme to the mainland, despite scientific advice to the effect that the animals would simply starve while trying to compete with the resident population. Few laypeople seem to have any grasp of the principles of natural selection whereby the majority of the offspring of species with litters above the replacement rate, must necessarily perish by starvation, disease or predation.

## The small herbivores: squirrels, rats, rabbits and hares

Finally, we should mention some small herbivores of relevance to vegeta-tion dynamics, as well as to the issues of naturalness and the effects of human interference. It is perhaps not generally known that such a familiar indigenous species as the red squirrel was driven to virtual extinction, even in Scotland, largely by deforestation; neither is it well known that rabbits, rats and brown hares are not indigenous to Britain.

Most people will know that the grey squirrel is an American import and is held responsible for the retreat of the native red. However, the native red squirrel had to be re-introduced to Scotland in the late 18th century, and after the nadir for woodland in Britain at the close of the 1700s, the native squirrel was very scarce in England – surviving mainly in the Peak District, Lake District and North Wales. By 1920 the native red had re-colonized most of Britain, but after introduction of American greys in 1876 it began a widespread retreat in the face of competition with the aggressive newcomer. The red squirrel now survive only in those areas where greys have not reached or seem at a disadvantage, such as the native pinewoods of Scotland; plantations in East Anglia and Snowdonia; or islands such as Brownsea, Isle of Wight, Jersey and Anglesey. It is, however, a widespread species from Scandinavia to the Balkans and across Eurasia to Japan.

The grey squirrel is acknowledged as a serious pest of forestry plantations because of its bark stripping and shoot nibbling habits. Yet, it now has few natural predators. Pine martens and wildcat were severely persecuted in the 19th century, as were raptors such as goshawk; all were efficient predators of squirrels.

Of the small herbivores, black and brown rats are not indigenous to Britain, and were not native to Europe either. The black rat (and house mouse) was established some time in the Middle Ages as a major pest of the urban environment, but was replaced by the brown rat *Rattus norvegicus* in the mid-1700s, when it spread from landings of timber brought from Russia (it is native to the Asian steppe). It has persisted despite a £50 million per year pest-control industry for its eradication, and remains abundant with estimates ranging from 7 to 40 million animals. It occupies about 45 per cent of agricultural buildings and 3 per cent of urban buildings. It has adapted to hedgerows and fields and even to seashore environments, thus forming an important element of the food web for many predators. Its affect on bird populations is incalculable, since any birds that are vulnerable to its predilection for eggs and young have long since altered their habits, died out (as in many documented island communities around the world) or become less abundant.

The rabbit is an earlier fellow-traveller of expanding human populations. It was brought over by the Normans, having been native to Iberia and North Africa, and has colonized dry short-turf grassland throughout Britain to a level of abundance where, both here and elsewhere (particularly Australia), it is a serious agricultural pest. Its damage to agriculture, estimated in the 1950s in Britain at £50 million, has inspired little short of biological warfare by governments worldwide.

The viral disease myxomatosis was introduced to Britain in 1953, perhaps deliberately for control purposes, but not through official channels. The virus weapon was developed from a South American rabbit-specific virus in laboratories in France and Australia, and an initial government trial on Skokholm Island failed. In 1950 the virus suddenly caught hold in Australia and decimated the plagues of rabbit that threatened that continent's agriculture as well as native flora. UK government legislation in 1953 actually forbade the dissemination of the virus, but it caught hold and spread rapidly, killing 99 per cent of rabbits in 1955.

The loss of such a large part of the food web caused ripple effects: overly suppressed downland orchids blossomed, field voles prospered in the long grass as did the weasel population feeding on them, but stoats were reduced and there was a widespread breeding failure of buzzards. It is estimated that whereas there were 100 million rabbits in 1950, they have been reduced to about 40 million today after populations have adapted. Another more virulent virus, Rabbit haemorrhagic disease (RHD), is yet to reach Britain, but in Spain it killed 90 per cent of the population, thus leading to knock-on effects on predators such as lynx and eagles.

As well as its effects upon grassland sward, the rabbit is still a major component of the food web in the British countryside, being a major prey item for foxes, stoats, weasels, badgers, buzzards, eagles, harriers, owls and crows. In Wales, perhaps because of the resurgence of polecats and the prevalence of buzzards, goshawks and kites, it is less common.

The brown hare *Lepus europaeus* arrived with the Iron Age farmers and was thus common in the English lowlands by the time the Romans arrived and commented upon it. The native mountain hare, blue hare, or Irish hare, *Lepus timidus* was probably formerly extensive in the uplands but had retreated and was confined to Scotland by the time records began. It was introduced to North Wales but is probably now extinct there – certainly brown hares are denizens of the lower pastures of the Rhinog. The mountain hare population of Scotland prospers under moor burning for grouse, and declines when that industry declines; it is thought that the poor success of the Lake District golden eagles is due to the absence of mountain hare, a staple prey item in Scotland.

Agricultural intensification has reduced hare numbers in eastern Britain, and the extension of forestry and the dominance of sheep have also reduced numbers in the western uplands. As this animal is also a major component of food webs, particularly for eagles in Scotland, strategies of woodland creation in the uplands and wood pasture corridors in the lowlands could have major implications. Wildlife-friendly corridors of wood pasture would likely benefit populations of hare in the eastern half of Britain where they have declined due to agricultural intensification.

The prevalence of these 'aliens', some of which are now 'keystone' species affecting the structure of plant communities, should give cause for reflection when other species, such as bison, Pardel lynx and even escaped panthers, are evaluated as potential additions to the British mammal fauna. I would argue that in these cases, nationalistic policies could give way to a more liberal policy of trans-locatory asylum!

# 8

# Restoring Ecological Processes: Bringing Back the Carnivores

In the US, the Wildlands Project is described as one of cores, corridors and carnivores. The large mammalian carnivores such as bear, wolf and lynx are considered essential to wildland. It is not just a matter of natural processes of predation, but central to the whole ethos of wildland. It is a mark of respect, or tolerance, and a willingness to accept some economic loss and personal risk in order to accord a certain sanctity to nature's ways. In the previous century the wolf was all-but eradicated across the US and the grizzly bear confined to the northern Rocky Mountains; the lynx and the mountain lion suffered equally. Each of these carnivores is now subject to recovery programmes. In Europe there is a definite move in this direction, with active programmes for re-establishing bear and lynx (in France, Spain, Italy, Switzerland, Austria and Poland) and tolerating the return of the wolf (in Norway, Germany, Poland and the Alps). The map in Figure 8.1 shows the current range of the wolf and bear, in Western Europe, and Colour Plate 6 shows the lynx and re-introduction projects. Britain cannot be truly wild whilst these former residents are absent, and we shall see that we cannot now argue that there is no room or that our ecosystems cannot support large carnivores.

The European programmes that I will outline below have not been without their problems, particularly in adjustments by the sheep farming and deer hunting communities. However, the data clearly show that these problems are of little economic significance, and that as cultural attitudes change, the carnivores are accepted. The ecological data also makes it clear that Britain, particularly Scotland, has ample room for wolf and lynx, though the bear might have to wait until forests recover their natural state of floristic abundance.

Wolf – shaded grey areas indicate the range and dotted grey lines of wandering individuals. Bear – dotted line indicates the range of Scandinavian, Russian, Carpathian, Dinaric and Balkan main populations, with small isolated group in Cantabrian mountains; + indicates remnants and re-introductions. (Sources: WWF and LCIE)

**Figure 8.1** *Distribution of the wolf and bear in Europe*

## The guild of carnivores

In a natural environment with a fully functional guild of herbivores, there is also a guild of carnivores of varying sizes and hunting strategies that are adapted to the size and behaviour of their prey. The two guilds evolve side by side and predation affects herbivore population, health and structure, possibly also limiting numbers and density and thus affecting grazing and browsing patterns. Such guilds are beautifully illustrated by Alan Turner and Mauricio Anton (1997) in '*The Big Cats and their Fossil Relatives*', and I particularly recommend the final chapters on environmental change and adaptation, as these place the differing sizes and hunting strategies within the context of the climatic cycles that have moulded the northern temperate ecosystems.

In the absence of such predator pressure, foraging behaviour, density and perhaps overall numbers are altered such that more intensive pressure is exerted by the herbivores on the vegetation. Resultant deterioration in vegetation cover can also affect other species as the structure of their habitat and availability of food changes. We have seen a classic example of this with red deer numbers in the Scottish Highlands. As we noted previously (see Chapter 3), the deer population has expanded to the maximum carrying capacity of the land and to a point where numbers may be self-regulating due to density-dependent mechanisms that limit breeding. The problem is that although deer numbers may now stabilize, they are at a density that prevents the forest from regenerating. In the presence of predators such as the wolf, foraging behaviour is significantly altered and deer herds, particularly in winter, are not able to congregate in sheltered locations. Such congregating can lead to the severe detriment of the vegetation. The damaging effects of herbivore density extend beyond the regeneration of tree seedlings: the shrub and field layer may be totally altered leaving less palatable species, grasses and mosses in place of an abundance of flowering and berry-bearing shrubs and tall herbs. These changes have a knock-on effect on the diversity of other life, particularly birds and insects.

In the mature forests of the Carpathians, where predators such as the wolf still exist, foresters will tell you that herbivores shun areas around the wolves' breeding dens for significant distances such that pressure on seedlings is reduced and there is notable regeneration.[1] As the wolves move their dens, so different parts of the forest experience the reduction in herbivore pressure. Perhaps because there are so few large areas of natural forest with herbivore and predator populations intact, these anecdotal observations have not been subject to detailed scientific assessment. Scotland's open moorland with large deer herds is not representative of most temperate forest habitat and such denning factors may not be relevant. However, there are further anecdotal observations from hunters in the Vosges and Jura, where lynx have returned, claiming a reduction in roe deer density, and this might also be expected to impact on vegetation. Even in the US, modern studies are few because wolves are only now returning to areas that can be surveyed scientifically, such as Yellowstone.[2] Data from Minnesota, where wolf numbers first recovered and where hunting fraternities keep detailed records, show that weather is the prime determinant of numbers for deer and moose.[3] However, generalizations cannot be safely applied to more southerly zones (where there are no severe winters) or across all herbivore species.

In addition to affecting numbers, density and grazing pressure, predators selectively kill the weak and the old, thus promoting the overall fitness of the herbivore population and its resistance to disease. Large predators such as the big cats will take adult animals, and the different hunting strategies will test adult fitness. Wolves will hunt in packs and subject deer to a trial of stamina before singling out a target animal, but in general, fit adult moose and larger deer are relatively immune: it is the old, the sick and the young that are taken. Smaller predators will exert pressure on population numbers by taking the more vulnerable young animals.

There is also a hierarchy around kills – with some carnivores operating as scavengers of other species' kills, sometimes driving the other predator off the kill and hence forcing that species to increase its kill rate. Wolves are known to drive puma off a kill, and bears will often drive any other species away. Scavenging birds and foxes also benefit from the presence of large predators, although in the case of foxes and smaller predators, their numbers are reduced by direct predation from the top predators such as big cats (lynx in particular) and wolves.

## The European carnivore guild

In addition to their functional role in the ecosystem, the big carnivores do, of course, have a magic of their own, introducing issues of risk, excitement, danger and loss. When we consider the formerly typical western European temperate forest fauna, we encounter some perhaps surprising data. Most people are familiar with mammoths and woolly rhino, but would perhaps not expect lion to be a significant member of the temperate or boreal landscape. Many people also think of the fabled sabre-toothed 'tiger' *Homotherium* as a prehistoric animal, but few can appreciate how *recent* this beast is in the palaeontological record. Further, despite my student studies of natural sciences including a substantial component of palaeontology, I did not appreciate the former presence in Europe of large panthers of a 'jaguar' type, with modern leopards present even during the intense cold of the glacial periods. I certainly had not appreciated how widespread the lion had become. These animals roamed the typical temperate parkland forests, alder swamps, upland birch and crags, pine forests and dune slacks that we associate with the 'near to natural' nature reserves of Britain today.[4]

It is the big cats that have suffered more than any other carnivore. Wolf and bear are still present in many countries of Western Europe, from Norway in the north to Spain and Greece in the south, but both lion and leopard are now extinct in this continent. The sabre-toothed cat (it was not closely related to the tiger) may have hung on in Britain until the last glaciation, and certainly survived until the immediate post-glacial period in America.

Thus, any large herbivore guild, such as the fauna of Bialowieza (often presented as the nearest to a complete boreal or temperate forest ecosystem) still lacks the large cats capable of downing the largest herbivores. There are ample post-glacial fossils of lion in Poland, now regarded as an extension of the then widespread Asiatic subspecies, and although the lion is an open country animal and disappeared as the steppe fauna was replaced, it must be assumed that leopard hung on in the forests, despite the paucity of fossil remains. Further, without human interference, lion would have found habitat and ample prey in the large riverine meadows formerly maintained by the mega-herbivores.

There would be a case, therefore, for the introduction of large cats into such faunal assemblages, provided the habitat was extensive enough, and aside from any political or humanitarian considerations. Clearly, the latter would be deciding factors, as the major difference between big cats and wolves, the current top predator, is that they are quite capable of killing people. Puma, which are much smaller than lion, kill several people each year in the US. Indian lions regularly kill villagers, and so, of course, do their African cousins. However, from our safely denuded European viewpoints, we still call upon Indians and Africans, Russians and Amerindians, not to exterminate their big cats and to live with the risk. In the US it would now be unthinkable to pursue a policy of extermination for the mountain lion and there are even moves to rehabilitate the jaguar in the southwest. How much more weight our exhortation would carry were we also prepared to accept these risks! There would be an argument for establishing a small population of the endangered Asiatic lion at Oostvaardersplassen.

The remnant primeval forests of eastern Poland are not the only area of Europe with top predators. The main area for wolf, lynx and bear is the Carpathian arc stretching from Slovakia through Romania and the Ukraine. In Scandinavia, the big three predators are supplemented by migration from their Karelian strongholds in northern Russia. There are sizeable populations of bear in Slovenia, and a few wolf and lynx ranging through the Balkan states. Wanderers from these populations have begun repopulating the Alps. Small populations of wolf and bear live in the Abruzzi Mountains of Italy and there is a healthy population of wolves in northern Spain.

Many European countries have been struggling hard to protect their populations of these predators and to encourage an influx from the eastern states; they have even trans-located animals (bear and lynx) to re-occupy their former ranges. In Britain these three carnivores were formerly present. The lynx, somewhat enigmatically, disappeared before any cultural record of its presence, and the bear is also a distant Medieval memory, but wolf hung on until about 300 years ago, having adapted to the loss of forest and was clearly exterminated by humans. Having considered the ecology of their current European sites, I have absolutely no doubt in my mind that with suitable restoration of habitat and herbivore numbers, these three animals could be returned to Britain. We shall therefore review European experience and the species' ecology with regard to potential re-introduction.

## Lynx

Of the great carnivores in Europe's heritage, the lynx is curiously silent when it comes to a cultural relationship. Bear and wolf figure strongly in fable and are clearly honoured in the culture of the Celts, but the lynx, despite its special character and powers, is strangely absent. Its very existence in Britain is shrouded in mystery. Until 1980, there were no references to it as a former member of the British fauna, although one late-glacial fossil had been found in Kilgreany Cave in Ireland. The naturalist Corbet, writing in 1974 in the first edition of the handbook of British mammals, made no reference to lynx. The same is even true of Stuart's *Pleistocene Vertebrates of the British Isles*, an extensive fossil

Upper – Scandinavian; Middle – Central and Eastern European; Lower – Spanish     Drawing: Peter Taylor

**Figure 8.2** *The European forms of the lynx*

history published in 1981. Yet, by the time of Derek Yalden's *History of British Mammals* in 2000, a plethora of data from post-glacial sites in Britain was available for review, including that from a cave in Sutherland where a complete 'sub-fossil' skeleton had been carbon-dated to AD 170, the time of the Roman occupation. Lynx are secretive animals, even in the fossil record. Their existence in Celtic Europe must have been well-known to the artists and jewellers, yet there are few images.

## Natural pre-history

The earliest lynx-like cat appeared at the beginning of the Pleistocene, and is represented in fossils ranging from China, through Asia to Italy, France and Spain. This ancestor, known as the Issoire lynx, had a typical short tail and the characteristic dentition of modern lynx, but was longer in the face and shorter in the leg – rather like a short-tailed puma. The eminent Finnish palaeontologist Bjorn Kurten thought that modern forms developed as an adaptation to hunting the hare as chief prey. In Europe, during the Middle Pleistocene, a population must have been isolated in the Iberian Peninsula where it became a specialist predator of rabbit and small game birds. This population began to differ sufficiently to form a new species, so that when its range eventually reconnected with the more easterly populations in Southern France, no intermediate forms appeared in the fossil record, indicating no inter-breeding.

Throughout the last glacial period, the Eurasian *Lynx lynx* and the Iberian or Pardel *Lynx pardina* remained similar in size, but after the end of the last glaciation, the Pardel lynx became increasingly smaller, shrinking to almost half the size of the largest Scandinavian forms. These changes are likely to be related to prey size and killing strategies – with the northern European forms regularly preying on roe deer or reindeer, and the Iberian form on rabbit.

At the end of the last glaciation, the Eurasian lynx ranged throughout Northern and Central Europe, the Balkans, Asia Minor, Persia, Tibet and the entire northern taiga belt. It was not confined to forests, but roamed in open semi-desert country where it inhabited rocky terrain with scrub. The lynx of Central and Eastern Europe take a large proportion of roe deer in their diet, as well as young red deer, and northern lynx take a proportion of reindeer. This may represent post-glacial expansiveness in the absence of a pantherine cat, such as leopard or lion. It is curious that the Pardel lynx became smaller in post-glacial times in the absence of other feline competitors. Perhaps human competition reduced the available large game, as well as climate change and human intervention reducing the canopy forests in favour of Mediterranean scrub to which the Pardel lynx is now confined.

## Lynx ecology

Lynx vary in their ecology: in the north of their range, they are a large predator, with males weighing at most 45 kg (average 30 kg) and with females weighing in at 20 kg; the Iberian species weighs about half that at 9 kg average for a female up to 12 kg for a male. The larger animals are powerful enough to bring down adult roe deer and have a fabled standing leap of 5 m. Territories in the north can range up to 500 km², but average 100 km² in better habitat; in central and southern Europe this reduces to 20–30 km², and down to 4–20 km² in the best of the Spanish habitat.[5]

Prey species vary according to the populations and ranges: in the Altai, for example, deer represent 60 per cent of the diet, whereas in Tartar ranges, hare constitute 66 per cent. In Sweden, roe deer and reindeer make up 80 per cent of the diet. In the Bialowieza forest of Poland hare represent 50 per cent, mice 15 per cent and roe deer only 7 per cent, whereas animals in western European forests have a larger take of roe deer. In Spain, the Pardel lynx is primarily a rabbit specialist, with small game birds such as partridge, rodents and a few young deer also taken. The recent decimation of the rabbit population (down to 5 per cent of the 1950 population), firstly by myxomatosis and then by rabbit haemorrhagic disease (RHD), has doubtless contributed to the demise of the lynx in Spain. The IUCN now report that the Pardel lynx is confined to about 11,000 km² of breeding range, where it exists in many isolated pockets.[6]

Derek Yalden (1999) provides some useful figures on Bialowieza: an area of 580 km² supports 15 lynx (38 km² each) as well as 32 wolves [some authorities, Mallinson (1978), for example, assert that wolf will not tolerate a territorial overlap – others make no references to this]. Prey animals in Bialowieza are drawn from a population of 3700 red deer, 2700 roe deer, 3400 boar, 170 elk and 250 bison. Mathiasson and Dalhov (1990) give territorial figures of 300–1000 km² for Scandinavian lynx and 10–250 km² for the smaller European forms.

Lynx will take domestic sheep and large game birds, though these are usually peripheral to their diets. However, re-introduced populations in the Vosges and Jura have had a reputation for killing sheep. In the provinces of Ain (France) and Valais (Switzerland), where there may now be over 100 lynx, they are reckoned to take between 3000 and 5000 roe deer annually from a population of 168,000 (3 per cent); the Alpine carnivore conservation group KORA puts a figure of 0.4 per cent for losses in sheep. This population of lynx has angered not only shepherds, but also deer hunters concerned at the competition. Hunters claim that the presence of lynx immediately depresses deer numbers (which have no other predator than man). However, about 10,000 deer are killed every year by cars on the region's roads and it is clear that the hunting fraternity are not basing their hostility on rational or economic grounds.

## Current populations and re-introductions

The main population of the lynx in Europe is in the Carpathian Mountains
of Romania (1000–1200 animals estimated in 1962, with the latest survey
of 2001 suggesting 2000), and in Scandinavia (2500–2800 animals in
2001). The Baltic countries and Finland receive incomers from larger
populations in Russia. In the Carpathians, Slovakia has a population
estimated at 400; Poland had 300 in 1963, but numbers had declined to 100
in 2001. In the Balkans the population may be decreasing with 50–70 in
Albania, Macedonia and Serbia. The current population in the Dinaric Alps
(Bosnia, Croatia and Slovenia) has prospered from re-introduction and now
numbers about 130. In Scandinavia, Finland holds the largest population,
thought to be 500 in 1990 and now numbering 870, with Sweden having
200–300 in the 1960s (it almost went extinct at the turn of the century), but
rising to an estimated 1500 in 1998 and 1800 in 2001. Norwegian lynx are
decreasing where they have been subject to culling and illegal hunting as a
result of heavy depredations on free-roaming sheep flocks.

Throughout the 1960s and 1970s lynx were regularly hunted – in one
eight-year period in Norway, 286 were killed; in Czechoslovakia in 1963, 80
were killed. In Romania about 100 were shot per year. In Sweden hunting
was banned in 1986 but started again in 1995, with a quota of 168 of which
97 were taken. The WWF report that in 1998 the Norwegian population
was estimated at 500, with 117 being shot under licence in that year alone.
WWF's estimate of the 'European' population is about 7000, which includes
the large population of European Russia and the Baltic States.[7]

There is no doubt that lynx can be eradicated from suitable habitat even in
quite remote regions. It was extinct in Germany by 1846, despite extensive
forests in Bavaria and the Alps; in Austria it has been extinct since 1872 and
in Italy since 1910. In France the last one in the Massif Central was killed in
1875 and the last killed in the Alps was in 1909. The lynx is more vulnerable
than the wolf – which survived in the remoter regions of Italy.[8]

It would appear that the Scandinavian populations are reasonably robust;
perhaps the same is also true in Poland, the Czech republic, Slovakia and
Romania, but recent research shows declines in the Balkans, doubts about
Romanian estimates and problems with the newly introduced and expanding populations in the Alps (100+), Jura (75) and Vosges (25), largely due
to their unpopularity with the hunting fraternity.[9]

There is a long history of re-introductions for lynx in its former range in
Western Europe. Mathiasson and Dalhov (1990) report attempts made in
Germany in 1938, but most projects took place in the late 1970s in France,
Austria and Switzerland. After successful re-introduction in the Jura (not
wholeheartedly welcomed by shepherds, despite compensation arrangements), the early 1980s saw introductions to the Vosges mountains, when
two wild-caught males and one female were released and radio-tagged.

Two additional five-year-old animals (a pair) were added from Riber Zoo in Derby, England, and reported at the time to have been of the southern 'subspecies' the Pardel lynx, which pre-historically had certainly overlapped with the Eurasian lynx in southern France. By 1987, six animals remained in the Ribeauville Forest, preying largely on rabbit and deer.

In 1974 three pairs of Slovakian lynx were released in Slovenia's Koccvjc Forest and Inner Carniola (600 km²), and by 1976, 15–17 individuals were present. The current population of 130 in the Dinaric Alps has grown from these re-introductions. Wanderers from these Alpine populations have been tracked in northern Italy where there is now an eastern Alpine population of about ten. The Bohemian population is also the result of re-introductions and now stands at about 75 animals – with colonization of the Bavarian Forest from the Czech side (about 12 and decreasing).

In Spain and Portugal the formerly stable population of *Lynx pardina* has crashed since the 1950s to a few hundred in fragmented pockets of scrubland. In their recent report, WWF estimated it at 800 animals but this would have meant only 13 km² per territory: if 20–30 km² is more realistic, then the breeding population may then have been as low as 400. The latest data show further declines with some estimates as low as 150–200 animals, and a captive breeding programme is envisaged by the Spanish authorities. IUCN regard this as the most endangered species of the cat family and a candidate for the first 21st century extinction of not only a European mammal but also of any cat worldwide.[10]

## The potential for re-introduction to Britain

There is no doubt that lynx was a key element of the British fauna throughout the formative period of the larger European fauna. It is an adaptable animal, showing great variation in size and prey preferences, and ranging from rocks and scrubland to dense forest. It may be vulnerable to damp, but is otherwise very cold-adapted. Its presence has a marked depressive effect on numbers of small deer. Provided there are ample populations of its main prey species, it prefers to hunt in forests and its depredations on livestock (outside of Norway) are minimal, especially if preventative measures are taken. It has demonstrated a capacity to prosper from re-introductions (in the Alps, Jura, Vosges, Dinaric Alps and Bohemian Forest), even to levels that call for culling – where animals may wander from preferred habitat and attack livestock.

There can be little doubt that sufficient prey and habitat exist in Scotland, which has excessive deer numbers and ample forests. In northern Britain, the forests of Kielder are extensive and hold roe deer. In Wales, there is a paucity of deer, though rabbit, hare, pheasant, rodents and the young of feral goats would provide prey in the Rhinogydd, and there are fallow deer in Coed-y-Brenin. Dartmoor has an abundance of game – roe deer, rabbit and pheasant, though predation of feral ponies, or their foals at least, could be a problem in terms of public acceptability.

The possibility exists of re-introducing a hybrid grouping – with animals of northerly size and disposition released in Scotland (perhaps of Norwegian and Swedish origin, where there are currently licensed culls), animals of central European origin released in Wales, and controversially, no doubt, of Spanish origin released in southwest England (Dartmoor). Such releases should only be contemplated *after* appropriate conservation policies are in place, such as the designation of large core areas in Wales and southwest England, or suitable safeguards and compensation agreements in Scotland and northern England, where there are already large, relatively remote forested habitats.

The importance of professional groundwork and commitment is made clear by the successes and failures of various re-introduction projects. These have been reviewed by the KORA project, based in Switzerland, which operates an online data-base. [von Arx and Breitenmoser (Breitenmoser, 1990, 1998; KORA, 2001) provide a summary in *ECOS*.]

The introduction of the Spanish species to an area where it was not formerly known (there are no fossils further north than central France) is controversial and would contravene current IUCN guidelines. However, these guidelines are not adapted to the current real world of alien invasions and climate change. There is an argument for setting up another population of Pardel lynx as a safeguard should disease strike in Spain, where there is also still heavy loss of habitat. The smaller lynx would be better adapted to the terrain and prey species around Dartmoor, where the non-indigenous rabbit and pheasant are common.

One further element in this equation is what we might call 'goshawking' – the deliberate release or accidental escape of animals kept privately by individuals of various motives. Britain's now thriving population of goshawk grew from falconers' 'losses' and is made up of a mixed bag of Scandinavian and Continental races. Lynx are regularly sighted in the British countryside, and one animal of unknown provenance was shot on the Norfolk–Suffolk border in 1990.[11] Recently a group of Scottish hunting activists threatened to release 20 animals in protest at the ban on hunting with hounds – presumably with the intent of then hunting the cats. This phenomenon is not, however, restricted to the lynx. Much larger cats have been deliberately released!

## Big cats in Britain

The living 'big' cats encompass the lion, tiger, puma, jaguar, leopard, snow leopard and cheetah. Europe has in times past hosted lion, leopard and cheetah. Of these, we can assume that lion and cheetah were a feature of the more open habitats of a warmer inter-glacial period or of the cold tundra and warm steppe phases of glacial and post-glacial environments, but the adaptable leopard appears in all climate phases. It was also a feature of all past British ecosystems prior to the present post-glacial episode. It occupied caves in the Mendips even during the coldest phases of the ice ages, and ranged widely across Europe, with a few post-glacial fossils in Italy. Quite when and why this resilient animal should have disappeared is a bit of a mystery.

There is, however, growing evidence that 'naturalized' panthers are already at large in Britain, with black leopard leading the sightings! Two close friends of mine have encountered black panthers in the English countryside, and my brother, an experienced naturalist tour guide, saw a puma attacking pheasants in Hampshire! The relatively staid *Field* magazine carried an article in the year 2000 in which estimates of several hundred individuals were made, ranging from puma and black leopard to the small jungle cat *Felis chaus*.[12] There are regular reports of encounters real enough to cause police helicopters to be scrambled and troops of army sharpshooters to be called out. Sheep farmers tend to know when a large cat moves into the region, but appear quite stoic in the face of a generally disbelieving establishment.

*Field* magazine, reporting on the issue in March 2000, interviewed the Wildlife Liaison Officer for Durham County Police Force, Sergeant Eddie Bell, who had personally sighted a puma and who stated 'most gamekeepers in the area will admit privately to knowing they are there, but are wary of being ridiculed'. Bell had been keeping track of sightings for the police force for ten years, and reckoned there were 8–10 puma in the region, 1 or 2 lynx and 1 caracal lynx! Sightings had been constant over a ten-year period, with about 60 out of 280 reports a year proving reliable.

The best sighting from an experienced naturalist is documented in Trevor Beer's *Beast of Exmoor*.[13] Beer began to investigate the reports of panthers on Exmoor throughout the early 1980s. He collated all reliable records, analysed the characteristics and concluded that both puma (20 per cent of sightings) and black panther (black variant of the leopard) were present. There were no reports of spotted leopards. His little book reports many of the sightings and descriptions, often by trustworthy field naturalists, and it makes enlightening reading. In 1984, after visiting a midden of deer remains for six consecutive weeks, he had his first sighting of a black pantherine cat at close quarters.

Beer's description is slightly at odds with the expectation of a leopard, in that the animal is rather longer-legged and fleet of foot, with a relatively smaller head – almost a black puma. There is a wonderful drawing in the book. Nevertheless, Beer believes his animal was leopard rather than puma. Black puma are not unknown in their American range, but there are no

Drawing: Trevor Beer

**Figure 8.3** *Large pantherine cat seen on Exmoor, 1984*

records of them being imported to the UK, as black panthers clearly were. However, inquiries with the import authorities have thus far not revealed any detailed records of imports, nor of any system of post-import checks on the eventual fate of the animals. Customs and Excise do not keep records, and it is down to the licensing departments of DEFRA to keep track – my enquiries there are ongoing, but so far have not turned up any system of logging imports, or, alarmingly, their subsequent fate!

Whatever their origin, black panthers were a favourite pet of gangster-land bosses, and many animals were cared for by animal trainers. Large cats could still be readily procured in Northern Ireland in 1997, when *BBC Wildlife* reported on the range of cats that had been let loose, shot, or found in garages and lock-ups. It talked also to dealers. Lynx and puma were no problem to procure at £400 a pair. Even tigers had been discovered kept in country houses.

It appears now to be established that these cats escaped, or rather were released, from captivity. In the early 1970s regulations were brought in to counter both the risk and animal welfare considerations of such beasts being held as 'pets'. The resultant obligations were onerous, and many owners may have simply turned their animals loose rather than sending them to zoos (which could often not take them) or having them put down. One such animal trainer has admitted to a *Times* reporter that he released both a puma and a black panther on the moors above Sheffield in 1974 (the *Times*, 29 January 2000). The trainer Leslie Maiden once owned more than a dozen big cats; he knows of several other owners who did likewise in the Pennine region.

For many people it is inconceivable that so many large and potentially dangerous cats could be living in Britain. There are few documented records by experts. Derek Yalden (1999) reports in his book the escape of two clouded leopards *Neofelis nebulosa* from London Zoo; although one was recaptured immediately, the other was not captured for several months until an irate farmer discovered what had been killing his sheep. The ability of leopard to remain secretive and unobserved is legion. I spent 3 months in close association with them in a Kenyan montane forest and despite the abundance of fresh tracks (often following mine by a matter of minutes!), I never saw a single animal. Quentin Rose in the *Field* article tells the story of an incident in the suburbs of Johannesburg in South Africa: a vehicle carrying a wild leopard due for translocation crashed and the animal escaped; that night the alarmed authorities set traps and much to their consternation caught seven separate individuals on the one night! Despite the ability of these animals to remain hidden, there is a huge amount of evidence from ordinary people, the police and farmers, many of whom report the animals moving around in broad daylight and with little evident fear of humans.

There is thus little doubt that a small population of pantherine cats could maintain itself in the British countryside preying on abundant small deer, pheasant and rabbit. What is surprising is the wide range of rural countryside in which sightings have been reported. At some stage, when final 'proof' is forthcoming, a policy will have to be developed, either of tolerance and safeguards, or of eradication.

## The European leopard

Although the lion is relatively well known not only as a fossil but also in historic times from Greece and Turkey, the fully functional European temperate forest also had an intermediate cat as part of the predator guild – the leopard – which took primarily medium-sized ungulates and wild boar. Yet this cat does not feature in the historical record. It currently occurs, though in small numbers, no further away than the southern mountains of Turkey, and there are little-known relic populations in Palestine and the Sinai wilderness.[14] In eastern Russia, the Amur sub-species occupies cold temperate forest.

There are a small number of cave paintings of spotted cats, several post-glacial fossil sites in Italy, and more surprisingly, late glacial fossils in Britain. The leopard thus has as equally long a history in Europe as the lion. Furthermore, it is present in both glacial and inter-glacial periods, showing typical adaptability to forests and open mountainous or cold environments. The latest British fossils are at Robin Hood's Cave (Cresswell Crags, Derbyshire) dating to the period of intense cold of the last glaciation, and also at caves in Somerset. Its range during the Pleistocene had a northern boundary across the Midlands of Britain, through Liege, Thuringia,

Moravia and the Transylvanian Alps. Sixty-nine fossil sites were logged by Stehlin in 1933 (cited in Kurten, 1968), with Kurten commenting that there have been many more since. He assumes that leopard were about three times less abundant than lion, but also points out that solitary forest animals are less likely to be fossilized.

It seems inconceivable that the post-glacial European forests and Alpine regions did not contain leopard until even later than the lion that were a feature of ancient Greece. Yet it is entirely unclear what became of them. European leopard were larger than their African cousins, which average 70 kg. It is curious that leopard should have survived through to the last glaciation in Britain and to post-glacial times in Italy, and not have colonized the subsequent forests of this current inter-glacial as they had done in all previous inter-glacials. Their prey species would have been undiminished and this cat has a large range of adaptability, from the snowy forests and rocky wastes in cold climes to temperate and tropical woodland and savannah and desert. It would also appear to be relatively robust to human persecution, having thrived in Africa and India until recent times, and having hung on in Turkey, Palestine, the Arabian Peninsula, Persia, and eastern Russia despite human pressure. Much of this is former territory of the lion, which survived in southeast Europe well into the historical period. Is it possible that the exigencies of the fossil record, coupled with human indifference, left the leopard unnoticed and that it died out in Europe much later than supposed? Considering the late extinctions of aurochs and bison and the survival of wolf, lynx and bear in Eastern Europe, the loss of the leopard is something of a mystery.

With regard to risks to human populations from leopard, these are low when animals occupy remote areas with abundant prey – only in heavily populated areas of Africa and India do leopards regularly predate humans. However, in Britain the only areas comparable in size and prey availability to other small leopard outposts are in Scotland, where the 2000 km² Caledonian Forest core area proposed by Alan Featherstone could accommodate a small population of cold-adapted animals such as those of the Amur race. Given the sighting of black panthers in Fife and the capture of an adult puma of unknown provenance near Inverness in 1980, there may already be a naturalized population at work on the deer problem!

## Wolf

If the leopard may be regarded as of low risk to humans, despite the fear factor, the wolf has an even lower, almost zero risk, yet it has been subjected to the most persistent and effective eradication programmes visited upon any mammalian predator. By the mid-1800s it was extinct not only in Western Europe and Britain, but over the whole of the US outside

**Figure 8.4** *Wolf*
Drawing: Peter Taylor

of Alaska, bar a small island in the Great Lakes. Yet a look at where it survived in Europe – northwest Spain, Portugal, Italy, the Balkans and Greece, the Carpathians, Finland and European Russia, shows that many cultures have also tolerated its presence. For the most part, populations of this most adaptable predator have been forced to retreat to rugged mountain or forested terrain. In the areas of southern Europe where it has survived, it has done so despite a long tradition of livestock husbandry in these remoter regions.

This pattern of toleration among southern and eastern Europeans and radical extermination on the part of their western and northern counterparts may represent different economic circumstances, but there is also a powerful psychological element at work such that the wolf has become the most 'political' of animals in recent conservation programmes. It seems to inspire fear and loathing out of all proportion to its depredations on livestock, and certainly in relation to its risks to human life.

In the latter regard, there are no reliable records of serious harm to humans in Western Europe or America, yet the myth of wolf attack still survives. In Norway, recently, the government exterminated a wolf pack (at a cost of £200,000) largely due to pressure from livestock interests, but in the public debate, the concern for human life was also a major feature. In

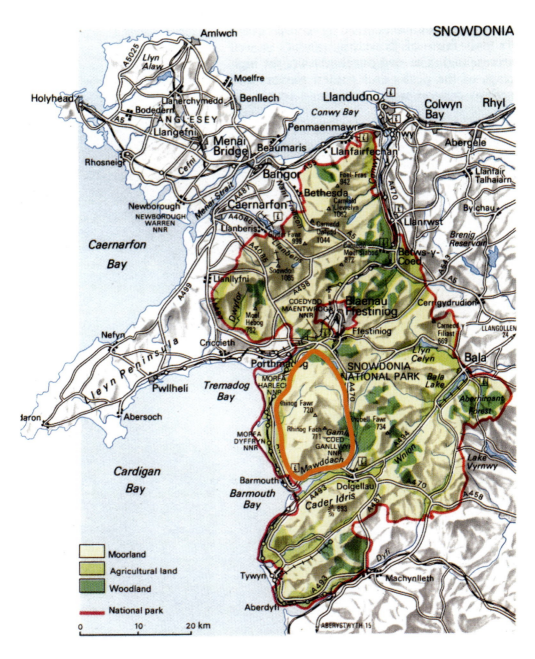

Proposed core area marked in orange

*Snowdonia National Park*

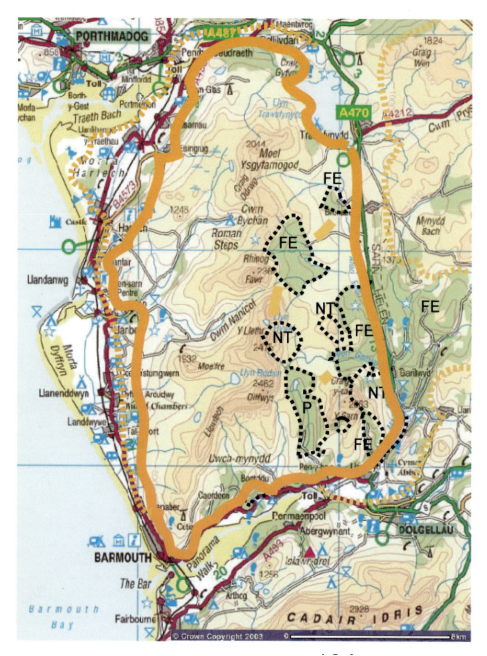

Areas in the south-east corner owned by potential cooperating partners (FE Forest Enterprise and NT National Trust). Private plantation forestry (P) could be purchased and land in-between targeted for acquisition or management agreements. The larger area outlined in orange is a potential core area, with buffer zones of wood pasture and forestry marked with dotted orange line.

*Rhinogydd*

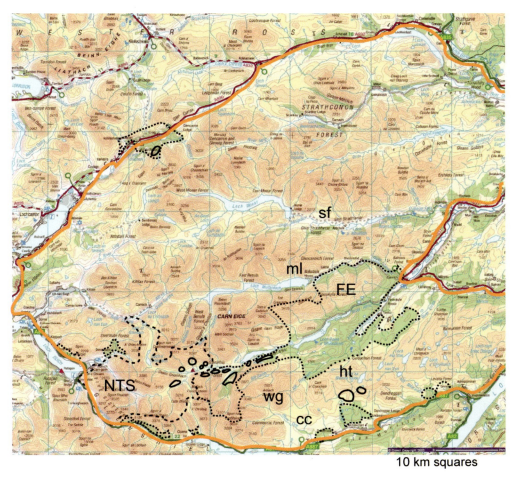

10 km squares

Reproduced from Ordnance Survey map data by permission of Ordnance Survey, © Crown copyright

| PUBLIC LAND | | | |
|---|---|---|---|
| FE | Forest Enterprise | NTS | National Trust Scotland |
| **PRIVATE ESTATES** with planting agreements | | | |
| sf | Strathfarrer | ml | Mullardoch |
| cc | Ceannacroc | ht | Hilton |
| dg | Dundreggan | wg | Wester Guisichan |

Solid line: Tfl exclosures for planting or regeneration.
Broken lines: Forest Enterprise and National Trust boundaries.
Orange line indicates extent of potential core area proposed by Trees for Life.

*The Glen Affric core area*

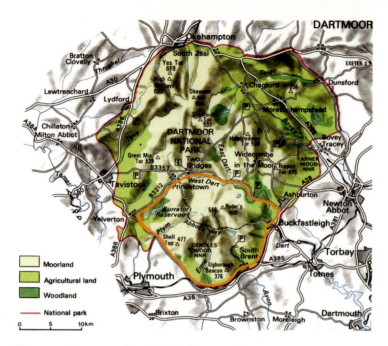

The prospective core area is outlined by the orange line.

*Dartmoor National Park*

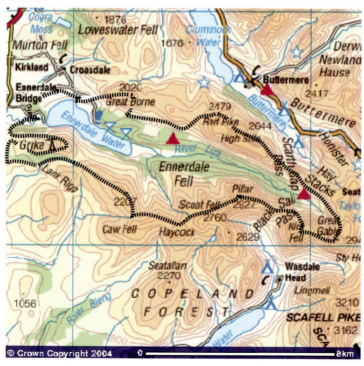

Reproduced from Ordnance Survey map data by permission of Ordnance Survey, © Crown copyright

The project area is outlined by the dashed line.

*Wild Ennerdale*

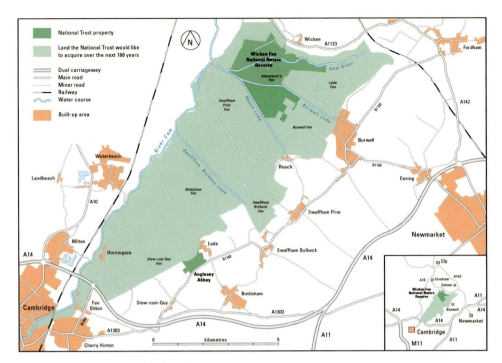

*The National Trust fenland project*

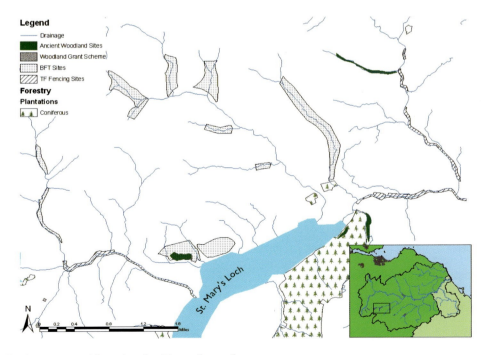

*Riparian corridors in the Tweed catchment*

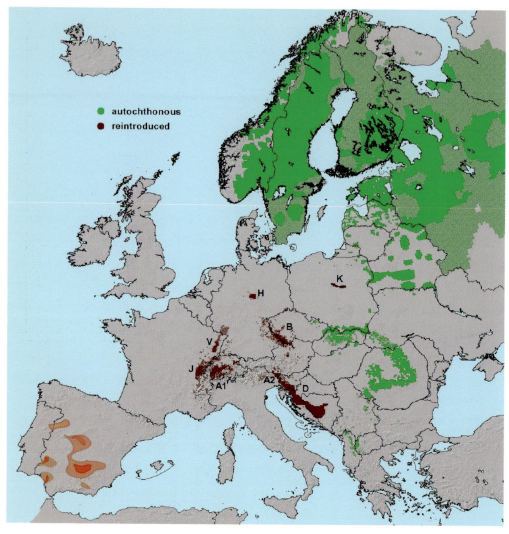

Constantly occupied areas are in darker shade. Re-introduced populations: B = Bohemian–Bavarian, D = Dinaric, A = Alpine (with western A1 and eastern A2 subpopulations), J = Jura, V = Vosges–Palatinian, K = Kampinow occurrernce, H = Harz occurrence. Orange: breeding territories (dark) and range of Iberian lynx.

*Current distribution of the Eurasian and Iberian lynx in Europe (modified from von Arx et al., 2004)*

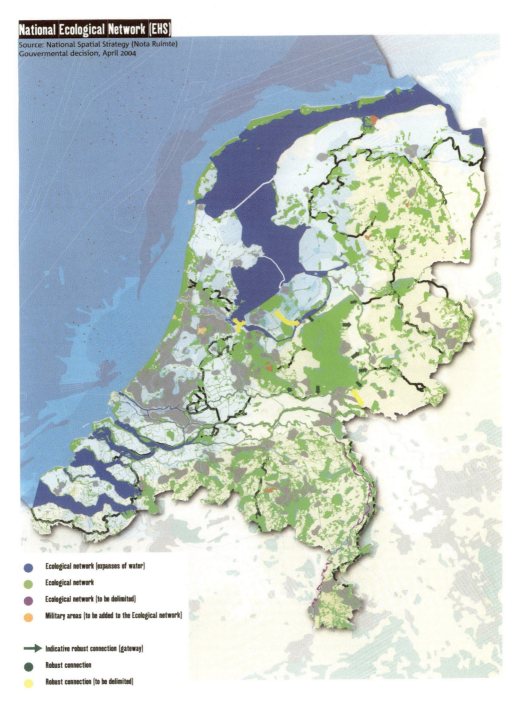

- ● Ecological network (expanses of water)
- ● Ecological network
- ● Ecological network (to be delimited)
- ● Military areas (to be added to the Ecological network)

- → Indicative robust connection (gateway)
- ● Robust connection
- ● Robust connection (to be delimited)

*Connectivity in the projected Dutch ecological network for 2018 (from Hootsmans and Kampf, 2004)*

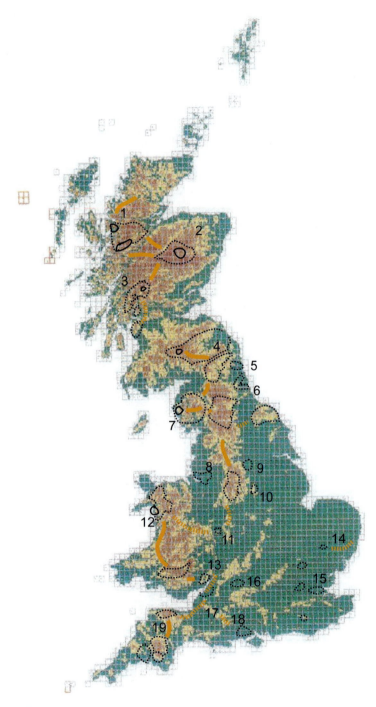

Solid line: prospective core areas.
Broken line: National Park, Community Forest and catchment project areas.
Orange line: solid – good potential for Forest Habitat Networks; broken – problematic corridors.

*Cores and connectivity*

1 Ben Eighe NNR and Affric forest initiatives.
  *Difficult to connect across the Great Glen to Cairngorm, but extendable to
  Inverpolly NNR in the north, and Knoydart to south-west.

2 Cairngorm National Park contains major wild forest reserves of RSPB at
  Abernethy and NTS Mar Lodge.
  *Connectivity south-west to Loch Lomond and Trossachs.

3 Loch Lomond and Trossachs NP contains Woodland Trust's Glen Finglas and
  RSFS Cashel Farm initiatives.
  *Connectivity to Argyl Forest Park to south, but difficult to cross Central
  Lowland area to Ayrshire Forest Park in the west or Southern Uplands in the
  east.

4 Tweed Valley Catchment project containing Carrifran in the west.
  *Good connectivity to Kielder Forest Park and Northumberland NP to South.

5 The Great North Forest.
  *Community Forest with some potential connectivity to Northumberland NP
  and Kielder.

6 The Tees Forest.
  *Community Forest on urban fringe with potential connections to North York
  Moors NP to south and Yorkshire Dales NP to the west.

7 National Trust Ennerdale project in Lake District NP.
  *Connectivity to the north-west and south-east compromised by the M6
  motorway.

8 Mersey Forest and Red Rose Community Forests are urban fringe projects
  between Liverpool and Manchester with difficult connectivity due to motorways.

9/10 South Yorkshire Forest and The Greenwood.
  *Community Forests around Sheffield and Nottingham with potential links to
  Peak District NP to the west.

11 Forest of Mercia.
  *Urban fringe Community Forest for Birmingham with Shropshire hills to the
  west, but difficult connectivity to the Pennines or to Welsh wild land.

12/13 Rhinogydd UNESCO biosphere reserve and Snowdonia NP.
  *Potential connectivity throughout Snowdonia and Cambrian Mountains south
  to Brecon Beacons NP (13) and east to Forest of Dean.

14 Cambridgeshire Fens (NT project).
  *Difficult to connect to other areas, e.g. Norfolk Broads NP to the east, Epping
  Forest and Community Forests of Thames Chase and Watling Chase north of
  London (15) or across to Great Western Forest (16) around Swindon, or to the
  Sussex Weald south of London.

17/18 The Forest of Avon.
  *Community Forest around Bristol with potential links south-west to Exmoor
  via Mendips and the Somerset levels, but difficult connectivity to Forest of Dean
  and New Forest NP (18) to the south-east.

19 Dartmoor NP.
  *The Moor Trees project could connect north to Exmoor and with Tamar
  Valley project in the west but M5 motorway is a problem for corridors to east.

February 2002 a seven-year-old boy was killed by a pack of 23 dogs running wild in a village 200 km northwest of Oslo and close to the wolf zone, yet the authorities had failed to respond to the villagers' warnings of danger after children had been harried. The dogs were subsequently shot. In the same year the Norwegian Institute for Nature Research published a report showing that in the peak periods of wolf persecution in the 19th century, when tens of thousands were killed, there was not one single record of a wolf attack. Dogs hospitalize around 4000 people a year in Norway.

In terms of livestock damage, disease, stray dogs and motor vehicles account for far greater mortality, and in modern studies in wolf areas where there are livestock, only around 1 per cent of stock are taken by wolf. Things may have been different in the 17th and 18th centuries when natural prey numbers were drastically reduced. There have also been times when human populations were more vulnerable – such as in war and famine, when wolves in Russia reportedly preyed on weakened humans. However, the depth of the response and single-mindedness of the eradication programmes is beyond rational explanation, particularly in the US, where there were vast areas of wilderness with little or no habitation or livestock.

It is as if the darkest elements of human nature – bestiality, sexual depravation, and genocidal killing, have been ascribed to one of nature's shyest and most efficient predators, one that may also be seen by the hunting and farming fraternity as a direct competitor not in terms of the damage that it can inflict, but in terms of its presence as a 'beast' of mythic proportion.


## History and ecology

The last wolf in Britain was shot in Scotland before the end of the 18th century, and by the middle of the 19th century the species had been eradicated from most of Western Europe, including the wildland of the Alps and Pyrenees. In the US the grey wolf was eradicated by the 1920s, even in the remote regions of the Rocky Mountains and the wilderness of the southwest; the red wolf of the southeast became extinct in the wild with a small population maintained in zoological parks. Ostensibly, the European persecution was driven by cattle- and sheep-farming interests, and the only strongholds left were heavily forested regions where there were few livestock, such as the Carpathians, Karelia in Russia and northwest Spain. In the US, many sub-species became extinct, and only the Canadian forests contained reservoirs from which the species could later repopulate the border forests of the northern US.[15]

Whatever the aetiology of this perverse attitude – bears get a 'better press' in fairy tales, despite their greater danger to humans – attitudes mercifully changed in the 20th century as the conservation ethic grew. In the US, there came a tolerance of wanderers from Canada, followed by an active re-introduction programme in the 1990s. In Europe there have been no direct re-introduction programmes, but the lessening of persecution has allowed wanderers to re-colonize from the eastern states, so that France, Germany, Switzerland and Norway have recently been faced with the issue of tolerating small breeding packs.[16] In Spain, the population in the northwest has remained robust and has colonized agricultural areas. In parts of Romania, the main stronghold outside of Russia, wolves are a feature of city life in Brasov much as the urban fox is in England.[17]

In all these cases of re-colonization or re-introduction, the wolf has aroused intense political debate – pitting modern conservationist ethic against fear, loathing and self-interest largely from hunting and farming communities that perceive their livelihoods to be at stake. In these debates there is a growing effectiveness of communication based upon fact, and as we see with lynx and bear re-introduction programmes, public education is crucial to the success of any project.

In terms of their ecology, wolves are the end-product of a complex of 'dog' experiments from cat-like, bear-like, hyena-like and dog-like dogs from the Eocene! All but the dog-like dogs and the racoon-dog went extinct. The first wolf appeared in the Cromerian or mid-Pleistocene (750,000 to 350,000 BP), along with the larger dire wolf, which was rare in Europe and commoner in North and South America. The dire wolf, which has a large hyena-like head, disappeared as part of the post-glacial extinction. There were also dhole (*Cuon alpinus*), or Indian hunting dog, in Europe in the immediate post-glacial times, but these are now confined to India and South East Asia. We should also note that hyena were common in Europe throughout the recent glacial and inter-glacial periods and can still be found as close as Palestine.

There are not now the huge Serengeti-like mixed populations of ungulates that were a feature of inter-glacial Europe and of the period immediately following the last ice age, and so the full ecological role of the wolf cannot be readily understood. Wolves have been reduced to living in remote mountains and forested areas, and often do not form packs.

Even in the US, the ecology of wolf as a predator of ungulates is only now being studied in depth. It is evident that a complex web of interactions exists. For example, in addition to effects upon ungulate behaviour and dispersal, the efficient kill rate of wolves has a knock-on effect on other carnivores and scavengers – bears tend to benefit by pushing wolf off the kill, whereas puma lose out, often being directly killed by the pack or chased off their own kills. Wolves also predate coyote. Data from Yellowstone is equivocal about wolf effects on numbers, as the limiting factor for elk (red deer) and moose seems to be the severity of winter. A fit adult red deer can defend itself successfully against wolf attack and therefore fawns and sick or malnourished animals are preferentially taken. In Minnesota, a non-mountainous region of extensive forests and the major US stronghold for wolves (producing 2000 cubs per year), both deer and moose numbers have increased as human hunting pressure has eased, despite the presence of wolf and bear – weather again being the limiting factor.

In Europe, the wolf has been forced to retreat to mountainous and forested regions where deer and moose are sparsely distributed. In summer the animals feed largely on rodents, hare, rabbit and roe deer; in winter they turn to bigger game such as red deer and elk. Packs tend to be small and made up of a single breeding pair and their offspring. It is perhaps not generally appreciated to what great extent the prey animals of wolves have been reduced in Europe – red deer and ibex were extinct in Switzerland, for example, by the mid-1800s, and many European countries experienced drastic reductions in large herbivore numbers. Over much of their range, loss of habitat and prey led wolf into conflict with livestock and to their subsequent persecution.

Curiously, three countries maintained a tradition of mountain pasturing of sheep using fierce shepherding breeds of dog to protect the flocks from wolf attack – Italy, Spain and Romania. In these countries livestock farmers have lived with the wolves and wolf populations have remained robust.

Wolves have a problematic relationship to domestic dogs, which they seem to single out as prey, taking almost no notice of human habitation and the risks attached. Dogs, more perhaps than any other domestic animal, have a special place in the human heart – almost diametrically opposite to that of the wolf! This has led them into conflict with shepherds and ranchers who might have otherwise tolerated the loss of small numbers of stock.

## The return

The 20th century saw an upturn in the wolf's fortune. War in Europe led to increases in wolf numbers in Eastern Europe, although the situation seemed to take a turn for the worse when Romanian livestock interests led a government-sponsored programme in which wolf numbers plummeted from a post-war high of about 5000 to less than 1000 in the 1960s. However, more enlightened attitudes in the 1970s saw the population in the Carpathians recover to about 3000 and a strengthening of immigration through Slovakia to the Czech Republic, Poland and Hungary; wolves from Croatia have expanded their range into Slovenia and the Alps. In the 1990s Poland's wolves were crossing the border into Germany, and Slovenia's had wandered to the eastern Italian Alps. There has been a steady colonization of the western Alps by wolves from northern Italy (the Apennine population) into Switzerland and France. Wanderers from the French Alps have crossed the corridor of roads into the Massif Central and recent tracks have been found in the Pyrenees.

In Scandinavia, where one might expect a more tolerant attitude from the strong wilderness ethic, wolves have nevertheless suffered eradication. In the far north, Sami herders of reindeer effectively created no-go areas for wolves. I recall on a visit to Scandinavia in 1975 how I was assured there were no wolves left in Sweden and Norway, and that one I thought I had seen crossing in front of me on a northern road at night was most unlikely to have been a wolf. However, immigrants from Finland eventually began breeding again in Sweden south of the Sami zones in the late 1980s and early 1990s, with the population now standing at about 25 individuals, some of which are breeding in Norway along the Swedish border.

The formerly robust Finnish population suffers heavy hunting pressure – there are estimated to be less than 100 animals, and 50 were shot under licence for sport in the five years to 1998. The robustness of this population was maintained by immigration from Karelian Russia, but since the break-up of the Soviet Union, the state has been heavily logged and immigration had been severely reduced by the end of the 1990s. The Russian population is estimated at between 80,000 and 120,000 individuals.

Thus, the situation in Europe is quite dynamic and one from which many lessons need to be drawn when, as is currently mooted, wolves are re-introduced to Scotland.[18] Firstly, it is obviously not necessary for wolf conservation to have a population in Britain – they would be isolated from the European gene pool. Of greater importance would be to safeguard corridors of contact between isolated populations on the Continent. Secondly, any programme aimed at restoring natural predation to the Highland deer population must expect enormous political opposition from sporting and farming interests.

It this latter regard, useful material for public education could be gleaned from experience in Minnesota, where there are information centres with wolf-watching facilities (penned areas). In most areas of that state, hunters take 20–30 per cent of the deer population, and wolves take 5 per cent. Wolf predation is not the limiting factor for deer herds – as most of the animals they take would not survive the winters anyway (natural fawn mortality can be 70 per cent). However, herds are likely to be fitter, and by being dispersed, in better balance with the vegetation. In Scotland the wolf areas would not extend over the large areas currently over-populated with deer, and wolf predation would not affect sport shooting, as wolf seldom predate the larger males of interest to hunters.

We could anticipate that when considering the core areas around Glen Affric, that a robust population would produce wanderers and colonizers of other areas. Issues would arise of culling, sporting licences, and the killing or trapping of individuals that persistently attacked domestic stock or domestic dogs. It is unlikely that Britain's upland sheep economy, already massively subsidized and vulnerable, could take on board the changes in shepherding practices that have worked well in Southern and Eastern Europe. For this reason, the spread of wolves to southern areas of Scotland and the forests of Northumberland (surrounded by sheep country) is unlikely to be tolerated.

This situation would change, however, if the upland economy were to evolve in favour of forestry and smaller-scale livestock husbandry in wood-pasture systems involving hardy cattle – and we shall examine this in discussions of future strategies for re-wilding large areas.

## Problems of re-introduction

The re-introduction of wolf thus faces an array of political problems contingent upon the poor level of education and understanding that exists among both urban and rural people in Britain. Farmers may be foremost in opposition, but the wolf might also excite the interest of animal rights groups unhappy about the 'cruel' end suffered by deer, or even by those who welcome the wolf but oppose any shooting of 'offending' animals.

Sporting groups have also proven remarkably irrational and resistant to factual data. Foxes currently cause economic losses, especially in upland sheep country, and yet they have not been subject to extermination policies. Wolves will predate fox in Europe (as will lynx), and if they have a choice of large ungulate prey, prefer that to sheep, whereas fox do not have the same choice and predate the more vulnerable lambs.

In northern Spain, where wolf numbers have been robust and where economic conditions are difficult, the local authorities have auctioned three licences per year for sport shooting at £4000 per wolf, but there is no effective compensation scheme.[19] Of the 1500 population, 700 are thought to be killed annually because of this failure to compensate for damage.

In Poland as late as 1998, with a population of 600–800 animals, permits were issued to shoot 90. In Norway there has been a very public battle between conservationists on the one hand and hunters and sheep farmers on the other. The Government initially veered towards eradication of a pack that had set up close to the Swedish border, but then agreed to designate wolf zones and no-go areas. Wolves would be allowed in the Osterdalen valley where there are moose and deer, but in neighbouring areas of sheep rearing, over £1 million has been spent to hunt down errant wolves (a wolf kill costs about £17,000). In the 1990s 425 sheep were killed and compensation paid.

Similar problems of acceptance have emerged in France, where two individuals appeared in Mercantour National Park close to the Italian border in 1992. By 1997 there were 20–25 animals, but illegal killing reduced this to 12–15 by the following year. The local administration appeared to collude in the deaths, with little effort expended on either public acceptance campaigns or investigating the deaths. Sheep losses over the period 1993–2000 averaged less than 500/year and £200,000 per year was being paid in compensation ('News of the Earth', *BBC Wildlife*, August 1999). If these statistics are correct, then compensation is running at £400 per animal! However, central government is also spending on guard-dog training schemes and new pens for better protection, and appears committed to allowing the wolves to return.

As with the task of tolerating lynx or bear, stakeholders may use misinformation and local politics to gain public support and flout the legal protection afforded wolves in the European Union. In a report in the *Times* (12 February 2001), a Norwegian sheep farmer named Ulvik (ironically Norwegian for Wolf!) related how she was kept awake at night at the thought of what wolves could be doing to her sheep up on the mountain – yet she was not pressed for statistics on lambing deaths, fox attacks, or disease from sheep essentially left out in the elements because it is not economic to provide better care.[20] Likewise, the hunting fraternity often accounts for very large takes of ungulate meat – in Brandenburg, for example, 4.7 million kilograms of game were killed in 1991–1992 in an area of 29,000 km² – adequate to support 2500 wolves. In many such circumstances, stray dogs and foxes exact a far heavier toll on sheep, as do motor vehicles on deer.

The risks to humans have proven almost non-existent in recent decades. There were no documented serious attacks on people in the US or Canada in the 20th century, and none in Western Europe. North American experience is not very relevant to Europe – wolves populate areas where they do not come into regular contact with humans, and a policy of segregation operates. In Western Europe there is not the option of segregated areas and wolves usually maintain their distance from habitation after centuries of persecution. In modern times when they may be protected and tolerated, problems could arise if wolves became over-familiar. For example, there was a recent wolf attack on Vancouver Island as a result of the public feeding local 'friendly' wolves – the person concerned panicked on contact and lost a part of his scalp.[21]

The 'urban' wolves in Carpathian towns appear to present no problems as they scavenge on rubbish tips (as do bears) and are regularly seen walking past residential areas early in the morning! Domestic dogs are at greatest risk from these interlopers, who breed within a few kilometres of the city limits and will kill small dogs. The embryonic population in Germany suffers the reverse: inter-breeding with domestic dog, leading to concern for genetic purity. The offending hybrids were live-captured – Ilka Reinhardt gives an account of the problems of this pack that lives close to an industrial town in *ECOS* 25 (3/4).

Given that wolves are now returning to their old ranges in the Alps, the forests of Saxony in Germany, possibly also the Pyrenees, and are encouraged to do so by enlightened governments, there is every chance that a future for them could exist in Scotland. In many respects it is more suitable as a habitat. Wolves from problematic populations in Norway and Sweden would be the obvious candidates, although some consideration should be given to cross-breeding this stock with the Spanish or Eastern European wolves to increase the genetic diversity of what would be an inbreeding British population.

This would, however, also be a European precedent; there have been no deliberate translocations of wolves. The current expansion has occurred due to the persistent movement of individuals from core areas in the eastern countries. The first appearances have met with hostility and commonly the death of the animals concerned. This was the case in Norway and Hungary, countries not bound by the Berne Convention. Even after a decade of breeding, as in the case of the French Alps, the populations are not secure from local efforts to eradicate the animals by shooting or poisoning.[22]

The situation requires some thought: if newly established populations are allowed to prosper, they will then start to colonize other areas with less-optimal habitat and availability of wild prey. Compensation schemes could then prove expensive. Also, measures to deal with wolves in areas where they are not welcome – as in the Norwegian experience – are likely to attract protest from animal welfare groups.

We can turn to the US for some insight into the problems of translocation and re-introduction of animals to their former range. As noted, after decades of government-sponsored eradication, the grey wolf was absent over virtually all of its historic range, and some sub-species, such as the plains wolf, became extinct. There was a small remnant population in Wisconsin, Michigan and the Minnesota woods, and the latter began to prosper under protection as an endangered species to reach over 2000 by the end of the 20th century. In the last few decades, wanderers from Canada began to appear in the Glacier National Park in Montana and the Cascades Range in Washington State. In 1995 and 1996, 65 wolves were captured in British Colombia and Alberta and released into Yellowstone National Park and the Idaho Sawtooth Wilderness. The introduced packs were doubling their numbers each year.

The success of the re-introductions was by no means problem-free. Intense opposition from ranching interests led at one point to a judicial order to remove the wolves from the Yellowstone National Park. The re-introduced packs had been accorded the status of 'experimental, non-essential' and hence could legally be captured and returned to Canada or destroyed. The Canadian government refused to take them back, as did zoos, and the judicial ruling was overturned on appeal. However, a large part of the success against the livestock lobby was an efficient compensation scheme at full market value, as well as extensive public education and majority support for the project. There are schemes now mooted for the Olympic peninsula in Washington State with funding of $200,000 for a feasibility study.

The future of the grey wolf in the northwestern states now looks assured, as many areas suffer from overgrazing by moose and red deer. In addition, Yellowstone has proven the tourist value of wolf, with additional income from visitors travelling great distances to see wolves. For the Park the annual 'existence' value is estimated at £5 million, and for the states of Montana, Wyoming and Idaho, business worth £15 million per annum has been generated. This experience has shown that appropriate education, public relations, and compensation schemes, together with the marketing of wolf eco-tourism can win over entrenched interests from the livestock and hunting fraternity.[23]

There has also been a recovery plan for the southern Mexican wolf, C. *Lupus baileyi*, which many regard as extinct in the wild, although there may be a few still living in remote areas of northern Mexico. Any wanderers into the US had previously been shot on sight by cattlemen. Between 1977 and 1980 the last known wolves in Mexico were captured and taken to the US as part of a captive breeding programme. There is now a captive population of 169 in the US and Mexico, and in 1997 a holding area was created in the Apache National Forest of Arizona for release into the Blue Range Mountains. In March 1998 three packs comprising 11 individuals were released, but by November half had been shot and the remainder recaptured.[24]

The programme is still moving ahead with new pairings and releases and has so far cost $7 million over 20 years. The losses have been due in part to local hostility, but road deaths and virus infection from domestic dogs have played a part. The captive-bred wolves also have to learn how to survive in the wild – which Yellowstone's wolves, wild-captured in Canada, did not. This programme has also failed to get sufficient local support or revenue for local businesses in what is a relatively unvisited area dependent upon ranching and hunting permits. Attacks on cattle and valuable cattle dogs have been frequent. It is an uphill task made worse perhaps by selecting areas that were too poor in natural prey and too close to ranching land. Greater success is anticipated for releases into the much larger adjacent Gila Wilderness in New Mexico. These programmes should yield useful lessons for British projects of re-introduction as compared to the European experience of repopulation by migrant individuals.

## Bear

The bear is the last of the usual 'big three' carnivores (with lynx and wolf) that are considered for re-introduction in Britain. It shares with the lynx

**Figure 8.5** *Bear*
Drawing: Peter Taylor

various programmes in Europe of active translocation, but not the release of captive-bred animals. However, the brown bear *Ursus arctos* is not *primarily* a carnivore, being largely vegetarian (approximately 75 per cent). Its main diet is a mixture of roots, tubers, fruit and berries, as well as grubs and, of course, honey! The remaining 25 per cent consists largely of young mammals, such as deer, or carrion. In wolf country it will often succeed in taking over kills.

As an opportunistic predator of stock, with perhaps an undeserved reputation for ferocity in relation to man, it has been persecuted and eradicated over its former range in Western Europe. It has managed to hang on in Northern Spain's Cantabrian Mountains, the western Pyrenees, Finnish forests, the Apennines of Italy and in the Balkans, with its main strongholds in the east, the Romanian Carpathians and Russian Karelia. As with the wolf, eastern immigrants have repopulated Sweden and Norway and moved into the eastern Alps. The French authorities, alarmed at the dwindling population in the Pyrenees, began a translocation programme in the 1990s using wild-caught Slovenian stock; Austria has also undertaken a project.[25]

Bears present bigger problems than lynx or wolf. Finding suitable habitat is not a simple matter because the original flora, rather than an abundance of ungulate prey, must provide its basic needs. This requires substantial areas of relatively natural forest and remnant bear populations have remained small and fragmented despite several decades of legal protection. Such forest is still common in Eastern Europe and Scandinavia, but has undergone severe degradation in northern Spain and the Pyrenees, where both populations are now close to extinction. In such cases, translocation is unlikely to help – the forests themselves require better protection. Brown bears seem to require a degree of remoteness and a lack of disturbance, unlike their black bear cousins.

The European brown bear is the same species as the American grizzly, but much smaller and far less of a risk to humans. Grizzlies account for several fatalities a year in the US and Canada, but their European cousins are far less aggressive. In Scandinavia there was only one fatality from unprovoked attack in the whole of the 20th century, but in Romania, where bears and humans regularly encounter each other in mountain pastures, Macdonald reports 12 people were killed and 94 injured over a recent eight-year period.[26]

## Re-introducing the bear to Britain

Reasons for re-introducing the brown bear to Britain cannot readily encompass arguments based upon a keystone ecological function, nor could we argue that a British population would contribute to a European or worldwide species conservation programme. We are left with the simple argument of wholeness: the forest is incomplete without the bear. It is therefore unashamedly our own sense of loss that would motivate its restoration.

The time of the bear's disappearance in Britain is not recorded with as much certainty as the wolf. Rather like the lynx, it disappeared sometime after the Roman occupation. Its Welsh name of aarth gives the Artro river in the Rhinogydd its name, as it does to Arthur, the bear-king, at a time when Celtic clans may still have had shamanic connections to totem animals. In common with traditions in North America, the bear 'holds the dream' and sleeps to awaken, as Arthur in prophesy would to reinstigate Albion, the sacred relationship to the land.

It is doubtful if anywhere other than the Scottish core area would be large enough to sustain what would be an isolated population. In this respect, the carrying capacity of these western glens is a matter for further research. The area has been severely over-grazed by deer for centuries and the structure of the crucial understorey of shrubs has been altered. Comparisons of the flora of these areas with parts of northern Sweden would be instructive and it would be likely that animals from this area, rather than the more productive regions of Slovenia, where stock has been sourced for the Pyrenees, would be the best candidates for re-introduction. Northern animals are larger and adapted to longer winters. In Roman times, the Caledonian bear was fabled as the largest and fiercest bear in the amphitheatre.

## History and ecology of the European bear

The brown bear appears to have evolved in Eurasia in the late Pleistocene, from whence it colonized North America after the last glaciation. In

Western Europe it appeared to coexist with the cave bear *Ursus spelaeus* until the latter died out in the immediate post-glacial faunal extinction – either due to the activity of man, or competition with *U. arctos*. It became the most widespread and variable of all the bears – ranging from the 1000 kg colossus of the Kodiak islands of Alaska to the 250 kg *U. a. pyrenaica*, and in colouration from almost black in Siberia to pale fawn in the arid zones of Central Asia. A small population lives in the Gobi Desert, and the species is very adaptable, able to occupy the alpine and tundra zones, boreal and temperate forests, steppe and desert.

The ecological element of most relevance to any re-introduction pro-gramme for Britain is the home range. This differs for males and females.[27] The males are solitary and the female forms a family unit, staying with her cubs for two years. Thus, female territories are smaller, in Scandinavia 120–130 km$^2$, whereas males encompass a territory of 1500 km$^2$. Alpine bears have smaller ranges, sometimes remaining in a single valley of 60 km$^2$. The Sarek reserve in northern Sweden supported bears throughout the period of persecution in the 19th and early 20th centuries and encompasses about 3600 km$^2$ but has a further 2000 km$^2$ of protected zones around it. It can clearly be seen that the Caledonian proposal would support only a small population of 10–20 family groups and only two or three territories for the males (assuming first that the degraded forest is allowed to regenerate). Such a population might be self-sustaining but it can also be expected to export wandering males and this underlies the need for wildlife-friendly corridors.

The recent history of bears in Europe is one of precipitous decline, eventual protection, and then re-colonization from the east, with a few programmes of translocation. Bear hunting in Scandinavia was a cultural activity until early in the 20th century, and by that time bears were restricted to the far north of Sweden. After protection, numbers gradually increased in Sweden – a rise from 300 in 1952 to 600 in 1980, and in Norway from 50 in 1960 to 150–230 in 1986. In Finland the population increased slightly from 400 in 1979 to 450 in 1985 and there is still migration from Karelia where there are approximately 3000. The popula-tion in the rest of European Russia rose from 20,000 in 1979 to 30,000 in 1983 and has always been regarded as stable – though increased logging in the boreal forest in the 1990s must have had some impact. The animals are afforded protection in Norway and Sweden but in the latter a maximum annual kill of 5 per cent has been allowed; however, no licences were required in Finland where hunting has been severe and the population maintained by immigration.

The Eastern European or Carpathian population also experienced an increase in the latter half of the 20th century, from Poland (40 in the Tatra), the Czech Republic and Slovakia (400 in 1979, 700 in 1988), and Romania (5700 in 1979, 6300 in 1988) and is regarded as stable and at the optimum for the habitats, though there have been recent doubts about Romanian population estimates. Poland re-introduced bear to the Bialowieza forest in the 1950s but there have been no recent reports.

The Balkan population has not fared so well. Between 1954 and 1979 the Yugoslavian population increased from 700 to 2600 and there was contact with the Greek population (100 in 1979), Bulgarian (450 in 1959, 850 in 1987) and Albanian populations (500–800 in 1987). However, recent wars and increased economic deprivation have taken a toll. The pre-war Bosnian population stood at 1300 but reports of virtual eradication of game and illegal shooting, plus bear casualties from innumerable land-mines, and the collapsed state of an economy where wildlife, once a valued heritage, is now a luxury, do not bode well for the future.[28]

However, the Dinaric Alps of Slovenia have fared better with a modern estimate of 400, and wild-captured Slovenian bears have been an export item to Austria and France, as well as providing a migration route into the Italian Alps. The alpine population in Italy numbers about 10–15, whereas the long-surviving population of the subspecies *U. a. marsicanus* in the Apennines (Abruzzi region) numbers 35–60. A few breeding bears are reported from the Austrian Gaitalier Alps and Otztal, where three Slovenian bears were released but the release programme was halted due to local pressure, particularly from bee keepers.

Further west the populations have declined. In the Pyrenees the bear hung on after centuries of persecution by shepherds in some of the eastern valleys and numbered about 200 in the late 1930s, dwindling to less than 20 by the late 1980s. The last stronghold of the French population, in the Val d'Aspe, was threatened in the 1990s with the upgrading of a little-used road through the region and the building of yet another tunnel to Spain. That this should happen in an EU country committed by law to protect the habitat of an endangered species is hard to comprehend. As if in recompense (there was considerable public outcry), the French government instigated the translocation programme with Slovenian bears to augment the population of this recognized sub-species *U. a. pyrenaicus*. The population – the only bears in France since extinction of the Alpine population in 1937, was optimistically estimated at 20–30 in 1987, but by the mid-1990s it was doubted if more than five bears survived. The authorities licenced logging roads in the last of the key areas at the same time as compensation schemes for shepherds and the announcement of a translocation programme! Such translocation programmes cannot be regarded as sensible as long as the basic habitat needs of the bears are not respected.

The translocation programme began in 1996 with three Slovenian bears and an allocated budget of £1.1 million, 75 per cent provided by the European Union's LIFE programme. One bear was killed by a French hunter 16 months after release, the hunter claiming to have fired in self-defence. This bear had three cubs with two known to have survived. One other bear crossed into Spain and was also later killed by hunters. The hunting fraternity in Spain have been virulently opposed to the French scheme. Again, the local hunting and shepherding interests are responding largely out of ignorance and long-standing prejudice, seeing bears as an indication of a past history of rural backwardness. This irrationality is born out by the small scale of the bear's depredation on stock in Spain (4 sheep were killed compared to the 3000 killed by dogs, avalanches and lightning in the same time period). However, future co-operation between French and Catalonian authorities looks likely, and the former government is committed to the translocation programme. It remains to be seen whether the habitats get the restoration they need, particularly the closing of logging roads.

Further west in the Cantabrican Mountains, the traditional stronghold of *U. a. pyrenaicus*, the same story of habitat destruction and decline, despite legal protection of the animals, has left the Spanish bear on the brink of extinction. In 1986 the population had been estimated at 100 and had declined to 70 by 1990 – a 30 per cent drop in 4 years! In addition to habitat fragmentation, largely due to EU-funded infrastructural projects such as hydro-electric dams, reservoirs for irrigation, new roads and tourist developments, all in or near prime bear habitat such that migration routes are affected, the population also suffers a high level of poaching by trophy hunters. Only in the last decade did the government instigate an effective compensation scheme for livestock and beehive damage, thus reducing vengeance killing.

In response to the precipitous decline, the local governments of Asturias and Castilla-Leon have instigated a 'bear recuperation plan' over 200,000 ha of the prime bear territory, and this includes the appointment of forest guards and heavy fines and prison sentences for poachers. In Castilla-Leon two large natural parks were announced with strict protection over 320,000 ha of bear territory. However, these measures apply largely to the protection of the animals themselves and these areas are still subject to roads and hydro-electric projects that will fragment the habitat.

There appear to have been few attempts at eco-tourism in relation to bear populations. It might be expected that bear would be as much a draw in Europe as wolf have been in Yellowstone. The brown bear has the disadvantage of not howling or making itself very visible, but it ought to be possible to further eco-tourism in the region based upon the presence of bears and the quality of some of the remaining forests. In a recent visit to the Large Carnivore Initiative for Europe (LCIE) project in the Carpathians, local eco-tourist enterprises reported success with bear-watching at carefully selected feeding sites supported by forestry authorities. In this area, bear hunting (with trophy licences fetching $10,000, a very large sum by rural Romanian standards) has been a major source of revenue for the State and local hunting fraternities that now own much of the forests. The annual cull is estimated at 10 per cent of a population of between 3000 and 5000 bears, but there are some doubts expressed by LCIE experts and naturalists in Romania as to the accuracy of population data.

One site on the edge of Brasov, Romania's second city, can almost guarantee a night-time close encounter with bear – as close as 20 m, unguarded and unregulated, by the light of a street lamp on the edge of a housing estate, as the local bears forage in the rubbish skips! As a result, taxis and small mini-buses can be seen parked after 10 pm in the small service road to the flats. While I was there, reckless teenagers taunted the very skittish bears, and so far there have been no casualties. The Romanians take a commendably relaxed view of these risks. Though this would provide an ideal opportunity for a commercial enterprise and for education (and safeguards), something of an unlicensed wild-night experience would then be lost.

## Other predators: the wildcat, polecat and marten

The large carnivores tend to get special treatment in the discussion of re-wilding because they have keystone status in the regulation of ungulate numbers and grazing behaviour. However, in Britain consideration also needs to be given to the smaller carnivores that are absent due to a long history of persecution. Scotland still has wildcat and pine marten, but the wildcat is extinct in England and Wales; the marten's status in the core area of the Rhinogydd is uncertain, though there are continuous records from other parts of Snowdonia and sparingly from the Cambrian mountains; the marten is long absent from Dartmoor. The Joint Nature Conservancy Council and the Vincent Wildlife Trust have carried out recent surveys and found the pine marten still hanging on in its traditional relict areas of the North Pennines, North York Moors and the eastern Lake District – though the positive data is dependent mostly on sighting and a few road kills, scat surveys showing very few signs in these areas. The Vincent Wildlife Trust's view was that re-introductions into these areas should await further research, but that a more southerly outpost (such as Dartmoor would provide) could be appropriate.

The pine marten is a secretive, nocturnal animal, with ranges in Scotland where it is largely confined to pine forest, varying from 250 ha to 3400 ha of woodland. Its main food in Caledon is field vole. In Ireland, populations can be denser, with one 140 ha woodland site supporting 10–12 animals, feeding largely on birds and berries. Although a woodland animal in Scotland, in much of Ireland and apparently also in England and Wales, it prefers rocky crags and scrub.

The polecat was extinct in Scotland until re-introduced to the Western Highlands and has maintained an expanding population in Wales; it certainly occurs in the Rhinogydd, but is still absent from Dartmoor, where it could readily be re-introduced to the core area.

There have been no proposals to bring back the wildcat to Wales or England, in part, perhaps, because of the large population of feral cats and the certainty of cross-breeding. With regard to genetic purity of wildcats, studies in its European strongholds have shown 40–70 per cent remain pure bred even in the presence of feral cats. This is another example of scientific values that may be out-dated. The domestic cat is the same species and inter-breeding with feral cats may well lead to improvements in the species overall functional capabilities. Throughout its range, the wildcat is a forest animal, preferring large undisturbed areas. Any population of feral-cat hybrids would likely occupy those areas on the fringe of such forests, areas which are in themselves already replete with artificial habitat and alien species – thus, on a functional level, a wild/feral predator would be an asset. The fabled 'Kellas cat' in Scotland – a very large black feral–wildcat hybrid, appears to be an instance where a new phenotype could evolve. I have seen large, wild black feral cats in the Rhinogydd that have raised kits in the woods adjacent to agricultural land and been efficient predators of squirrels and rats.

If the fringe areas of the Rhinog are home to feral cats, how much more beneficial and closer to the natural situation it would be if there were wildcats in the remoter parts of the hills and forests, even assuming there was some interbreeding in the less wild parts of their range. As efficient predators of rabbits, rats and squirrels they would go some way to redressing the balance of these populations, and should be considered as introductions for the large areas of forest in northern Britain, such as Kielder, areas of the Lake District and North Wales. This would parallel a project in Bavaria where a programme begun in the 1980s has so far re-introduced 350 captive-bred wildcat and has recently started radio-tracking studies.

The otter is present in all three core areas, although it declined in the last few decades in Snowdonia for no apparent reason, and only in the last ten years has it begun to recover on the Afon Dwyryd, spreading up into the Rhinog. It has also recovered on Dartmoor.

The status of the American mink in the core areas is uncertain, but this is an 'alien' species that is doubtless here to stay. It causes much consternation: being held accountable for the demise of the water vole as well as impacts on waterfowl and fisheries. It is perhaps less well appreciated that Europe has its own mink, *Mustela lutreola*, which has been persecuted to such a degree that it hangs on in southwest France, parts of Spain and eastern Europe only. It is virtually indistinguishable in the field from the American species. This is a good example of an 'alien' causing a functional replacement where the European species has disappeared, and it may have a competitive edge in the European strongholds. Thus, our own wildlife would probably have had to adapt to this predator, were it not for the fortunes of post-glacial geology and the English Channel. There is also some evidence that where otter have recovered from former persecution, mink have declined.

## Concluding on predators

There can be little doubt that the demise of British as well as European predators has been as much a consequence of human fear and irrationality as of economic damage or loss of habitat. In Eastern Europe the risks to life as well as stock are balanced by acceptance as well as some economic gain from hunting. Throughout Europe stock losses are now compensated. Habitat fragmentation has seriously affected lynx and bear, though the wolf has proven more adaptable, and new programmes of larger reserves and wildland corridors, together with strategic translocations, have some potential to allow numbers to recover. As the paradigm shifts towards the re-instatement of natural processes over larger areas, particularly with wild grazers, British wildland proponents must begin to consider the re-introduction of lynx, wolf and possibly also the bear and hence the reinstatement of predator–prey dynamics.

Even without these charismatic animals (which it has to be admitted, are very hard to see in the wild), consideration of extending the range of the smaller predators is long overdue.

# 9

# The Healing Forest

One morning, in the first year of my time at Llety'r Fwyalchen, with the dew still heavy and the air cold, I walked out and no more than 10 m from the house I found a grass snake coiled on the path. I instantly leapt, grabbed it by the throat, bundled it into a lidded bucket and hurried back to the house to get my camera. Slowly I leant the bucket on its side and waited for the snake to emerge into the picturesque background of pond and rockery that I had created. For a few seconds nothing happened, then suddenly there was a blur of movement as the angry snake rocketed out and into the greenery before I could fire the shutter. I sat contemplating what I had done. Old responses, old habits. I could have knelt down slowly and quietly at the first encounter, closed my eyes and awaited the images or thoughts that might then have flowed onto the screen of my receptivity. And the snake – of all the symbols, of all the opportunities! It never happened again in the seven years that followed. It would take six years to break the habits of a lifetime of separation, objectification and use of nature for my own personal ends.

In relating the account of my time in Coed Eryri, I shared something of the healing that I experienced in my contact with the deeper ecology of the forest. I had come to the mountains with a deep malaise – a division of masculine and feminine, rational and intuitive, and that habitual objectify-ing of the natural world. I recoil now at my behaviour in those first few months, but I gradually became alert to every visitor, from the small and exotic humming bird hawk-moth that stayed for hours at the honeysuckle, or the magnificent Iceland falcon that quartered overhead only a few months after I had wandered the wastes of its homeland hoping but failing to catch a glimpse. I became accustomed to listening to the inner whispers of knowledge that every bird, or tree or flower could precipitate and there grew the slow realization that whatever voice it was that spoke, or image that formed, it always had relevance for my own personal unfolding.

The truth of the eastern sages, that there is no real separation but a continuum of consciousness, began to dawn in the simplest of its meanings – all beings are dancing within a greater dance of space and time, and that dance is choreographed. Synchronicity rather than coincidence is the unavoidable consequence. Whether one *realizes* this nature of things, is simply a matter of awareness. What begins at first as openness and acceptance of the *possibility* evolves into a knowledge based upon the reality of experience.

This is ultimately what I had been moving towards in yogic and shamanic training.[1] It did not conflict with science, but complemented it. Science is mental knowledge gained from separation and observation. There is another knowledge gained from unified consciousness – a world of feeling, intuition and dream. We can choose to operate from either mode and there is no contradiction. The question is – what benefits may come from each? What can come from *feeling* the flight of a raven or falcon as if you *are* it, or reading portents from encounters, or taking a lesson in patience and timing from a young osprey waiting for hours, head bobbing, assessing the distance to the fish, their closeness to the surface, and timing its foray to perfection? In receptive mode, there is enjoyment, and awe and mystery, but mystics have never held much appeal in this our modern culture. With science and medicine we can cure the sick and feed the hungry, yet such knowledge when allied to greed, fear and aggression has also caused us to pillage the planet, prosecute ever more horrific warfare, expand our population to breaking point and provoke a destabilization of the global ecosystem.

It is well appreciated that we are at a major turning point in our evolutionary history. Popular writers such as Bill McKibben in *The End of Nature* and more recently Colin Mason's *The 2030 Spike* have communicated the message of the scientific community's warnings about the greenhouse effect and carbon dioxide emissions. Humanity is now the single most pervading ecological force on the planet, and sometime within the next few decades a number of factors will combine to bring about massive change. Either humanity wakes up to the scale of cooperative response required, or large-scale famine and resource wars will become all-pervasive.

Despite there being widespread agreement on the urgency [with some dissent from the eternal optimists represented by writers such as Lomborg (2001) and governments unduly influenced by global business interests], no real progress has been made in the decade since the Rio Declaration. How is it possible for governments to ignore substantial majority opinion and do so little? Why do so many people simply shrug their shoulders and accept this situation? I can find no answer in any of the sciences. Economists have supposed a collective individual self-serving model of an essentially unconscious mechanistic market – but I find that model simply serves the political ideology of the elites who benefit from that particular political economy. There are also powerful motivations towards cooperative structures, community, aid and ecological sustainability. The question we have to ask is why the balance is one way rather than the other, and through what means we may bring about a rebalancing. This, I would suggest, is the most urgent of 'healing' missions.

It is my intuitive feeling that beneath the conscious motives of national security and economic interest, lies a primal fear of nature and her cycles of abundance and scarcity, growth and death, vibrancy and decay.[2] How else are we to explain the irrational consumer behaviour that accumulates not only vast wealth, but results in an obesity problem and an obsession with security that characterizes the world's leading economic power?

This power has set the political agenda on a global level, even in the widespread opposition that manifests in reaction to it. In the previous century, that opposition took the form of collectivized power versus the supposed power of individual freedom – both calling themselves democratic, and both pursuing an essentially materialistic and technocratic agenda of security. In this century, the opposition to what is now called 'modernity' has evolved into something almost tribal and theocratic. Each of these forces appears disconnected from feminine values of love, community and ecology. They are locked in combat, as if fighting their own shadows and fearful projections, and in that, they effectively lock up the creative resource and prospective future of humanity. This single failure must rank as the greatest threat to a harmonious ecological outcome as we approach the 2030 spike.

Yet, how often do we see the issues of world peace, terrorism and global security connected to our conservation agenda? Briefly and distantly at the Rio Declaration and Agenda 21; but hardly at all in the day-to-day workings of nature reserves, Wildlife Trusts or the Joint Nature Conservation Committee. Wildlife and nature conservation are backwaters of the psyche. We have failed to take on the message of Rio: that everything we do has consequence in physical ecological terms; and even more so, that underlying our failure must lie a form of cultural denial that prevents that action.

In this chapter I want to approach this malaise: the lack of will, the cultural denial and the prospective power of nature, as symbolized by the forest, to work as an ally in the healing process. In the final chapter I shall propose that this country undertake a major initiative demonstrating a commitment to natural process and cycles, based not upon survivalist rhetoric, but on the sacredness of nature and its power to heal the human condition.

## A healing peace

Peace is more than the absence of war. In that kind of peace, the manic consumerism of materialist culture will just as severely invade that peace, albeit in two or three decades. Peace must embody a calming of that materialist frenzy. It is my understanding that to become truly peaceful, the human psyche must be at peace with the dark aspects of its own nature, and for that, in my own experience, there has to be contact with the deeper security that lies *within* nature.

This level of awareness cannot come from objective study. The so-called 'laws of nature' will reveal only the patterns. If conservation as an endeavour limits itself to the scientific and eco-tourist paradigm it now so strongly embraces, it surely will be sidelined in the immense conflict and bonfire of resources that now looms. There is a chance, I believe, to turn things round – it requires the embracing of the power of nature to heal the human soul. If we can acknowledge this and begin to put our immense wealth and resources into restoring the earth, then I think we have a chance.

Is there a single element of natural wisdom that is so fundamental and able to be grasped by everyone and that has the power to cause the necessary shift? I think there can be only one. If one watches the natural world as much with the inner eye as the outer, if one becomes receptive to the feeling nature of ourselves as well as the feeling in nature around us, then something inescapable arises in consciousness – everything about us is in peace. Paradoxically, this includes predator and prey alike.[3] Yet this peace is inordinately difficult to feel and to foster. Our Western industrialized stimulated minds are constantly in motion, thinking about yesterday and tomorrow, memories and fantasy, and above all, worry. The Western economy is geared to the perpetuation of worry. To be at peace and happy with what one has, would bring the whole unstable edifice crashing down. A mere 1 per cent fall in consumer spending, or even a failure of year-on-year growth, is seen as threatening 'the economy' in terms of unemployment and social instability.

We in the industrialized nations have become so accustomed to worry and stress that it is hard to imagine a contented state of peace, abundance and a world without striving to improve one's circumstances. When industrial nations imperialized tribal societies they lampooned their lack of industriousness, seeing contentedness as laziness or fecklessness. Yet these societies were in balance with their resources. Most had a conception of the earth as a benevolent mother. Indigenous peoples knew the mother earth's graces and her dangers. Indeed, even some of the spiritual teachers at the foundation of the great civilized religions, who were in themselves non-industrial, indigenous and tribal, have extolled those graces and taught their disciples the fundamentals of trusting the divine purpose that flows all about them.[4]

Such a trust – that would transcend the basic fears of enemies and the exigencies of nature – relies upon a *transcendent* state of consciousness, an identification with a higher spiritual reality that lies both within the human heart and outside of it, within nature, and of which human consciousness is a part. From this level of awareness arises an acceptance of the darker side of life, and hence the dark side of nature, and this acceptance is the key to spiritual strength and happiness. All such teachings have led the seekers of spiritual strength deeper into their own natures and have used contact with outside nature to bring that about. Once the spiritual aspirant becomes rooted in an internal experience of the presence of divinity, then all outward worlds lose their fearful hold and the human then truly flowers as a being of love, trust and devoted action.

In this state there can be no great fear of death, for the mind has not identified with the separate existence of the temporary body and ephemeral personality. This is the soul level of wisdom that has been lost by industrial peoples, and I am convinced that without its retrieval there can be no healing.[5] It can be approached through any of the great religions, though with difficulty, and usually through an esoteric and reclusive training. Yet all of these great teachings allude to the power of nature to confer this deepest insight. This, then, is the ultimate medicine of the forest, its trees and flowers and animals. Once met on the level of soul, their voice is our own voice but newly found. And beyond each individual, the unified forest speaks of a grand harmony in the orchestration of all beings. Merely to be in the presence of such harmony imbues the human soul with some subliminal understanding, if not of a hankering memory of wholeness (I am not convinced there *was* a paradise lost), then of a future atonement.

Perhaps it has long been the nature of the evolving human animal to experience separation and fear, and the object of all spiritual teaching to transcend that fear through the experience of unity. In Buddhist and Hindu tradition, the forest and many of its powerful creatures are allies in the process of healing that separation. In Christian, Judaic and Islamic tradition, the allies are the birds and flowers of the desert. In our own ancient and Celtic past the forest was not a place to *visit*. It was not separate from daily life, and in that time before civilization, our language would have had no word that categorized nature as other than ourselves. The earth beneath our feet merged imperceptibly into the land of rivers and mountains, swamps and grasslands, open areas and thickets. It was the dwelling place and provided food, clothing and shelter. It was *mother*, rather than *other*. Only gradually, as man settled into agriculture, did the forests recede to be named as something beyond our normal life. The medieval English word 'forest' has its linguistic roots in the Latin for 'outside'.

It is as if the outside began to shrink, first as humans settled and cities grew, and then finally as the wild remnants of forest became 'royal' preserves. A dichotomy of town and country, civil and wild, artifice and nature gradually led to a duality of concept: nature and the natural, set apart from man and the man-made, and where once the divine had permeated everything, new religions evolved that would confine it to one realm, that of the human. Gradually the old ceremonial connections to wild nature were demonized,[6] and those who lived beyond the boundary of the civil world – the *pagans* (literally, those outside who had no protection) and the *heathen* (literally, those who lived on the heath) were then classified as without God.[7]

We are, perhaps, only half-emerged from the religious paranoia of the past where pagans and heathens were slaughtered not only as ungodly, but as sub-human; the words and concepts live on in mass consciousness, and the habitual assumption remains, that the divine, though one spirit, only exists within the human heart. It is this that must be healed.

Modernists have yet to emerge from the later stages of our cultural history where scientific rationality took the separation a stage further – neither nature nor man presupposed a divinity, and hence what man willed and desired became central. Modern man looks to the forest as a resource. Modern forestry still sees itself as delivering multi-purpose public goods in the market economy – recreation, wildlife conservation and landscape-quality as well as marketable timber. That this is political correctness is only appreciated by meeting foresters who dare not express their spiritual connection to the forest in an open way. If the forest teaches them to be a more humble and peaceful human being, then it must do so in private.

Thus have forests shifted in meaning according to the culture of the times. They have become a metaphor and an icon for that which lies outside: at different times – places of dark threats and a refuge for bandits, outlaws and dangerous animals; places with special laws to protect the privilege of royal hunting grounds; plantations marching across landscapes to our imperious will. And now in recent times, as the planet faces a crisis of climate change, human population explosion, soil loss and water scarcity, the restoration of forests has become a major tool for the protection of life-sustaining ecosystems.

At the start of the millennium, however, there is a discernable movement that sees forests as a metaphor for the restoration of that deeper sense of wholeness that we have lost. In Genet's poetic story *The Man Who Planted Trees*, a barren land is restored to fruitfulness by the human sower, slowly, selflessly and with an eye to future generations. As the trees come, the dry winds cease, the dust settles and the mountain streams begin to flow again. Flowers and butterflies and birdsong return to the villages, and the human soul begins to smile and hold hope for the future. It is more than metaphor – the trees carry a living power that impacts the human psyche. By their presence, their growth, their strength, their different characters and the life that they foster about them, they infuse that sense of wholeness and well-being.

## The emergence of spiritual values in modern conservation: healing the wounds of industrialization

This relationship of wholeness is nowhere better articulated than in the practical conservation work spearheaded by Trees for Life in Scotland, but it has also surfaced in an unexpected and perhaps overlooked form in the work of government agencies. The Forestry Commission in Scotland was already engaged upon restoration of the ancient Caledonian pine forests and became Alan Watson Featherstone's very supportive ally. In England and Wales, with forest cover long reduced to a paltry few percent of its former glory, the Forestry Commission had, until recently, become a by-word for crass economic mass production and the alien destruction of treasured upland landscapes. In the past century, forests had become ugly. For many who value the aesthetic of landscape and wild places, plantation forests were a scar upon that land. Campaigns were mounted to limit the impact upon wildlife and tourism and to educate city-dwellers into what should be or could be in their place. In 1995, the British Association of Nature Conservationists (BANC) caught the shift in consciousness with its conference, *21st Century Forests*: conservationists and foresters were beginning to bring beauty back into the landscape.

There is now a growing perception of the forest as healer of the wounds inflicted by urban and industrial civilization's ugliness. In the early 1980s the Countryside Commission embarked upon a remarkable programme of Community Forests, twelve areas, each of the order of 100,000 ha, being targeted and each within easy travelling distance of large centres of population and urban dereliction, such as Newcastle's The Great North Forest, Middlesbrough's The Tees Forest, The Red Rose and Mersey Forests of industrial Lancashire, the South Yorkshire Forest near Sheffield, The Greenwood near Nottingham, Birmingham's Forest of Mercia, Swindon's Great Western Forest, East London's Thames and Watling Chase, Bristol's Forest of Avon and Bedford's Marston Vale. The idea also sparked the Scottish Lowland Forest between Edinburgh and Glasgow.

These 'forests' would aim to create new woodland at about 40 per cent overall cover in a patchwork of agriculture and villages on the edge of the urban areas. Forest development offices were set up and staffed with cooperation from Local Authorities, local businesses and wildlife and community groups. Each forest would have an identity, with the communities contributing towards fund-raising, planting and educational work. Within this concept, the arts, such as sculpture, music, poetry and theatre, added meaning to the endeavour, and ancient crafts, such as hurdle making and charcoal production, were reactivated. Whether articulated or not, the underlying ethos was of a forest as a potential healing experience. Since its inception, the idea has generated further initiatives that now include 'urban forests' that penetrate the city, for example, in Cardiff and Belfast, with an Urban Forestry Unit in Birmingham and a large new National Forest over 200 square miles of the English Midlands that includes many scars of industrialization.[8]

The conception of the forest as a healing power is ancient knowledge, and what has surfaced now is perhaps an unconscious rediscovery of that force. For millennia the forest has been a source of healing herbs and medicine. In our modern culture we tend to think of that healing in terms only of medicinal effects: some herbs have healing properties and once discovered they can be harvested, perhaps even processed to extract the 'active' ingredient, and then administered.

This is to limit our understanding to those areas accessible to science. Scratch even the most scientifically qualified medical herbalist of today and you may still find a deeper understanding, often deliberately hidden.[9] Each individual herb may cure this or that ailment – and doubtless there are active ingredients that can be extracted – but the place of that herb in the forest and its intimate relationship to the broader healing, not just of physical, but of emotional and spiritual malaise, is a matter not of some accident of evolution, but of deep process and design.

If we stay focused on the physical levels of reality at the current limits of science, then we cannot explore further the intricate relationship that plants in particular have to the sun, our planetary system and, indeed, to the galaxy beyond – something that herbal lore holds central. The inner eye of the shaman and healer perceives these relationships. Indeed, all aspects of the human condition are also perceived as aspects of a larger galactic nature. This level of reality cannot be readily explored within a scientific paradigm that separates physical reality from consciousness; although, even that separation is on the verge of breaking down. Physicists now appreciate that physical reality is merely a lower vibration than the invisible realities of electromagnetic waves. Yogis have long recognized that consciousness is a higher vibration of these waveforms. It is *all* a light show. The whole is held together by unseen dark energies and dark matter that in some parts of the universe consume light, and in others, birth it as stars. The central gravitational reality is still mysterious and undescribed, whether termed 'great attractor' or 'black hole'.

Science still seeks a unified theory of every force that moves the universe – and of course, it is sought 'outside' as measurement of something *we* can all agree on, or at least, the majority of scientists can agree on. Thus, in its hubris, human consciousness ultimately creates, by agreement, the nature of reality. But whatever reality is there described, it cannot be the whole. The intelligent ape that peers down the microscope has another reality behind the eye – an immense world of poetry and song, art and beauty, love and the struggle to love, as well as a world of shadows, of fear and loathing, histories of resentment, jealousy and anger, and the dark will to dominate, humiliate or abuse. The shadow directs the microscope user as often as any nobler purpose does, and for the most part, it is unacknowledged. Any 'unified' theory must, one would think it obvious, include what lies behind the eye of the beholder.

## Towards a science that looks within

If science has been a separation – a looking 'outside' of ourselves – the 'forest' has been a symbol for the natural world as a separate reality to be studied and manipulated. Yet now something new is happening. Our sense of loss and our love for the trees and wild places has opened us to the power of that which appears to lie outside, and where, in that openness, we let something *in*, something of the healing power that is nature. It inspires us, it awakens children to joy, to art, music, dance and poetry, and it awakens the child in the adult to awe and natural majesty.

That the forest has this dimension to its healing is evident even within our current material culture. A perusal of the many brochures for the Community and City Forests, and attendance at the art, sculpture, poetry and drama events instigated by their programmes, will readily display a sense that the forest has come to represent the healing power of wild nature from which an urbanized man has become separated. It is as if the wholeness of the forest itself has the power to recreate wholeness within the human spirit. In the forest that is outside of our selves, there is no judgement, no right and wrong that frets out vitality, and where trees are old, where the process of death and decay is evident, there is a tangible sacredness.

Not all science has been concerned with the outside. In the 20th century, science as 'psychology' began to explore the world of the 'unconscious', finding its most erudite expression in Carl Jung's *Modern Man in Search of the Soul* and the development of humanistic psychologists as opposed to 'behavioural' psychologists – those regular scientists still focused upon the apparently objective realities of mammalian physiology and cognition for all manner of managerial purposes. Jung's study of man's inner world built upon the psychotherapeutic beginnings of Freud and began to elaborate the patterns of both the individual and collective mind. What started as an attempt by 'doctors' to heal the emotionally dysfunctional, developed into a broader and more positive view of the psyche as possessing a will to 'individuate' and grow within an encompassing field of a collective psyche. Jung's great though largely marginalized contribution to scientific thought has been to begin mapping this level of reality.

Jung's lineage of psychotherapy works primarily with verbal expression – counselling and analysis, and where dreams and symbols have come to figure strongly in the landscape of the mind. He pays due homage to the shamanic realms of animal totems and synchronicity. It is nevertheless still a world for the healing of trauma – from childhood abuse, rape, violence and oppression in its grossest form, to the more subtle worlds of dominance and hierarchy. In its most developed form, it has a purpose in the healing beyond trauma – as the rebirth of the individual soul in its power to love and to participate creatively in the social world. In a sense, the collective and unconscious mind is the matrix, the birth-giver, from which any individual mind must be born. The individual point of consciousness gathers from the matrix the elements that will make up its individual identity.

To be a fully functional soul, the individual mind must have access to a functional reality in the collective mind of its culture. In a damaged culture, one that has no language, no form, no symbol or ritual for the beneficence of mother earth, the individual soul will experience an inexplicable sadness, loss and alienation.[10] Much of the modern market economy relies upon this psychological alienation, without which it could no longer grow and continue to degrade the earth. Separated peoples are then easily led into fear of their neighbours and into the ever-greater accumulation of weapons of defence.

These are largely unconscious processes and only in the 20th century have we evolved a science of those processes. The studies of Freud, Jung, Reich and others, utilizing some elements of the scientific method – cataloguing and case studies, the search for patterns and correlations of cause and effect – though not readily amenable to experimental methods, have been among the major developments of Western culture. The 'unconscious' mind has been mapped and related to organ dysfunction and disease, psychological stress and spiritual growth, all very largely in the realm of *medicine*. We have discovered the absence of soul through the medical consequences of losing it.[11]

Our modern concept of 'soul' has expanded in the last 50 years, as has our concept of personal individuality. Seldom, however, is this depth of psychology made a part of the sociology of nation states, modern economies and the drive to domination and war. These approaches to psychological damage as 'soul' damage are still compartmentalized and not yet integrated with medical science. The prevalent paradigm still views the physical body as a mechanical system prone to invasions or breakdowns. Almost every doctor's surgery now has access to counsellors and therapists and the relationship of psychological stress to illness is well appreciated, but the linkage is usually through the presentation of physical symptoms, and the motivation largely that of performance management. If an individual wishes to pursue the healing of the psyche at a deeper level, then he or she must enter the private realm of 'therapist' and client. Society as a whole has no motivation to help in that quest.

Modern medicine still holds to a largely mechanistic world view, though it has built bridges in the past two decades not only to psychotherapy but also to the hitherto spurned worlds of homeopathy, developed in the West, and acupuncture from the ancient East. It is here, in the interweaving currents of modern and 'complementary' or 'holistic' medicine, that we may find a small bridge to a future, more inclusive science. However, even humanistic psychology has its perceptual limits and compartments. Psychologists still deal with the human entity as if it were a bounded individual. Human consciousness is perceived as residing totally within the individual and presumed to reside at some relevant bodily level. In my view, this is like trying to locate the orchestra one listens to on the radio within the circuits of the little electronic box on the windowsill. If particular components of the receiver are damaged, the music will distort. And if elements of the orchestra are missing, there is no symphony.

Suppose that it is the same with the plants and animals of the forest, of which we are still one. Each species exists within an orchestra of form that goes beyond the mere physical. There is a symphony that is playing beyond the human ear. In our long departure from the forest, our culture has lost the words to describe it. For such language we can turn to other cultures that have not wandered so far from that which birthed them. In their teachings, native peoples have many naiveties of perception that can lead us to dismiss everything they perceive. They know little of the chemistry of photosynthesis or history of the ice ages, but in other respects, they have developed techniques of perception that far outstrip our limited scientific methods and the world view spawned thereof. Where we have made outer realities our journey-ground, they have voyaged inward. These journeys inform their world and language and have built a consistent body of knowledge. They have tuned the receiver inside to finer frequencies, and above all, they have been willing to listen to the whole orchestra.

In all of these different cultural assemblages, with their varying myths of creation, causality, purpose, perception of disease and techniques of 'medicine', there is one common factor – a perception of spirit. Every being, human, animal, plant, mountain, river and even stone and crystal, exists within a world of spirit. The sun is not just a heating and lighting unit, it is spiritual grandfather to some, father or mother to others. The earth is not simply soil and rock, but fertile mother, sentient, loving and at times fiercely dark in lessons to her errant offspring. In our past and too often present arrogances, we have pretended to know better – yet even in our science, we know there to be truths in these perceptions. We are quite comfortable in acknowledging apes as our ancestors, but not frogs. And though we are made of ancestral dust and water, not without the sun could we have been birthed. We just don't celebrate these facts. We take them for granted. That is to say, there is no gratitude.

Native peoples have not come to hold these world views from belief – a common misperception – though they may now be maintained as such in what is left of the original communities, but by direct *perception* and ritual relationship. It is Western civil society that has built a world of belief mediated by priesthoods, whilst 'reality' is honoured largely as economy, commerce and warfare. In societies where direct experience of the divine presence is fostered as the norm, the world of the divine spirit is a world where the divine and the human are not separated any more than father and son or mother and daughter are separated. The creative power is not projected *beyond* nature – it resides within nature, and is *represented* by the sun, the moon, the ocean, the earth and the forest.

The so-called primitive human psyche knows from whence it has come, and that its brothers and sisters live in the same forest. And for the individual, redemption is not a promised land beyond the boundary of this life; it exists only in the here and now, the present moment of the very present forest. If one looks to the writings of Native American teachers such as Jamie Sams, that redemption is about love in the face of all the human frailties that are not love. It is the same story as that of civil society, but with one major difference: nature is an ally not an enemy.

We come to address these questions at the apotheosis of a Western culture that worships economy and has systematically ostracized the soul from daily life. Soulfulness has no expression in the normal business world. Homes and workplaces struggle to maintain a quality of soul in architecture and building, but everywhere, from offices and airport terminals, sprawling housing estates and motorways, we are afflicted by a built environment without soul. People who are born and grow up in these urban environments have little contact with the natural cycles that sustain them. There is born a culture of consumerism without depth that spawns its global icons of fast food and cinematic entertainment. And just like its most obvious global element, the Hollywood film, it is founded on fantasy: the freedom of the few enslaves millions in mindless repetitive 'jobs' at minimal wages who then hunger to escape into some consumer paradise; but above all, it is not sustainable, it is slowly destroying the very ecosystems that support it.

## Shadows in the psyche

There has always been a Western shadow culture; it has now reached such massive proportions that it can no longer be denied. One in ten citizens will suffer debilitating mental illness. Suicide is the biggest killer of young men. Narcotic drugs are so prevalent that the US devotes billions of dollars to a 'war' on supply. The medical use of anti-depressant drugs is a normal feature of urban life, especially among women. Violence to women and abuse of children is endemic. Obesity, especially in young children, is a Western disease that is now spreading to Russia and even China. In Southern Africa seven million people will die of AIDS by 2010 and life expectancy will drop to 41 years. There is a clear relationship between the

AIDS epidemic in Africa and the fragmentation of communities, migration of males to find work, and consequent breakdown of social and sexual mores. HIV infection levels at 30–40 per cent are highest in those small states supplying workers to the South African economy, such as Botswana, Lesotho and Swaziland.[12]

In the world of business, now the dominant force in a global culture, humanity has abandoned even the ethics by which, in the personal world, it would otherwise live. That there are now, after several centuries of gradually globalized markets, special investment funds (which are but a fraction of total funds) that can be termed 'ethical and environmentally sound' is testament to the betrayal of humanity inherent in the normal practice of business.

That the Western psyche is sick, disturbed and dangerous cannot be admitted. That is the force of denial. It cannot be faced that there is not enough of a global resource to sustain Western societies, and also it cannot be faced that the market can never deliver global equity. Rather uncharacteristically and to its great credit, Western science has not colluded with the environmental denial.[13] That the emperor has no clothes began to dawn in the early 1970s and grew to a mass movement by the mid-1980s. What was initially a movement of resistance against soul-less, centralized and dangerous technology, symbolized by nuclear power, became a progressive and creative culture embracing renewable energy, organic agriculture, sustainable forestry and the protection of wild areas. In those early decades, these ideas were regarded as 'alternative' by their holders and cranky by the mainstream; however, by the 1990s they had become accepted wisdom and embodied in the global declaration for sustainable development at Rio.

In recent years a new organic architecture has sought to bring habitation and nature together in a marriage of form and sustainable building materials. Organic agriculture, whilst loudly focused upon food safety and soil conservation, also has an underlying ethic of animal welfare and an honouring of natural cycles and processes. Even the business world stirs – a recent article in the *Financial Times* headed 'Spirituality in Business' recognized the soul-destroying nature of a corporate world that had lost sight of the core values of humanity, and reported that Price-Waterhouse, a leading management consultancy, had started to send its managers to the Findhorn Foundation for courses in personal discovery. Meaning, purpose and identity crises are surfacing and these apparently affect the all-important efficiency of business affairs![14]

These early attempts at retrieving the soul in the corporate world may have begun as a response to failing motivation, but at least they are a recognition of where the problem lies. If such seeds can prosper in the thorny ground of corporate finance, then it is but a short step to conservation biology and economic forestry! The disjunction between conservation science, resource economics and the 'sacred' is not now as great as it was. Some ecologists and anthropologists have at least begun to realize the value and potential of native systems of 'ecology' and 'conservation' that are based upon deep observation and rules of sanctity.

## Steps towards a sacred ecology

One such is the anthropologist Fikret Berkes, whose recent book *Sacred Ecology* provides case studies of Cree Indian culture in sub-arctic Canadian 'wilderness', where aboriginal peoples have used and shaped the most apparently pristine of environments. He argues that 'conservation' ethics needs to take on board the cultural dimensions of such use and further, that traditional knowledge – in this case, that of the Caribou migrations, numbers and health of animals – though based upon oral history held by certain elders and not strictly scientific in form, needs respect not only in its own right as part of a cultural heritage, but also as a successful system of predictive knowledge complementary to ecological science.

Berkes argues that enlightened management systems for natural resources would include indigenous peoples not only as part of the ecosystem, but as part of the management at both a practical and philosophic level. It might be expected that the argument would end there – he is Professor of Natural Resources at the University of Manitoba – and in general the 'sacred' has been merely a descriptive element in the anthropology of indigenous knowledge and practice. In a final chapter, entitled 'Towards a Unity of Mind and Nature' he states:

> Until only a few years ago, the spread of modern, rational, scientific
> resource management was considered a part of "natural progress". The
> problem is that Western scientific resource management, despite all of its
> power, seems unable to halt the depletion of resources and the
> degradation of the environment. Part of the reason for this may be that
> Western resource management, and reductionist science in general,
> developed in the service of a utilitarian, exploitive, dominion-over-nature
> worldview of colonists and industrial developers . . . best geared for the
> efficient use of resources as if they were limitless, and consistent with the
> laissez-faire doctrine still alive in today's neoclassical economic theory.
> But utilitarianism is ill-suited for sustainability, which requires a new
> philosophy that recognizes ecological limits and strives to satisfy social as
> well as economic needs.

He goes on to argue that traditional ecological knowledge and practice demonstrates that world views and *beliefs* matter – 'almost universally one encounters an ethic of non-dominant, respectful human–nature relationships, a sacred ecology, as part of the belief component of traditional ecological knowledge.'

Fikret Berkes has the advantage of having *experienced* the reality of an indigenous relationship to nature, and perhaps therefore, the very personal reality of the reciprocity within such a culture. My feeling is that this alone is the key to a fusion of sacred and scientific ecology. The latter may have grown more humble in the light of its now very obvious limitations of prediction and control, but until a largely urbanized political and scientific corpus get to experience the sacred dimensions of nature other than as romantic idyll or recreational frolic, scientific ecology and resource management cannot begin to incorporate the sacred other than as a marketable attribute of some indigenous culture ripe for eco-tourism.

This was the work we began within Coed Eryri at Cae Mabon. We had to go beyond the philosophical and analytical to the direct spiritual experience of the individual in which the forest *becomes* sacred and the true value of nature is as an ally in the retrieval of this essentially human experience of a greater soul. There are very deep Native American and neo-classical Druid teachings of the 'medicine wheel' that seek to align elements of the human soul to the 'four directions' of East, West, North and South. It is an essential rebalancing of the psyche whereby the cooler, rational, knowledge-oriented North is balanced by the passion, fire and fecundity of the South; the West of individual creativity and inventive dreaming must be balanced with the surrendered ego and spiritual teachings of the East. Animal totems are invoked in the process of learning that the medicine wheel initiates.[15]

How often does anyone from the Western, rational, material culture (in effect an amalgam of North and West, to the exclusion of East and South – which often then harbour 'enemies') engage upon a personal journey to reintegrate these elements of the psyche? There are immense cultural barriers to the 'soul healing' that needs to take place. Most people cannot even begin to make the journey. It is no accident that psychotherapy for individuals grew out of the needs of those unable to contain their emotional trauma and failing to function in Western society. In a sense, they were the ones approaching sanity – in whom the soul broke through and began its long journey into healing. For the rest of imperial and militaristic Europe at the time, the unfeeling denial of emotion, caring, human unity and alienation from nature was regarded as sane. Much the same force now operates against true sanity in a modern world of huge defence budgets and collective insecurity.

How is this to be healed? There are at least signs that industrial society sees the need to heal itself. 'Healing' is now becoming an accepted concept and exists within what is known as 'complementary' or 'alternative' medicine, a system that is much more fundamentally concerned with causes rather than symptoms, in contrast to modern 'patch-up' medicine. The concept of 'therapy' itself relates more to healing than cures, and there has been a gradual acceptance and growth, particularly in the fields of family

therapy and counselling, but also a gradual blossoming of dance, movement, drama, music and art as therapeutic processes.

What then has all this to do with the forest? Most of these healing
therapies work on the individual, the dysfunctional elements of society. The
problem is, as Reich observed, that it is often the structure of society that
creates the dysfunction. We need a healing process that connects the
growing strength of the ensouled individual to the greater whole that is
both social and universal, and to such an extent that it transforms global
consciousness. Anything less will likely see the ecological demise of
humanity within the 21st century.

## Complementary maps of reality

For this task, we need a new map, and we might turn to some of the very
oldest systems of medicine concerned most fundamentally with healing at
a causal level, rather than repair or management of symptoms; systems that
also do not perceive the body as a superficial mechanical and chemical
system. Traditional Chinese medicine is a mixture of careful observation
and listening, detailed case history, and intervention with herbs and
acupuncture needles. Since the mid-1970s numerous schools of traditional
Chinese acupuncture have been training students in Britain, and it has
grown in acceptance within the medical profession.

Though some healers within this field may limit their explanations, and
even their goals, to relief of symptoms – there are 'medical' acupuncturists
as well as 'medical' herbalists and homeopaths (those who learn simply
which remedies tend to effect a relief of symptoms) – the traditional
practitioners have both a different map of reality and a wider goal of
healing.

This map concerns the description of the underlying 'energy' body, its
field or form, the flows within its channels and its relation to energy flow
in the environment. Acupuncturists have mapped the subtle pathways and
nodes within the human body as exactly as geographers would map the
streams and tributaries of a great river system. It is into these 'meridians'
that the needles are inserted. All organ systems of the body receive vital
energy from these flows, and if the flow becomes blocked or clogged or
slowed or feint, then the organ system will suffer. A practitioner requires
months of training to locate and identify the pulses and their varying
qualities – a sensitivity as yet beyond the most sensitive of technical
instruments. There are six pulses in each wrist, each pulsing with one of a
dozen different qualities. These pathways can be affected by emotional and
mental states, trauma, stress, attitude and accidents.[16]

At the deepest level, a person's spiritual integrity and well-being helps to
energize the pathways, and conversely, the emotional and physical world

feeds back through these pathways to their spiritual health. In traditional Chinese acupuncture, the ultimate goal of the physician was to help align the spirit to the divine presence.

In herbal medicine also, the scientific mind has continually failed to grasp what is on offer. It limits itself to seeking the 'active' ingredient, the magic bullet that will cure the symptom. And certainly, active ingredients *are* isolated and *do* work – such as the compounds of the Madagascan periwinkle that have aided recovery from leukaemia, or the extracts of the yew tree that have benefited AIDS and cancer patients. Extracted cannabinols are set to legitimize the medical use of cannabis for relieving chronic pain, without the 'high'. The greatest pain reliever of the Western world's medical chest is still the extract of opium poppy, and quinine from the bark of a Peruvian tree was the mainstay of malaria treatment for a century or more. In the latter case, the founder of homeopathy, Samuel Hahnemann (1755–1843), was inspired by the actions of this plant remedy to his vibrational doctrine of similitudes – the bark induced fevers similar to malaria.

Undoubtedly, one reason for this limited vision is the industrial pharmaceutical imperative of business and profit. If the extract can be refined and simplified, patented, tested, manufactured and bottled, distributed and transacted with the minimum of involvement on the part of others – then it makes money. If the herb remained whole, with the added complexity of regulating doses, careful monitoring and additional remedies to moderate side-effects, all of which require time with an experienced practitioner, then the economics would flow in a rather more decentralized way. For this latter reason, many such complementary methods *are* expensive at the point of use, even though the remedies themselves may be cheap. But perhaps more importantly, the herbal practitioner used herbs and symptoms *within* a cultural context of spiritual realities, and in the consultation time of an hour or more, deeper emotional and spiritual realities related to those symptoms could be addressed. In this multi-layered, highly sensitive and skilled approach, the plants are obvious allies *in that process*.

Thus it is that, for reasons of scientific prejudice and economic stricture, conventional Western medicine does not address ailments of the spirit, and barely touches the emotional and mental states (other than in the management of depression). It perforce limits itself to seeking 'cures' rather than seeking 'healing'. These plants offer far more than cures for the symptoms of disease, but we need to wade slowly now into the deep end of this inquiry.

Just as we can embrace with awe and wonder the fact that a whole symphony can exist in the ether about us, right now, even if we turn off the radio. Indeed, a myriad symphonies, and conversations, and languages are all about us, encoded in great complexity and with the potential for emotional charge, mental interest and spiritual uplift – all, that is, if we have the means to access them. Pictures and movies too! Yet the medium that holds the information and transmits it over great distances has no substance and is not discernable to human sense organs. Were we to go back 200 years, when no instrumentation could detect an electromagnetic wave, such a phenomenon would have been beyond credence, even, and perhaps especially, to most scientists.

The relevance that this has for the 'healing' realms is more than analogy. The energetic body that responds to homeopathic remedies, that channels *chi* and *prana* (the yogic equivalent) through the meridians that vitalize the organ systems, exists on a similar plane to the electromagnetic waveforms so capable of encoding and transmitting the symphony. However, there is also another shared reality, and far more easily accessed. As with all human art, the symphony first existed not in the orchestra but in the composer's personal dreamworld. Every artefact of the human story is founded upon the ability to dream another reality.

## The unifying dream

It is a bizarre science that concerns itself so much with the circuit boards of life, the molecular structure of plants, the sequences of genes, the chemistry of the brain, and yet ignores the dreaming. The more bizarre when all of science's greatest breakthroughs came from those who could listen and act upon their intuitions – which in essence is an opening to a dream reality. Intuition, which can be learned and perfected, is all about 'listening', and it can be as visual as it can be auditory. It is essentially a passive act of surrender, but it takes a disciplined mind to let go into that silence.

We are deep enough now to consider the underlying reality in the healing power of plants and animals. They exist *within* a field of dream as old as evolution itself. This is the shaman's reality. The animals have already been dreamt. They are at one with creation, which is an unfolding dream. We, however, are different. We are not at one with this creation. We have dissented big time. We don't like parts of it. We think we are above it, or in control of it. We are at least aware of our origins: we surmise from our science (remembering that all theories are to be regarded as temporary) that our sun had a birth time and will one day die, and that our planet was itself born from its dust clouds. As scientists we at first only noticed the visible play of matter – the clouds of dust and waves of light. Only later, with a more sophisticated methodology did we apprehend an underlying reality, a unity of gravitational waves and the supposition of dark energy (we can measure the consequences of its presence but not its substantive reality). It was a huge leap to realize that matter and energy were not separate realities. Is it that much more of a step to realize that matter, energy and consciousness are also not separate? Curiously, in this regard the novelist Philip Pullman, in his acclaimed trilogy for children *His Dark Materials*, has taken a step that most scientists are not yet able to contemplate.

If the underlying reality *is* consciousness, then we come to the most fundamental of all realities – that everything that exists first exists as part of a dream, an unfolding story that we have called evolution.

Suppose that the underlying energetic reality, the dark matter, energy, or ether that is currently seen as passive, is not only originally creative but also *receptive* to human consciousness. After all, humans have evolved not only as part of the dream, but as dreamers themselves. At present we see this only with a time lag between imagination and the world becoming organized by the will of the creative agent, for example, as architect, inventor, technologists or artistic creator. But just as those agents of creative thought are all embedded in a collective reality from which they draw inspiration, and upon which they must build, the deeper collective reality has the power to mould the ethereal future, the dream that is *yet* to unfold.

On a smaller scale, usually that of the individual human soul in search of healing, the shaman healer enters that deeper reality on a dream level – the practitioner has to project his or her own consciousness into that dreamworld. In that healing work, the animals and plant powers are allies in the process. Changes are effected in ordinary reality by first instigating changes in the underlying dream reality.

Rarely is it possible to gain any kind of trustworthy insight into shamanic practices – the shamans do not usually speak our language, and why would they bother? Furthermore, the language that would alter the dream reality is not necessarily one that would come readily to a Western mind. We are used to the symbolism of sacrifices, pleading and prayers for intervention; but we cannot expect readily to understand the training and state of mind required to directly enter the realm of the unconscious dream substrate and effect changes.

However, in one Western shaman we have a person of sufficient grasp of both worlds for communication to take place who has been willing to share the story of the rigorous training required. For a moment, imagine you are a good field naturalist, you love animals and you are asked to prove how in tune you are with the natural order of things by going into a game park and plucking a whisker from one of the lions. In the case of Martin Prechtel, it was the jungles of Guatemala and the whisker of a wild jaguar. Prechtel passed his test, not so much by courage, of which there was an abundance, but by trust, at which point the jaguar *came to him*. His story, told in *Secrets of the Talking Jaguar* (1999), is the personal history of a traditional training of a medicine man who communes with animal spirits in an alliance for the healing of the human condition. He was born of Swiss and Native American parents and brought up on a reservation in the US –

a bit of a teenage misfit, who married early and met the all-too-common difficulties of an indigenous soul searching for meaning in such a damaged culture.

As his marriage and community life foundered, he had a vivid dream of a village of unimaginable beauty, with its native community intact, by a deep blue lake surrounded by lush forested mountains. He set off on a journey south, guided by instinct, and when that failed, by the unseen hand of his dream. By 'chance' he crossed from Mexico into Guatemala and found himself in the village he had seen in his dream – Santiago Atitlan, by the lake and the then intact forest. An old man jumped him from behind, accosting him for taking so long to get there.

Thus began his training. The old man was the most revered Indian medicine man in Guatemala and announced that he had 'dreamt' Martin to him to take on as an apprentice. The training takes years; it is an instruction in all the old ways of the indigenous Mayan culture. Herbs and healing are central, but also we are given a window into the rich and astonishingly intricate world of ritual. The indigenous soul of the Mayan village, indeed, the Mayan culture, is kept vibrant by a constant stream of devotion to the Gods.

In weaving the story of his own evolution, Prechtel paints pictures of the intricate wonder and meaning of Mayan language, costume, dress, music, prayer, food and relationship to nature. What is at first an obviously simple and hard existence is revealed in great depth, meaning and beauty. Despite the hardships, there is much laughter and great love. He wins his spurs through ordeal and constant practice of ritual to finally qualify as shaman.

His teacher then announces that he, the teacher, will die in a few days' time. He knows the time and manner of his death and that his work is now complete – for Prechtel had received the knowledge of the ancestors. He foretells that in a few months the village will be destroyed and the Mayan culture all-but exterminated. He is told to return to the United States and teach what he knows. The old man duly died and Guatemala experienced a military coup and a vicious ethnic cleansing. The old world of balance was finally laid waste in the name of modernity. Martin Prechtel now lives and teaches in New Mexico and occasionally comes to Europe to run workshops on ritual practice.

In his final chapter he talks of the 'indigenous soul' and how it must be kept alive at all costs. As we look at our own countryside, we know that only too well; there is an acute lack of soul. We have no jaguars – no bear or wolf or lynx, reminders of the limits of our human power should we momentarily surrender our technology. Look also at our farms and villages – the old buildings had balance, harmony with the hill, the copse, the meander. Now, despite our huge wealth, we have a welter of corrugated sheds, tacky boxes and neat gardens, fields barren of birds and flowers, with 'nature reserves' on the edge, never central, hardly respected.

We have a lot of work to do. We have called it ecological restoration, but what has been lacking is still soul. Prechtel makes a plea, that without a soulful relation to nature, a richness is lost. This we can learn from the indigenous soul of the shaman as healer. From so-called primitive cultures we can access a wisdom we have lost. My only doubt is: for Martin Prechtel, this wisdom was won at great personal risk and huge devotion, and I know of many trainee shamans in Britain, from neo-native Druid and Wiccan to imported Yogi and Native American, but have yet to meet anyone who has broken through to the level of consciousness that he describes.

Yet, we *are* dreamers. We have the power of creation. No other species on earth has been given that. It was our gift when we left the garden. For good or evil.

So, to our healing. It is not a question of cures. My father died of a cancer that could not be cured. It was a painful ending. He almost drowned in his pulmonary fluid. The doctor had given him a few hours once his heart had failed to pump the blood from the lungs, and he was left alone. The ward nurses and sisters held a space of angelic quality, but it would not have reached him in his dire state. He was in great fear. He very nearly died with no healing. In those final hours, however, his spiritual dimension made its final push through the prejudice, fear, pride, the immense guilt of the years, and he asked for help. I count myself immensely fortunate to have been by his side at that moment, and to have been able to offer the gifts I had received. He began to work with the ancient yogic breath and to embark upon the healing journey.

I do not know who and what he encountered, because he could not talk, but I could feel and at times sense the energetic work. Five days later, after no food or water and no medical intervention, his spirit crossed the threshold with a confident joy, shorn of guilt, self-forgiven and at one with life. His shrivelled body glowed with health; there was a smile on his face and a deep peace in his final sigh as we kissed him. His death was a healing. His cancer was a healing. Had he keeled over with a heart attack whilst gardening and had gone in seconds, there would have been no such healing.

Healing is about atonement, not about curing symptoms. Sometimes the physical symptoms disappear, sometimes they don't. Healers are often aware that the disease is the cure in progress. There is a lesson for the body and the mind and the spirit. Disease is a fact of nature and its prevalence is well revealed in fossil bones of everything from big cats to gorillas. But in humans, disease exists at the physical, mental and *spiritual* levels. Most healers experience the spiritual level as primary cause, then the mental, then the emotional and then the physical. The body is always the last to register the discord, and by then it is often too late to affect a 'cure'. The healing process can engage at any of these levels. Body work releases stored emotional energy from the musculature. Alignment work such as osteopathy and chiropractice corrects postural patterns that can arise from wayward attitudes and a lifetime of holding and tension. Analysis and psychotherapy can address guilt, resentments, fears and childhood trauma – essentially mental conclusions, which have gathered emotional charge that can also then feedback into physical and emotional release. We now have the immense heritage of Jung with its rich exploration of symbol and archetype in the unconscious mind – and perhaps the single most important articulation of our evolutionary destiny – the individuation of the soul.

In these processes of healing, growth and personal unfolding, herbal medicines have the power to affect not only emotional and mental states (and hence the physical too), but also deeper underlying spiritual malaise. There are remedies that lift and strengthen the spirit in its constant battle against despair and doubt, and in its willingness to love, to be humble, to forgive and to trust in the divine unfolding. And it is in these realms beyond ailments and physical distress that the spirit powers of plants and animals can be most effective: plants can strongly aid the constitution physically, emotionally and psychically; animal powers can lend strength of will, courage, industriousness, determination and divination of the path.

The animals and plants exist in the dreamworld. They may not dream as we do and they cannot create, but they can join with us in *our* dream. Our mind has the power to include them by choice. They already exist in the greater mind, into which we can expand; but until we do so, they cannot be other than what they are as animals and plants in the slowly unfolding dream of evolution. Once we enter that expanded reality and invite them into our process of evolution, they will respond as willingly and as readily as the faithful dog offered a run in the meadow. When we make that move, it is as if we become co-directors of the film and they are willing and very able actors who want the work.

The oak, for example, has many ecological functions, but when connected to the human psyche it becomes an expanded being of heart and strength, joy and light; in contrast, the yew occupies the realm of death and rebirth, of darkness and the underworld powers of regeneration. All of the trees have different qualities. The remedies developed by Edward Bach are decoctions of the essence of flowers, many of which are trees.[17] They are largely used to treat mental and spiritual states. There are correlations with herbal medicine, and even with legendary and mythic Celtic lore – the Druids had a tree-alphabet that was also a monthly calendar, with each month having an association with a particular tree, and to them, the oak *Derwen* was the *doorway*, as befits the heart. As with Beethoven, there is no scientific treatise thereupon.[18] This is something all the dreamers know because it is a consistent experience of the spirits of these trees as met in the dreamworld.[19] It is the job of the healing herbalist to know this. It would be no surprise to a Druid elder that the oils of the yew *Taxus* had provided a cure for failure of the regenerative powers of the blood and immune system. Everything connected to the yew is connected to that realm.

In my own work I have come to view all animals and plants as handmaidens of the creative dream. A dream that has dreamt us as its eventual co-dreamers! It is the nature of the Great Mystery known to all peoples, even our own, that we cannot know the creator other than by the process we see unfolding. *Evolution* in the language of its conceptual birth, carries within it the sign of its purpose, which we know anyway to be *Love*. In that word, love is reversed – for it is love from which we were born and to which we must return. It has always been the greatest human challenge to have faith in that process. All of creation knows our journey into love. The yogis teach that when all of our energies are in harmony, when we are at one with the divine source, the vibratory power that energizes all life, then we can experience only love. Then are we one with the creator.

The healing journey is thus fundamentally a quest for harmony with the creative power. Whereas each of the animal spirits has a particular healing power to address the small disharmonies, the forest in its wild and natural state teaches the harmonies of nature itself. In the symphony of the wildwood there is no disharmony. In its wholeness it holds and reflects the Great Mystery. To be whole, we must be able to experience wholeness. The soul-less, for the soul can be lost, will enter the wildwood and it will be an empty place. But to those just awakening to the depth and connectivity of their soul, the forest will sing the song of awakening; to the weary and humble, it will offer solace and strengthening; and to the joyful and playful, the questers and explorers, it is a *doorway* to the stars!

# 10

# The Land In-between: Wilding Agriculture

Thus far, we have looked at the cores and corridors that as wildland advocates we would like to create. However, the land in-between the reserves is a problem area of great complexity and is subject to global economic forces that presage great change. The intensification of agriculture over the past few decades has led not only to an impoverishment of biodiversity on agricultural land, there are also signs of significant deterioration in the fauna and flora of isolated small reserves.[1] Concerns over the ability of such isolated reserves to allow adaptation to climate change have made the issue of size and connectivity more pressing. In response to these pressures, conservation bodies have been engaged in a two-pronged strategy of extending reserves by purchase, and hence control, and trying to influence agricultural policy over the land in-between. In the wilder perspective, any programme of returning large herbivores and some of their predators would require larger-scale reserves and connectivity between them, which can only be developed within the context of land use for agriculture or forestry.

In the case of forestry, there has been a radical shift in practices, in the structure of the industry and in the role of government agencies towards multi-purpose landscape-sensitive forestry. Latterly, there has also been some embracing of the wildland ethos in joint projects with Forest Enterprise and voluntary bodies such as the National Trust, and the future looks very positive. We shall look at the role of forestry in more detail in the next chapter. The situation with agriculture is not so assured. Powerful forces of change are at work, ranging from major problems of disease, changes in global markets and consumer preference, global pressures to reduce subsidies for production and an ageing workforce to a growing concern at the destruction of wildlife in the general countryside.

It is now widely recognized that there is a crisis in farming and the government has instigated a number of reviews, in particular following the Foot and Mouth epidemic of 2001. There are also government plans for the complete overhaul of all agencies with remits for the countryside, such as the Countryside Agency and English Nature, towards an integrated land management agency. Such changes might further landscape-scale conservation planning.

## Landscape-scale intervention

As we have seen, there is already a discernible shift in emphasis among nature conservation bodies to consider landscape-scale change. In addition, as we noted in Chapter 5, the Environment Agency and water companies already have catchment-based plans for water quality, fisheries and wildlife, and the inter-agency Land Use Policy Group has been studying landscape-scale regeneration of woodland cover, concluding that the uplands offer the greatest prospects. Land use in the uplands is already in a state of flux, with large areas of uneconomic hill farming subvented by the taxpayer, a livestock community still recovering from Foot and Mouth Disease, and the future evolution of General Agreement on Tariffs and Trade (GATT) threatening to end all production on marginal land. On the positive side, there is public support for more native broadleaf forests and international recognition of the benefits of carbon sequestration, as well as a growing understanding that recent severe floods and water quality issues are linked to a long history of deforestation and soil degradation. These economic and environmental forces present both a crisis and an opportunity for land use in the hills, and wildland corridors may offer ways of meeting many of the current objectives for the local economy and communities.

In the lowlands, the picture is less favourable due to the high returns and high land prices associated with agricultural use; however, networks can be built around river corridors, gravel pits, worked-out peat deposits and coastal defences, as well as building mosaics with core areas where there is sufficient wild woodland, heath or marsh.

Before we explore these new avenues, all of which have embryonic projects, it is worth examining the foundation upon which nature conservation currently rests. Much of the infrastructure was laid down in the post-war years when agriculture was less intensive and farmland rich in wildlife.

## Infrastructural inheritance

Most of this infrastructure – in the form of National Nature Reserves, Sites of Special Scientific Interests and the reserves of the County Wildlife Trusts, as well as management policy for the largely secondary habitats they contain – was conceived within a paradigm of protection that originated before the global forces of the past two decades became evident. These forces include pollution-induced global warming, acidification and increased nitrogen deposition; global markets for food and pressure on production costs; and increased animal and animal product movements leading to the spread of disease and greatly increased frequency of alien introductions.

In past decades, protected areas served to defend against major development or outright persecution, but as they have become surrounded by intensive cultivation, their boundaries cannot offer sufficient protection from pollutants, pesticides, alien introductions and other effects, such as drainage and water abstraction. Above all, small populations are isolated. Even small fauna such as butterflies, moths, beetles and dragonflies, when adapted to specific habitats, can disappear from small reserves (see for example discussions on the enlargement of Wicken Fen, by the National Trust[1]).

These pressures have been increasingly recognized by the conservation community and have given rise to several programmes and a discernible strategy that seeks to enlarge nature reserves (the RSPB has been particularly active on wetland sites and in the Caledonian Forest), to create wildlife corridors, reform agricultural policy, address individual vulnerable species and habitats through a Biodiversity Action Plan, and control alien introductions. In response to these issues, cooperative endeavours have been common across the voluntary sector and a great deal has been achieved. These restoration programmes have focused most recently on extending reedbed habitat, wet grassland and lowland heath, with the latter receiving several million pounds of support from the Heritage Lottery Fund and with chalk grassland restoration on Salisbury Plain winning £2 million from the EU LIFE Fund. Although there is little in the way of collated statistics among all these organizations, this process of habitat restoration and woodland creation has doubtless added significantly to the area of land devoted primarily to nature conservation.

The last decade has also seen extensions of agri-environment schemes such as Wales' Tir Cymen and Tir Gofal, Environmentally Sensitive Areas (ESAs) and Countryside Stewardship, the Community Forest programme and continually upgraded farm woodland grant schemes.

These welcome developments have, however, coincided with disturbing data relating to several key indicator bird species that have shown a catastrophic decline in the past decade – lapwing (42 per cent), corn bunting (74 per cent), grey partridge (78 per cent), skylark (60 per cent), tree sparrow (87 per cent) and song thrush (50 per cent) among others, such that it is obvious that all is far from well with the British countryside.[2] This decline has been most marked on English and Welsh farmland, but it also extends to data from undisturbed habitat in Scotland, where declines of skylark, meadow pipit, dunlin and golden plover have been equally severe. The most obvious cause is a continued intensification of farming, both of western grasslands and eastern arable land, and this degradation also appears to affect wintering populations from undisturbed habitats. In addition, there has been a marked decline in small mammals, such as hare, water vole, common shrew and especially the field vole, upon which many predatory species are dependent.[3] Similar large-scale losses have been noted for insect life generally, but especially for once-common moths and mayflies.

The continued decline comes at a time when wildlife should have stabilized after the massive habitat losses of the previous four decades and most particularly after the introduction of agri-environment schemes such as Countryside Stewardship. In the previous decades, between 1977 and 1987, 50 per cent of lowland heath was lost; between 1987 and 1995, 60 per cent of herb-rich grassland was lost; and since the war, 50 per cent of ancient woodland has gone. There is some indication in recent government monitoring that losses have stabilized, but nevertheless, at a very low level. Agri-environment schemes as they now stand can be expected to do little to make up these losses.

The picture from a species perspective is not entirely negative. New habitat initiatives coupled with better legislation and protection have led to conservation gains, especially with regard to birds, with increases for marsh harrier, osprey, red kite, goshawk, sparrow hawk, honey buzzard, little egret and even the first breeding crane to return to England.[4] Other animal groups have a few success stories – pine marten has increased in Scotland, polecat are spreading, otter are recovering well and roe deer continue to re-colonize their former range. However, outside of woodlands and wetlands, once-common butterflies, moths and flowering plants have registered steep declines, even in the last decade.[5] The problem lies with the ever-increasing intensification of agriculture and its inability to reform itself.

## The problem of intensive agriculture

The process of intensification has occurred in the UK both in the eastern counties on arable land (where mixed farming has declined, hedgerow loss has been severe and large fields are now devoted to arable crops alone) and in the west with intensification of grass production with the loss of herb-rich meadows to monocultures of rye-grass, early mowing for silage and a gradual reduction of mixed farming. There is now an east–west divide between pasture and arable land, and throughout Britain, small-scale features such as woodland and scrub have been rooted out, ponds filled in and streams canalized. Even within National Parks with readily available grant schemes and advisory expertise, many farmers have continued to destroy ancient flower-rich hay meadows, especially along river valleys, and to convert rough upland pasture to sown and fertilized grassland.

These changes in farming practice have arisen both from powerful economic forces and conservatism on the part of the farming community in their failure to embrace a new paradigm for sustainable agriculture. The economic forces are largely beyond both farmers' and governmental control: consumer pressure for cheap food, supermarket dominance of the food markets and hence pressure on prices at the farm gate, the liberalizing of world markets for food and animal feed, and the vagaries of the 'green pound' in the EU currency system. These forces could have been better combated by a coordinated approach to sustainability on the part of farmers (the NFU in particular), government, and NGOs concerned with the countryside. Many of the pilot projects such as Countryside Steward-ship developed by the Countryside Commission and taken up by the Ministry of Agriculture, Fisheries and Food and payments for farms in Environmentally Sensitive Areas suffered from limited funds and the fact that they were voluntary schemes.

In the face of these problems, conservation bodies have focused a great deal of attention and resources upon reforming the Common Agricultural Policy (CAP).[6,7] It is rightly seen as the engine of destruction, having subsidized food production to the detriment of the environment across Europe for five decades. The CAP intervenes in the market to guarantee producers a minimum price, taxes imports from overseas in order not to undercut that price, and pays out subsidies on an area and headage basis for crops and livestock. This costs the European taxpayer about £30 billion/year and £3.5 billion finds its way back to British farmers. It has been argued that UK food would be 14 per cent cheaper without import barriers supported by the CAP and which amount to another £6.5 billion as the cost of underpinning the price system.[8] This would work out at roughly £500/annum per household, or nearly £10 per week on the food bill.

The main thrust of environmental reform has been the expansion of agri-environment schemes, whereby subsidies can be channelled into environmentally beneficial practices. These schemes (known now as Pillar 2 expenditure) account for only 4 per cent of the total CAP budget (the rest goes on Pillar 1 crop and livestock subsidy), but they appear to offer the only way forward in halting the destructive impact of the production subsidies, and then potentially reversing the decline.

The aim of CAP campaigns is to transfer as much of Pillar 1 money to Pillar 2 schemes (known as modulation), or to make receipt of Pillar 1 funds conditional on compliance with environmental regulations (known as cross-compliance). The main stumbling block is that those farmers who would lose most from reduction of Pillar 1 funding – the large corporate holdings where there is little left to conserve – are not those who would gain from current Pillar 2 projects, and they have considerable power to block reform. In the first round of reform, Pillar 2 schemes will be integrated into funding via the regional agencies under the rubric of Rural Development and an 'entry level scheme' will cover all agricultural land along the lines of Tir Gofal. The main CAP payments will shift from production-based (for example, livestock payments) to area-based entitlement with a necessity for compliance with minimal environmental standards – in wildlife terms, the maximum achieved thus far has been the requirement for 2 m strips of uncultivated land along hedgerows and 1m along ditches or streams.

The whole subsidy system is already under pressure from GATT; other international producers of meat and grain have complained of price subsidies and import duties. Given the trend towards liberalized markets, the system needs to find a justification to provide farmers with income support; high on the agenda for change is support for the environment and rural community life.

Without any subsidies at all, European farming would alter radically. Firstly, the market would have to compete with cheaper foreign produce, and prices of basic commodities would fall. This would drastically affect marginal producers, particularly upland livestock and the smaller arable farmers, of whom large numbers might be expected to cease farming. The resultant shake up would lead to amalgamation of holdings across Britain (and in other countries with a tradition of small producers) and the disappearance of upland farming communities, with potentially great social distress. This problem has led to an entrenched opposition to reductions in subsidies, particularly from the French farming lobby, but also from British farming interests that are loathe to embrace restrictions related to environmental goals and equally determined to maintain subsidies. These interests have slowed the pace of modulation in the UK, which since the reforms of 2000 could have moved to 20 per cent (see above), but instead has risen from a base of 2.5 per cent to 4 per cent.

Very few countries have attempted to phase-out subsidies entirely. New Zealand is hailed as one example, where subsidies were phased out in the 1980s and as predicted, farming contracted in the uplands (to be replaced by forestry or scrub) and many small farmers went out of business. However, producers now compete effectively in the world market, and New Zealand GDP per capita, drawn largely from an agricultural base, is now higher than in the UK. Agricultural holdings were at the outset, however, traditionally much larger than in the UK.

The increasing pressure to liberalize global markets has been accompanied by other forces that presage change for the agricultural community. The EU itself is enlarging to include Eastern European countries that have a large agricultural base, thus straining the EU budget further as well as threatening wildlife-rich habitats that in many ways provide reservoirs for species now rare or extinct in Western Europe. In this respect, CAP reform has never been more urgent, and a more integrated wildlife-friendly system could be of enormous benefit in rewarding these countries for their natural assets.

Added to these economic factors are the recent concerns over animal and human health following the major and very costly catastrophes of Bovine Spongiform Encephalitis (BSE) and the Foot and Mouth Disease (FMD) epidemic (dealt with in greater detail below). The former has led to grave public disquiet about the quality and health risks from meat and the latter has led to unease over issues of animal welfare, the power of the livestock industry to affect major areas of public policy in rural communities, and the financial risks of an industry exposed to increased transfer of global diseases in a liberalized global market for animal products. There has been a marked increase in those following a vegetarian diet and a subsequent depression (both financial and psychological) in the British livestock industry.

The loss in quality of food and the environmental degradation caused by intensive production have led to a rapid growth in the 'organic' food market and thus to some extensification of production – though Britain has lagged behind continental Europe and still has only 1 per cent of production under organic regimes, compared, for example, with Austria at 20 per cent.

The CAP response to these global trends is expected to accelerate when the global agreements on trade (GATT) work their way through into policy for the next decade. There is a general expectation of the phasing out of all production subsidies. This, in itself, would bring considerable 'environmental' benefit when viewed in terms of pesticides and fertilizer use, but there would be social and cultural impacts that would have major implications for habitats – for example, with many marginally economic grasslands losing their grazing stock and converting to scrub. It has long been understood that the most successful conservation strategies rely upon local communities being involved and gaining economic benefit. Hence, there has been an emerging agenda on the part of conservationists to direct subsidies to maintenance of semi-natural grazed habitats such as moorland, heath and wet pasture, but with lower stocking densities. The farmers are then compensated in the form of agri-environment payments.

However, there is strong global resistance to forms of 'hidden' subsidy and environmental standards affecting a free market (an agenda pursued by nations with little care for environmental safeguards). Few environmentalists see the global market and absence of subsidies as an ally. There would be little support for a policy that imported cheap food from areas in the world that had already sacrificed biodiversity and community for mass production. It is now more generally recognized that cheap food is not something that rich Western nations should aspire to – and it is cheapness, more than the farmer's embrace of industrial production, that has driven the degradation not just of our own countryside, but of large areas of the world's forests in the drive for ranching lands and export earnings.

At this stage, it is difficult to predict outcomes. The pace of CAP reform is agonizingly slow. British conservation interests have pushed for an increase in the modulation of funds, and UK farmers have expressed a willingness to cooperate but prefer such schemes to be voluntary, and one has to doubt that the heart of the large farming corporations really lies in that direction. However, the direction that the reforms are moving would require all EU countries to move towards a modulation of 20 per cent, as well as the capping of funds available for the largest farms and a gradual reduction in overall subsidy expenditure (3 per cent per year until a 20 per cent reduction is reached). In the case of smaller farmers in the uplands and other marginal lands, faced with dwindling incomes, a change of heart is already apparent, and there is an accelerated take up of agri-environment funds.

As an indication of the importance of dwindling incomes in precipitating change, UK farmers' average income per head has been quoted as being as low as £3500 for 1999 and as high as £13,500 for 2000, and this is universally recognized as a major crisis. Livestock farmers on marginally productive land (virtually all of the English, Welsh and Scottish uplands) would have had no net average income were it not for subsidies. In other words, farming costs equalled the income from sales, and as the great majority of farmers would have been at the lower end of the scale for net incomes, they will be in receipt of social benefits to provide their families with a living wage. Only the larger farms in the uplands produce a living wage, and even then, only by virtue of subsidies.

Urgent efforts are thus underway to support farming so that traditional rural community life can be maintained, and in the wake of the devastation caused by the FMD epidemic, there are a number of government reviews emerging relating to food production, health and the environment. The first of these, the Curry Report on the future of British farming, identified the subsidy modulation process as crucial to the future environmental health of the countryside, and this applies with particular strength to the uplands. This report was instigated in the wake of the impact of the FMD epidemic, and before commenting on the report, it is worth looking in some detail at that crisis because it exposed several important vulnerabilities of modern livestock practice to the global changes of the past two decades, and a great many of Britain's nature reserves rely upon grazing regimes to maintain secondary habitats.

## Animal and human diseases: consumer response to BSE and FMD

The FMD epidemic, which lasted from the autumn of 2000 to the summer of 2001, was a major shock to farming communities as well as to a horrified general public. An estimated eleven million animals were destroyed, with a compensation bill amounting to over £2.7 billion, of which £1.25 billion was for direct livestock compensation, £700 million for clean up and £470 million for animal welfare. All this expenditure was incurred to protect an export industry worth less than £500 million per year, but at an estimated cost to the tourist industry varying from another £3 billion (government estimates) to £20 billion (according to the Institute of Directors). Perhaps just as important as the financial cost was a profound psychological impact, the consequences of which are hard to gauge. The public were faced with images of mass executions, rotting corpses and millions of burning bodies with massive black smoke from the funeral pyres hanging over the British countryside. Farmers, very largely the most economically vulnerable hill farming communities, were faced not only with bankruptcy, but with a military-led operation of such punitive insensitivity that many were left in the most profound despair, both for their livelihood and their country.

Tim Adams, reporting in the *Observer* (10 February 2002) on a visit to the hardest hit Cumbrian communities one year after the onset, and just as export restrictions were being lifted, found farmers he had met during the epidemic still profoundly pessimistic about their futures. The communities reported an increased drift from farms, with many valleys holding virtually no prospect of young people taking up the family farm. There was still much bitterness against the Ministry of Agriculture, Fisheries and Food (MAFF) – with one landowner commenting, 'they planned it like a war . . . First they panicked everyone . . . then they killed the farmers' stock.' Conspiracy theories and a distrust of government were widespread, but equally disturbingly, one sheep farmer commented, 'You can't say you don't feel damaged spiritually. It is like a bereavement, but there is no burial site.'

Adams also highlighted the cultural divide that still exists between well-meaning conservationists keen to get the farmers onside with agri-environment reforms and hard-bitten hill farmers. He attended a seminar by Lord Haskins, coordinator of the government task force on farming, where a listless and resigned farming community listened to a catalogue of future perils – reform of CAP, global pressures, consumer demands and environmental pressures – all with a sense that there could be little future for upland sheep farmers.

The telling fact of the disease itself is that from an animal welfare and food quality perspective it is not particularly serious – rather like a heavy bout of flu – but as many countries have eradicated the disease, they will not import meat products from countries not vouchsafed as clear of it. This affects the export of all meat products. The alternatives to culling are either to accept the disease and loss of exports, dealing with each outbreak with smaller-scale culling and vaccinating adjoining herds, eventually relying upon building immunity, or to vaccinate the entire national herd at repeat intervals of six months. The latter is not regarded as practicable and vaccination of animals close to the centres of infection can only be used in tandem with culls, as was practised on the Continent with the small outbreaks there. However, within the current structure of export markets and the scale and rapidity of animal movements in the livestock industry, none of these alternatives are particularly robust.

The scale of the operation to contain FMD is difficult to comprehend, as is the psychological stress it caused in a shocked farming community and a disturbed public. Rural communities were divided by the policy – apart from the reaction to the severity of government policy, those farmers with infected herds that were culled were compensated, whereas those with healthy herds who were not allowed to get their animals to market were not. This division of communities was further exacerbated by the lack of adequate compensation for the tourist sector – thousands of small hotels and 'bed & breakfasts' lost custom as the countryside was effectively closed to walkers and others seeking recreation for as much as 6 months. One result of this, at least, was the realization in government and elsewhere that tourism was a bigger contributor to the rural economy than agriculture.

All this chaos was caused, ostensibly, by the import of infected meat that ended up in pigswill at a far-from model farm in Northumberland. Its rapid spread also highlighted the huge scale of animal movements across the country. The problem for the future lies not so much with the policies of culling and vaccination, which have received most discussion, but with the probability of repetition and the inherent vulnerability of Britain's intensive animal production methods. If FMD were to become endemic – it can hardly be imagined that another massive cull would be sanctioned – and thus some form of accommodation to the disease would have to be made, then Britain's livestock industry would lose its export markets and contract further.

To add to these troubles, there are rising concerns among scientists that the UK sheep stock could have been infected with the BSE agent. The first scientific studies to investigate the situation were marred by incompetent sourcing of test material, but theoretical studies point to the possibility that the indigenous scrapie agent, a prion disease that has BSE-like effects on sheep, though once thought not to affect humans, may also be able to jump the species barrier. I can remember from my student days that Creutzfeldt–Jakob Disease was more prevalent among African Arab tribes with a penchant for eating sheeps' eyeballs, a part of the anatomy close to the brain and rich in nervous tissue. If the BSE agent can transfer to sheep, or the sheep scrapie-prion mutates, this would be a potentially fatal blow to upland farming communities.

The loss of sheep and cattle in the hills has prompted studies of the effects on nature conservation, and as expected, there are some gains where over-grazed vegetation recovered, and some losses where too many stock were confined and unable to be moved (particularly severe on Lundy Island). Some conservation programmes using domestic stock for grazing were affected. On the one hand, Stephen Harris of the Mammal Society contemplated the potential for bringing lynx back to Britain if sheep farming declined and woodland developed ('In the shadow of death' *Wildlife* December 2001), and on the other hand, Graham Harvey warned of the threat to conservation from the loss of grazed habitats (*Wildlife* April 2001).

Stephen Harris has also warned of the potential for FMD containment policies to affect Britain's native mammal populations. A wide variety of animals can host the virus – ranging from hedgehogs to deer, and including wild boar. The difficulty of culling and the dispersal of hunted animals offer some protection from the ferociously extensive policies seen with domestic livestock; however, the potential risks of transference count against policies to re-introduce large herbivores to wild areas.

One further legacy of FMD, coming on top of the BSE debacle of the previous decade, has been an accelerating shift away from red meat – partly on health grounds, partly out of animal welfare concerns – and to an increased market for organic meat. In Britain, the proportion of people claiming to follow a vegetarian diet has risen from 3 per cent to 10 per cent in the last decade. There has also been a shift towards chicken from beef, with a 10–20 per cent reduction in sales of red meat. These shifts have already affected the economics of livestock production, and if maintained, would have major implications for land use. Large areas of lower-grade grain production are devoted to livestock feed and therefore arable farming is also affected.

There is at least one consequence of this crisis that has some potential for good: the public awakening to the true costs of unsustainable agriculture on an environmental, animal welfare and rural community level. To this end, the government instigated the Policy Commission on the Future of Farming and Food, and also reorganized its departmental structures in response to widespread criticism of MAFF – now effectively subsumed in the Department of Environmental and Rural Affairs.

## The Curry Report: A Policy Commission on the Future of Farming and Food

This policy commission was set up largely as a response to widespread public disquiet at the methods used to contain FMD, the suffering both of animals and rural communities, the huge costs and the general demise of Britain's agriculture. Views expressed in the wake of the epidemic had often been extreme, with otherwise sensible economists and political commentators showing an almost contemptuous disregard for farming, arguing that uneconomic agriculture in the countryside should cease and the rural economy should shift to leisure and wildlife opportunities for city folk.

The Commission was chaired by Sir Don Curry, a former head of the Meat and Livestock Commission and himself a farmer. In its foreword, the report states, somewhat anodynely:

> ... the trauma of Foot and Mouth Disease caused many people in the farming and food industry to think about what they do from first principles.

Despite its 140 pages, the report is thin on detail and replete with well-worn argument and generalities, albeit in the right direction – more localized production and connection to local markets, higher quality distinctive products, better welfare conditions, better training, retirement packages (significantly!), advice and education, and accelerated modulation of funds into agri-environment schemes and organic farming.

Simon Gourlay, former president of the NFU (1986–1991), on publication of the Curry Report told the *Independent* in February 2002, that though it contained many fine proposals, he had heard most of it before under previous governments, and that an agricultural reform group with the cooperation of the Prince of Wales, the NFU, Ministry of Agriculture (MAFF) and the EU Commissioner had made similar recommendations ten years ago – only to founder in the battle of vested interests.

Thus far, British farmers can expect the modulated funds to increase from 2.5 per cent to 4.5 per cent by 2006. The Curry Commission recommended an acceleration to 10 per cent by 2004 and the full 20 per cent by 2006. The problem is that these funds redirect money from production subsidies to agri-environment schemes under the England Rural Development Programme (ERDP), and will at present, take money away from 'successful' and 'efficient' farms (as seen from the industry perspective) in order to sustain uneconomic enterprises in the margin (a new area-based Hill Farm Allowance, ESA–Countryside Stewardship and Organic Farming conversion scheme). The NFU has thus resisted any drop in direct subsidy, as the large producers with virtually no environmental assets will be capped to fund farming in environmentally sensitive areas.

The Curry Commission recommended that a new countryside stewardship scheme should be available to virtually all farmers, and that new government money – matching funds from the treasury, should be available – of the order of £280 million over three years. The new money should support a 'broad and shallow' tier of stewardship payments for which most farms in lowland England would be eligible, and based upon whole-farm audits (with simplified bureaucracy and aided by information technology and GIS to identify environmental assets). This scheme would complement the present ESA-oriented specialized schemes for more clearly identifiable natural assets. In many ways, this approach is already being pioneered in

Wales under Tir Gofal, but I could find no references to this scheme in the Curry Report, or to the lessons to be learned.

Within the 140 pages of the report, lay one page concerning the benefits of organic farming, which simply stated that the sector had endeavoured for over 50 years to develop 'a system of farming that embodies sustainability in an environmental, social and economic context', addressing such public concerns as 'animal welfare, biodiversity, rural employment and the links between the health of the soil, plant, animal and man' and in so doing 'the organic sector has stimulated a growing demand for its food'. Curry then concludes that ongoing public support is justified, that it be included in the new agri-environment scheme, and recommends a strategy for organic food production covering issues such as research, development, standards and marketing, addressing all parts of the food chain in much the same way as for conventional supply chains.

This is rather symptomatic of the more general problem: agriculture is seen as a business, an industry supplying public goods, and organic production thus a specialized sector of that industry supplying a niche market. That organic production also has proven solutions to many of the sustainability problems facing industrial farming such as soil erosion, long-term loss of soil fertility, biodiversity losses, rural unemployment, pesticide pollution, fears over genetically modified organisms (GMOs) and general food safety, though mentioned by Curry, still does not lead to any great embracing of organic methods. Perhaps it is a simple matter of a business and industrial mentality, which conservationists have also encouraged, in which farmers see not just organic produce as a niche market, but redshanks and curlews too. There simply does not seem to be any real appreciation that farms are also ecosystems, the sustainability of which the quality of life and human survival itself depend upon.

Having been part of the long-term scientific and ecological lobby for sustainable food production (irrespective of its biodiversity or spiritual dimensions), I can now reflect upon the grudging concessions that have been made, no doubt engendered by 'the growing demand for its food'. Most organic farms are small-scale family enterprises run by people committed to the land and the processes of nature, from which the farming techniques have been learned. Those farmers I have known well over 15 years (one farming 500 ha of wheat, oats, sheep and beef in Oxfordshire, and another a large National Trust mixed farm in Wiltshire) have all faced ridicule until the last few years, despite consistent success in a premium market. Their farming practices have not been developed out of some opportunistic response to a niche market, but as an extension of their spirituality, a caring for the life and bounty of the land, their animals and the communities they supply.

The personal factor is not something any government commission is going to comment upon, whether it is the desolation experienced in northern England or the spiritual strength of the organic farming movement, but I believe it is crucial to the future of farming. As agri-environment schemes are extended, they will be available to a large part of the farming community that has been industrially minded and mentally disconnected from the cycles of nature and the spirit of their land. It is this cultural failing that needs to be addressed in the training and education of farmers in colleges that have until now focused exclusively on technology, chemicals and business acumen, in which the environment or nature is seen as just another product to be delivered to the more discerning customers.

These comments notwithstanding, some farmers have been exemplary in understanding what is at stake and doing something about it. Philip Merricks runs the farming estate at Elmley Marshes National Nature Reserve (NNR), and this reserve has achieved much more than a halt to declines, having increased wader counts significantly on the wet meadows by judicious use of DEFRA's agri-environment schemes. In *Agri-environment – Some Thoughts from the Marsh* (2003) he discusses the forthcoming changes, the potential merger of Countryside Stewardship Schemes (CSS) and ESA, the new trials of Entry Level Schemes in England and the all important changes of attitude required in the farming community towards their responsibilities, as well as for consumers and taxpayers regarding the wildlife heritage of farmed land – where the greater part of Britain's wildlife heritage has to find its habitat. In the same issue of *ECOS*, Ian Hodge and Alan Renwick (2003) of the Centre for Rural Economics Research at the Department of Land Economy, University of Cambridge, who reviewed agri-environment schemes for DEFRA, put forward four elements of reform, arguing for an entry level scheme that covers a substantially greater proportion of agricultural land, the 'broad and shallow', coupled to three elements of 'wildlife, landscape and resource enhancement' – the higher tier in which creating new habitat can be funded; 'collective initiatives for enhancement' in which competitive bids could further cooperative ventures; and 'community engagement' which would draw a wider range of actors into land management.[9]

To some degree, these integrated schemes have already been pioneered in Wales through Tir Cymen and Tir Gofal by the Countryside Council for Wales (CCW), which some time ago combined the roles of nature conservation, agricultural reform and rural development. It remains to be seen whether such schemes can do more than halt the declines, and in this respect, grazing marshes and wading birds may not be such a useful guide – Philip Merricks makes the telling comment: 'getting the habitat right for breeding waders means that it won't be far wrong for most of the other wildlife interests'. Such gains are not to be gainsaid, but most grazing marshes are secondary habitat with natural processes arrested by domestic stock. If we are to see large areas with wild grazers such as deer, cattle and horses, as in the Netherlands, then agri-environment schemes need to be integrated with support for core areas and networks of wildland.

The prospects are not good – consultants to Northumberland National Park and the Countryside Agency looked into the social and economic benefits of wildland policies on two large 3000 ha holdings that currently receive agricultural subsidy for hill cattle and sheep. A strict wildland policy with no qualifying grazing would have major problems accessing suitable schemes to replace the subsidies upon which upland farms depend, and the study concluded that under current support schemes, re-wilding would have negative social and economic impacts, even assuming that there was some compensation in eco-tourism.[10]

## Tir Gofal: an integrated agricultural support system

In many respects, the kinds of proposals made by the Curry Commission are already in train in Wales. In the quest to support the ailing upland farming economy and restore some of the damage of the past few decades, the Welsh Assembly in 2000 extended the Tir Cymen pilot schemes to the whole of Wales with the title Tir Gofal. Here, 'whole-farm schemes' apprise a number of nature conservation, cultural landscape and archaeological features for which farmers are paid maintenance grants to safeguard or improve. There are obligations to conserve and manage broadleaf woodland, hedgerows, stone walls and archaeological features, heath and unimproved grassland. Habitat enhancements, such as streamside corridors, creation of ponds or wetlands, and the restoration of flower-rich meadows, though eligible for payments, are optional. Similar schemes have been operated on a smaller scale throughout England under the Countryside Stewardship Scheme, and special whole-farm schemes in ESAs. An important feature of the new schemes is the ability to monitor and restrict livestock density in sensitive habitats.

The English schemes, especially the ESA/Stewardship programmes in England, were limited in extent, and like Tir Gofal, voluntary. They have not been taken up on a sufficient scale to have arrested decline even in these sensitive areas (little more than 10 per cent of agriculture) and may have been of only local significance. The Countryside Agency is now piloting larger-scale Land Management Initiatives in several sensitive 'countryside character' areas in an attempt to provide a similar focus to the stewardship schemes.

The Tir Cymen scheme was piloted in a few areas of Wales, including Meirionnydd in southern Snowdonia. Tir Gofal largely repeats the Tir Cymen focus upon landscape maintenance – especially the preservation of field boundaries and natural features, but can also reward creative conservation. The areas of potentially significant impact are the creation of streamside corridors, woodland, new wetlands and buffer zones of unimproved land adjacent to important conservation areas. It remains to be seen how far the scheme is primarily a defensive line against further degradation (welcome nevertheless) or can contribute to some restoration of past losses such as hay meadows, upland heath, streamside vegetation and wetlands. Much will depend upon the will and creative imagination of farmers and their advisors.[11] The total budget for Wales in 2000 was only £3 million and this rose to £6 million in 2001. This is adequate for between 500 and 700 farms per annum out of a total in Wales of 27,000. Thus, at £8000 per farm, if half of farms are involved a budget of £80m would be required.

If the National Farmers' Union were lobbying for such funds as enthusiastically as conservationists, there might be more progress, but it is the exceptional farmer who embraces a more soulful role as landscape manager and conservationist, and the NFU still represents the old business paradigm. I strongly believe that efforts to dress this more enlightened role in the language of business – producing environmental *goods* such as ponds and hedgerows for discerning *customers*, is a mistake, and that there needs to be a cultural shift to a new paradigm of loving care and responsibility. A linguistic analysis of farming journals would reveal more than a simple business mentality: the industry is replete with macho military vocabulary relating to wars on pests and invaders, as well as an industrial fervour for big machines and new chemicals.

The industry has aspirations to compete in world markets and the justification is entirely economic. The countryside is relegated to an obligation, either because of cultural attachments or environmental interests, and the industrial farmer expects to be paid for meeting that obligation. It is hardly surprising that farmers have drawn such little sympathy in the midst of their collective plight.

This growing lack of sympathy may well determine their future in a world where political commentators wedded to the ethos of global trade and liberalization of markets are quite prepared to see farming cut back on a grand scale. Battle lines are already drawn between a ruthless market-oriented future in which farmers, having sided with the dominant ideology, suffer a similar fate to coal miners and steel workers; and an almost welfare-based system of support for the socially disadvantaged (with the latter supported by conservationists intent on maintaining their favoured agriculturally-dependent habitats).

If the liberal marketeers dominate, then many thousands of small-scale family businesses, many of which care passionately about the fabric of the countryside, its wildlife and community, will disappear. On the better land, the holdings will be bought up by larger farms, boundaries will disappear, and the homes sold off to country commuters, tele-cottagers and people retiring from city life. Such amalgamations fuelled by subsidies over the past decades have brought in major corporate players such that they now produce most of the basic commodities. Just 9000 large cereal growers produce 60 per cent of British production, with 10,000 dairy farmers producing 60 per cent of milk. There is no incentive for these large producers to diversify even into woodland with some economic use, let alone non-productive habitats for wildlife such as wetland. If grant schemes were to match the income per hectare of these operations, they would swallow a huge proportion of the subsidies for very little gain. The very poor take up of woodland grants on farmland in England, compared to similar schemes in Scotland, is entirely due to the differential in land values and incomes. In Wales, holdings are smaller and largely pastoral, and as incomes have fallen, the take up of Tir Gofal has increased.

The crux of the problem thus lies in the extent to which agriculture in eastern England has aspired to world markets with a minimum of constraints, and in western England to the production of cheap dairy products for the supermarket chains. In large-scale production of cheap products, costs are high and margins of profit are small and I see no way in which a voluntary system that has to match incomes per hectare will succeed. The experience of the Farm Woodland Grant Scheme and the difficulties faced by Community Forests and the New National Forest should be enough evidence of this. Any broad-based scheme that would involve mainstream production, as proposed by the Curry Commission, would entail huge costs – 20 per cent of modulated funds amounting to £1 billion (with 50 per cent coming direct from the UK Exchequer) and at a time when the general political mood to subsidies is negative. If that money proved ineffective, it could lead to as great a political backlash regarding 'conservation' as the current 'production' subsidy has done, and there must be serious doubts as to how effective 'broad and shallow' schemes can be when they are largely untried. Nevertheless, change is afoot, and Countryside Stewardship and ESA schemes will be replaced in 2005 with a two-tier, whole-farm system available throughout England, a system similar to Tir Gofal as a 'broad and shallow' entry-level subsidy, but again, voluntary in its take-up.

## The limitations of agricultural support systems

There is little statistical data to show that 'greening' mainstream agriculture actually brings much biodiversity benefit.[12] Notwithstanding the successes on Elmley Marshes, in my current backyard of the Somerset Levels, designation as an ESA and the availability of funds over the last decade has not managed to reverse the decline of key wet grassland species such as whinchat and lapwing. Whole-farm schemes in wetlands have limited effect in those circumstances where neighbouring farms still operate with modern drainage techniques. Furthermore, there can be direct conflict between certain environmental benefits, such as reduction in fertilizer inputs and numbers of certain target species, such as waders. Studies in Holland of a major scheme in which hay-cutting was delayed to allow wading birds to breed showed a *fall* in wader numbers. This flagship EU scheme, using £1.7 billion of funds, also included restrictions on fertilizer inputs, which then affected invertebrate densities and food availability.

The RSPB has reported some success with farmland birds on arable land where stubble has been allowed to remain over winter, and although these successes are not to be gainsaid, they are coming from a very low starting point, with losses across a whole range of farmland bird species of the order of 50–80 per cent over the past decade.

One case history of a committed farmer motivated by the loss of birds on a 500-acre farm he took over in Hertfordshire is very instructive (*Independent*, 30 January 2002). The family farm had historically followed the national trend away from mixed farming to cereals, and working out of his own budget and investing of the order of £50,000, Edward Darling found that the loss of profitability from his first attempts to 'green' production (following conservation advice) made the farm economically unsustainable. He had used less fertilizer, left stubble throughout the winter and planted more spring crops. Through trial and error he began a programme of separating areas devoted to wildlife from those devoted to food production – instead of reducing inputs on cropland, he created new habitat: 'The result is that the numbers of a whole range of species have escalated and it is fabulous. The whole farm is alive.' Numbers of partridges and skylarks trebled, and with them other birds, bees, butterflies and wild flowers.

Darling welcomed the prospect of new agri-environment money in the wake of the Curry Report, although he has clearly achieved this without such support. Had he converted to organic production, the organic premium might have helped with the cost of the original extensification. This example does, however, show that there is an alternative to lowering inputs and changing planting practices, and it can be effective provided the motivation and expertise exists.

Conservation strategy with regard to farmland has been focused upon greening the CAP, with policies often being developed by buying farms and testing the various prescriptions – examples being the RSPB in leaving stubble and margins, raising water levels etc.; the Woodland Trust in mixed planting, pasture and wood pasture; and the National Trust in various schemes to reduce grazing. These efforts may halt declines and possibly reverse trends, but there may be greater benefit from enlisting farmers in targeted habitat creation through the use of nature maps and networks as described in Chapter 5. To a small extent, Tir Gofal provides for habitat creation, but there is no strategic thinking regarding networks – something that would require local leadership.

A large-scale programme of targeted habitat creation could be funded by CAP, though one would not expect imaginative progress until such time as the old paradigms of MAFF had been laid to rest (Philip Merricks believes there has been a major change in ethos with DEFRA). Some key schemes could attract money from the National Lottery, but a broader scheme could also be funded by a combination of carbon taxes (there are advantages for carbon sequestration) and a sustainable land tax on all non-organic food. A hypothecated tax of this kind would likely be more acceptable as well as communicating the unacceptability of 'cheap' food – at 2 per cent of consumer spending on fossil fuel and non-renewable electricity sources and 2 per cent on non-organic produce, it would yield several hundred million pounds per year, enough to begin a radical programme of habitat networks, which we discuss in the next chapter.

In such a programme of targeted habitat creation, current restraints on agri-environment schemes would have to be removed: for example, the CSS only allows 10 per cent of the farm area to be used for habitat diversification and is still focused upon the conservation paradigms relating to secondary grazed habitat with the funding agreement only extending to ten years. Farm woodland grants are limited to 40 ha and extend for only 15 years. This may be adequate to further streamside and riparian corridors, but not for the removal of domestic grazers from large areas of heath, and it is problematic in the support of wood pasture on a similar scale.

## Organic farming and sustainability

There is a widespread appreciation that land farmed organically is better for wildlife, soil fertility and water quality. Scientific surveys have shown lower environmental impacts and increased biodiversity, as well as increased employment and the creation of more local marketing of produce.

As early as 1989, in the days when organic farming was regarded as a rather quaint irrelevance by industrial farmers and their representatives, my own research group in Oxford provided one of the first such scientific reviews (authored by Charlie Arden-Clarke, who now works on GATT issues at WWF headquarters in Switzerland). It was extraordinarily difficult to fund and took us three years with help from, among others, the WWF; my former colleagues still get requests for the review from institutes around the globe.[13]

At the time of that review, there had been very few comparative field trials of organic production systems with conventional agriculture. Many more field trial comparisons have since been carried out and confirm the overall benefits both to sustainable production and biodiversity. So much so, that the Curry Report, somewhat shyly in a few paragraphs out of the whole analysis, admitted that organic methods answered all of the problematic issues of food quality, marketing and environmental degradation that had arisen in conventional agriculture.

Ultimately, consumer demand for better food and environmental quality, reflected in the willingness to pay 'organic' premiums, may be the most potent driving force of change in the next decade or more. The pace of such change in continental Europe has seen as much as 20 per cent of Austrian production switch to organic methods in the past decade, with Germany, Denmark and France not far behind. The UK organic sector accounts for about 2 per cent of farming and consumer demand cannot be met by local sources – one of the principles of organic production, and much organic fruit and vegetables is sourced in Holland, Germany, Denmark and as far away as Israel and Egypt.

However, the prospects are not entirely rosy. In July 2002, the *Independent* reported that the UK organic food market was approaching £1 billion/year, yet one third of all UK producers were operating at a loss. Only a small proportion of the home market is met by UK producers, and despite an acceleration of organic conversions, the number making more than £10,000/year profit had fallen from 56 per cent in 1979 to 38 per cent 2002. The flood of cheaper foreign imports coupled with the take up by supermarkets had forced prices below the level of production costs for many small producers. Thus, the same global forces that pressure conventional farming, coupled with high local costs for British farmers (rental, land prices, labour etc.), threaten to undermine the potential for organic production to green British agriculture.

I do not think that the greening process is likely to do more than arrest the current decline in abundance and diversity of wildlife. The UK government has hardly led the modulation of funds towards environmental schemes: only 12 per cent of agricultural holdings in England have been part of Countryside Stewardship or other schemes, and although the Welsh Assembly has pioneered the greening process with Tir Gofal, that scheme has limited funds, and a great deal of the activity is little more than tidying up farms. Tir Gofal has a potential to create new habitat and certainly to safeguard what has been left, but how far this arrests the current decline may not be known for 10 years.

The most that can be expected in response to the Curry Report is that a shift towards more environmentally friendly farming will begin, and that the decline of farmland species will be halted. If such a shift changes the consciousness of farming away from the macho-industrial mentality that has dominated the past towards an attitude of care and even some reverence for nature, that will be a major achievement. At best, it may form a supporting context for a more proactive approach that targets change in specific areas. What is needed to effect real change in mainstream agriculture is far more fundamental than these schemes, which may be little more than tinkering with a system that is at base unsustainable.

In this regard I can do little more that state what I feel is required, but in the certain knowledge that it will be another ten or 20 years before a political and economic environment evolves sufficiently to support it: ultimately, all farming must become organic and the consumer must pay through higher prices. At present, an unjust economic and political system rewards the irresponsible consumer (who pays the cheapest prices for commodities) and penalizes the responsible customer with the penalty of a higher proportion of their disposable income being paid towards society's general environmental benefit in cleaner air, water and more abundant wildlife.

Government will immediately defend its cheap food policy on anti-inflation grounds as well as protection for the economically vulnerable (a large sector of the population), much as it has done with regard to fuel prices and fuel poverty. There is a general aversion to regulation and 'interference' in consumer choice, but none of the arguments hold water, because all manner of regulations, some with considerable cost implications, exist on matters of consumer safety in other areas, for example, in fire regulations. Those on low incomes for whom food is a major expenditure can be protected by enhanced benefits and better education on diet and health.

I see no good reason why organic or near-organic standards should not be laid down for British agriculture, with a timetable of compliance on a par with targets set for other sustainable objectives, such as renewable energy. If this added 20 per cent to the cost of basic foods it would add perhaps 10 per cent to the social security bill to help the poor, but would hardly be punitive to the majority of households for whom food expenditure is not more than 20 per cent of total outgoings. If it meant a significant shift of expenditure away from other consumer areas, this would be balanced with more money directed to rural communities and employment, not to mention cost savings in pollution control and potential losses from further disasters associated with intensive livestock practices.

There would be an expected loss in yields of basic commodities, but this comes at a time when advocates of unregulated consumer choice already propose that we produce less and rely upon buying cheaper food from overseas. Such losses in yield could readily be compensated for by an educated shift to less meat in the diet. At the very least, government should now instigate research into the economic, social and environmental implications of a transition to organic production in all dairy products and cereals. There is already sufficient data for such a study. This could be followed by the land use implications of recent and potential future shifts to vegetarian diets and a thorough analysis of a livestock and poultry industry subject to organic standards and enhanced animal welfare. The Royal Commission on Environmental Pollution could engage upon a strategic study much as it did with regard to climate change and energy policies.

## A dual strategy: ecological farming practices and targeted habitat creation

It is my conclusion from this complex of interacting factors that a dual strategy is required: support for organic standards of production and a strategy of targeted creation of wildlife habitat. And as I shall argue in the final chapter, I believe that what we do here in Britain may have some influence on what happens elsewhere. As Eastern European nations come under the CAP – Poland, Slovakia, Lithuania and Estonia, in particular, some of the most valuable wildlife environments in temperate–boreal ecosystems will suffer the pressures of intensification. Poland contains the only remnant primeval forest at Bialowieza, and this should not remain a laboratory or living museum piece when it can act as a reservoir for the rejuvenation of a large tract of wildland in that region. If Bialowieza were to become isolated and surrounded by intensive agriculture, it would be a major opportunity lost. The Polish government has already submitted plans for major EU-funded infrastructural development in the area, including a motorway that would cut Bialowieza off from neighbouring forest areas (after intense lobbying, the Polish government has promised to carefully review the route). US meat companies have already earmarked Poland as the 'new Iowa' for pig production. In Belarus, there are already drainage developments underway that could affect the hydrology of the forest.

In Holland, as we have seen, there are well-developed landscape-scale initiatives, with some core areas for natural processes, and discussion about wildlife-friendly corridors for returning large herbivores and their predators. In Britain, we have the space for several flagship core area projects, and a newly developing infrastructure and ethos to support a network of wildland corridors. This potential (and its problems) is illustrated in Colour Plate 8. What we do now in the next ten years could affect thinking and policy in other key countries, but I believe we have to do far more than rely upon the slow reforms of the CAP. An acceleration of organic production and support for core areas and connectivity offers the most dynamic way forward. In the next chapter we shall look at those elements of new thinking that can lay the foundations for such change.

## The separation of farming and wildlife

First, I would argue for a distinction to be made for all farmed land in the national parks. In my view all farmers in national parks should be required by statute to participate in higher-level schemes when requested to do so by the National Parks Authority. At present, farmers in national parks take up stewardship schemes on a voluntary basis, but these should be compulsory and the extra funding made available. All the evidence points to farmers in such 'less favoured areas' gaining from such schemes.

However, there is little doubt that many farms in the uplands cannot be economic, even with the benefit of subsidy, and there is a general flight of young people from the industry. Those farms that come on the market in strategic zones for wildlife should be purchased by the park authorities and managed accordingly, perhaps in association with experienced land managers such as the National Trust. In a core area, that would mean holdings being allowed to develop into woodland or wood pasture. The National Trust recently purchased the Hafod y Llan hill farm on the flanks of Snowdon, and rather than put it out to tenancy, manages the land in such a way as to maintain the agricultural element but bring back woodland and montane scrub cover. Much as I would prefer to see a wilder policy – using wild grazers – this is a step forward for over-grazed hill land and a model for buffer zone management. The current Tir Gofal scheme is flexible enough to fund most of the changes that would be required in a buffer zone around core areas. National Park Offices could gain specialist knowledge from traditional wood pasture systems in countries such as Spain and Portugal, and help to provide information and an identity for this form of husbandry throughout Wales. Such a cultural shift could be part of a wider rejuvenation of cultural and linguistic identity.

In this respect, the communal purchase of uneconomic hill farms presents an alternative to purchase by large voluntary bodies such as the National Trust, Woodland Trust or RSPB. Land with character but of less value to these bodies could form the basis of community enterprises, in which the owners do not need to extract a living from the agricultural use of the land. The pioneering purchase of Moelyci in Snowdonia[14] will make a valuable case study for Welsh and perhaps also English uplands, and mirrors communal land reform in Scotland. Such communities need to be able to access appropriately tuned agri-environment/diversification funding tailored to part-time, non-industrial farming practices.

The situation in England, and Dartmoor in particular, requires further study – the Moor Trees group has focused upon the establishment of new woodland and intends to finance a study of the broader farm and moorland environment with regard to planting, regeneration and biodiversity. The various agencies are discussing habitat networks within the National Park. However, the woodland pasture systems in the Rhinogydd could well provide a model for the development of the pasture zones around a core area in the lower part of Dartmoor. Outside of the national parks, with their potential for core areas, we need to prioritize habitat networks on a landscape scale in the farmlands of the uplands, lowlands and coastal areas, and we shall look at this in the next chapter.

# 11
# Targeted Habitat Creation

The conclusion from the forgoing chapter is that reform of agricultural support may lead to lessening of the relentless intensification of arable land and grass cropping, but the signs are that for eastern Britain, this will do no more than halt the decline at what is now a very low level of abundance and diversity, and that if we are to reverse this decline, a programme of targeted habitat creation on a landscape scale is required. In the uplands of western and northern Britain, whole-farm support schemes with environmental criteria, such as Tir Gofal in Wales, may regenerate degraded moor and heath and create small areas of new habitat, but in an ad hoc manner. A strategy of targeted habitat creation using Forest Habitat Networks and river corridors could provide a focus for landscape-scale wilding projects. Such a programme of creative re-wilding, rather than protective conservation, may also have a wider public appeal.

A strategy of targeted expenditure on cores and corridors parallels recent thinking articulated by Chris Baines (*Wildlife* June 2002) on an initiative of conservation charities and government agencies for a 'Rebuilding Biodiversity Group' as well as the thinking of the inter-agency Land Use Policy Group outlined in Chapter 5. The Rebuilding Biodiversity Group aimed to explore issues of direct political and economic importance in an attempt to make wildlife central to the solution of several major problems: flood management and water quality, coastal defence, the carbon balance and climate change, economic recovery from FMD, reliable food production and healthy urban living. Baines outlines how 'joined-up' thinking can operate on a landscape scale, for example, to deal with the problem of flooding in lowland Britain.

The record floods of 2000 caused £3 billion in insurance claims, yet rainfall patterns have not altered significantly. The damage was caused by a combination of decades of over-grazing in the uplands, land drains to improve pastures, and canalization of rivers – thus leading to rapid run-off. Baines advocates using the context of the recent Water Framework Directive of the EU, which requires a whole-catchment approach to managing both quantity and quality of water. The Group wants to focus on one river catchment as an opportunity to show how ecological land management could work in practice, and the Tweed project outlined in Chapter 5, would be ideal in this regard, especially with its connections to Carrifran in the uplands.

One of the undoubted problems of conservation in the past has been its limited appeal to the broader public – the growth of membership in RSPB, the National Trust and Woodland Trust notwithstanding, it has made little headway against the main agendas of agriculture and industrial growth. Sites of 'special' scientific interest, or 'special' areas of conservation or protection, hardly grab the imagination and are often focused upon protecting esoteric treasures of actual interest only to specialists. The one significant large-scale programme of land-use change for public benefit has had wildlife as a bonus rather than a goal, and that is the planting of amenity forests close to urban areas in the Community Forest programme. This programme of targeted land-use change (not necessarily involving changes in ownership) has married elements of wilder land with amenity, education and productive use and will contain much useful experience for other large-scale strategies of land-use change, in particular the issue of *identity* and ownership of the project for local communities.

In all this new thinking, the rather older programme of targeted habitat creation – the former Countryside Commission's Community Forests – has proven remarkably visionary and successful. As outlined in Chapter 9, this project was conceived as a creative programme of new forest on the urban fringe with multi-purpose aims relating to amenity, wildlife and forestry. These areas would create a bridge between urban areas, some severely degraded and derelict, and the wider countryside, providing schools and communities with opportunities to become involved in planting and educational projects. Each forest had its own management group and sought sponsorship from local businesses.

The Community Forest experience provides a useful model for study. Such large-area schemes on what is expensive land are rightly regarded as very long term with regard to aims for tree cover, and the slow progress has been due mainly to the inability of government grant schemes for new woodland to provide sufficient financial incentives compared to agricultural land use.[1] The schemes have been successful in areas of amenity planting, riparian corridors, coordinated river restoration and new flood-plain woodlands, with some involvement also in woodchip energy crops such as coppiced willow providing for local markets (pioneered near Swindon). Further study of the lessons derived from river restoration, flood plain woodland and riparian–urban wildlife corridors within these schemes would be most useful for other lowland initiatives.

## Whole-farm and whole-catchment approaches in the uplands

In the uplands of Britain, the introduction of whole-farm integrated subsidy schemes may bring a reduction of grazing, widespread planting of broadleaf woodland, the blocking of drains and use of wetland habitat to cleanse water. These, along with the reduction in the use of fertilizers on improved pastures and less-intensive sheep-dip and pesticides use, would all contribute to solving the problems of flood damage and the costs of water treatment. In addition, directing smaller-scale attention to stream sides – as currently envisaged in Tir Gofal where farmers can be paid to extend the 1 m margin around streams to 6 m with fencing and planting (with later removal and access of livestock also allowed) – if carried out on a large scale, would provide thousands of mini-corridors that could also be extended into lowland areas.[2]

Whilst whole-farm subsidy schemes integrated with environmental objectives may go some way to greening upland farming, major landscape-scale ecological restoration requires large areas of new broadleaf woodland.[3] The inter-agency review group (LUPG – Land Use Policy Group; see Chapter 5) tasked with looking at the problem of large-scale establishment of new woodlands focused upon 'New Wildwoods' (largely as a result of the failure of English and Welsh policies to increase the planting of broadleaf native woodland generally) and concluded that a *wildwood* would have wider appeal and leverage for funding. The Group was welcoming of input from the grassroots and Adam Griffin, Stanley Owen and myself attended two of the seminars focusing on Wales and southwest England. We were able to communicate much of the vision of Trees for Life, Coed Eryri and Moor Trees with regard to wildland cores and corridors, and this is reflected in the final report. However, we all found that thinking within the agencies and the leading charities, such as the National Trust, was already well advanced and extremely encouraging.

The seminars showed how far the agencies and the leading conservation bodies had taken on board the concepts of large-area initiatives, particularly the need for cooperative endeavours. I found everyone open to new ideas, and was particularly impressed by the thinking of the Forestry Commission. However, the agencies still seemed to see the issue purely in terms of trees, and there was a danger that our well-developed concept of a wildwood core area would be watered down in an effort to find a new message for an essentially old and failed policy of increasing native broadleaved woodland. The concepts of defragmentation, linkage and large-area planning were all soundly articulated, but the problem areas related to the degree of management and the political requirements to further economic and social interests, especially access and recreation. We discussed the different management approaches to core areas of true wildwood and buffer zones with corridors, but the LUPG had little enthusiasm for the cultural dimensions of wildland, wildwood and re-wilding, most especially when it might relate to re-introducing exterminated forest species.

The Group has developed an approach based upon George Peterken's Forest Habitat Networks, where a mosaic of habitats and a variety of management styles operate. Within the mosaic there would exist a core area with corridors and connections, although these are largely seen as benefiting the flora and general landscape, rather than in the context of larger forest mammals. In its brief survey of sites the Group included Glen Affric and the Rhinogydd, adding the North Pennines (Geltsdale – though with little enthusiasm from their colleagues in conservation agencies in the area), the mid and northern sections of the Cambrian Mountains (Tywi catchment and Elan Valley), the Scottish Borders and Ennerdale in the Lake District. The preference, however, is for many relatively large schemes (by English standards, 1000 ha is a very large scheme), rather than one very large scheme, such as something on the scale of the Trees for Life project or our targeted sites on Dartmoor and in Snowdonia.

Nevertheless, the final report of June 2002 gave cause for some optimism, particularly in the attitudes of the Forestry Commission and the Welsh Assembly with regard to public lands. The stage is now set for a major initiative in wildwood creation with large areas of new woodland, in some cases building upon remnants of ancient near-natural woods and restructuring plantations, with an essentially wildlife ethos. What is required is a financial and policy instrument that will turn this potential into trees. The way forward with the greatest potential lies with the willingness of the Forestry Commission to re-wild significant areas of plantation to form a core area, and for this to act as a focal point for other landowners such as the National Trust – exactly the situation pertaining in the Rhinogydd and successfully developed in Glen Affric.

The major stumbling block to expansion beyond Forestry Commission lands will be funds for the purchase or lease of agricultural land. In the cases we reviewed in Chapter 5, such as Cashel and Glen Finglas, access to public funds, whether lottery or various woodland grant schemes, is usually predicated on provision of public amenity in the form of access and visitor facilities. This is fine and necessary in buffer zones where it is important to provide new employment opportunities and maintain tourism (in Snowdonia and Dartmoor particularly), but it compromises schemes for truly wildland where such facilities should be minimal and any additional visitor pressure discouraged. In this respect the Carrifran project, funded largely by small donations from committed individuals, and where access is open but facilities minimal, provides a more useful model.

The LUPG surveyed several areas in some detail, looking at both ecological and institutional issues in each region. The North Cambrians were favoured because of the large land holdings of the Forestry Commission (effectively owned by a sympathetic Welsh Assembly) and the existence of agency-supported groups such a Tir Coed, with visions of re-establishing large-scale near-natural Atlantic oak woods. The Tywi headwaters had been earmarked for study, particularly with the possibility of converting maturing conifer plantations. The Pennines were also looked at in detail, an area where tree cover is acknowledged as the lowest in upland Britain. However, with little tradition of forestry and many moorland sites of special conservation concern, only small areas at the western end of Wensleydale and in the northwest Pennines at Geltsdale suggested themselves for large-scale wildwoods. In the Southern Uplands of Scotland there are already initiatives of the Borders Forest Trust and the Southern Uplands Partnership promoting Forest Habitat Networks.

In lowland England the potential is much reduced because of the high value of arable land and limited traditions of forestry. Exceptions are the Sussex and Surrey woods, with proposals already made for using similar principles to Forest Habitat Networks (Sussex Wildlife Trust[4]). However, there are also projects to revitalize ancient forests such as Rockingham and Sherwood, and as noted, Community Forest projects that could conceivably include smaller-scale wildwoods. The LUPG concluded that targeting riparian strips of woodland and other semi-natural habitats linking individual woodlands within these zones was the best way forward, with action led by the Woodland Trust, Wildlife Trusts and other voluntary organizations.

However, if large-scale new woodlands in the uplands and riparian corridors of lowland wildland are to become a reality, significant new funding will be required, and this is unlikely to come quickly enough from reform of agricultural subsidies, or on a sufficient scale from the leverage funding of conservation organizations such as the Woodland Trust and the RSPB or from the National Lottery. In these cases, there is the added complication of responsibilities to members and the general public with regard to access and to local communities with regard to economic opportunity. New funding for wildland needs to come from sources that would not of necessity compromise the ethos of wildland. In this respect, I have been a long-term advocate of carbon sequestration, despite its unpopularity among environmental campaigners.[5]

## Climate change, carbon dioxide emissions and renewable energy: opportunities for targeted funding

Global warming introduces another major element of change into the conservation and land-use equation. It is now regarded as 'very likely' (IPCC Summary Report[6]) that the global average temperature is rising at a rate not seen at least this side of the last ice age, and this is expected to translate into rapid warming in polar regions with concomitant effects on temperate forest ecosystems. I am not personally convinced of the link between carbon dioxide emissions and temperature anomalies, but the precautionary principle ought to commit governments to reducing atmospheric carbon, whatever the evidence for effects, and new broadleaf forests can be a small part of that strategy. My lack of conviction arises from a palaeo-ecological perspective: it is well-known that the Holocene (the past ten thousand years) has been an unusually stable climatic period. The earth's rhythmic cycles are normally peppered by chaotic episodes of rapid temperature fluctuations connected with oceanic circulation changes, and these are far from understood. The globe is quite capable of warming without human help, and it does so in response to solar cycles.

The IPCC is less forthright on this issue than might be supposed from governmental pronouncements – first, they ascribe a 10 per cent chance that global warming is an artefact of measurement (seeking a world average from a series of regional disturbances) and second, they ascribe a 30 per cent chance that if real, it is due to natural causes. Scientific hypotheses normally require a 5 per cent probability of error, and ideally, 1 per cent. The uncertainty relates to the role of water vapour in the climate model: it accounts for 110 units of temperature-forcing with an error bar of 10, wherein the computed forcing power of additional carbon is 3 units – the 'noise' in the system readily drowns the expected signal.

However, there has been an international response to reduce the pollution from fossil fuel burning, with targets set in the UK for renewable energy substitution, largely as a percentage of electricity generation. A large proportion of the renewable energy resource is located in the countryside, for example, short-rotation coppice, biofuel crops such as oil-seed rape, forest residue power stations, small-scale hydro-schemes and wind turbines, or in sensitive coastal areas as with tidal barrages. Estimates of the land take vary, but biomass crops could extend to 800,000 ha and under some scenarios take up to 15 per cent of arable land. Wind turbine deployment is set to expand from about 500 MW with less than a thousand turbines to 5000 MW with another three thousand machines.[7] Large corporations have already targeted extensive areas of the Scottish Highlands and Western Isles, the North Pennines, the Cambrian Mountains, Cornwall, coastal regions and some large estuaries, and there are recent government moves to counter local objections on the grounds of landscape impact.

There are crucial wildland implications of what is essentially industrial energy production in the countryside – such as the intrusion of wind turbines and access roads (the Welsh Assembly has mooted the whole Plynlimon massif as a turbine zone), hydro-schemes on remote wild rivers, barrages on estuaries, and the industrial processing of wood, where wood-chip power stations can source material up to 50 km distant and can be expected to put pressure on all 'unmanaged' woodland in the vicinity. The current lack of appreciation of wildland values is demonstrated by the indiscriminate support of onshore wind turbine sites by environmental groups such as Friends of the Earth and Greenpeace, with only the National Trust and the government's Countryside Agency expressing deep concern at the change of character and feeling with the clear loss of wildness.

In this regard, my own consultancy work over the past three years has focused on developing modes of communicating the issues and forming inputs to the planning process, the last line of defence for crucial wild areas that also hold significant renewable energy resources. Working with the National Trust, we produced a booklet *Call for the Wild* which set out the value of undeveloped wildland for human spiritual needs, as well as for animal species dependent upon undisturbed habitat. The Trust constrained the analysis to that of a protective rather than proactive advocacy, in keeping with its obligations as land managers to farming tenants, and could not, at that stage, embrace the re-wilding of farmed areas. However, the Trust has embarked on two major initiatives to re-wild the fens near Cambridgeshire and the fells of Ennerdale in the Lake District, and lessons from these projects will inform land management in other areas.

The intrusion into rural areas of industrial-scale renewable energy production is already creating conflict, particularly with regard to changes in the visual character and feel of an area, which are important for tourism-based industries, as well as the general psychological wellbeing of a significant proportion of the population. There are few planning aids for the visualization process, especially with regard to strategic siting and choices of technology.

In an attempt to remedy this, I set up the small consultancy *Ethos* to develop the use of virtual reality software in visualizing change, and with a commission from the Countryside Agency we explored issues relating to renewable energy and the English landscape.[8] The visual techniques have great potential to illustrate the choices that planners can make – of the differing technologies of supply and their environmental consequences. The location, size and ownership of wind farms, for example, make a huge difference to their intrusiveness and acceptability in rural communities, and although our most treasured landscapes, such as national parks, Heritage Coasts and areas of outstanding natural beauty (AONBs), are reasonably well-protected, developments on their periphery can destroy that sense of isolation and wildness so important to their character.

The project has also explored coastal retreat scenarios and afforestation of the uplands, although largely in respect of energy policy scenarios. The visualizing techniques could be used to good effect with wildwood development, the greening of agriculture and the siting of corridors, and at *Ethos* we have been exploring ways of developing the software with the University of East Anglia, which has a unit modelling coastal salt marsh and climate change responses.[9]

However, the prospective impact of measures to meet the Kyoto obligations is not entirely negative. The restoration of large tracts of near-natural forest, reduction of grazing on upland pastures and the use of re-wilding techniques in forestry have significant implications for carbon balances – and this has recently been embraced by the Kyoto protocols to the Climate Convention and recommended by the Royal Society.[10] Our upland soils have been losing carbon for hundreds of years, either through overgrazing and reduction of soil organic matter, the drainage and subsequent oxidation of peaty soils or the planting of short-rotation conifer crops on peat (which results in a net carbon loss).

## Carbon sequestration and wildland

All of Britain's soils have been steadily depleted of organic content as agriculture has intensified. The effect is not limited to over-grazed moor and heath or peaty soil that has been drained and opened to plantation forestry – virtually all arable soils have experienced a reduction in carbon content (and would benefit from organic practices).

The natural regeneration of upland forests and the cessation of commercial short-rotation production (30–40 year cycle) in favour of native broadleaves (or Caledonian pine) either as wildwood or for firewood (with the use of much longer cycles of smaller-scale less-intrusive felling of timber) have the potential to reverse these carbon losses and act as a carbon sink for a small but significant percentage of the UK's emissions. Moreover, there is the rapidly emerging potential of funding for such forestry based upon carbon taxes and credits per tonne of carbon sequestered.

As yet, no schemes have been worked up. The British government has tended to be sceptical of carbon sequestration because of the size of the UK's emissions and the small amount of land resource available. However, as part of a larger strategy of ecological restoration, even a small contribution to the carbon equation from the UK's land bank would make a potentially big difference to the viability of wilder forests in Britain's uplands.

In 1989, whilst working on these issues in the lead up to the Rio summit, I came across the initiative of the US company AES, a provider of 'turn-key' operations for the electrical power industry. AES built and operated power stations on behalf of utilities worldwide. In the US they had just commissioned several gas-fired stations under agreements that the carbon emissions would be offset by planting trees in Central America. At my research group in Oxford in the late 1980s we had become sceptical of the US technical fraternity who were then looking to 'manage' the world's forests for carbon sequestration, with several supposedly scientific studies under way to identify the size of global resource. There were even proposals to clear cut the great forests of the taiga, store the carbon and replant with genetically modified fast-growing trees! At the Political Ecology Research

Group (PERG) we were anxious to counteract this madness and at the same time to draw attention to the power of carbon-offset programmes to direct funds into ecological restoration.

At the time, Britain had a single state-owned power supplier – the Central Electricity Generating Board (CEGB), with Sir Walter Marshall as its head. The CEGB was about to be privatized, and AES were looking to begin operations in the UK. I met with their chief executive as they arrived in London to look for offices and quizzed him about the Central American schemes. I was struck by his genuine desire to do something to restore degraded ecosystems. AES was working with aid agencies (and gaining leverage funds) to identify appropriate strategies to provide fuel-wood to take pressure off the natural forests, to protect existing forest and to regenerate natural forest in degraded areas. The schemes were funded out of the profits from the stations commissioned in the US.

I approached Walter Marshall, and after much debate, the CEGB decided to fund a PERG research programme on the potential for such a scheme in Britain. We embarked upon a land-use study and an appraisal of the carbon-sequestration potential of UK woodland. Data was scarce, and it was clear that little relevant work had been done. However, we arrived at a rough figure of 2.5 tonne of carbon per hectare per year as a reasonable expectation for natural forest restoration projects (about three times that yield may be obtained for wood grown directly as biomass-fuel on good arable land). About 1 million hectares of degraded formerly forested land (moor and heath) could be identified which was of low conservation status (not SSSI heathland or blanket bog) along with a further one million hectares of marginal pasture land.

In its final report in 1990 (*An Assessment of the Feasibility of Large Scale Afforestation in Britain to Offset Carbon Dioxide Emissions*) PERG proposed hybrid schemes whereby much cheaper large-scale ecosystem restoration would be undertaken in Africa alongside more expensive schemes in the UK.[11] In this way, Britain could help restore the planetary carbon balance in a way that was economically feasible, aided overseas development and dealt with its responsibilities in its own back yard. The restored forests would also be large enough for the re-introduction of formerly eradicated mammals such as boar, beaver, moose, bear, lynx and wolf, thus also meeting the UK's obligations under the then forthcoming Biodiversity Convention and the new EU Habitat's Directive, which had given authority to the concept of habitat enhancement and restoration after decades of preservationist and protectionist programmes.

Sadly, our hopes for turning the vast resources of the CEGB and the UK electricity consumers on to an AES-style restoration programme foundered with the denationalization of the CEGB and the regeneration of the private profit motive. The economists at Powergen and National Power could see no obvious benefit to the new companies, and AES, though active in the new deregulated market, did not need to use its green credentials to get contracts.

In one other European country, however, these ideas did take off, and Forests Absorbing Carbon Emissions (FACE) developed in Holland, led by the utilities and supported by many city councils and consumers. To date, FACE has put significant funds into the restoration of over 300,000 ha of African degraded land (in national parks), as well as into planting programmes in Holland.

In recent times, others have progressed self-taxing schemes in Britain. There are two major UK-based carbon offset programmes – Future Forests and Climate Care. Both have sought to provide a package to industry and consumers whereby a percentage of carbon emissions can be offset.[12] A variety of companies have taken up the schemes but it remains to be seen whether the large-scale response that is required will be forthcoming.

Environmental groups and government agencies remain sceptical of the schemes. Climate Care has recently overhauled its programme to take account of the criticism relating to diversion of focus from emission controls and has evolved a package that involves efficiency in the UK and forests planted largely in Africa (in cooperation with FACE). The work of Future Forests is rather more problematic because they plant trees largely in Britain and do not approach the issues of emission control and company audits with the same rigour. Planting trees in Britain, especially as part of amenity programmes around cities, is very expensive, and claims that a household's carbon emissions can be offset by a £25 annual donation and the planting of no more than a handful of trees is hard to reconcile with the figures that we produced and the emission profile of the average household at 6 tonnes C/annum. From discussions with their scientific advisors at Edinburgh's Centre for Carbon Management, the future lifetime carbon credit is assumed in the annual offset payment, rather than the annual carbon sequestration in the year of payment. It is a valid approach, in that the amenity tree is guaranteed protection and management and will eventually sequester a tonne or more of carbon, but it is of limited potential given the high costs of amenity planting. Furthermore, companies can offset only a small proportion of their emissions and still gain publicity, and few large companies have so far opted for the full carbon-neutral option.

A better approach would be to fund larger-area schemes, in Scotland for example, either by purchase of land or management agreements. It would take 2–3 ha of new planting at 2000 trees per hectare to offset that first household-year, but the woodland would sequester at that rate for at least the next 100 years, eventually sequestering over 200 tonne/ha. If land is purchased for wildland programmes, the ongoing management costs are very low. Much higher annual costs are incurred if landowners are paid for management at rates that would compete with current incomes per hectare. The removal of subsidies for livestock would alter the equation in the English and Welsh uplands considerably.

## Wildland and the integration of future land-use issues

Perhaps the times are becoming more favourable for linking these sets of problems. A potentially unpopular consumer carbon tax could be packaged as a climate levy that would regenerate wildwoods over much of the British uplands. The costs of land purchase or management (according to core area, buffer zone or corridor status) could be shared with a number of agencies – Forestry and Farm Woodland Grants, Countryside Stewardship, Tir Gofal and the HLF. It is what the American company AES termed 'leverage' funding – one initiative on carbon sequestration in an area leading to access to funds for community development, eco-tourism and wildlife enhancement. We shall return to this theme in the next chapter on strategies.

In all of this, stands the conservative, subsidy-dependent upland farming community and the challenge to sustain livelihoods. In some areas, agri-environment schemes can offer such communities a lifeline – particularly in the conservation of secondary habitat such as herb-rich grassland (in the Dales, for example) or heather moorland (Exmoor, the Pennines, North York Moors and the Berwyns, among others) – but in other areas, perhaps in the majority of uplands where acid grassland or bracken predominates, there is a tremendous opportunity to create woodland corridors. A significant proportion of that new woodland could be wildwood, with no economic use, as a means of restoring ecosystem health not only to the uplands, but as part of a wider watershed management policy for water quality, flood control, biodiversity and carbon balancing.

Government has recently expended vast sums, £3 billion on FMD alone, as well as £60 million per annum on upland farming subsidy, and faces similar billions for the annual expenditures on flood control and sea defences. The landscape is not robust against climate change and will become increasingly expensive to maintain by traditional practices. In the longer term, investing in ecological processes of flood control and maintenance of water quality will make sound economic sense. Re-wilding is an option that goes much further than wildlife and recreation – on a large enough scale, it would contribute to a more robust and healthy landscape, encourage eco-tourism and help sustain upland communities in the face of future economic and environmental changes.

## River restoration and Forest Habitat Networks

In conclusion, therefore, I believe that we already have the institutional framework for major landscape-scale re-wilding in Britain. The basis has been laid in both thinking, planning and practical projects related to Forest Habitat Networks, a concept developed by George Peterken for SNH[13] and embraced by the inter-agency LUPG in its New Wildwoods project, and in the catchment-based wild rivers projects supported by the River Restoration Centre and the Environment Agency, as perhaps best exemplified by the Tweed and Tamar catchment projects.

These two conceptual frameworks could act to *target* land purchases by all conservation-oriented organizations, especially those now embracing a broader ethos of re-wilding and creative habitat work, such as the Woodland Trust, RSPB, the National Trust, the Wildlife Trusts and the Forestry Commission. If the focus is upon riparian woodland (and other habitats such as reedbed, meanders, heath and rough water meadows), then effective wildlife corridors can be created through relatively sterile agricultural landscapes. These targeted purchases could be combined with greater emphasis on the part of the agencies involved in agri-environment support schemes upon streamsides with 6 m margins, as contained in the pioneering Tir Gofal scheme.

There is, however, a danger that attention will be distracted and large sums of money will not be made available for making major inroads into agricultural landscapes using quite ordinary riparian corridors and greater woodland, by the current preponderance of expenditure upon both the maintenance and extension of *secondary* habitat such as heathland, wetland and especially reedbeds for the more charismatic and rarer species. This approach is driven by the UK Biodiversity Action Plan (UKBAP) targets and a focus upon rare species (mostly birds) often on the margins of their European strongholds (for example, the bittern, golden plover, merlin, hen harrier, marsh harrier and black-tailed godwit). Large organizations such as the RSPB have institutional commitments to visitor facilities, access and public amenity. Public money for these schemes is often tied to greater access and provision of such facilities. Large amounts of funds have been garnered for extending heathland and reedbeds that would, under wildland conditions, experience natural processes of succession that would be less than favourable to target species, as well as to visitor attendance. Nature-gardening on a grand scale has its place, but surely not at the expense of a broader strategy. There is a need for both approaches, but there are already signs that after the instigation of these heathland and wetland projects, government and lottery money may not now be forthcoming for new projects. It may well be that new money for cores and corridors will have to come from forestry grants, the agri-environment budget and innovatory carbon schemes.

## Ecological Networks in the Netherlands

In the Netherlands, however, government has recently spearheaded targeted habitat creation with the intention to buy land as well as to subsidise the private sector to do so. In its 2004 National Spatial Strategy the government of the Netherlands embraced the concept of cores, corridors and ecological robustness in a major programme for the expansion of nature-area consisting of wildlife reserves acting as core areas, and corridors of connectivity between them.[14] By 2018, over 280,000 ha are projected for development by enlarging existing reserves and creating corridors and buffer zones, with 60 per cent to be purchased by government, and 40 per cent by subsidised private organisations and farmers (75 per cent and 65 per cent respectively).

This major programme followed intensive public consultation in 2000 on issues of robustness to climate change, fragmentation of habitat, and public recreation. With public support, government has begun not only to enlarge areas, but to dismantle obstacles to connectivity such as inappropriately sited industrial developments, and to provide tunnels and bridges for wildlife movement across motorways and railways. River corridors are a prime means for establishing connectivity. The planned Dutch Ecological Network (see Colour Plate 7) will eventually link to a Pan European Ecological Network.

# 12
# Stepping Stones to a Wilder Policy

In the previous chapters I have outlined what could be achieved for specific sites and the wilding of the countryside in-between: core areas that are essentially sanctuaries of nature; buffer zones that take account of the special wildlife needs of the core areas, but which are integrated with compatible economic activity; and wildlife-friendly corridors that link these key areas. Within the natural sanctuaries, ecosystems must be restored to include the guilds of herbivores and carnivores that are essential to the evolutionary processes with which most of our wildlife has evolved. In addition to these essentially biological elements of wildland, there are aspects that relate to the human need for wildness. The core areas must be free of intrusive development and, as far as practicable, artefacts of past industrial and agricultural uses should be removed.

There are many conservation achievements that already provide us with stepping stones relevant to our core area proposals:

- The national parks have worked consistently towards conserving biodiversity despite having a remit to balance nature conservation with economic interests, and although past recommendations for core areas of wilder land (Edwards Commission[1]) have not been implemented, the general constraints on development have at least safeguarded potentially viable core areas on Dartmoor and within Snowdonia; in Scotland, recent cooperative endeavours within the voluntary sector, such as the Royal Society for the Protection of Birds, the National Trust for Scotland and the Woodland Trust, have begun to establish large areas where the main focus is upon habitat restoration.

- the once monolithic and economically oriented Forestry Commission has evolved a modern multi-purpose forestry ethos which includes restoration of native woodland, diversification of plantations, conservation of biodiversity and the devolvement of management to community enterprise, including the sale of less viable plantations.

- There has been a very large increase in the memberships of conservation organizations such as the National Trust, RSPB, Woodland Trust, and the county Wildlife Trusts, such that the financial resources available for initiatives, especially the purchase of land and expensive habitat restoration, have increased considerably.
- Initiatives to restore the natural flow and riparian habitats of Britain's rivers have begun with several successful pilot projects that have gained support from county councils, the water companies and government agencies.
- A greater awareness of the urban fringe and 'ecology in the city' has brought the concepts of ecological restoration and creative conservation to a wider range of communities; in this respect the Community Forests and City Forests, involving thousands of young people and community organizations, have paved the way for wildlife corridors into the heart of urban centres.
- Farming practices are under review after serious failures relating to public health (vCJD) and animal welfare (foot and mouth disease) that have impacted upon the economics of the countryside, especially livestock farming and the tourist industry; the world economic environment is also moving towards the removal of subsidies – an uncertain development, but one that appears to have the potential both to liberate marginal land from agriculture, and also to further conservation practices through agri-environment subsidy, as now pioneered by Tir Gofal in Wales; several decades of experience now exist with various Countryside Stewardship schemes for Environmentally Sensitive Areas, Woodland Grant schemes and Land Management Initiatives, all of which could be expanded in a broader policy of redirecting production subsidies towards environmentally benign practices.
- Greater access to funds for creative initiatives now exists through the auspices of the National Lottery, with the Heritage Lottery Fund, which has already made substantial grants for land purchase and has articulated an interest in large-area schemes.
- A potential supporting factor for afforestation arises under the Kyoto Protocol, which recommends carbon sequestration as part of a strategy to adapt to climate change; the onset of man-induced climate change also furthers concepts of robust habitats, food and fuel production, which may also aid in re-wilding.
- Finally, the last fifteen years since the European Union's Habitats Directive have given Britain an obligation to enhance habitats as well as to protect them and, where conditions are favourable, to include the potential for the return of former elements of the fauna exterminated by man; a small start has been made by Scottish Natural Heritage in the programme for the re-introduction of the beaver to its former range.

These developments have all converged at the beginning of this new millennium to produce a remarkable resurgence for wildlife in Britain. In the last decade we saw the National Trust for Scotland purchase large areas of former sporting estates – in the Cairngorm with Mar Lodge (30,000 ha) and in Glen Affric with the West Affric estate – and the National Trust in England and Wales recently purchased 3000 ha on Snowdon. The managerial philosophy of these organizations, though seeking a balance between economic interests and conservation, is increasingly open to concepts of re-wilding. Indeed, in some localities, cooperative projects have begun – for example, at Ennerdale in the Lake District National Park, with a reduction in stock numbers and restoration of montane habitats, and in the fens of Cambridgeshire with flooding and restoration of reedbed and carr. The National Trust for Scotland has furthered pinewood restoration at Mar Lodge and the Trees for Life group has been carrying out activities in West Affric.

In addition, the John Muir Trust has accumulated land for 'wilderness' in Scotland, largely from an aesthetic or spiritual perspective, and is keen to extend its purchases from Scotland to England and Wales. The Trust is also open to concepts of re-wilding and the importance of natural processes as part of the wilderness experience.[2]

Such successes have led some conservationists to a bright and optimistic outlook (Chris Baines in 'The future for nature' in BBC Wildlife), an optimism also reflected in a number of press articles on Britain's gradually increasing biodiversity count – for example, Amelia Hill in the Observer on 22 April 2001 with the headline, 'UK teams with life as species beat extinction'. Hill's article highlighted increasing numbers of fox, badger, pine marten, otter and polecat, as well as orange-tip and white admiral butterflies, and various newly colonizing dragonflies. We could add the success stories for peregrine, osprey and kite; re-introduction of the white-tailed eagle; recovery of the black grouse; and colonization by little egret.

There is a problem, however, with this approach. Although I would agree with Baines that we are at a turning point in recent history, and that the efforts of the past 50 years are worth a great deal if now directed with the future environment in mind, I am not convinced by the biodiversity indices. This use of indices illustrates what we might call the 'Lomborg' effect (after the optimistic world outlook of the Danish environmental writer): focusing upon those data that support the argument, without truly evaluating the meaning of the data in relation to environmental change.[3]

## The UK Biodiversity Action Plan

There is a major question in this regard surrounding the UK's Biodiversity Action Plan (UKBAP) – the main plank of government strategy for nature conservation. It focuses upon species, and although not to the exclusion of habitats, which have their own action plans, it presents difficulties when ascribing value and priority to those species. Many of the species are selected because they are declining or are threatened with extinction, but at times, only in Britain, and although references are made to international status and whether they are on the edge of their range, much practical interpretation and prioritizing neglects this fact.

A great many species in the plan are obscure, difficult to separate and meaningless to all but the experts in their fields – the different eyebrights *Euphrasia* species, ground beetles, rare mosses and liverworts, and even the different fritillary butterflies – with many dependent upon secondary habitats of often fleeting appearance in the natural succession of vegetation, or on the extreme edge of their range. Some may be arctic alpines with a global distribution, or common in Scandinavia and relict here (e.g., the Snowdon lily *Lloydia serotina*), and for which little can be done but to monitor and protect. Others, the bittern or stone curlew, for example, can be justification for huge expenditures on habitat restoration, such as reedbed and chalk grassland, which require constant maintenance.

As might be expected, the majority of species of conservation concern are dependent on man-made habitat that has been marginal to agriculture for centuries, but which has been a casualty of recent economic forces – either through neglect or intensification. Given that only 2 per cent of Britain's woodlands are ancient semi-natural woods, it is not surprising that a small percentage of the species of concern live there – and as the decline of native woods had been halted by the time of the UKBAP, few species are therefore 'threatened'. As Peter Marren observed in the pages of an *ECOS* issue devoted to BAP (vol 21 no 2, 2000), the action plans presented a real danger of directing resources to the maintenance of a status quo – lots of small isolated nature reserves intensively managed to protect their habitats from nature itself. Whilst acknowledging the gains in knowledge over the last 50 years he warns:

> While both ecological and related philosophical knowledge have made
> great leaps forward over the last two decades, the BAP process is stuck in
> an interventionist, hierarchical and isolationist approach that is founded
> upon circumstances and policies 50 years ago . . . it is not a long term
> solution. It will continue to keep nature at arms' length.

This illustrates a major weakness with scientific nature conservation: there are policies that scientists and conservation managers pursue that reflect their own professional interests and limitations as much as, and often more than, the interest of the general polity. This may save many an obscure species, and I do not wish to gainsay the importance of scientific conservation and the pressures it has been able to put on other political and economic agendas in the battle for the countryside – but government agencies and NGO bureaucracies can collude over action plans that justify their own particular commitments and professional interests, one of the greatest of which is the role of management. When we advocate wilding, we necessarily envisage less management and more natural succession, which will be to the detriment of species dependent upon managed secondary habitats. In the wildlands project as outlined here, we have carefully chosen sites that do not engender conflict with other conservation goals – there is scope for *both* approaches, but it is worth reminding ourselves that the UKBAP is essentially a policy of stasis that seeks to protect many species that would decline in numbers if natural processes were dominant.

In the previous chapter, we noted that whatever the gains that could be seen (and oddly, so many concern predatory species!) and whatever index of diversity one chose, the *abundance* of a great many farmland and woodland species had severely declined. This has been best documented for birds and wild flowers, but it would also apply to butterflies, amphibians, reptiles and some small mammals such as the field vole and water vole. Regarding once-common species, the BAP may work positively for the general situation where its target species are both charismatic and occupy more general habitats – for example, the lapwing, skylark and song thrush. Recovery plans for these species necessarily involve reversing major agricultural trends.

## BAP and the candidate core areas

We could take a numerical approach and add up all the species of current conservation concern in these areas – those to which the UKBAP pays particular attention – but this would be to miss the main point of such core areas, which is to re-establish some of the *processes* of our natural environment. An area of 400 km² of Caledonian pine forest or an area of 100 km² of Atlantic oak woodland that can find its natural dynamic with the effects of fire, wind, climate change and herbivore and carnivore densities, free from the domineering influence of man, has a value in itself. There may be few 'rare' species, indeed, common species may become commoner, but some rare element of the wildness of nature will have been restored.

The main faunal and floral changes we could expect from a wilding programme in the three core areas are outlined below.

### Caledon

*Assuming a secure area of about 2000 km² with corridors extending west to Ben Eighe and Knoydart*

This area provides a unique opportunity for the return of the large mammal herbivore and carnivore guilds: boar, beaver, bison, elk, wild forest cattle and pony; wolf, lynx, and bear. It already holds significant populations of red and roe deer and populations of smaller mammals – red squirrel, mountain hare, wildcat, pine marten and otter. The polecat is missing and could be re-introduced. Of the important Caledonian bird species, it holds osprey, capercaillie and Scottish crossbill *Loxia scotica*, but it is not regarded as the major stronghold of any BAP priorities and could readily accommodate a wildland ethos that favoured forest species and the return of large mammals.

## Rhinogydd

*Assuming a core area of 20,000 ha and a buffer zone extending to the Arenigs and Coed y Brenin forests*

These hills currently hold no indigenous large herbivores, but have the capacity to support re-introduced red deer (there are no free-living herds in Wales and very few in England), roe deer, wild cattle, wild ponies, boar and beaver. There are fallow deer in the Coed y Brenin, which, with more contiguous woodland, would likely colonize the area. The feral goat in the northern rocky areas is a valued constituent of the local fauna. The area could also support a small population of elk. Of the carnivores, the wolf is problematic in the present day, given the prevalence of sheep farming in the surrounding hills, and could only come back if large areas of Snowdonia as a whole reverted to wilder land. This area would almost certainly be too small for a viable bear population; however, lynx are a definite possibility, given the amount of forest and assuming wild herbivore numbers increased. The hills already support healthy populations of rabbit, pheasant and hare as prey items, but such a predator would still present problems for any neighbouring sheep pastures – a suitable buffer zone would rely upon forestry and the use of livestock more robust to this small predator, such as wood pasture with suckler herds of cattle.

Of the rarer smaller mammals, the otter is present, pine marten may still be and polecat is a major feature of the region. Red squirrel has given way to the grey. The wildcat could be re-introduced and the pine marten population supplemented with stock from Scotland and Ireland.

It would take of the order of 200 years for newly created woodland to acquire even a small part of the biodiversity features of mature Atlantic oak woodland with its rich bryophyte flora and a field layer of plants that are characteristic of ancient woodland, but this area has the potential to increase the current area of relict oak wood

The biodiversity gains from new mammals would not prejudice species of current concern, because heathland and moorland could benefit from wilder grazing regimes. The current bryophyte flora of Atlantic oak woods is a feature of a few gorge woodlands that benefit from sheep grazing, but these are on the periphery of the hills in what could be buffer zones managed with domestic stock.

## Dartmoor

*Assuming a 10,000 ha core area in the southwest, buffer zones of 10,000 ha in the northwest and forest corridors along the Dart woodlands in the southeast*

The Dartmoor area already contains several species of BAP priority – and these are generally associated with open moorland, heath and grassland. The zoning plan for wilder management can accommodate these areas, which are either in the north or the southeast of the National Park. The southwest core area could provide a significant extension of the more southerly type of wet Atlantic oak wood – a woodland type that has been reduced to relict status in a few river valleys.

This area has already been re-colonized in recent times by roe deer and the naturalized sika and supports a population of feral Dartmoor ponies. It could certainly support additional wild boar, beaver and red deer. Consideration should be given to replacing the ponies in the core area with the more primitive Exmoor type, but this would require some study as inter-breeding with Dartmoor pony stock would need to be avoided; wild-type cattle, either Chillingham or Heck might be sufficient.

Of the smaller mammals, the polecat, wildcat and pine marten are absent and would be candidates for restoration. Otter is present. The population of rabbits, hare and pheasant would support the introduction of the smaller lynx (perhaps an extension for the non-native but threatened Iberian species).

Dartmoor has several important bird species – the ring ouzel, in particular – that are a feature of the open high ground, but the proposals would take account of the need to keep this ground open; grazing regimes should ensure that this remains possible through minimal intervention. Most of Dartmoor's BAP priority species are associated with Rhos pasture, blanket bog and other habitats in the north, central and eastern areas, with the southwest holding Atlantic oak wood priorities, which would therefore benefit. A rejuvenated forest could support goshawk, kite, osprey and honey buzzard, which are regular visitors but have yet to re-establish themselves.

Any perusal of the BAP lists, those for Snowdonia and Dartmoor in particular, will reveal intensification of agriculture as the main damaging force. This applies across the board – to loss of upland heath, overgrazing of upland woods, montane grassland and scrub, drainage of wetlands, reseeding of pastures, early cutting for silage, grubbing out hedgerows and infilling ponds, and to sheep-dip use and the poisoning of stream fauna. Thus, any added pressure to reform the CAP towards sustainable agricultural practices will be of value, but it is likely to take a decade or more just to halt the decline. BAP baseline data, often related to 1990, carry the danger of setting a halt to the decline as a political goal, rather than reversing it. For this reason, I believe we need a strategy that has the potential to work more quickly than the reform of agriculture, one that includes the conservation of natural processes and focuses on land that can be taken out of agriculture.

## Essential elements of a wilding strategy

In my view the following should be our priorities:

1 *Purchase of land*  Given the size of the areas and likely costs, there will need to be a policy of cooperation among the major land-owning conservation bodies, and this can best arise through an agreed strategy that relates to specific sites and priorities where the different organizations can purchase strategic sites within an overall plan; there may also be a role for communal purchase and collective management by groups able to diversify into eco-tourism and educational sectors, independent of agricultural incomes.

2 *Wilding of agriculture*  There has to be a system of cross-compliance in key areas where voluntary uptake has been too patchy to be effective; parallel to these initiatives, separation of agriculture and wildlife in the form of new habitat in strategic farmland locations should be used in parallel with other reforms towards less-intensive or fully organic systems of production.

3 *Government agencies*  Government agencies tend to take the middle road at all times, trying to placate or involve all stakeholders, when bolder strategies are required in some areas – the major initiative of the Community Forests by the Countryside Commission shows what can be achieved.

4 *Education*  The general public needs to have a better understanding of the processes of nature and especially the role of large carnivores and the nature of risks. The voluntary sector still has a largely 'nature needs scientific management' ethos, and the forestry sector, though perhaps now leading with modern practices incorporating biodiversity and recreation, could play a crucial role in the development of forest pasture systems, the use of wild herbivore species, corridors and the return of large predators.

## Obstacles to progress on wildland

Before embarking on an outline for such a strategy, we need to carefully consider those forces that work against the re-wilding of large areas, because any such strategy that fails to take account of them, will likely fail:

- consumer pressure for cheap food and fuel, and government policies that make a priority of minimizing inflation – these factors promote intensive agriculture and the poor siting and development of renewable energy resources
- attitudes within the community, especially among farmers, towards wildland (seen as retrogressive)
- the expectation among farmers that subsidies should support a farming business mentality as well as community values, but also the absence of appropriate subsidies or grants for re-wilding the landscape and future stewardship of such areas
- the strategic location of infrastructure such as roads, ports, airports, telecommunications, quarries and energy technologies in crucial corridors and their effects upon migration, fragmentation and genetic isolation; as well as the sense of remoteness, quiet and wildness of the core areas
- lack of consultation on issues that bring change to the countryside and a general public aversion to top-down planning (usually an entirely healthy state of mind) – but the current situation demands the opposite, a commitment to long-term, adequately financed, community-based education and outreach programmes on the part of government agencies; especially important for development of renewable energy sources, deployment of wild herbivores such as cattle and the re-introduction of large carnivores
- public ignorance and fear of 'beasts' such as large cats, wolves and even boar, wild cattle and elk
- the fear and aversion to 'economic' diseases of livestock, such as FMD, on the part of farmers and ministries, for which wildlife may act as a reservoir
- the cultural aesthetics of wild and beautiful land that is also treeless, but thereby affording great views and easy rambling – a balance will have to be struck between regeneration of forests and the love of open land
- the prevalence of species-oriented thinking based on rarity that would preserve habitats that if left to themselves would regenerate a closed canopy forest with a different and perhaps more mundane association of species – this goes hand-in-hand with a management ethos of continual intervention
- the concerns over 'purity' and provenance of introduced stock and concepts of alien and non-native fauna where functional equivalents are proposed.

## Areas of special interest to conservationists

Of the above issues, all but the last two are issues of general concern and matters of public policy in which all conservationists need to be informed and engaged. In regard to the issues of species-oriented thinking, concern for rarity, purity and provenance, I believe conservationists need to examine the way in which their own professional interests determine matters in not entirely scientific ways, and certainly ways that might not represent the public interest upon which conservation depends. As a community of interest, we have to be aware of how old thinking and the vested interests of the profession can bind us to particular policies. There is an obvious connection between the orchestrated programmes of the UKBAP and the required role of managers and interveners to maintain habitats. In addition, a huge amount of survey work, ecological analysis and target setting has been generated.

In this regard, there can be blind spots relating to selection of important species and their 'decline' due to habitat changes that are the result of natural processes, or species that may be rare in the UK but have their stronghold elsewhere, such as many specialists of open moorland and heath, reedbeds and water meadow.

This issue also affects forestry policy and even the mode of establishing and maintaining new woodland, irrespective of species concerns. The Land Use Policy Group addressed the issues of what constitutes a 'wildwood' and how it can be 'managed', but when it came to recommendations for funding, it was dogged by the current political requirement for public money to deliver economic and social benefit to the rural community. Some of that benefit could come from management jobs, whether of the forest, wildlife or visitors.[4]

Necessary though the issue of economic benefit is for the general rural environment, it should not rule out exceptional policies for exceptional and limited areas where natural processes could be allowed to operate out of a fundamental love and respect for wild nature and with rather less in the way of management jobs. In this respect, Toby Aykroyd (2004) has worked up proposals in 'Wild Britain' (see *ECOS* 25 3/4) for a balance of wildland values and economic potential that have formed the basis of a great deal of discussion and lobbying for major changes, particularly in the uplands.

As we shall argue, such special areas can also bring social and economic benefits, but this is not the prime motivation, nor should it determine the grant structures for all 'new wildwoods'. One further limitation of this initiative is that it is fundamentally tied to the notion of a 'forest' or woodland as being entirely a question of trees and natural processes, whereas, as we have argued, grazing regimes and predators are essential components of a natural forest.

## Areas of natural sanctuary

With respect to the new wildwoods proposals, there is a danger that the potential for large-area coordinated action will be lost in favour of a host of smaller broad-brush schemes that compromise the wildland ethos of scale, the presence of large mammals and natural processes of grazing (as well as risks to humans). Both approaches can work side-by-side. I propose that we begin by selecting three core areas of sufficient size to accomplish these aims:

1  The recognition of core areas, with special designation as areas of natural sanctuary, one each in Scotland, England and Wales (and also perhaps a joint project between the counties of Northern Ireland and Eire to identify a suitable area).
2  The provision of a Wildlands Challenge Fund that would initially provide funding for the purchase or management of core areas within the national parks and would invite proposals from other areas.
3  A specific targeting of funds from forestry and agricultural support systems in 'buffer zones' and corridors in which practices are modified to support the objectives of the core areas.

My own choice is clearly Glen Affric, the Rhinogydd and Dartmoor, as these areas have many of the factors likely to contribute towards success: substantial National Trust land, Forestry Commission sites, large areas with little infrastructural development, protection against industrial intrusions such as wind turbines, and the presence of potential buffer zones and linking corridors to other semi-natural areas. Affric and Dartmoor also have locally active community groups engaged in tree planting, seed collection, research and lobbying, as well as the capability to be involved in major expansion programmes.

In my view, there needs to be a designation that encompasses both conservation objectives for nature and the spiritual dimensions of the human response and valuing of nature. 'National' and 'Parks' never quite did that for me – certainly not in Britain, where the parks attract millions of visitors and have no core area designations. 'Nature Reserves' is problematic too – like all reservations, there is something peripheral in the meaning. 'Special Areas of Conservation' is too esoteric and of course 'Sites of Special Scientific Interest' even more so. We need something new. 'Wildwood' can be applied to small woods. Wildlands is closer, but perhaps, as in the US, is best applied to the project and strategy. I think we need something that respects the sanctity of nature and natural processes, but at the same time implies a human value in its existence – hence *Area of Natural Sanctuary*.

There is a long way to go before wildland and natural processes are accepted as requiring special designation and planning. Plans for each of the three Areas of Natural Sanctuary proposed here should evolve with the direct involvement of the communities concerned; however, vision and strong leadership is required if schemes are not to founder in an effort to please all stakeholders. The essence of the vision would be outlined and interested parties invited to make a contribution to specific ends, as practised by Moor Trees in their *Wild Dartmoor Forum* and the well-attended conference *Toward the Wild.*[5] Key issues for presentation would be:

- the establishment of contiguous areas of wildland in which there is no exploitation of resources (timber, grazing, water extraction or hydro- or wind-power)
- limitations of access (controlled numbers of walkers, campsites, students etc.) preferably by removal of incentives to enter the area rather than measures of direct control (but where necessary these should be employed): examples would be the closure of access roads, the provision of educational material at the periphery (requesting walkers to keep to certain routes) and of information on alternative attractions nearby (such as eco-tourism, working farms and study centres)
- the removal of barriers to animal movement such as fences and walls within the core area, access to corridors, and the restoration of the natural flow of rivers
- the establishment of 'quiet area' status with restrictions on over-flights from private, commercial and military planes and helicopters; controls on developments in the buffer zones in terms of noise and light and the attraction of large numbers of visitors
- where traditional visitor sites exist – such as in Glen Affric, Cwm Bychan and around the southwest fringe of Dartmoor – either roads in the core area and buffer zone should be closed to all traffic (if this can be agreed with the local community) or locals be provided with keys to locked gates (for traditional local amenity) or given free access to otherwise commercial taxi operations using battery-powered vehicles; other roads with little tourist use could be closed to all but local essential traffic – these would apply especially to the buffer zones in the areas outlined and used by the local farmers, suppliers, trades-people, and farm-based eco-tourists.

The 'wilding' process can consist of a mix of managed initiatives that will provide employment, but a reduction of management overall will necessarily involve compensatory agreements. Managed initiatives would involve:

- development of tree nurseries using local provenance seed; this could be coordinated with an educational project for all schools in the region with each school receiving funds and advice for setting up nurseries and collecting seed (thus allowing both science and art to contribute to the raising of awareness)
- the planting of whips on land where grazing has ceased, and protected trees in areas where rabbits, goats or deer are a problem; the 'sabre' method developed by Steve Watson in North Wales is labour intensive

and ideally suited to schools and community programmes: funds could support managers and educationalists as well as landowners and tenant farmers

- working groups can also be employed on the phased removal of stone walls (which can be breached and otherwise allowed to decay), the protection of significant archaeological features and the removal of various industrial artefacts; professional local contractors could deal with the removal of dams, reservoirs and pylons; in the buffer zones power lines and telephone wires could be usefully buried in a phased programme
- transport programmes for Affric and Cwm Bychan, which have traditional holiday spots close to the centre of the area, would include employment for taxi drivers (and guides) and fees for parking at the taxi points
- future populations of herbivores (deer are already plentiful in Affric but scarce in the Rhinogydd, and when introduced will require culling, at least until the forest becomes more robust; a suitable penned area in the buffer zone could show examples of all the animals in a wildlands programme) for example, wild horse, cattle, elk, deer, wolves, lynx, beaver etc., and would generate employment and income locally with potentially high visitor numbers
- in the distant future, carnivore populations will require management intervention in the buffer zones, where culling should be overseen by expert marksmen for the humane killing of those animals that create problems
- where former commercial forestry is extant – such as in the Rhinogydd – there would be a phased programme of felling and replacement with native species at conservation densities, or simply leaving felled areas to regenerate, which is usually a rapid colonization by birch, willow and rowan and the gradual encroachment of oak (the seeds of which can be transported some distance by jays).

In the case of the removal of management from large areas:

- The three candidate core areas would all regenerate quite well without any intervention once stock were removed: bracken zones can move quite quickly to woodland and there are large areas of bracken in the Rhinogydd and on Dartmoor; bare grassland would require scarifying at first and seeding with a colonizer such as birch. Thus, these areas would require little input and offer employment only through the provision of wardens.
- Removal of management from suitable woodland – such as fences from pockets of ancient woodland and non-intervention after the felling of exotic conifers – would also require little future input in the core area, but managed woods would still be a feature of the buffer zones and offer suitable employment for small-scale timber production and craft work.

Given the plethora of grant schemes currently available for woodland management, native woodland regeneration and whole-farm schemes, as well as access and tourist facilities, none of the above presents problems once an area is targeted; the main issue is education, access to funds and *sufficient* incentive to replace current land-use practices. The establishment of a local office that facilitates negotiation of grant schemes would help with integrating a strategy. Each of the current grant schemes would require a little tweaking and possible top up, which should be the job of the core area (and buffer zone) office with access to the Challenge Fund.

Within this scheme there is the potential to add two elements that have proven effective elsewhere. The first is the operation of a 'land-bank' in which the core area office seeks to purchase suitable good-quality grazing land as it comes onto the market (and even functional farms) such that farmers in key strategic places within the core area or buffer zone can be offered alternative land. One such scheme is operated by the Parc d'Amorique in Brittany where farmers are compensated for the development of wet fields caused by the re-introduced beaver. The second element is the coordination of the two major landowners of wildland and forest in the UK, The National Trust and Forest Enterprise, such that strategic blocks of land can be managed for re-wilding with knock-on effects upon adjacent land or areas between their holdings.

These two processes could be particularly effective in the Rhinogydd and on Dartmoor. In the case of the Rhinogydd, the southeast part of the hills contains a patchwork of National Trust and Forest Enterprise holdings. Reduced stocking levels (and replacement with special breeds of cattle) would affect adjacent land. Forest Enterprise could replace existing blocks of exotic conifer with native trees. Both organizations could seek to purchase adjacent blocks of land with appropriate help from the Challenge Fund.

## Wilding agriculture and the urban fringe

We have outlined a general strategy for agricultural land (Chapter 10) in which new separated habitat is created. This can run in parallel with policies to green mainstream agriculture, such as reducing inputs, restoring mixed farming, grass leys and extensive livestock husbandry, and needs to be applicable to almost any farming environment where corridors and buffer zones are important. The strategy also needs to target resources where they can be most effective and where leverage can access other funding – hence the focus upon river corridors within agricultural areas. This also applies to urban initiatives that are so crucial for taking the wilding message to our largely urban culture.

There are discernible shifts towards landscape-scale integrated plans for wildlife. The RSPB has begun to carry forward a larger-area landscape-oriented programme of habitat restoration [see *Futurescapes: large scale habitat restoration for wildlife and people*, Royal Society for the Protection of Birds (2001)] with the programme striking a balance between recreating woodland in certain landscapes – for example in the Caledonian Forest, in pastoral areas in the west of England and Wales, and wetland woods in the fens – and restoring *existing* habitat, such as lowland heath, montane heath, downland, lowland wet pastures, hay meadows and less-intensive arable farmland. This approach is wholly appropriate for the broad balance of habitat restoration and biodiversity in the wider countryside. It has the merit not just of restoring the abundance and diversity of species, and of ameliorating the aridity of much of eastern Britain's arable deserts, but of providing recreational enjoyment close to urban and industrial centres. The programme also has great potential to contribute to a strategic approach to corridors linking core areas.

It is not therefore a question of *either* wildland with minimal management *or* restoring habitats that depend upon management, such as reedbed or heath, although a choice between the two options would have to be made in some areas. In most cases current conservation policy would favour the latter, and we can expect problems in extending major corridors of woodland across upland habitats, for example, in the North Pennines. There should be room for *both* approaches: the core area proposal takes the best of the current possibilities for large-area initiatives, and a system of corridors would rely upon a great deal of secondary habitat creation and management. Many upland habitats in corridor zones would benefit from reduced grazing and the development of a mosaic of habitats, as proposed in the Forest Habitat Network approach. The core area wildland proposal is thus one horn of a two-horned approach and it brings in qualities that are not catered for in a habitat restoration, mainly BAP-oriented approach.

## Government agency

How far is it possible to get government agencies on board for a programme of core areas and corridors of wildland that goes beyond the current conservation paradigm? I believe there are already some very positive antecedents:

- The Countryside Agency, CCW, SNH, Community Forests, DEFRA and the Forestry Commission are all committed to the expansion of native woodlands through either planting or regeneration programmes, and as reported, the inter-agency Land Use Policy Group has recommended a Forest Habitat Network approach for new wildwoods, as well as having endorsed a 'core area' concept.
- The Forestry Commission has already taken on board the concept of Forest Habitat Networks and taken some measures to re-wild some of

its upland plantations and create streamside corridors of native trees in commercial operations, and thus its grant schemes would already support wilding in the uplands; in the lowlands, new woodland could be supported in strategic locations (as currently practised for Community Forests and the New National Forest) and there is great interest in the use of flood plain forests for water management.

- The Environment Agency and River Restoration Centre have already worked successfully with local authorities and water companies to develop Local Environment Action Plans (LEAPS) on a catchment basis, and would support more floodplain forestry and streamside protection in the uplands.

- DEFRA could look favourably upon grant schemes that would focus on targeted areas as well as broad schemes that are geared more to income support than to the environment; if global market pressure reduces the funds available, targeted habitat creation is likely to deliver more benefits.

These are ambitious plans for those agencies and departments that have had little experience of long-term strategies and whose resources have been used primarily to monitor and protect existing habitat, but not out of keeping with the initiatory work of the Countryside Agency in England or Scottish Natural Heritage working with the Forestry Commission and NGOs in the restoration of the Caledonian Forest. The Countryside Council for Wales has participated in developing the New Wildwoods concept, and the agency is committed to a long-term strategy for doubling the extent of native woodland in Wales.

What is now required is for inter-agency initiatives, such as those pioneered by the Land Use Policy Group, to be followed up by a long-term, well-funded strategic plan. This may best be initiated by NGOs and supported by the agencies (with grants and research), but the LUPG forum of regional seminars is an ideal format for integrating plans and dealing with conflicting issues. With such ambitious targets, the good work on Forest Habitat Networks and wildwoods needs to be further integrated with wilding issues relating to secondary habitats, bird conservation, water catchment initiatives and the re-introduction of large mammals).

## Education

Many of the ideas related to wildlands are relatively new to the conservation community in Britain and Europe, but less so than in the US where large-area ecological restoration has been a major feature of conservationists' strategies. The major impetus in Britain has come from the voluntary sector, in particular, a huge effort on the part of Trees for Life in Scotland, involving both practical examples and inspirational teachings. From the outset, Alan Featherstone has invested a great deal of time and creative ability in communicating ideas to a wide audience of conservationists, local communities and schools. Moor Trees has followed this example with school tree nurseries and outings for planting. Steve Watson in Snowdonia has pioneered community involvement in his labour-intensive 'sabre-planting' schemes in which potted trees 5–6 years in age are transported by hand into remote locations.[6] Future wildlands must first be created in the heart and the imagination of the communities in which they will be situated, for however valuable they may be to biodiversity, carbon and water cycles, or to the spiritual recreation of the general populace, they will not be truly sustainable unless supported by local people.

An educational strategy is thus required that addresses our own community of conservationists, many of whom will think re-wilding too ambitious and conflicting with current conservation values and practices, and a broader constituency of communities, particularly those involved in farming, forestry and game shooting. Schools should be a major focus for educational materials and projects. I would personally go further and suggest that 'nature conservation', though captivating for younger children, inspires very few teenagers, and that a broader concept relating to wildness and the wilding of the heart as well as the land might gain a greater constituency.

There is a huge interest among young people in outdoor adventure sports, and yet many of these simply use wild places and physical risk without fostering any real contact or understanding of nature and natural processes. Educationalists could contribute greatly by balancing such programmes for young people with episodes of quiet observation and vision quest, as pioneered by Eric Maddern and others at Cae Mabon.

Thus, in addition to teaching about the importance of water, carbon balances and environmental crises, we could add to the curriculum the history of Britain's fauna and flora, the persecution and needless eradication of predators, the overall poverty of the present countryside and the successes of many pilot projects in ecological restoration. We need to teach children, by example, that they can make a difference in their immediate world, and how to stay active and effective agents for change in a world that will desperately need creative solutions.

# 13
# Straight to the Heart:
# A Wildland Strategy

If Britain were to embrace a wildland ethos by setting aside one large area for each of the three nations, it would set a marker for the world. The Dutch ministries have worked together on a 5000 ha wild area and plan corridors. Britain is not as crowded a country as the Netherlands. Wildland could be created and safeguarded as a natural sanctuary on a much larger scale – of the order of several hundred square kilometres. It would send a signal to all developing countries whose wildlife policies we currently hope to influence. If that project were to involve the active study of the return of eradicated large mammals such as elk, forest cattle and ponies, with lynx, wolf and bear, we could have greater hope of influence in countries that now seek to safeguard the tiger, lion and leopard. Furthermore, we would be contributing significantly to a new ethos of toleration for predators that is slowly gaining ground in the Alps, northern Spain, Germany and Scandinavia. Above all, we would be signalling a move beyond the past conservation paradigm to a more creative and extensive philosophy, one already apparent in the current projects we have outlined, but hitherto not embraced in all its potential.

## The Three Nations Proposal

The selection of three large-area schemes with flagship status would be the beginning of a broader strategy that would extend to wildland schemes using Forest Habitat Networks (FHNs) and riparian corridors. Each of the core areas has programmes in train, representing a variety of interests and levels of action. In the Caledon core area, the vision is evolving within an overall strategy of cooperation between Trees for Life, Forest Enterprise and the National Trust for Scotland. In the Rhinogydd, the Coed Eryri vision has yet to inspire cooperative action, but the National Park Authority already has a policy for quiet use and minimal development. The LUPG took on board the characteristics of this area in its appraisal of large-area schemes, though seeming to prefer the Cambrian Mountains to the south. The Rhinogydd has the advantage of National Park protection (particularly from wind turbines now encroaching upon the North Cambrians) and significant holdings by the National Trust and the Forestry Commission. On Dartmoor, the Moor Trees group is currently raising funds for a detailed feasibility study for regeneration of the tree cover.[1]

In all three areas, the vegetation, if left to itself and mediated by natural levels of grazing, would eventually regenerate forest cover; this could happen more quickly with active planting programmes. There would be an impact upon the open habitats and a change in the balance of species, but in each case there are neighbouring areas with high conservation status where these open habitats would be maintained – for example, both north and south of Caledon throughout most of the Western Highlands; the northern, southern and eastern parts of Snowdonia; and in the north of Dartmoor and nearby Exmoor. A detailed perusal of the BAPs for Snowdonia[2] and Dartmoor[3] shows very few conflicts – none that cannot be accommodated by careful planting and regeneration schemes or judicious grazing by introduced herbivores.

Whilst not offending against BAP targets, and in many cases contributing to them (especially for Atlantic woodland, Scots pine, montane heath and scrub), these core areas would primarily contribute to a uniqueness of scale in the returning wildwood. This has inherent value, as we have argued, and should not necessarily be judged by its contribution to the species-oriented action plans.

The Caledonian Forest proposal centred on Glen Affric adds to extensive work already underway in the Cairngorm Mountains, with the added perspective of a more remote wilderness element and the potential for the re-introduction of large mammals. The Rhinogydd would provide an opportunity to reverse the decline of Atlantic oak wood, and the hills also hold fine examples of montane heath that could be kept open by the use of wild herbivores such as the tarpan-like Exmoor ponies and aurochs-like Heck cattle, thus providing an example of balancing traditional conservation interests regarding heathland birds, insects and flora with the broad wildlands concept. Dartmoor presents great challenges with regard to commoners' rights, domestic stock and traditional grazing practices but can contribute significantly to the regeneration of the more southerly Atlantic oak wood type as well as montane heath. Dartmoor and the Rhinogydd are both in areas with highly developed tourist industries and farming communities, providing opportunities to study the implications of re-wilding programmes for the rural economy in the buffer zones.

These three core areas have a mixture of habitats – woodland and montane heath or grassland, with river valleys and lakes, and in the case of England and Wales, wood pasture for livestock. They do not include examples of lowland heath, fenland, lowland wet pasture, arable farmland, downland or urban habitats – all of which are important when considering the UK biodiversity strategy and its priorities. However, these essentially secondary habitats will be more important when considering the creation of linking corridors, as they will necessarily involve management agreements with farming, forestry and other interests.

## Land purchase

There is no substitute for ownership when it comes to managerial decisions! But it is not conceivable that enough land could be purchased, and thus land under conservation ownership has to act as both a sanctuary and a pilot showing the way for the management of neighbouring land. The owners of neighbouring land must have access to grant schemes that effectively compete with current incomes. The advantage of having three select areas is that initial pioneering wildland grant schemes would be targeted and limited.

In the core areas, direct ownership is conceivable only in Scotland because of the pattern of ownership and size of the estates. In England and Wales, this will be problematic in areas with commoners' rights over the Rhinogydd and Dartmoor. In Caledon, there are already large tracts of land in the ownership of sympathetic organizations – the Forestry Commission and the National Trust for Scotland. The former has already earmarked its Glen Affric holdings for minimum intervention management, the removal of non-native trees and restoration of native Caledonian pine, and has cooperated with Trees for Life in the fencing, regeneration or planting of new areas; the National Trust for Scotland purchased the West Affric estate with a commitment to restore the forest and to work cooperatively with the Trees for Life programme. Nearby large estates may come on the market. The RSPB has already purchased land in the northeast of the core area, and the Woodland Trust, National Trust for Scotland, and John Muir Trust should be encouraged to follow suit, with help from the Heritage Lottery Fund.

In the Rhinogydd, both the National Trust and Forestry Commission have large holdings, and large private plantations of exotics of Sitka and larch also regularly come onto the market. There are complexities here of common grazing rights, but the strategic purchase of a few key farms could lead to reduced grazing pressure, particularly in Cwm Bychan. This is wild country, and the John Muir Trust might usefully consider extending itself to Wales in these hills, which are wilder than the North Cambrians and protected from wind turbines. In the southeast of the hills, the National Trust and Forestry Commission could collaborate on an overall strategy on land in-between their properties. On Dartmoor, the National Trust has a large estate in the southwest corner, the main area of interest, but commercial forestry plantations are smaller in scale, and commoners' agreements are also a complicating factor.

In buffer zones to these areas and corridors radiating out, reliance will have to be made on encouraging management regimes through funding agreements as well as some strategic purchases. Purchased land, particularly large farms or commercial forestry plantations, could act as pilot projects for the encouragement of neighbouring landowners.

With regard to land purchases, government agencies and the National Park Authorities have grown averse to ownership, and have sought to implement their policies through the funding of management agreements on private land, or by matched funding for purchases made by the voluntary sector. This may not present much of a problem. Organizations such as the National Trust and RSPB have the required managerial expertise, have been successful in gaining matched funding, and certainly appear to be moving towards large-area initiatives. There remains a question as to whether this will be adequate to encompass the full spectrum of restoration we would wish to see in core areas. These organizations and The Woodland Trust are all committed to open access, education, and finding cooperative ways forward in communities with economic interests. This works well for protective conservation based solely upon species, but may not be adequate where wildland policies are required, such as the removal of stock; the cessation of game fishing, stalking and grouse shooting; and the larger-scale restoration of forest cover. Those bodies focused upon species, such as the RSPB, have been less concerned with the aesthetic issues of wildness as impacted by wind turbines, power lines and telecommunication towers, where they are shown not to impact on abundance or diversity.

In this respect, the National Trust has a more holistic approach: some of its values are expressed in the preservation of parks and gardens, whilst other projects value both wildness (the *Call for the Wild* campaign to further the sense of wildness in areas threatened by intrusive developments) and habitat restoration (in the fens and Lakeland fells). The RSPB has a tendency to open up remote sites to visitors and the motorcar, and many of my own favourite haunts have lost a certain sense of mystery as a result of visitor centres and car parks – though the birds are still there. However, the RSPB in the past ten years, in working on a larger-scale regeneration of key habitats such as reedbeds and heathland, has demonstrated many of the techniques of habitat restoration, particularly on land degraded by past industrial or agricultural activity, such as old peat-workings on the Somerset Levels.

There are now unprecedented opportunities for the purchase of 'economic' forestry plantations in key areas (in particular where ancient native woodland was replaced with exotic species). Sadly, many opportunities were lost in the first wave of selling from the Forestry Commission, but sites continue to change hands. Sizeable areas – several hundred hectares were for sale in the Rhinogydd in the late 1990s along the Vale of Ffestiniog, one of the most important sites of relict Atlantic oak woods, but the conservation bodies could not then see the value of purchasing 300 ha of Japanese larch and Sitka spruce neighbouring an SSSI of bryophyte-rich gorge woodland. As part of a more strategic plan, this might now be a different proposition.

Other players could contribute to such a strategic plan. The County Wildlife Trusts regularly purchase land and obtain matched funding, and although largely concerned with protecting threatened habitats, they have long been concerned to purchase land adjacent to nature reserves and place it under appropriate management. There has been a gradual acceptance that many nature reserves are too small, exist in a fragmented landscape and are vulnerable to climate change. An opening thus exists for cooperative endeavours. In the southwest region of England, the County Wildlife Trusts have already announced an intention to study landscape-scale programmes.

The Woodland Trust, though historically much concerned with the purchase of threatened woodland, has also been purchasing strategic farmland with an aim to planting new woods, either close to its holdings or as part of a broader strategy – such as Community Forests or, as in Glen Finglas in Scotland, a cooperative endeavour to regenerate ancient Caledonian deciduous as well as pine woodland.[4]

One relatively recent element in these endeavours has been the willingness of water companies to cooperate with management agreements over large areas of their holdings. The water companies account for significant land ownership in upland Britain; although less relevant in our three selected core areas, they could be important in the corridor areas of the uplands and with regard to river restoration projects acting as corridors in the lowlands. These companies face a certain dilemma regarding wilding: domestic livestock have kept the land open but make the water supplies vulnerable to diseases caused by *Cryptosporidium*, commercial forestry using conifers has tended to acidify the water, and whereas native broadleaves would neutralize acidity and remove disease risks, they would increase transpiration losses in the watershed.

On an aesthetic level, reservoirs with their access roads reduce the sense of wildness. Similarly, hydro-schemes add dams, roads and power lines. In Caledon, most of the lochs have lost their natural status, affecting both the ecology of the loch and natural flow of the river. Ultimately, installations in a few core areas could be removed at the end of their working lives, and natural regimes restored. Their contribution to the Highland economy as a whole is relatively small and compensation schemes should be available. In the Rhinogydd, a few of the lakes have pipelines and small dams as drinking water sources, and these could more readily be removed or better disguised. National Park policies protect the Rhinogydd from intrusive telecommunications or wind turbines, but the situation with regard to small-scale hydro-development on rivers is a cause for concern. There is also a large lake at Trawsfynydd that has been artificially raised for hydro-power and has a nuclear reactor site in the process of being decommissioned. This site could act as a showpiece for natural restoration of a site despoiled by industrial development despite being within a national park. The regenerated margins of the lake would doubtless support beaver (there is a similar nuclear lake site with beaver in Brittany).

Finally, there is the yet-to-be-explored potential of the electricity generating and distribution companies, as well as consumers, becoming involved in carbon sequestration projects. If the large corporations became more involved in these schemes, which have great potential, then another big player could enter this theatre.

Here then is the crux – great resources exist, both in experience and finance. What is required is a coordinated strategic plan that maximizes those resources and ensures that things happen on the ground. The many discussions and meetings that arose from the conferences of the 1990s contributed to developments such as habitat restoration and less-intensive management practices. The time is now ripe to focus resources upon some agreed core areas and corridors, as well as the re-establishment of herbivore and carnivore guilds. In this book we have proposed three viable core areas; others exist on a similar scale in the North Pennines, but do not have a community ground-up initiative to support them.

## Buffer zones

The core areas in each initiative should be surrounded by buffer zones in which economic activity takes place but in such a manner as to support the objectives of the core areas. Thus agriculture and forestry would be less intensive and eco-tourism and study or work groups would be encouraged. In this respect grant systems already exist and these could readily be modified for the specific needs of the sites.

In Caledon the larger area of nearly 2000 km$^2$ requires little in the way of a 'buffer' because the adjacent land is not intensively farmed or forested, though there are sporting interests. What is required is a series of wild forest corridors reaching out to the National Nature Reserves of Ben Eighe and Inverpolly. Forestry interests in the area can already apply for special grants to convert to native pinewoods, and this scheme has proven very successful throughout the region. Deer stalking and salmon fishing should not present problems in the support of the longer-term vision for the return of animal species such as the bear, wolf, lynx, boar and beaver. The latter may raise objections from salmon fishing interests, but as there are no immediate prospects of returning the beaver to the Glen Affric area, there will be time for education and the experience of the Knapdale project to convince fishing interests that fish populations do not decline in beaver areas and may be enhanced.

Active forestry in buffer zones is not likely to be detrimental to core areas of wildland if managed with biodiversity in mind. Native pine or birch woods grown for timber, if felled and extracted sensitively, would be the most appropriate land use in areas contiguous to the Glen Affric project. If a proportion of old trees are left and stands are not clear-felled then biodiversity is not likely to suffer and there will be little visual impact in the area. In addition, planting can leave large margins for a streamside vegetation of alder, willow and aspen. Access roads in buffer zones can be sensitively constructed with limitations on noisy sports vehicles and other activities that would be detrimental to the wild character of the Natural Sanctuary. In Wales, areas contiguous to the Rhinogydd and currently heavily grazed by sheep could support wood pasture in a combination of organic beef production and active forestry using native species.

In Coed Eryri, the buffer zones that I have proposed would contain most of the currently working farms and in-bye land on the tops of the lower hills in the west overlooking Morfa Harlech and Dyffryn Arduddwy, in the north above the Vale of Ffestioniog, and around Trawsfynnyd to the northeast. The National Trust already owns pasture–woodland in the southeast near Coed-y-Brenin. This buffer zone also contains several actively managed forestry plantations, both private and Forest Enterprise. In relation to the forest, there is an opportunity for private operations to be purchased or grant aided for conversion and Forest Enterprise is already looking at ways in which some of its holdings can be returned to native species and managed for conservation.

In the buffer zone, newly converted plantations and new woodland corridors could support low-intensity timber use, extraction by horses and local marketing of timber and firewood. The Harlech Estate has an old timber yard and ancient sawmill that could be renovated and used to process local timber for local uses. In this respect, the National Park and Gwynedd County Council could further the use of local timber in buildings and various local infrastructure projects. The estate felled several mature pines in a copse suffering from wind-throw and planked the timber for use in the construction of new barns.

The major decision point will relate to the current intensive sheep grazing on in-bye land that reaches well into the western parts of the hills. These fields are generally poor in biodiversity – there being very few remaining herb-rich meadows. The Tir Gofal agri-environment scheme that many of the hill farmers are taking part in is unlikely to reduce sheep numbers sufficiently to affect regeneration of woodland – which would likely be fenced under the scheme. What is required is for certain farms in the core area (Cwm Bychan particularly) and in the periphery (as in-bye land lower down supports sheep that are also ranged higher up) to be brought out of production or converted to wood pasture for cattle – with no subsequent replacement of sheep on the common lands in the core area.

In the buffer zone, it would be ideal if sheep could be phased out in preference to cattle and the farmers became engaged in the creation of woodland pasture systems as currently found in the 40 ha of Llety'r Fwyalchen and on the National Trust land in the southeast of the hills. This would require some imaginative development of Tir Gofal and additional funding for the low-intensive management that would ensue. Traditional farmers may be reluctant to phase out their sheep, but this may happen anyway as the GATT changes work through and upland livestock rearing becomes uneconomic.

In Dartmoor, the upper parts of the grass moorland in the southwest are grazed by sheep and cattle, and there are commoners' rights for ponies. There is less good-quality in-bye land than borders the Rhinogydd, but much the same arguments apply. The ideal would be for greatly reduced grazing in the southwestern sector and for the phasing out of domestic stock in favour of special breeds of cattle and wild pony.

Each of the local offices could identify priority habitats – relict ancient woodland, riparian strips, upland scrub and heath, lake margins etc. – as well as opportunities in schools, seed collecting, nurseries and general awareness. In Caledon, the Trees for Life group already has an effective team that could be supplemented by a Challenge Fund and representation from the agencies, National Trust for Scotland, etc. The administration of the Challenge Fund, land banks, and integration with other sources of finance would also fall to the local offices. Strategic purchases and management agreements could then follow.

## Forest networks and riparian corridors

We have explored the principles of corridors but have not yet looked at the best sites. In this latter regard, we are dealing with a much more complex situation, and there has been only a minimal amount of research to demonstrate the principles and practices. I think the situation calls for a major review and a degree of research on the part of government agencies.

The FHN concept developed in Scotland provides a useful model for a wildland corridor strategy in the uplands. The network concept links woodland through a mosaic of other habitats, such as open heath, grassland and bog; thus, important upland habitats are safeguarded whilst at the same time increasing woodland cover. Linked networks would be essential to provide large herbivore populations with sufficient opportunity for genetic exchange and winter migrations.

Such a network approach can apply to virtually the whole of the English and Welsh uplands (see Colour Plate 8), linking the Borders forests of

Kielder and Eskdale with the North Pennines, the Lake District, the Yorkshire Dales, Forest of Bowland and the Peak District. Linking these areas with a corridor to the Welsh Hills more than 60 km away across the Cheshire Plain would be a great challenge – there are options across the plain to link with the Rivers Dane and Weaver, and across the plain of the Dee south of Chester to link up with the Clwyd Hills, Clocaenog Forest and Snowdonia. Another route lies to the south via the River Dove towards Cannock Chase and across Shropshire via the Severn Valley, the Shropshire Hills, and the Berwyns to Snowdonia and the Cambrian Mountains.

The Cambrian Mountains, already heavily forested with commercial plantations, could be subject to an overall FHN plan linking the north and south of Wales, and then east via Afon Monnow from the Black Mountains across to Monmouth and the Forest of Dean. An even greater challenge would be an FHN link across the upper Severn Estuary south of Gloucester to the southern Cotswolds and Mendips, Somerset Levels, across to the Quantocks, Exmoor and Dartmoor in the southwest, and the River Yeo to north Dorset, Wareham Forest, Cranborne Chase, Ringwood and the New Forest.

This ambitious strategy is not greater in scope than the Community Forest initiative, and given long term commitment, is feasible. There are major obstacles in the M6 and M5 corridors, but these may be negotiable via east-west river corridors, underpasses and future 'over-passes'. One great value of establishing a strategic plan on this scale, is that infrastructural development – housing, roads, airports, etc. – can be monitored and directed to less sensitive areas.

## Species re-introductions

If we are to consider a programme of re-introductions based upon functional components of ecosystems, then it would be sensible to make those additions only after the land areas have been secured and the vegetation sufficiently restored. A start has been made in Scotland with beaver, and Glen Affric could support a greater diversity of herbivores and has adequate prey for the wolf, but the main problem is political acceptance of potential risks to domestic livestock. Other areas, such as the Rhinogydd and the Cambrians, could begin with small groups of Heck cattle, Konik or Exmoor ponies, and red deer. A start could be made by purchasing land in these areas and establishing breeding herds, as has been practised in Holland and Poland. The Large Herbivore Foundation would readily supply stock, and this has already happened with Konik horses at Wicken and Minsmere.

A greater leap forward could be made by bringing back a charismatic carnivore such as the lynx. The return of the lynx would set a precedent for the return of a mammalian carnivore (and political reaction in Britain could be determined), with the ground being laid for the other large carnivores. Although there would be expected opposition from sheep farmers, an educational programme based upon experience from France and Switzerland would go some way to alleviating fears. Compensation schemes should be in place before any releases take place. Initial target areas need to be carefully chosen, and I would suggest three sites in Scotland – Glen Affric, the forests of Galloway, and the Borders/Kielder. Re-instating the lynx to Wales or southern England would be more problematic, given the prevalence of sheep rearing in the uplands, and in Wales, the paucity of deer.

Another immediate project would be the re-introduction to Dartmoor of the three extirpated small carnivores, pine marten, polecat and wildcat. Additionally, the pine marten in North Wales could be supplemented by releases from Ireland to add to the genetic base and perhaps aid colonization of the craggy rock areas.

Of the herbivores, the elk is a prime candidate – but not until large core areas have been secured and vegetation restored. This animal has the capacity for rapid population growth, and a policy of control would need to be agreed, perhaps involving licensed hunting in the buffer zones. Wild boar could be re-introduced to the Caledonian Forest in an immediate programme, and would, by all accounts, further the natural generation of the pinewood. Roe and red deer should be re-instated in Snowdonia, with a red deer herd established on the Rhinogydd. Again, questions of culling will have to be established in advance.

In the course of researching this book I have been fascinated by the two enigmatic British treasures of wild white cattle and primitive Exmoor ponies. I feel that these gems are undervalued, doubtless as a result of the obsession with genetic purity and nativeness. These animals retain a wildness and enough of a genetic heritage to enable them to fill the functional niches of tarpan and aurochs. They should both be used in preference to domestic 'rare breeds' that require husbandry for the larger area schemes. As wild animals they would be less likely to trigger a reaction from animal welfare groups concerned at the health and survival of these animals under wild conditions.

## The heart of nature: wild to the core

It has been a difficult task to shake myself free of old ways of thinking about nature and conservation. For decades conservation has been on the back foot, focused upon protection, and losing ground in attempts to ameliorate the impact of agriculture and forestry. The future now looks brighter – at least for reversing the decline of species – but is also fraught with the risk of losing other elements of nature, the very processes that created the species we show concern for. Just as we are learning ways to respect those processes and let go of some of our old values (in *some* areas, rather than across the board, as there will always be a place for managed habitat maintenance), there are new threats to wildness, such as intrusive wind turbines, telecomm towers and increased military over-flights and training. We should be careful as 'conservationists' not to lose sight of the wildness at the heart of nature. I believe it has a far stronger appeal to the general public than species-oriented conservation can ever hope to attain. If we can embrace this wildland ethic, we will be strengthening the wildness of our own hearts and coming closer to nature both within and outside ourselves.

# Endnotes

## Introduction

1  There has been much recent discussion on wildland, definitions and principles of management in *ECOS* (see Fenton, Taylor and Fisher, 25 (1) and the special re-wilding issue summarizing practical experience of wildland management, 25 (3/4) 2004).
2  See IPCC (2001) Summary for policy-makers, 2–10
3  Bill Adams reviews these trends in *Future Nature* and Chris Baines outlines the potential contribution habitat creation and natural processes can make to environmental objectives in his discussion of the Rebuilding Biodiversity Group agenda in *BBC Wildlife* (June 2002).
4  The relevance of the consumer is made clear in the government's recent response to the crisis in farming and food production in the report of its independent inquiry under Donald Curry (Policy Commission on the Future of Farming and Food).
5  Derek Yalden's most excellent *History of British Mammals* gives a thorough account of the historical demise of Britain's large mammals.
6  The most exciting examples in Holland involve the introduction of wild cattle, ponies, and red deer into wetland nature reserves, such as the 5600 ha Oostvaardersplassen, where intervention is minimized (see Whitbread and Jenman, 1995). In North America the *Wildlands Project* (*www.wildlandsproject.org*) has proposed large corridors for migration of herbivores and predators between core areas of wilderness.

## Chapter 1 The Wild Side of Natural

1  See Steve Carver's website *www.geog.leeds.ac.uk/staff/s.carver/wildbrit_web* for discussions of perceptions, parameters and policies relating to wilderness in Britain, Europe and America. Carver and his team have been developing indices of wildness and mapping the wilderness continuum (see Carver et al, 2002).
2  See *The Future Eaters, an ecological history of the Australasian lands and people* by Tim Flannery for an account of the impact of humans on Australian mega-fauna. See also *The Eternal Frontier* by the same author for an account of palaeo-Indian impacts upon North America.
3  Shepard Krech gives a telling account of the impact of later Native American hunting and use of fire to regulate game in *The Ecological Indian: myth and history*. Though its conclusions should be treated with caution – see this author's review in *ECOS* 21 (1), 100–102.
4  See J.A. Estes et al (1998) 'Killer whale predation on sea otters linking oceanic and nearshore ecosystems', *Science* 282, 473–476.

5   See Yalden (1999) and Kurten's *Pleistocene Mammals of Europe*.
6   This discussion is featured in *ECOS* 24 (3/4).
7   I presented a piece on the nature of death at the *Nature in Transition* conference at Lancaster University, the proceedings of which were available at the time on the National Trust website.
8   See Flannery's *The Eternal Frontier*, 300–311, in the chapter entitled 'The fatal impact'. John Muir's *Eight Wilderness Discovery Books* were compiled in 1992 by Diadem. I can find no evidence that he was aware of America's ecological and palaeo-Indian past.

## Chapter 2 Coed Eryri

1   Extracts from 'Coed Eryri' in *Reforesting Scotland* 13, Winter 1995, 10–13.
2   William Condry's *Snowdonia National Park* in Collins' New Naturalist series, though written in 1966, is still one of the best overviews of Snowdonia's natural history, perhaps indicating that not a lot has changed. Jim Perrins in *Visions of Snowdonia* gives an up-to-date account of community life in the hills and Michael Leach's *The Secret Life of Snowdonia* captures the ethereal quality of the mountains and wildlife.
3   Extracts from 'Coed Eryri' in *Reforesting Scotland* 13, Winter 1995, 10–13.
4   Extracts from 'Coed Eryri' in *Reforesting Scotland* 13, Winter 1995, 10–13.
5   See *www.caemabon.co.uk* for details of the educational programmes.
6   The Western scientific mind determines much of our mode of relating to nature as observer or analyst. Tribal peoples have developed an inner dimension best described as a dreamworld, where the spirits of animals and plants take on a more intimate two-way relationship. I recommend the work of Jamie Sams, first in the form of her oracular system *Medicine Cards*, and her *Dancing the Dream . . . the seven sacred paths of human transformation*. For an inspiring account of shamanic training and the life of a healer bound closely to nature, Martin Prechtel's *Secrets of the Talking Jaguar* is without parallel.
7   In 1998 the National Park produced the *Snowdonia Biodiversity Action Plan* which listed 49 species plans and Habitat Action Plans.
8   See Martin Prechtel's autobiographical work, *Secrets of the Talking Jaguar*.
9   Graves' *The White Goddess* explores the origin of poetic inspiration and contains some of the earliest attempts at retrieving the soulful elements of Celtic myth and ancient lore relating to trees, language and symbol.
10  See 'Return of the animal spirits' in *Reforesting Scotland* 15 Autumn 1996, 12–15.
11  *The Tir Gofal Farmer's Handbook* produced in March 2000, is available from the Countryside Council for Wales, and the special Snowdonia National Park pack from the SNP offices, Penrhyndeudraeth, Gwynedd.
12  In later years I was to work alongside teachers such as Elizabeth Brooke and Iona Fredenburgh at Cae Mabon as they re-introduced *Plant Spirit Medicine*, the techniques of deep intuition and listening in respect of herbal medicine.

## Chapter 3 Caledon

1   The denudation of the original extensive Caledonian Forest is the subject of some debate. Recent studies of climate, peat deposits and pollen histories show that the post-glacial pine forests shrank considerably as the climate became cooler and wetter and that by 5000 BP it was considerably reduced over large areas of blanket bog. Human intervention by grazing probably hastened the natural processes such that by pre-industrial times, it

was reduced to 4 per cent of its original splendour. Hugh Miles and Brian Jackman's *Great Wood of Caledon* illustrates the magnificent beauty of this forest.

2   Discussion of this Scotland-wide problem can be found in SNH's *Red Deer and the Natural Heritage*. Some recent practical experience of selective culling of hinds at Creag Meagaidh NNR is reported by Crispin Hayes in *Reforesting Scotland* 24 Summer, 17–18.

3   See Alan Featherstone's 'The Wild Heart of the Highlands', *ECOS* 18 (2), 48–61. The Findhorn-based Trees for Life organization can be contacted at *www.gaia.org/treesforlife*.

4   See Derek Yalden's 'Opportunities for re-introducing British mammals', *Mammal Review* 16, 53–63.

5   Reforesting Scotland has a website *www.reforestingscotland.gn.apc.org* and publishes the quarterly journal *Reforesting Scotland*.

6   The John Muir Trust is the only trust dedicated to buying and preserving wildland. Details at: *www.jmt.org*

7   The issues of land reform, wildland and community social and economic interests are featured in *ECOS* 23 (1), with articles on the community management of the former state forest at Abriachan, the Assynt Crofters Trust and RSPB's work on bringing economic benefits to local communities.

8   The need for education is clear from the demise of the Highland Wolf Fund, which failed to raise support and money for a feasibility study of re-introduction. These issues are reported by Diana Holt in *Reforesting Scotland* 26 Summer 2001, who found almost total opposition from all statutory bodies, and in particular deer societies and shooting interests.

9   See Gibbons et al, *The New Atlas of Breeding Birds in Britain and Ireland*, p100.

10  See Dennis R., *Ospreys*.


# Chapter 4 Dartmoor

1   *Dartmoor* by Lee Frost and Ian Robertson provides a stunning photographic tapestry of the hills and woods; the *Dartmoor National Park Management Plan* of May 2001 gives an account of the various issues of wildlife, local communities, tourism and planning; English Nature and Dartmoor National Park Authority have produced a very clear summary of biodiversity issues *The Nature of Dartmoor: a biodiversity profile*.

2   Adam Griffin can be contacted at *moor.trees@ukonline.co.uk*. The report *Towards the Wild* of the conference at Dartington Hall, November 1999, showcases the excellent promotional work of Moor Trees.

3   See *Dartmoor National Park Management Plan* 2001.

4   See *Action for Wildlife: the Dartmoor Biodiversity Action Plan*, Dartmoor Biodiversity Steering Group, Dartmoor National Park, Newton Abbot.


# Chapter 5 The Potential for Networks and Corridors

1   *New Wildwoods*, Land Use Policy Group, JNCC, Peterborough.

2   See *www.wildennerdale.co.uk* and 'Wild Ennerdale – letting nature loose' in *ECOS* 25 (3/4) 2004.

3   The 'Wild Ennerdale' partnership and plans are described by George Browning and Rachel Yanik in *ECOS* 25 (3/4).

4   See *www.carrifran.org.uk* and 'The Carrifran Wildwood Project' in *ECOS* 25 (3/4) 2004

5   For a description of the site, the vision and a discussion of the principles, see Adrian Colston, 'Beyond preservation: the challenge of ecological restoration' in Adams and

Mulligan eds, *Decolonising Nature*, Earthscan, and 'Wicken Fen – realising the vision' in *ECOS* 25 (3/4) 2004.

6   See Friday L.F. and Moorhouse T. (1999), *The Wider Vision* Cambridge University Press.
7   See Tony Whitbread 'From weald to wild' in *ECOS* 25 (3/4) 2004.
8   See the River Restoration Centre website *www.therrc.co.uk*. The Centre, at Silsoe College, produces a newsletter on projects. Also particularly relevant as it is close to Dartmoor, is the Westcountry Rivers Trust *Tamar 2000 Project*, email: *wrt@wrt.org.uk*.
9   See Luke Comins' account of the Tweed Project from a rewilding perspective 'Rewilding the Tweed' in *ECOS* 25 (3/4), 24–28
10  See 'Wild Britain – a partnership between conservation, community and commerce' in *ECOS* 25 (3/4), 2004.

# Chapter 6 Restoring Ecological Processes: the core vegetation

1   See F.W.M. Vera (2000) *Grazing Ecology and Forest History* CABI Publishing, Wallingford.
2   Following the pioneering work of Paul Martin (see *Quaternary Extinctions*), Tim Flannery developed the thesis of mega-faunal extinction by looking at the knock-on effects upon forest dynamics of the removal of this level of vegetation processing, both for Australian and American fauna. The same principles apply to European temperate forests, which held elephant and rhino in previous inter-glacials.
3   See for example the excellent discussion paper in English in the special issue of *Vakblad Natuurbeheer* (2002) (this special issue from the Dutch ministry LNV was supported also by the Danish Nature Agency and English Nature, two agencies showing more interest in natural processes, particularly grazing regimes).
4   This debate on naturalness and grazing regimes by James Fenton, Peter Taylor and Mark Fisher is featured in *ECOS* 24 (3/4), and also in 25 (3/4), a special edition on re-wilding themes where Keith Kirby of English Nature outlines the potential for wild grazers.
5   George Peterken (1981), John Rodwell (1991) and Oliver Rackham (1980) offer different classifications, with Rodwell also co-authoring a very clear and practical booklet for the Forestry Commission *Creating New Native Woodlands* (1995). Derek Yalden (1999) also gives a relevant pre-historical account (Holocene) of Britain's changing climate, forests and mammal fauna (pp 63–137).
6   See The National Vegetation Classification system, centred on Rodwell's work at Lancaster University (1991) and published in the series *British Plant Communities* (see especially Vol. 1. *Woodland and Scrub*).
7   See Kurten (1968), Yalden (1999) and Stuart (1982) for the fossil history of hippopotamus in Europe.
8   See Yalden (1999) 91–92.
9   Yalden (1999) summarizes the loss of forests and fauna from Neolithic to Roman times, 128–129.
10  See English Nature note from *keith.kirbyenglish-nature.org.uk* and discussion forum http://forums.ceh.ac.uk:8080/~naturalised-grazing.

# Chapter 7 Restoring Ecological Processes: the herbivore guild

1   Whitbread A. and Jenman W. (1995). 'A natural method of conserving biodiversity in Britain', *British Wildlife* Vol 7 (2).
2   There is a website *www.wwf.pl/bialowieza* that gives details of the forest and its management.

3 See Kurten (1968) 72–74.

4 Anecdotal information from hunters in the Vosges and Jura suggest depression of roe deer numbers in lynx territory, although data from hunting returns and road kills does not support a significant impact on numbers.

5 Geert et al of Alterra 'Make way for the European Ecological Network' in *Vakblad Natuurbeheer* (51–53).

6 See Roberts' *The Holocene*, 63, for figures relating to rhythmic contraction of forests.

7 Palaeontological data are drawn from Kurten (1968), Yalden (1999) and Stuart (1982).

8 See Flannery *The Eternal Frontier* for an account of the land bridge and exchanges between Eurasia and America, 206–229.

9 See Yalden (1999) 32.

10 Whitehead (1953) provides a thorough account.

11 Both Whitehead (1953) and Yalden (1999) 157 discuss these issues, with the latter convinced of a domestic origin.

12 See Yalden (1999) 97.

13 Whitehead (1953) provides an account of the Hecks' work. These cattle have since been used as wild grazers in some Dutch and Polish nature reserves.

14 Jaap van Leeuwen et al 'Health risks between large herbivores, farm animals and man', *Vakblad Natuurbeheer* May 2002.

15 See Morrison (1994) 146–148.

16 Joep van der Vlasakker (personal communication), *flaxfield@skynet.be* and *www.largeherbivore.org*. See also the website *www.exmoorponysociety.org.uk* and the works of Dr Sue Baker at Exeter University; in particular, 'Exmoor ponies – Britain's prehistoric wild horses?', *British Wildlife* 9(5)

17 See Mathiasson and Dalhov (1990) 201–207.

18 See Morrison (1994) 170–171 and Mathiasson and Dalhov (1987) 235–238.

19 See Mathiasson and Dalhov (1990) 157–159 and Morrison (1994) 149.

20 Martin Goulding (2003) *Wild Boar in Britain* Whittet Books. See also *www.britishwildboar.org.uk* for latest sightings.

21 Information about these programmes is available at *www.scotsbeavers.org.uk* and *www.snh.org.uk*; see also *www.kentwildlife.org.uk*

22 See Taylor (2002a) 'Beavers in Britain: laying the foundations', *ECOS* 23 (2), 23–26.

23 Yalden (1999) gives details of the distribution.

# Chapter 8 Restoring Ecological Processes: Bringing Back the Carnivores

1 I had heard this recounted several years ago, but on a recent trip to the Carpathians I talked to foresters and carnivore experts and was struck by the absence of any detailed studies of the interaction of herbivores, predators and forest regeneration. I suspect that forest regeneration effects are marginal and that the main determinants of forest structure are long-term chaotic events such as wind-throw and fire.

2 See M.K. Philips and D.W. Smith *The Wolves of Yellowstone*, Voyageur Press.

3 See Mech L.D. *The Wolves of Minnesota*, Voyageur Press.

4 Kurten was of the opinion that all the lions, including the large British cave lion and American lion, were sub-species of *Panthera leo*.

5 Accounts of lynx ecology and history in Europe can be found in Mathiasson and Dalhov (1990), Mallinson (1978) and Morrison (1994). Peter Jackson reported on problems with sheep and hunters during the re-introductions in the Jura Mountains 'Shepherds neglect to smile . . .', *BBC Wildlife*, June 1989, 401.

6   The IUCN website contains much up-to-date data on cat species ecology and conservation issues, including Iberian and Eurasian lynx, *www.lynx.uio.no/catfolk*; see also *www.lcie.org*

7   See WWF (1999) 'Europe's Carnivores: a conservation challenge for the 21st century', *www.wwf-uk.org*

8   See Breitenmoser (1990) *Status, Conservation Needs and Re-introduction of the Lynx in Europe* Council of Europe. Strasbourg and Breitenmoser (1998) 'Large predators in the Alps', *Biological Conservation* (83) 279–289.

9   Council of Europe (2001) *Pan-Alpine Conservation Strategy for the Lynx*. Strasburg; KORA (2001) *The Balkan Lynx Population: History, Recent Knowledge on Status and Conservation Needs www.kora.unibe.ch*

10  See Peter Jackson in the *Independent*, 'Iberian lynx nears extinction', 16 June, 2002; see also Jorge Bartolome 'A creature great and small', *BBC Wildlife*, August 2001, 22–26 for up-to-date account of Iberian lynx issues, as well as the WWF website.

11  Chris Moiser et al (2002) 'On the prowl . . . lynx in the British countryside', *ECOS* 23 (2) 9–13.

12  Higginson L. (2000) 'Big Cats in Britain', *The Field*, March issue and Peter Taylor (2002) 'Big cats in Britain: restoration ecology or imaginations run wild' in *ECOS* 23 (3/4). See also *www.bigcats.org*

13  Trevor Beer (1984) *The Beast of Exmoor: fact or legend*, Countryside Productions, Barnstaple.

14  The IUCN cat group website [provides good data on relic leopard populations and their ecology].

15  See David Mech *The Wolves of Minnesota* for detailed discussion of history, ecology and management. A residual population in the Lake Superior National Forest area numbered about 700 in 1950 and has increased by 4 per cent per year to about 2500, which now ranges south into Wisconsin.

16  There appears to be no overall review, but several reports in *BBC Wildlife*, e.g., Chris Hellier's 'Alpine shepherds cry wolf', January 2000, and 'Wolf witch hunt' document attempts by hunters and shepherds to eradicate newly colonizing wolves in the French Alps; a brief review in *New Scientist* by Reinhard Piechocki 'Who's afraid of the wandering wolf?', April 1994, documents their arrival in Germany and gives up-to-date numbers for Europe. Oliver Klafke provides further reports on accommodation to migrants 'The company of wolves', *New Scientist*, February 1998.

17  The occurrence of wolves within the city limits of Brasov is under research by the Large Carnivore Initiative for Europe; see Christoph Promberger 'Project Wolf' in *BBC Wildlife*, July, 1999.

18  Whilst Scotland would undoubtedly support a population of wolves, much as Norway or Sweden does, given the over-population of natural prey, the oft-mooted re-introduction has met with little support. Roger Panaman's Highland Wolf Project (reported in the *Independent*, 29 March 1995) failed to gain funds for a study. In a recent review of the issue (*ECOS* 23 (2) 2–7) he remains optimistic, but in my view under-estimates not only sheep farmers' opposition, but that of the hunting fraternity in Scotland. Diana Holt's 'Should wolves be reintroduced to the Highlands of Scotland?' provides a more realistic perspective, following canvassing of stakeholder groups in the region (*Reforesting Scotland* 26 Summer 2001, 38–40). See also *www.wolftrust.org.uk* for world news, European papers and the Scottish visionary project.

19  See Chris Hellier, 'Alpine shepherds cry wolf', *BBC Wildlife*, January 2000.

20  See Ann Treneman's 'Wolves to the slaughter', *Times*, 12 February 2001.

21  Reported in Joanna Streetly's 'Wolves between the worlds' in *BBC Wildlife*, December 2000.

22  See Boitani L. (2000) *Action plan for the conservation of wolves in Europe*, Council of Europe and also the Carpathian Large Carnivore Project *www.clcp.ro*

23 Keith Highley gives an account of the Yellowstone experience, 'Out of the woods', in *BBC Wildlife*, September 1998; Rupert Isaacson reports on Yellowstone and Montana's experience in 'Chances with wolves' in *The Geographical*, July 1999.

24 Ray Nelson gives an account of the Mexican re-introduction programme 'The lure of el lobo' in *BBC Wildlife*, July 2000.

25 *BBC Wildlife* has reported on various projects and their problems over the years. The small Spanish population is described by Teresa Farino, 'The littlest grizzly', March 1989; the problems faced by this population due to infrastructural developments were covered in June 1991; the Slovenian translocations to the French Pyrenees featured in December 1997 and August 1999, and their impact on the Spanish side in November 1998, with reports in October 2000 of some recovery in the Cantabrian Mountains following the Spanish Government's 1990 Brown Bear recovery Plan.

26 See David MacDonald (2001) 71.

27 Accounts of bear ecology and history in Europe are given by Mathiasson and Dalhov (1990) 181–186 and Morrison (1994) 103–105.

28 See *BBC Wildlife* report 'Wildlife in the wars', June 1999.

# Chapter 9 The Healing Forest

1 Ken Wilbur describes the different *levels* of awareness in his *A Brief History of Everything*, Chapter 12, 'Realms of the superconscious' (his particular interest in deep ecology provides some useful insights). Martin Prechtel describes his own initiations in *Secrets of the Talking Jaguar* and *Long Life, Honey in the Heart*. There is also the classic *Autobiography of a Yogi* by Paramhansa Yogananda. Additionally, Wilbur has some fine paragraphs describing the relationship of the yogic experience of the witness – that which has no locus and no identity – to the *causal* level of consciousness. However, the earliest description of states of consciousness rests with the *Siva Sutras*, 8th century writings on the nature of reality (see Jaideva Singh's commentary).

2 See 'The nature of death' in proceedings of the conference Nature in Transition, National Trust, 2000.

3 In Peter Levine's *Waking the Tiger: healing trauma*, he speculates that the capacity to be traumatized is a product of a human evolution from prey to predator in which the rational mind overrules the instinctive, thus leading to the repression and blockage of energy that the therapist eventually causes to be released.

4 The epitome of peaceful and balanced but civilized society must rest with Buddhist communities, some of which have prospered for over a thousand years with little technological change, balanced populations and a deep respect for the natural world. The fundamental teachings of the Buddha related to *transcendence* not just of struggle and suffering, but of ego–identity and thus all fear. Original Christian teachings also drew heavily on natural metaphor – such as the 'lily of the fields', where the spiritual aspirant is taught to trust in the divinity that resides both in the human heart and in the heart of a nature imbued with sacredness.

5 Martin Prechtel and other writers have called this the 'search for the indigenous soul'. Ken Wilbur accounts the industrialization process as responsible for the loss of inner consciousness and objectification of nature – with the romantic poets then idolizing that separated entity, and science according it sole significant reality. Our modern ecological consciousness is still caught in that mental trap, where surface reality is seen as our essential support service.

6 The ancient Greek God of the forest, Pan, the universal, wild and instinctive formed the basis for the cloven-hoofed, rams-horned devil of Christian symbology.

7  It is generally not recognized that a 500-year western European persecution of women, demonized as 'witches', purged all trace of feminine deities and herbal medicines that were based upon a ritual connection to natural divinity. This holocaust, with few scholarly and accessible accounts within our educational system, ritually executed hundreds of thousands perhaps millions of women (the historian Barbara Walker provides some documentation of the 'inquisition' in her *Women's Encyclopedia of Myths and Secrets*).

8  See websites: *www.communityforest.org.uk* and *www.nationalforest.org*.

9  I have known several professionally qualified medical herbalists also trained in the modern Order of Bards, Ovates and Druids, who use an invocation of the spirit of the plant as well as the material infusion or essence of an herb. However, the healing is understood to be taking place on a *spiritual* as well as a physical level, and it is this level that is denied relevance by modern medicine.

10 The 20th century existential crisis of Western philosophy, typified by Sartre, hardly turned to a mother earth for its soul's ease but that was perhaps part of the lostness; the 'return to the Goddess' now prevalent in feminist writings is held by Wilbur still to be mired in separation and mythic yearning. For the yogi, only the internal integration of male and female elements of consciousness promises wholeness.

11 See Helen Graham's *Soul Medicine: restoring the spirit to healing* for a succinct account of the historical perceptions of soul in medicine and for a scholarly account of modern practices, particularly the rise of bodywork, bio-energetics, analysis, Jungian work and the gradual resurgence of soul-oriented healing in medical practice.

12 See Dan Smith's *State of the World Atlas* and the Worldwatch Institute's *Vital Signs 2003–2004*.

13 The message of the Stockholm and Rio environmental summits has been consistent, as has the work of the Inter-governmental Panel on Climate Change – though only on the identification of the ecological problems of unsustainable development models, rather than the psychological and political forces that might drive them. The publication of Lomborg's *The Skeptical Environmentalist* also provoked a storm of criticism in scientific circles.

14 See Richard Barrett's *Liberating the Corporate Soul: building a visionary organisation*, Butterworth-Heinemann, 1998

15 See Jamie Sams' *Medicine Cards* and *Dancing the Dream* and Leo Rutherford's *Elements of Shamanism* for the more practical approach, together with the anthropologist Michael Harner's classic *Way of the Shaman*.

16 See Kaptchuk's *Chinese Medicine: the web that has no weaver* and Liu's *Traditional Chinese Medicine*.

17 There are numerous books on the Bach flower essences, see Wright's *Flower Essences* and Ramsall and Murray's *Questions and Answers: Clarifying the Basic Principles of Bach Flower Remedies*.

18 There is an assumption among many scientists and within the general medical profession that the majority of complementary therapies are 'unproven' as if they would somehow fail the tests of science were science to be applied. There are two issues here: (1) scientific medicine's own house is hardly in order, with a history of apparently efficacious drug treatments withdrawn due to unforeseen consequences, and with virtually all data on effectiveness kept secret for 'commercial' reasons (often related to marginal improvements of a few percent – with many remedies thus proving ineffective in the *majority* of cases); and (2) science has very limited means for testing the subtle aspects of mood, spiritual wellbeing and their health consequences, but in recent cases, surveys have found complementary therapies, particularly homeopathy and acupuncture, to be effective for chronic ailments. This issue is treated in a British Medical Association report of the Boards of Science and Education on Alternative Therapy 61–75 in Saks' *Alternative*

*Medicine in Britain* and also in Helen Graham's *Soul Medicine*, which has useful accounts of homeopathy and other vibrational remedies.

19 There are numerous works by Philip Carr-Gomm, chief of the Order of Bards, Ovates and Druids, that introduce concepts of the dreamworld or otherworld, healing, and the animal and plant spirits, e.g., *The Druid Animal Oracle*, *The Rebirth of Druidry* and *Druid Mysteries*; however, the classic work by Carlos Castaneda *The Art of Dreaming* should be read to gain a perception of the darker side of 'dream' work that is also prevalent in Prechtel's writing. Virtually all shamanic writing describes encounters with 'evil' and ensuing battles – see also this author's autobiographical account *Shiva's Rainbow*.

# Chapter 10 The Land In-between: Wilding Agriculture

1 A good example of local declines in a nature reserve, perhaps due to small size and isolation, is provided by Colston (2003) and Friday and Colston (1999) for Wicken Fen, which has lost Montagu's harrier and marsh warbler, swallowtail butterfly, large tortoiseshell, dark green fritillary, several moths and beetles, five dragonfly and 28 marsh plant species in the last 100 years.

2 David Gibbons and Mark Avery 'Birds' in Hawksworth (ed.) *The Changing Wildlife of Great Britain and Ireland*, Taylor and Francis, 2001.

3 Report of the Mammal Society in *BBC Wildlife*, January 1999.

4 See Gibbons et al (1993) *The New Atlas of Breeding Birds in Britain and Ireland 1988–1991* Poyser.

5 Hawksworth's *The Changing Wildlife of Great Britain and Ireland*, Taylor and Francis, 2001, provides reviews for the noted declines of butterflies and moths, amphibians and reptiles, certain bird species and small mammals.

6 See Dwyer J. (2001) *Paying for the Stewardship of the Countryside: a green print for future of agri-environment schemes in England*, Wildlife and Countryside Link, London.

7 See Green M. and Orme E. (1992) ESA's – Assessment and Recommendations. FOE, London.

8 See Lynn Hunt 'Reaping the benefits', *BBC Wildlife*, March 1998.

9 See Hodge I. and Renwick A. (2003) 'Developing agri-environment schemes – towards a rural environmental policy', *ECOS* 24 (2), 37–44. Details of the review can be accessed at *www.statistics.defra.gov.uk/esg/evaluation/agrienv*. See also Alastair Rutherford's 'A hall of mirrors: reflections on the 2003 CAP reform', *ECOS* 25 (2) 2004, in which the direction of current reform is laid bare: cross-compliance in Pillar 1 offers very little for biodiversity other than 2 m field margins and the rationale for Single Farm Payments (decoupled now from production) appears little more than continued financial support based on assets rather than need. It fails to support marginal livestock so important to many grazed habitats.

10 See the report by Natural Capital Management for the Countryside Agency – *The Social and Economic Effects of Developing New Wild Land in Northumberland*. This report considers the present funding structure and rather unimaginatively makes no prognosis relating to the future reduction or loss of beef and sheep subsidy, with which other forms of agri-environment subsidy cannot compete; nor does it make recommendations regarding support schemes for wild-grazers, corridors and core areas, even though it makes reference to the pioneering Dutch experience.

11 See also Stoate C. 'Behavioural ecology of farmers', *British Wildlife*, February 2002, which explores farmers' attitudes to wildlife schemes.

12 See Klein P. and Sutherland W. (2003) 'How effective are agri-environment schemes in conserving and promoting biodiversity?', *Journal of Applied Ecology* 40, 947–969. See

also Mick Green's 'More environment less agri' in *ECOS* 25 (1) 43–47 and James Robertson's 'CAP reform: turning the corner', *ECOS* 25 (1) 48–54.

13 See C. Arden-Clarke (1988) *The Environmental Effects of Conventional and Organic-biological Farming Systems*. Part I and II, RR-17; Part III and IV, RR-18 Political Ecology Research Group, Oxford.

14 See Della Fazey 'Seeing over the hill . . . a vision for community land ownership in Wales', *ECOS* 24 (2) 2003.

# Chapter 11 Targeted Habitat Creation

1 See *Community Forests Monitoring Report, 2000/2001* Entec Ltd., The National Community Forest Partnership and Evans S. *The National Forest: a case study in delivering change* The National Forest Company, UK.

2 See *Tir Gofal: Farmer's Handbook*. CCW, Bangor.

3 See Peter Taylor's 'Whole ecosystem restoration: re-creating wilderness' in *ECOS* 16 (2) 22–28 and 'Restoration forestry and the global ecosystem' in *ECOS* 14 (2) 2–8.

4 See Whitbread A. and Jenman W (1995). 'A natural method of conserving biodiversity in Britain' in *British Wildlife* 7 (2) and also 'From weald to wild' in *ECOS* 25 (3/4), 2004.

5 Peter Taylor 'Whole ecosystem restoration: re-creating wilderness' in *ECOS* 16 (2) 22–28 and 'Restoration forestry and the global ecosystem' in *ECOS* 14 (2) 2–8.

6 See Inter-governmental Panel on Climate Change *Climate Change 2001: Summary for Policy Makers* and *Technical Summary of the Working Group 1 Report*.

7 See Royal Commission on Environmental Pollution 22nd report *Energy: the changing climate* in which numbers of installations are given for various scenarios.

8 See The Countryside Agency (2001) *Visualising Renewable Energy in the Landscape of 2050*. See also *www.ethos-uk.com*

9 GIS Research Group, School of Environmental Sciences, University of East Anglia, contact Trudie Docherty at *T.Docherty@UEA.ac.uk*.

10 See Royal Society *The Role of Land Carbon Sinks in Mitigating Global Climate Change*, Policy Document, July 2001.

11 See Roger Kayes et al (1990) *An Assessment of the Feasibility of Large Scale Afforestation in Britain to Offset Carbon Dioxide Emissions*, Political Ecology Research Group, Oxford.

12 Future Forests can be contacted at *www.futureforests.com* and Climate Care at *www.co2.org*. The debate as to the long-term value of carbon offsets continues, with many scientists warning that in a warming world, the carbon will return through respiration on a much shorter timescale than previously assumed (see Fred Pearce 'That sinking feeling' in *New Scientist* 23 October 1999), and although the Kyoto Protocol is evolving towards furthering such offsets, the US Government's use of data suggesting its forests already absorb all of its emissions, causes many who might be sympathetic to carbon offsets, to oppose them as a potential distraction from emission control. Further, some large forestry corporations are looking to purchase carbon credits by planting fast growing *Eucalyptus* forests over hundreds of square kilometres in Africa, and thus direct the incentives towards highly technological single-issue programmes when ecological restoration could be a more holistic use of financial resources.

13 See George Peterken (1995) *A Forest Habitat Network for Scotland*, SNH.

14 See *Ecological Networks: experiences in the Netherlands*. A Working Paper of the Ministry for Agriculture, Nature and Food Quality by Monique Hootsmans and Hans Kampf (for information: h.kampf@minlnv.nl)

# Chapter 12 Stepping Stones to a Wilder Policy

1   See Edwards R. (1991) *Fit for the Future: Report of the National Parks Review Panel*, Countryside Commission, Cheltenham.
2   See the John Muir Trust website, *www.jmt.org*
3   For a short critique of Lomborg see Peter Taylor's 'Agendas of delusion: just who is manipulating environmental data?' in *ECOS* 22 (3/4) 101–104; a more detailed critique was posted on the BANC website *www.banc.org.uk*
4   See Rogers and Taylor *New Wildwoods: removing barriers to development and implementation*, LUPG, JNCC.
5   Information can be obtained on planting programmes etc, at *moor.trees@ukonline.co.uk*
6   See 'Sabres in the hills' by Steve Watson, *Tree News*, 2, 1998.

# Chapter 13 Straight to the Heart: A Wildland Strategy

1   Contact Adam Griffin at *moor.trees@ukonline.co.uk*
2   Snowdonia National Park Authority (1999) *Biodiversity in Snowdonia.*
3   Dartmoor National Park Authority (2001) *The Nature of Dartmoor: a biodiversity profile*; and *Action for Wildlife: the Dartmoor BAP*. See also *Dartmoor National Park Management Plan* DNPA, 2001.
4   Angela Douglas of the Woodland Trust reports on *Glen Finglas: the return of the forest* – the acquisition of 4000 ha of land in the Trossachs in Loch Lomond National Park, in which over 3000 ha of new forest is planned (*Reforesting Scotland* 23, Spring 2000, 23–25. See also *www.woodland-trust.org.uk*.

# References

Adams W. (2003) *Future Nature: a vision for conservation*, Earthscan, London

Akroyd T. (2004) 'Wild Britain – a partnership between conservation, community and commerce, *ECOS* 25 (3/4), 78–83

Arden-Clarke C.A.C. (1988) *The Environmental Effects of Conventional and Organic-biological Farming Systems*, Part I and II, RR-17; Part III and IV, RR-18, Political Ecology Research Group, Oxford.

Ashmole P. and Chalmers H. (2004) 'The Carrifran Wildwood project', *ECOS* 25 (3/4) 11–19

Barrett R. (1998) *Liberating the Corporate Soul: building a visionary organisation*, Butterworth-Heinemann, Oxford

Bates S. (2004) 'Nature maps', *ECOS* 25 (3/4), 55–58

Beer T. (1984) *The Beast of Exmoor: fact or legend?* Countryside Publications, Barnstaple

Boitani L. (2000) *Action Plan for the Conservation of Wolves in Europe*, Council of Europe, *www.nature.coe.int/cp20/tvps23e.htm*

Breitenmoser U. (1990) *Status, Conservation Needs and Re-introduction of the Lynx in Europe*, Council of Europe, Strasbourg

Breitenmoser U. (1998) 'Large predators in the alps', *Biological Conservation* (83) 279–289

Browning G. and Yanik R. (2004) 'Wild Ennerdale – letting nature loose', *ECOS* 25 (3/4), 34–38

Carr-Gomm P. (2002) *Druid Mysteries*, Random House, London

Carr-Gomm P. (ed.) (2003) *The Rebirth of Druidry: ancient earth wisdom for today*, Element Books, Shaftesbury

Carver S., Evans A. and Fritz S. (2002) 'Wilderness attribute mapping in the UK', *International Journal of Wilderness* 8(1), 24–29

Castaneda C. (1993) *The Art of Dreaming*, Element Books, Shaftesbury

Colston A. (2003) 'Beyond preservation: the challenge of ecological restoration' in W Adams and M Mulligan (ed.) *Decolonising Nature*, Earthscan, London

Colston, A. (2004) 'Wicken Fen – realising the vision', *ECOS* 25 (3/4), 42–45

Comins L. (2004) 'Rewilding the Tweed', *ECOS* (3/4), 24–28

Condry W. (1966) *The Snowdonia National Park*, New Naturalists Series, Collins, London

Corbet G.B. and Harris S. (1991) *Handbook of British Mammals*, 3rd Edition, Blackwell, Oxford

Council of Europe (2001) *Pan-Alpine Conservation Strategy for the Lynx*, Council of Europe, Strasburg

Council for National Parks (1997) *Wild by Design: an exploration of the potential for the creation of wilder areas in the national parks of England and Wales*, CNP, London

Countryside Agency (2002) *Visualising Renewable Energy in the Countryside of 2050*, Countryside Agency, Cheltenham

Countryside Council for Wales (2000) *Tir Gofal: farmer's handbook*, CCW, Bangor

CRER (2002) 'Economic evaluation of agri-environment schemes', report for DEFRA, Dept of Land Economy, University of Cambridge, Cambridge

Curry D. (2002) *Policy Commission on the Future of Farming and Food*, Cabinet Office, London

DEFRA (2002a) *The Strategy for Sustainable Farming and Food – Facing the Future*, DEFRA, London

DEFRA (2002b) *Agri-Environment Schemes Framework Document: a consultation on the future of agri-environment schemes*, Expanded version, DEFRA, London

Dennis R.H. (1991) *Ospreys*, Colin Baxter, Lanark

Dwyer J. (2001) *Paying for the Stewardship of the Countryside: a green print for the future of agri-environment schemes in England*, Wildlife and Countryside Link, London

Edwards R. (1991) *Fit for the Future: report of the national parks review panel*, Countryside Commission, Cheltenham

Fazey D. (2003) 'Seeing over the hill: a vision for community land ownership in Wales', *ECOS* 24 (2) 51–56

Featherstone A.W. (1997) 'The wild heart of the highlands', *ECOS* 18 (2) 48–61

Fenton J. (2004) 'A new paradigm for uplands', *ECOS* 25 (1), 2–5

Fisher M. (2004) 'Self-willed land: can nature ever be free?', *ECOS* 25 (1), 6–11

Flannery T. (1995) *The Future Eaters: an ecological history of the Australasian lands and people*, Reed Books, Port Melbourne

Flannery T. (2002) *The Eternal Frontier: an ecological history of North America and its peoples*, Vintage, London

Forestry Commission (1998) *A New Focus for England's Woodlands: strategic priorities and programmes*, Forestry Commission, Cambridge

Friday L.F. and Colston A. (1999) 'Wicken fen – the restoration of a wetland nature reserve', *British Wildlife*, October, 1999

Geert W.T.A. et al (2002) 'Make way for the European Ecological Network' in *Vakblad Natuurbeheer*, Special Issue 'Grazing and Grazing Animals', Dutch Ministry LNV, Wageningen (gratis from *balie@ecinv.agro.nl*)

Gibbons D.W. et al (1994) *The New Atlas of Breeding Birds in Britain and Ireland 1988–1991*, Poyser, London

Goulding M. (2003) *Wild Boar in Britain*, Whittet, Stowmarket

Gow D. (2002) 'A wallowing good time: wild boar in the woods', *ECOS* 23 (2), 14–22

Graham H. (1999) *Complementary Therapies in Context: the psychology of healing*, Jessica Kingsley, London

Graham H. (2001) *Soul Medicine: restoring the spirit to healing*, NewLeaf, Dublin

Graves, R. (1948) *The White Goddess*, Faber and Faber, London

Green M. and Orme E. (1992) *Environmentally Sensitive Ares – assessment and recommendations*, FOE, London

Harner M. (1980) *The Way of the Shaman*, Harper, San Francisco

Hodge I. and Renwick A. (2003) 'Developing agri-environment schemes – towards a rural environmental policy, *ECOS* 24 (2)

Hole M. (1998) 'What Future in Farming for Wildlife?' *British Wildlife*, October 1998

Hootsmans M. and Kampf H. (2004) Ecological Networks: Experiences in the Netherlands. A working paper of the Ministry of Agriculture, Nature and Food Quality (from h.kampf@minlav.nl)

Intergovernmental Panel on Climate Change (2001) *Climate Change 2001: Summary for Policy Makers and Technical Summary of the Working Group 1 Report*, Cambridge University Press, Cambridge

Singh J. (1979) *Siva Sutras*, Motilal Banarsidass, Delhi

Jung C.G. (1966) *Modern Man in Search of the Soul*, Routledge, London

Kaptchuk T. (1983) *Chinese Medicine: the web that has no weaver*, Rider, London

Kayes R.J., Taylor P.J. and Arden-Clarke C.A.C. (1990) *An Assessment of the Feasibility of Large-scale Afforestation in Britain to Offset Carbon Dioxide Emissions*, Report RR-19, Political Ecology Research Group, Oxford

Kirby K. et al (2004) 'Fresh woods and pastures new', *ECOS* 25 (1) 26–33

Klein P. and Sutherland W. (2003) 'How effective are agri-environment schemes in conserving and promoting biodiversity?', *Journal of Applied Ecology* (40) 947–969

KORA (2001) *The Balkan Lynx Population: history, recent knowledge on status and conservation needs*, *www.kora.unibe.ch*

Krech S. (1999) *The Ecological Indian: myth and history*, WW Norton, New York

Kurten B. (1968) *Pleistocene Mammals of Europe*, Weidenfeld and Nicolson, London

Land Use Policy Group (2002) *The New Wildwoods Project: developing the role of large scale new native woodlands*, JNCC, Peterborough

Lawson T. (2004) 'Back to the future', *BBC Wildlife*, October

Leach M. (1991) *The Secret Life of Snowdonia*, Chatto and Windus, London

Levine P. (1997) *Waking the Tiger: healing trauma*, North Atlantic, Berkeley, California

Liu Y. (1988) *Traditional Chinese Medicine*, Columbia University Press, New York

Lomborg B. (2001) *The Skeptical Environmentalist: measuring the state of the real world*, Cambridge University Press, Cambridge

Macdonald D. (ed) (2001) *The New Encyclopedia of Mammals*, Oxford University Press, Oxford

Mallinson J. (1978) *The Shadow of Extinction: Europe's threatened wild mammals*, Reader's Union, Newton Abbot

Marren, P. (2000) 'Did the bittern read the BAP?', *ECOS* 21 (2), 43–46

Martin P.S. and Klein R.G. (eds) (1984) *Quaternary Extinctions: a prehistoric revolution*, University of Arizona Press, Tucson

Mason C. (2004) *The 2030 Spike: countdown to global catastrophe*, Earthscan, London

Mathiasson S. and Dalhov G. (1990) *In the Wild: wildlife in Great Britain and Europe*, Swan Hill, London

McKibben B. (1990) *The End of Nature: humanity, climate change and the natural world*, Bloomsbury, London

McVean D.N. and Ratcliffe D.A. (1962) *Plant Communities of the Scottish Highlands*, HMSO, London

Mech D. (2000) *The Wolves of Minnesota*, Voyageur Press, Stillwater, MN

Merricks P. (2003) 'Agri-environment – some thoughts from the marsh', *ECOS* 24 (2) 28–36

Miles H. and Jackman B. (1991) *The Great Wood of Caledon*, Colin Baxter, Lanark

Morrison P. (1994) *Mammals, Reptiles and Amphibians of Britain and Europe*, Macmillan, London

Muir J. (1992) *The Eight Wilderness Discovery Books*, Diadem, London

National Trust (1999) *A Call for the Wild*, National Trust, Cirencester

Natural Capital Management (2003) *The Social and Economic Effects of Developing New Wild Land in Northumberland*, Report to the Countryside Agency, Cheltenham

Perrin J. (1997) *Visions of Snowdonia: landscape and legend*, BBC Books, London

Peterken G. (1981) Woodland Conservation and Management, Chapman and Hall, London

Peterken G. et al (1995) *A Forest Habitat Network for Scotland*, Research, Survey and Monitoring Report No 44, SNH, Edinburgh

Philips M. K. and Smith D. W. (1998) *The Wolves of Yellowstone*, Voyageur Press, Stillwater, MN

Prechtel M. (1999) *Secrets of the Talking Jaguar*, Element Books, Shaftesbury

Prechtel M. (2000) *Long Life, Honey in the Heart: a story of initiation and eloquence from the shores of a Mayan lake*, Element Books, Shaftesbury

Pullman P. (2000) *His Dark Materials Trilogy: Northern Lights, The Subtle Knife, The Amber Spyglass*, Scholastic, London

Rackham O. (1980) *Ancient Woodland: its history, vegetation and uses in England*, Arnold, London

Rackham O. (1986) *The History of the Countryside*, Weidenfeld and Nicolson, London

Ramsall J. and Murray N. (1987) *Questions and Answers Clarifying the Principles of Bach Flower Remedies*, Mount Vernon Bach Centre, Oxford

Reinhardt I. and Kluth G. (2004) 'Wolves in Germany: lessons to be learned', *ECOS* 25 (3/4), 73–77

Rodwell J. (1991) 'British Plant Communities', Vol 1, *Woodlands and scrub*, Cambridge University Press, Cambridge

Rodwell J. and Patterson G. (1995) *Creating New Native Woodlands*, Forestry Commission Bulletin No 112, HMSO, London

Roberts N. (1998) *The Holocene: an environmental history*, Blackwell, Oxford

Rogers S. and Taylor K. (2003) *New Wildwoods: removing barriers to development and implementation*, LUPG research report, JNCC, Peterborough

Royal Commission on Environmental Pollution (2000) *Energy – the changing climate*, 22nd Report, HMSO, London

Royal Society (2001) *The Role of Land Carbon Sinks in Mitigating Global Climate Change* (report available on *www.royalsoc.ac.uk*)

Royal Society for the Protection of Birds (2001) *Futurescapes: large scale habitat restoration for wildlife and people*, RSPB, Sandy, UK

Rutherford A. (2004) 'A hall of mirrors: reflections on the 2003 CAP reform', *ECOS* 25 (2) 22–30

Saks M. (ed) (1992) *Alternative Medicine in Britain*, Clarendon, Oxford

Sams J. (1988a) *Medicine Cards: the discovery of power through the ways of animals*, Bear and Co., Santa Fé

Sams J. (1998b) *Dancing the Dream*, Harper, San Francisco

Scottish Natural Heritage (1994) *Red Deer and the Natural Heritage*, SNH Policy Paper, Edinburgh

Scottish Natural Heritage (2002) *Wildness in Scotland's Countryside*, Policy Statement No.02/03, SNH, Edinburgh

Smith D. (2004) *The State of the World Atlas*, Earthscan, London

Stoate C. (2002) 'Behavioural ecology of farmers: what does it mean for British wildlife?', *British Wildlife*, February 2002

Stuart A.J. (1982) *Pleistocene Vertebrates in the British Isles*, Longman, London

Taylor P. (1993) 'Restoration forestry and the global ecosystem', *ECOS* 14 (2) 2–8

Taylor P. (1995) 'Coed Eryri', *Reforesting Scotland* 13, 10–13

Taylor P. (1995) 'Whole ecosystem restoration: re-creating wilderness', *ECOS* 16 (2) 22–28

Taylor P. (2002a) 'Beavers in Britain: laying the foundations', *ECOS* 23 (2), 23–26

Taylor P. (2002b) 'Big cats in Britain', *ECOS* 23 (2) 56–64

Taylor P. (2004) *Shiva's Rainbow*, Ethos, Oxford

Taylor P. (2004) 'To wild or not to wild: the perils of "either–or" ', *ECOS* 25 (1), 12–17

Turner A. and Anton M. (1997) *The Big Cats and Their Fossil Relatives*, Columbia University Press, New York

Van Leeuwen J.M. and Van Essen G.J. (2002) 'Health risks between large herbivores, farm animals and man' in *Vakblad Natuurbeheer*, Special Issue, 'Grazing and Grazing Animals' LNV, Netherlands

Vera F. (2000) *Grazing Ecology and Forest History*, CABI, Wallingford, Oxford

Vithoulkas G. (1980) *The Science of Homeopathy*, Grove, New York

von Arx M. and Breitenmoser U. (2004) 'Re-introduced populations of lynx in Europe: their distribution, status and problems', *ECOS* 25 (3/4), 64–68

Walker B. (1983) *Women's Encyclopedia of Myths and Secrets*, Harper-Row, San Francisco

Watson S. (1998) 'Sabres in the hills', *Tree News* 2

Whitehead G.K. (1953) *The Ancient White Cattle of Britain and Their Descendants*, Faber and Faber, London

Whitbread A. and Jenman W. (1995) 'A natural method of conserving biodiversity in Britain', *British Wildlife*, 7 (2)

Wilbur K. (1996) *A Brief History of Everything*, NewLeaf, Dublin

WWF (1999) *Europe's Carnivores*, WWF-UK, Godalming

Worldwatch Institute (2004) *Vital Signs 2003–2004*, Earthscan, London

Wright M.S. (1988) *Flower Essences*, Perelandra, Warrenton, VA

Yalden D. (1986) 'Opportunities for re-introducing British mammals', *Mammal Review* (16) 53–63

Yalden D. (1999) *The History of British Mammals*, Poyser, London

Yogananda P. (1952) *Autobiography of a Yogi*, Harper-Row, San Francisco

# Scientific Names of Species

These are the scientific names of species where not mentioned in the text

## Plants

alder *Alnus glutinosa*
alpine saw-wort *Saussurea alpina*
ash *Fraxinus excelsior*
aspen *Populus tremula*
baneberry *Actaea spicata*
barren strawberry *Potentilla sterilis*
beech *Fagus sylvatica*
bilberry *Vaccinium myrtillus*
bird cherry *Prunus padus*
black currant *Ribes nigrum*
bluebell *Hyacinthoides non-scripta*
bog whortleberry *Vaccinium uliginosum*
bracken *Pteridium aquilinum*
bramble *Rubus fruticosus*
celandine *Ranunculus ficaria*
common violet *Viola riviniana*
cowberry *Vaccinium vitis-idaea*
cow wheat *Melampyrum pratense*
crab apple *Malus sylvestris*
creeping lady's tresses
crowberry *Empetrum nigrum*
devil's bit scabious *Succisa pratensis*
downy birch *Betula pubescens*
dog's mercury *Mercurialis perennis*
elder *Sambucus nigra*
enchanter's nightshade *Circaea lutetiana*
field maple *Acer campestre*
frog orchid *Coeloglossum viride*

foxglove *Digitalis purpurea*
gean *Prunus avium*
germander speedwell *Veronica chamaedrys*
globe flower *Troillius euopeaus*
golden rod *Solidago virgaurea*
gooseberry *Ribes uva-crispa*
greater stitchwort *Stellaria holostea*
ground ivy *Glechoma hederacea*
hazel *Corylus avellana*
herb robert *Geranium robertianum*
holly *Ilex aquifolium*
honeysuckle *Lonicera periclymenum*
hornbeam *Carpinus betulus*
juniper *Juniperus communis*
lady's mantle *Alchemilla glabra*
lime *Tilia cordata*
marsh marigold *Caltha palustre*
meadowsweet *Filipendula ulmaria*
mountain sorrel *Oxyria digyna*
northern bedstraw *Gallium boreale*
primrose *Primula vulgaris*
ling *Calluna vulgaris*
purple loosestrife *Lythrum salicaria*
raspberry *Rubus ideaus*
red campion *Silene dioica*
red currant *Ribes rubrum*
rowan *Sorbus aucuparia*
sanicle *Sanicula europaea*
Scots pine *Pinus sylvestris*
silver birch *Betula pendula*
soft hawksbeard *Crepis mollis*
spindle *Euonymus europaeus*
sweet woodruff *Gallium odoratum*
sycamore *Acer pseudoplatanus*
tormentil *Potentilla erecta*
valerian *Valeriana officinalis*
water aven *Geum rivale*
whorled Solomon's seal *Polygonatum verticillatum.*
wild angelica *Angelica sylvestris*
wood anemone *Anemone nemorosa*
wood avens *Geum urbanum*
wood false brome *Brachypodium sylvaticum*
wood sage *Teucrium scorodonia*
wood sorrel *Oxalis acetosella*

wood speedwell *Veronica Montana*
woodrush *Luzula sylvatica*
wych elm *Ulmus glabra*
yellow archangel *Lamiastrum galeobdolon*
yellow flag iris *Iris pseudacorus*
yellow pimpernel *Lysimachia nemorum*
yellow star of bethlehem *Gagea lutea*
yew *Taxus baccata*

## Insects

blue ground beetle *Carabus intricatus*
marsh fritillary butterfly *Eurodryas aurinia*
narrow bordered bee hawk moth *Hemaris tityus*

## Birds

bittern *Botaurus stellaris*
black grouse *Tetrao tetrix*
capercaillie *Tetrao urogallus*
corn Bunting *Miliaria calandra*
crane *Grus grus*
dunlin *Calidris alpina*
grey partridge *Perdix perdix*
golden eagle *Aquila chrysaetos*
golden plover *Pluvialis apricaria*
goshawk *Accipiter gentiles*
honey buzzard *Pernis apivorus*
lapwing *Vanellus vanellus*
little egret *Egretta garzetta*
merlin *Falco columbarius*
marsh harrier *Circaetus gallicus*
meadow pipit *Anthus pratensis*
pheasant *Phasianus colchicus*
osprey *Pandion haliaetus*
red grouse *Lagopus lagopus*
red kite *Milvus milvus*
ring ouzel *Turdus torquatus*
Scottish crossbill *Loxia scotica*
skylark *Alauda arvensis*
song thrush *Turdus philomelos*
sparrow hawk *Accipiter nisus*
whinchat *Saxicola rubetra*

white-tailed (sea) eagle *Haliaetus albicilla*

## Mammals

aurochs *Bos primigenius*
beaver *Castor fiber*
boar *Sus scrofa*
grey squirrel *Sciurus carolinensis*
elk *Alces alces*
fallow deer *Dama dama*
hippo *Hippopotamus amphibious*
otter *Lutra lutra*
puma *Puma concolor*
pine marten *Martes martes*
polecat *Mustela putorius*
Przewalski's horse *Equus przewalski*
rabbit *Oryctolagus cuniculus*
red deer *Cervus elaphus*
red squirrel *Sciurus vulgaris*
reindeer *Rangifer tarandus*
roe deer *Capreolus capreolus*
sabre-toothed cat *Homotherium latidens*
sika *Cervus nippon*
wildcat *Felis sylvestris*
wolf *Canis lupus*

# Index